The Sporting News

SELECTS

BASEBALL'S 25 GREATEST TEAMS

The Sporting News

SELECTS

BASEBALL'S 25 GREATEST TEAMS

Written by
LOWELL REIDENBAUGH

Co-Editors
JOE HOPPEL
STEVE ZESCH
CRAIG CARTER

Design
BILL PERRY
MIKE BRUNER

President and Chief Executive Officer
RICHARD WATERS

Editor/The Sporting News
TOM BARNIDGE

Director of Books and Periodicals
RON SMITH

The photographs on pages 155, 157, 158 and 160 were provided by the Society for American Baseball Research.

Published in the United States by THE SPORTING NEWS Publishing Co., 1212 North Lindbergh Boulevard, St. Louis, Missouri 63132.

A Times Mirror Company

Library of Congress Catalog Card Number: 88-42860

ISBN: 0-89204-280-X
10 9 8 7 6 5 4 3 2 1

First Edition

Contents

Baseball's 25 Greatest Teams

Introduction

More than 60 years have gone their inevitable way since the 1927 New York Yankees thundered across the national conscience. Six decades have come and gone, decades in which scores of pennant races and three major wars have been waged. Time has done its best to erode the image of those Yankees. Once vibrant and muscular, they exist today only in memories.

Heroes of all kinds have emerged and disappeared during the intervening years. The Yankee organization alone has sired dynasties of greater lengths, powerhouses that piled up more impressive statistics. But wouldn't life be one simple equation if mere numbers were used to measure greatness?

What honest-to-God baseball fan would silently accept some computer-derived miscarriage that determined superiority not by exploring the character and personality of a team of ball players, but by whether one particular team won more games, scored more runs or hit more homers than another? After all, didn't the ball players themselves —the men, the personalities—determine the club's success?

Frankie Frisch explained this more than 50 years ago when he led a hell-roaring gang of St. Louis Cardinals to the 1934 World Series title. There was a certain something, "a fighting spirit, a confidence, a determination to pull through," that pumped through the lifeline of a great ball club.

"You can search in the records for this spirit and you will never find it," Frisch said. "It isn't there. Batting averages don't express it, nor pitching averages, nor fielding averages."

The last thing the fan needs is a statistical rehash. Those are better left to large "stat" bureaus who care only that Joe Shlobotnik was 7-for-18 with a 3-and-1 count when the sun was setting over the right-field grandstand, not that Al Simmons was just so damned mad at that pitcher that he'd just as soon bounce a line drive off his head than get to first base via a base on balls.

The image of one team's greatness can only be really understood when we clomp spike-shoed into the musty clubhouses of yesteryear, bound onto the fresh shoots of green that have sprung up for a new season at Ebbets Field, the Polo Grounds, Sportsman's Park or sparkling new Yankee Stadium and learn about these men as players, fighters, competitors.

Picture those 1927 Yankees, "Murderers' Row," and their "Five O'Clock Lightning," the ringing drives that streaked high into a sea of grandstand patrons. There's the gazelle Earle Combs, the lanky line-drive machine Bob Meusel, the dangerous Italian prince Tony Lazzeri, the sculpted power of Lou Gehrig and the bulging Bambino himself, Babe Ruth. And if the sight of that fabled band alone wasn't intimidating enough, there would be Ruth, consoling the rival pitcher warming up, "Don't worry, you won't be around long," or the blunt Lazzeri grunting, "Sucker, we'll knock that ball right down your throat." What mentally stable pitcher, past or present, would want to go through the order one time, much less time and again over one season?

And what batter, probably even a couple of those Yankees themselves, could dig in comfortably against a 1954 Cleveland Indians starting rotation that had Bob Lemon, Early Wynn, Mike Garcia, Art Houtteman and Bob Feller whirling white heat and sailing benders and winning game after game after game after game?

That the '27 Yanks have remained the standard by which all other teams are judged certainly attests to their overall might. They had hitting, pitching, defense and that certain "something." They had so much of it that, pitcher Waite Hoyt explained, "We felt we were superior people."

In 1944, The Sporting News sought to resolve baseball's age-old question. In a poll of 140 members of the Baseball Writers' Association of America, the paper asked simply, "What, in your opinion, was the greatest baseball team of all time?" Seventy-one writers, or 50.7 percent of the respondents, voted for the 1927 Yankees. Only four other teams received at least five votes: the 1919 Chicago White Sox (15), the 1928 Yankees (13), the 1929 Philadelphia Athletics (six) and the 1913 Athletics (five).

More years passed. More heroes passed in review. And on June 8, 1963, The Sporting News reported the results of a similar poll. The Academy of Sports Editors, a Boston-based organization whose 100 members represented newspapers of at least 100,000 circulation, voted Murderers' Row baseball's great-

est aggregation ever by an overwhelming margin over the runner-up 1929-31 Philadelphia A's.

And now, more than a quarter of a century later, editors at The Sporting News have reassessed the question that is destined to live on. After thousands of hours of researching, re-evaluating and reliving countless thrills through yellowed news clips housed in the publication's storied vaults, the consensus held that the 1927 Yankees have yet to be eclipsed in superiority.

Twenty-four other teams were judged worthy enough of carrying the banner of greatness, teams that left their indelible marks on the scrolls of the grandest game on earth, teams that were blessed with fight, fire and a magic touch in magical seasons.

If there is controversy in the following pages, let it be directed toward the runner-up teams, numbers 2 through 25. Be assured, there was controversy in these chambers as well.

Number 1

The 1927 Yankees: First-Degree Murder

Joe Judge slumped like a helpless man, his will and determination draining onto the clubhouse floor in pools of sweat. "Those fellows not only beat you, but they tear your heart out," said the Washington Senators' talented first baseman. "I wish the season was over."

Hours earlier, an air of optimism had pervaded the Senators' ranks as they arrived at Yankee Stadium for a Fourth of July doubleheader against the defending American League champions. Only the day before, the second-place Nats had defeated the league-leading Yanks in the nation's capital for their 10th straight victory. By sweeping the holiday twin bill, Bucky Harris' cocksure club could whittle the New York lead to 7½ games and, just possibly, parlay that momentum into their third pennant in four seasons.

Fireworks exploded early and late that Independence Day in 1927. And nowhere did thunder crack the sky louder than at 4-year-old Yankee Stadium. Prodigious sluggers all, the Yankees whipped the Senators dizzy the first game, 12-1, then battered them helpless, 21-1, to pull 11½ games ahead.

Three months remained in the season. Joe Judge, his heart torn out, was content to go home with a semblance of strength and sanity. For that, he can be forgiven, for meeting the 1927 New York Yankees was like a date with trauma, an invitation to humiliation. Never did a more brutal band of baseball assassins pull on spiked shoes.

"We were good, a really great team," said Al Simmons, the hellbent left fielder for the 1929-31 A.L. champion Philadelphia Athletics, "but when you compare us with the great Yankee world champions who preceded us, we simply weren't in their class. I'm not trying to kid myself nor anyone else. I fought those Yankees as hard as any man in the American League, but when they got us into a tough series, they just batted our brains out."

These 1927 Yankees hammered a major league record 158 home runs, 102 more than the runner-up Athletics. They batted .307 as a team, .327 among the principal eight starters. Of the regulars, five batted over .300, four drove in more than 100 runs. Their five-man rotation and one ace reliever accounted for all but nine of their A.L.-record 110 victories. And from start to finish, the Yankees

Babe Ruth was the biggest gun in Yankee Manager Miller Huggins' thundering offensive arsenal.

Herb Pennock was the top lefthander on an impressive 1927 staff that also included
(clockwise from top left) Urban Shocker, Wilcy Moore, George Pipgras and Waite Hoyt.

were in first place, capturing the season series from each of their seven rivals. "It was equivalent to the performance of Othello suffocating Desdemona," summarized the 1928 Spalding Baseball Guide. "The Yankees spread their hands over the remainder of the American League's face when they began in April and their hands were still over the face when they finished in October."

The heart of the New York lineup consisted of Babe Ruth, Lou Gehrig, Bob Meusel and Tony Lazzeri. They were surrounded by Earle Combs, Mark Koenig, Joe Dugan and the catcher, Pat Collins, Johnny Grabowski or Benny Bengough. History remembers them as "Murderers' Row." Their mode of attack was known as "Five O'Clock Lightning," a term coined by Combs in reference to the hour at which the Yanks launched their winning onslaught.

These Yankees were swashbuckling bruisers, the greatest stars of the Roaring '20s—and they knew it. "We had a pride in performance that was very real," explained pitcher Waite Hoyt. "It took on a form of snobbery. We felt we were superior people." They monopolized the limelight and broke rules under moonlight. Each day, however, they reported to their unobtrusive "Mite Manager," a 5-foot-4, 145-pound elfin named Miller Huggins.

Huggins had stood up to high spikes and hot drives at second base in 13 National League seasons with the Cincinnati Reds and St. Louis Cardinals. He managed the financially- and talent-poor Cardinals for five seasons, twice into third place, before Sporting News publisher J.G. Taylor Spink helped set up a meeting between Huggins and Yankee Owner Jacob Ruppert for the New York post. Huggins took over in 1918, leading the Yanks out of the second division and to the A.L. pennant in 1921, 1922 and 1923.

Huggins' success, however, was not without strain. Many temperamental Yankee stars thoroughly resented taking orders from a man over whom they towered. Huggins stood up to Ruth in 1925, fining the game's greatest star $5,000 and suspending him for insubordination. The Babe seldom challenged Huggins thereafter.

"You will find that ball players who get too ambitious are always dumb," Huggins said. "They are easy to outsmart, but they usually outsmart themselves."

All the while, Huggins battled digestive ailments and declining health; in the final week of the 1929 season, he would die of erysipelas. "Managing Babe Ruth and the Yankees took five years from my brother's life," said Myrtle Huggins.

But in 1926, Huggins brought harmony back to the Yankees after turmoil helped drag them to seventh place in 1925. The Yanks took the '26 A.L. crown by three games before running their steamroller over the majors in 1927. And although the robust Yankee batting attack received the glory, Huggins pointed to pitching as the backbone of his club.

"The backbone of any ball club is the pitching staff," he said. "The New York Yankees are sometimes spoken of as an exception. I have heard it said their tremendous batting punch carries them through. Now I appreciate that batting punch as much as anyone, but no team would lead its league as we did in 1927 unless they possessed real pitching strength...."

On opening day, righthander Waite (Schoolboy) Hoyt bested Lefty Grove for his first of 22 wins. He wound up tied for the league lead in victories and second in earned-run average (2.64). Just turned 28, Hoyt had been pitching professionally since 1916 after gaining notoriety as a no-hit specialist for Erasmus High School in Brooklyn. "I just had too much stuff for those kids and all I had to do was buzz the ball by them," he remembered.

Hot-tempered and headstrong, he stuck by that philosophy, winning 19 games in both 1921 and 1922, his first two seasons in Yankee pinstripes, then 17, 18, 11 and 16.

"If Hoyt could curb his temper, he would be a better pitcher," Huggins explained in 1927. "There is no reason why he should not win 20 games every year. He has stuff and he knows how to use it. After the ball he pitched in the 1921 World Series, he should have gone to the very top." In an epic performance against John McGraw's powerful New York Giants, Hoyt pitched three complete games without surrendering an earned run.

Once past the smoke and fire of Hoyt, A.L. hitters were crossed up by the gentlemanly grace of Herb Pennock, a willowy lefthander of 6-feet and 160 pounds. Pennock would pitch in 23 major league seasons, a testament to his easy manner, and win 240 games. Relying on control and a superior intellect, he won 19 games in 1927, the same number he had won in 1923, his first season with the Yanks. In between, he won 20 games twice.

"His curve never scared anybody and there were games in which he didn't throw half a dozen fastballs," recalled Lefty Gomez, Pennock's teammate from 1930 through 1933. "What he had was control and psychology . . . he had a cunning, a way of staring down a batter and making him wonder what was coming next. . . . When he shook off a pitch, it didn't mean a thing. It was just to nettle the batter."

Exasperating hitters also was a specialty of Urban Shocker, a righthanded spitballer whom the Yankees had traded to the St. Louis Browns in 1918. Shocker won 20 games in four of his seven seasons in St. Louis (including a league-high 27 in 1921) before he was reacquired prior to the 1925 campaign. He was 12-12 his first year back, 19-11 in 1926 and

Despite his spectacular statistics, the younger Lou Gehrig learned a lot from teammate Babe Ruth.

18-6 with a 2.84 ERA for Huggins' 1927 powerhouse.

Tragically, the great righthander was dead of a heart condition the next September. In February, he had informed the Yankees he was retiring to pursue a business career. Actually, he feared he was a dying man after he dropped from 170 to 115 pounds. He regained the weight, rejoined the team in April but collapsed while pitching batting practice in Comiskey Park. He pitched only two innings in relief before he was released in July. On September 9, he died of an enlarged heart at 35.

Walter (Dutch) Ruether was 33 and completing the last of his 11 major league seasons in 1927. His extensive service, however, had not dulled his keen love of nightlife. As Ruth's occasional roommate on the road, he and the Babe starred in the nocturnal circuit. By day, Ruether was 13-6 in '27 while hitting a respectable .263, evidence of his proficiency with a bat.

"Do you know," Ruether said in 1925, "that I believe my whole pitching career has been a mistake? I have had good years, if I do say so myself (19-6 for Cincinnati in 1919, 21-12 for Brooklyn in 1922, 18-7 for Washington in 1925), but for all that I believe my natural position was at first base."

Stuck at an "unnatural" position, Dutch won 137 games in the big leagues.

George Pipgras succeeded for his determination to overcome wildness and a deliberate nurturing of his early career. Huggins liked the hard-throwing righthander's potential, but Pipgras was only 1-4 after pitching 50 innings over the 1923 and 1924 seasons. Reminded in 1924 that Pipgras was close to 25 years old, Huggins explained: "Few ball players under 25 are any good, as a matter of fact. Success in the major leagues is largely a matter of mental balance, which usually does not come to a man before he is 25. . . . Two years in the minors will cure him."

Brought back to the Yanks in 1927, Pipgras was eased into the rotation; at season's end, he was an impressive 10-3.

Rotating his strong starting five, Huggins was rewarded with 74 complete games. As a bonus, he got seven more from two righthanders out of the bullpen—one from Myles Thomas, 7-4 in his second season with the Yanks, and six from William Wilcy Moore, a 30-year-old rookie who wound up 19-7 with a league-leading 2.28 ERA in 50 games.

Moore was a balding, broad-shouldered cotton farmer from Hollis, Okla., who had meandered through the bush leagues for six years. He got the break he needed—literally—when he suffered a fractured wrist in 1925. Forced to throw sidearm due to lingering pain, Moore developed a sharp-breaking sinker that batters could pound only into the ground. In 1926, he was 30-4 for Greenville (S.C.) in the South Atlantic Association. That August, he was purchased by Yankees General Manager Edward G. Barrow.

Moore's skills on the mound were in sharp contrast with his talent at the plate. Ruth squinted at the newcomer's batting form and bet $300 to the pitcher's $15 that Moore wouldn't collect three hits all season. For nearly three months, Moore hacked away without success. Finally, on July 8, he rapped two clean singles at Detroit. Teammates fully expected Ruth to buy up the bet, but the Babe sat pat while Moore kept swinging. "My money's as safe as a church," Ruth laughed.

Wilcy's efforts paid off August 26 in Detroit when he topped a pitch from Sam Gibson. Arthur Mann, a veteran New York newsman, described the scene for The Sporting News some years later:

The ball hit the grass and rolled. Wilcy spat on his hands and lighted out for first base with all the speed of a hibernating turtle. Yankee players stormed from the dugout as Jackie Warner, Detroit third-sacker, waited for the ball to roll foul.

"Pick it up!" Ruth bawled. "Throw it! Throw him out!"

"No, no, no!" yelled other Yankees. "Let it roll, let it roll!"

Wilcy waved in glee as he thundered past the Yankee dugout in a crisp nothing an hour. Warner was still watching the ball roll when it decided to settle in a heelprint right on the whitewashed foul line. It was fair, and it was Wilcy's third hit.

Even more wondrous accomplishments were ahead for the son of the Oklahoma soil. On September 16 against Chicago, Moore shocked the Yankee Stadium customers with a home run into the right-field stands. The wallop left Wilcy 52 home runs behind the Babe, who cracked his 53rd round-tripper in the 7-2 victory, the Yankees' 100th of the season. Three days earlier, they had clinched the flag with a 5-3 decision over the Cleveland Indians.

At 32, Ruth reigned as the unchallenged hero of American culture. Years before, after baseball had been disgraced by the Black Sox scandal of 1919, the Yankee right fielder almost single-handedly restored the game to respectability. In 1920, Ruth walloped a record 54 homers; in 1921, 59. The nation was enthralled with the spectacular slugging of this charming giant.

By 1927, his affinity for bright lights, fast cars and women of a similar gait was well-documented: His gargantuan appetite toward life was as storied as his ability to pole mammoth home runs. But it was that glorious hitting that stirred the public and made the Yankees the most feared team of the 1920s.

Obtained from the Boston Red Sox (with whom he won 89 games as a pitcher) before the 1920 season, Ruth averaged 44 homers in his first seven Yankee seasons. He led the league in RBIs five times, in runs scored six times. In 1921, he set records with 171 RBIs and 177 runs (a mark that still stands). Five times he batted over .370, yet he won only one batting crown, in 1924, with a .378 mark. In 1923, his .393 average ranked second to Harry Heilmann's .403 mark with the Detroit Tigers.

Weeks before the 1927 campaign, the Bambino signed a three-year contract calling for $70,000 annually. "I know that Ruth will live up to the terms of this new contract," Ruppert said. "He is worth just what he has signed to accept and you're going to see him play great ball." To that end, Ruth smashed a major league record 60 home runs.

Ruth was greeted at the plate a record 60 times by Gehrig in the 1927 regular season.

With the Babe batting third and Gehrig fourth, the Yankees wielded a one-two long-distance punch that was deadlier than some *lineups*. No other A.L. team could match Ruth's 60 homers; only three topped Gehrig's 47, the most hit by anyone other than Ruth. *Excluding* those 107 home runs (which would appear in the runs scored and RBI columns), Ruth and Gehrig were responsible for 432 Yankee runs. Gehrig led the league with a major league record 175 RBIs. Ruth topped the circuit with 158 runs scored. They accumulated 864 total bases—417 for Ruth, 447 for Gehrig, who led the league in doubles (52). In addition, they were issued 247 walks—138 for Ruth, 109 for Gehrig.

In only his third season as the Yankees' regular first baseman, Gehrig was the single player capable of rivaling Ruth for power. He was a 6-foot-1, 212-pound block of granite with blue eyes and curly brown hair. A native of New York City and the son of German immigrants, he had attended Columbia University, where, he recalled, he "drove baseballs where they had not been driven before on the Columbia grounds."

Gehrig signed with the Yankees on April 30, 1923, but he spent virtually all of the 1923 and 1924 sea-

sons in Hartford of the Eastern League. He stuck with the Yankees in 1925 but sat on the bench through much of May while veteran Wally Pipp hit .244 as Huggins' first baseman. "I went to Hug and said, 'Trade me, send me someplace I can play every day, even St. Paul. Anything is better than this,'" Gehrig recalled.

"On June 1, Hug sent me in as a pinch-hitter. The next day, he called me into his office and said, 'Well, here is that chance you've been hollering for. You are the new first baseman of the Yankees.'"

Gehrig went 3-for-5 as New York defeated Washington, 8-5. It was the second of 2,130 consecutive games he would play in a Yankee uniform. On June 18, The Sporting News reported: "The substitution of Buster Gehrig for Wally Pipp at first base has provided the necessary punch, for Gehrig, so far, has walloped the apple for five home runs and is beginning to play his position like a veteran. Unless Gehrig becomes a cropper, Pipp will remain on the bench indefinitely."

Pipp did ride the pine, watching the 22-year-old Gehrig finish the season with 20 homers and 68 RBIs. In 1926, "Larrupin' Lou" batted .313 with 16 homers, 107 RBIs and a league-leading 20 triples.

"How did I learn to hit a long ball?" Gehrig reflected in 1930. "I'm not admitting that I can, but whatever I know about it I owe to Babe Ruth. He has been an untiring instructor and has spent hours and hours of his time showing me how to swing."

In typical Gehrig fashion, he was content to praise another.

"I'll tell you there is no man in the world with a bigger heart than the Babe," he said. "The saddest day of my life will be when the Babe swings the last time. I can tell you, too, that the biggest kick I have gotten out of baseball was in the last few days of the 1927 season when the Babe hit his 60th home run for a new record."

Gehrig must have reveled, too, in the ringing line drives of Earle Combs and Bob Meusel, Ruth's outfield mates.

Tall and lean, Combs was a 28-year-old gazelle from the Bluegrass Country of Kentucky and the Yanks' leadoff-hitting center fielder. Though his accomplishments were overshadowed by the mountains of praise heaped on Ruth and Gehrig, Combs led the league with 231 hits and 23 triples. He had a sweet swing, a flair for line drives and a .356 batting mark. In only his first season as a regular (1925), the lefthanded-hitting Combs had rapped 203 hits for a .342 average. His only drawback was a weak arm, but he compensated for that with his demon speed afield. That quickness induced Huggins to

Left fielder Bob Meusel often was overshadowed by the exploits of Babe Ruth and Lou Gehrig.

question Combs about his reputation as a base burglar.

"Down in Louisville," said Combs, "they called me 'The Mail Carrier.'"

Huggins smiled roguishly and replied, "Up here we'll call you 'The Waiter.' We have a couple of fellows around who can break windows in the next town. All you have to do is wait till they come to bat."

Combs never waited long with Ruth, Gehrig and Meusel, the No. 5 hitter. Meusel, a righthanded batter, knocked in 103 runs in 1927 and batted .337. In seven previous seasons with the Yankees, he had hit under .300 only once, in 1925, when he led the league in home runs (33) and RBIs (138).

A tall (6-3), loping left fielder, he often was accused of loafing, but his long legs actually carried him to the ball quickly and his rifle arm kept baserunners at bay. "Meusel's arm was the best I ever saw," said Bob Quinn, former president of the Red Sox and Boston Braves. "And I'm talking about strong arms, not merely accurate ones. Meusel threw strikes to any base from the outfield."

He also was described as the "coldest Yankee of them all" for his colorless expression, but Meusel simply never had to boast or make excuses. "What a player Bob might have been if he had been born with a different disposition," Huggins said. "He had everything to make him great—a good eye at bat, strength, a natural easy swing and that wonderful steel arm."

Of the eight American Leaguers who drove in more than 100 runs, the Yanks had four in Meusel, Gehrig, Ruth and second baseman Tony Lazzeri. Just 22 years old, "Poosh 'Em Up" Tony already was regarded as the top second-sacker in the circuit. As a rookie in 1926, he ripped 18 homers and drove in 114 runs. In 1927, he stroked another 18 homers, drove in 102 and batted .309 behind Meusel. His sudden impact was extraordinary, but his romp through the Pacific Coast League in 1925 had been a positive harbinger: 222 RBIs, 60 home runs and 252 hits in 197 games for Salt Lake.

The righthanded-hitting Lazzeri packed only 160 pounds on his 5-11 frame but he cracked line drives of the 400-foot variety with regularity. "It's because he worked in a boiler factory for years and developed wiry strength," explained Pennock. "It comes from eating spaghetti and drinking wop wine," sneered a "joking" Ty Cobb.

The proud Italian was more than a fence-busting slugger, however. He was tough, agile and surehanded around the keystone. "I've seen a few better second basemen, but not many," Huggins said. "He

Second baseman Tony Lazzeri weighed only 160, but still claimed his spot on Murderers' Row.

Jumpin' Joe Dugan, seemingly out of place with his gentle bat, gave the 1927 Yankees good defense at third base.

has a phenomenal pair of hands, a great throwing arm and he covers acres of ground."

Lazzeri's keystone colleague, shortstop Mark Koenig, also was serving his second season as a regular. Though his fielding was erratic—52 errors in 1926 and 47 in 1927—the switch-hitting Koenig was a dependable No. 2 hitter. He batted .271 as a rookie and .285 in 1927, collecting 62 RBIs each season.

"I was ordinary, a small cog in a big machine," the modest San Franciscan said in retirement. "The Yankees could have had a midget at shortstop."

Joe Dugan, nicknamed "Jumpin' Joe" for his practice of going AWOL as a young Athletic, rounded out the infield. Now 30, Dugan remained a good gloveman at third, agile and blessed with an artist's delicate hands. As a hitter, he had batted .300 twice in a career that began in Philadelphia in 1917. In 1927, he slipped to .269, his lowest mark since 1918.

Dugan delighted in telling a bit of lore that depicted the power of Murderers' Row. The Yankees, he explained, were engaged in a close game when Five O'Clock Lightning struck. Combs tripled to center, Koenig doubled to left, Ruth homered into the right-field stands, as did Gehrig. Meusel doubled, Lazzeri tripled and Dugan singled sharply to right.

"That'll cost you $100," Huggins told Dugan when he returned to the bench.

"What for?" came Dugan's astonished reply.

"For breaking up a rally," Huggins said.

Huggins rotated his crew of catchers, Collins, Grabowski and Bengough, who were known as "Slow" "Slower" and "Slowest" to some teammates. Their lack of speed mattered little, for Meusel (24 stolen bases, second in the league), Lazzeri (22) and Combs (15) were threat enough on a club that thrived on the long ball.

Despite their success in 1926, the Yankees were picked to finish second behind the Athletics in many preseason polls. On opening day, however, New York dialed in its wrecking machine by whipping a star-studded (Lefty Grove, Mickey Cochrane, Ty Cobb, Eddie Collins, Al Simmons) Philadelphia outfit, 8-3, then took two more games to sweep the series. The most noteworthy feature of the opener was Ben Paschal pinch-hitting for Ruth in the sixth inning. After fanning twice in three at-bats, Ruth asked Huggins to "get me outta there." Paschal singled and gained notoriety as the last man to pinch-hit for the Babe.

By June 1, the Yankees were only two games in front with a 28-14 record but they were looking more invincible with each week. Even Huggins, never given to winning pennants in the press, sounded a positive note.

"I have a much better ball club than last year," he said, "and if we don't run into misfortunes we ought to stay on top. . . . It's possible for us to take a slump at any time, but just now I'm not worrying a great deal. You see my boys are hitting the ball consistently and my pitchers are working very smoothly. The Yankees, as a team, have improved in every way.

"Gehrig, Lazzeri and Koenig, the young infielders, are showing the results of last year's experience by playing with more confidence and steadiness. Koenig is destined to become one of the finest shortstops in the majors. He is handling balls that he couldn't reach a year ago and is throwing wonderfully. Gehrig is the hardest-hitting first baseman I've seen and that is saying a whole lot. Lazzeri is the best second baseman in the American League today.

"Joe Dugan isn't hitting but his third-base play is excellent. In case of accidents to my regular infielders, I'll be well fortified. (Cedric) Durst can play first base, while (Ray) Morehart, (Mike) Gazella and (Julie) Wera are ready to jump into the other positions.

"The pitchers? They've surprised me, particularly Hoyt and Ruether. Pennock hasn't lost a game yet (he lost his first on May 27) and Shocker is coming along nicely. Moore . . . has done splendid relief work."

Moore's reputation as a fireman even started to color the conversation of his teammates. In Detroit one night, several players were attracted to a huge fire near the team's hotel. As the flames subsided and white smoke filled the air, Gazella turned to his companions and quipped, "We can go now. They got Wilcy Moore in there."

Twenty-one victories in 27 games, their best monthly mark, raised the Yanks' record to 49-20 at the end of June. They also breezed through July, building a comfortable lead with a 24-7 pace. Day after day, Yankee bats boomed and enemy pitchers retreated. The nimble-witted Dugan was inspired to coin another slogan, "Second time around"—If a pitcher retired the New York hitters his first time through the order, beware the "second time around."

Winning with ease was the Yankee trademark. It also chilled the public's interest in the pennant race —or lack of one—and diverted attention to the home run contest waged by Ruth and Gehrig. After they warmed up with four home runs apiece in April, Ruth hit 12 in May to take a four-homer lead. Gehrig's 11 circuit blows in the last half of June deadlocked the derby at 25 at the end of the month, but he moved ahead, 35-34, heading into August.

The race remained hot as Gehrig blasted No. 38 on August 9 to move ahead by three, but Ruth pulled even with single home runs on August 16 and 17 in Chicago, the first of which was historic-

Shortstop Mark Koenig was a self-admitted 'small cog in a big machine.'

ally significant. Facing Tommy Thomas in the fifth inning, the Babe drilled a pitch deep into right field. The ball "soared upward and onward," wrote a New York Times reporter, "in the general direction of the stockyards and there it may have come to rest on some surprised and unsuspecting steer." It was the first home run to clear the double-deck right-field stands at Comiskey Park.

Gehrig's 44th home run on September 5 tied the "Great American Home Run Derby" for the final time. The next day, Lou cracked a single homer in a Labor Day twin bill against the Red Sox, but the Babe smote three over the fence in Fenway Park. Ruth never looked back, corking his 17th homer of the month on September 30 against Washington to eclipse the record 59 he had hit in 1921. (Gehrig, upset by his mother's illness, hit only two more homers, on September 27 and October 1.)

The Yanks and Senators were tied 2-2 in the eighth inning when Koenig tripled off lefthander

Tom Zachary with one out. Ruth stepped in, Zachary unleashed a screwball and Bill Hanna of the New York Herald Tribune typed this dispatch in the press box:

> *This one broke over the plate . . . a screwball until it met the Babe's unruly bat. After that, it was a minie ball. It didn't go high and it did go on a line. Bill Dinneen, the umpire, crouched on the foul line and peered carefully into the distance to see whether it was fair or foul. It buried itself in the bleachers, 15 rows from the top, and was fair by not more than six inches. Still, it was fair, and the record was beaten. Count 'em—60!*

The following day, the Yankees claimed their 110th victory, an A.L. record that stood until 1954. Among those wins were 21 against the St. Louis Browns, who won only the last meeting of the season between the two clubs. The Yanks became the first A.L. team to top .700 in winning percentage (.714) and their 19-game advantage over the runner-up Athletics was the largest since the league was founded. It was the first of the Yankees' 14 100-victory seasons, a major league record.

New York dominated the league in every batting department. Ruth and Gehrig claimed the top two positions in home runs, RBIs, runs scored, walks, total bases and slugging average. Combs and Gehrig ranked 1-2, respectively, in hits and triples, Combs was third in runs scored and total bases, Lazzeri was third in homers. Gehrig, third in batting behind Heilmann and Simmons, was named the A.L. Most Valuable Player.

Among the league's pitchers, the Yankees claimed the first four spots in winning percentage (Hoyt, Shocker, Moore, Pennock), the first three in ERA (Moore, Hoyt, Shocker).

With Huggins' fifth pennant secured, the Yankees rumbled into the World Series to face the Pittsburgh Pirates. The Bucs couldn't match the Yankees' power—no team could—but they had hit a composite .305 with the likes of Paul and Lloyd Waner, Pie Traynor, Glenn Wright and Joe Harris gracing the lineup. Still, Huggins liked the chances of his juggernaut.

"It is my notion that we will outhit the National Leaguers," he said. "We have knocked over the best pitchers in our league, particularly when we have needed important games. It has made little difference whether they have been righthanded or lefthanded. There isn't a medium hitter in the Yankee lineup. The Pirates have no sluggers who compare with Ruth and Gehrig."

That acknowledged fact evolved into a popular piece of fiction that contended the Pirates lost the World Series before it ever began. The Yankees, the myth supposes, strode into Forbes Field for batting practice on the day before Game 1. Cowering in the stands, the Pirates watched Murderers' Row bash ball after ball into the outfield stands. By the time the Yankees laid down the lumber, the awe-struck Pirates were whipped.

"That's just silly," Paul Waner argued years later. "We weren't a scared club; why should we have been scared? We had just beaten out the Cardinals in our own league, the same team that had taken the Yankees in the 1926 World Series. . . .

"Lloyd is supposed to have said to me, 'Aren't they awfully big guys?' The only thing wrong with that is I wasn't even in the stands.

"As a matter of fact, we weren't overpowered. There were only two home runs in the Series, both hit by Babe Ruth. One of them was off a second-string pitcher, Mike Cvengros, after (Game 3) already had been lost. We weren't disgraced. We knocked Waite Hoyt out of the box in the first game, and lost, 5-4. . . . The last game was tied, 3-3, and in the ninth inning (when) John Miljus' high pitch got away from Johnny Gooch. That was the ball game. But in the four games, Lloyd batted .400 and scored half of our 10 runs. I batted .333. Didn't look as though we Waner boys were too scared."

Evidently not, but the Yanks made short shrift of

Center fielder Earle Combs strokes a hit in Game 2 of the 1927 World Series against Pittsburgh.

the Bucs, sweeping them in four games to claim their second World Series title. After Pipgras shut down the Bucs in Game 2, 6-2, in his first-ever Series appearance, Pennock boosted his postseason record to 5-0 with an 8-1 decision in Game 3. He retired the first 22 Pirate batters before Traynor and Clyde Barnhart singled and doubled, respectively, for the lone Pittsburgh tally. Moore earned the victory in the fourth contest, pitching a complete game in the only World Series start of his career. Koenig was the sparkplug of the Yanks' offense, batting .500 (9-for-18) to lead Ruth (.400, two homers, seven RBIs), Combs (.313, six runs) and Gehrig (.308, four RBIs).

The 1927 Yankee triumph was more than a victory over 15 other major league teams. It was a victory for the organization, something that gave rise to a couple of qualities known as Yankee tradition and confidence.

"The team and organization began to assume proportions of power and glamor," Hoyt explained some 25 years later. "As the Yankee teams gained in power, rival teams developed an increased awe. So much so that when an important game or series arrived, the opposition was plagued by needles of doubt while the Yanks thrived on inherent confidence.

"Some may look upon Yankee tradition as merely the intensity of spirit, an infallible belief in themselves. I think it to be more than that, for I am conscious of the long hours of advice and guidance Miller Huggins gave to the early teams.

"Huggins called it 'attitude.' It was an attitude which included baseball intelligence in its highest form. Huggins demanded awareness. The Yankee bench during a ball game knew a deportment as rigid and stiff as a third-grade classroom directed by a New England schoolmaster. Huggins tried to surround himself with players who, if they weren't book-smart, were baseball-smart and eager. As a result, he usually had players to whom a stiff game was a delight.

"In this thing called tradition, you will find not only the handiwork of Huggins, but the personalities of all former Yankees. Despite Ruth's tendencies toward peccadillos, the Babe was an alert player. You've heard it said he never threw to a wrong base. Ruth wanted to win. In that sense he was a great pacemaker. We had the high-speed performance of Ruth; the eagerness of Gehrig, which was never stated; the baseball intelligence of Lazzeri; the spontaneous reflexes of Dugan—and also Irish wit; the iron will of a thorough and clever man, Earle Combs; the competitive spirit of the pitchers and, believe it or not, the silent and almost indifferent nonchalance of Bob Meusel.

"These characteristics established Yankee tradition—tradition in a sense that a family is known as a progressive unit, with father and sons contributing toward stability and success."

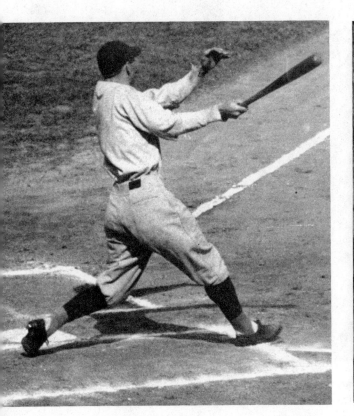

1927
FINAL STANDING

Club	W.	L.	Pct.	GB.
New York	110	44	.714	——
Philadelphia	91	63	.591	19

BATTERS

Pos.	Player	G.	HR.	RBI.	B.A.
1B	Lou Gehrig	155	47	175	.373
2B	Tony Lazzeri	153	18	102	.309
SS	Mark Koenig	123	3	62	.285
3B	Joe Dugan	112	2	43	.269
OF	Bob Meusel	135	8	103	.337
	Earle Combs	152	6	64	.356
	Babe Ruth	151	60	164	.356
C	Pat Collins	92	7	36	.275

OTHER CONTRIBUTORS (20+ Games): Benny Bengough, Cedric Durst, Mike Gazella, Johnny Grabowski, Ray Morehart, Ben Paschal, Julie Wera.

PITCHERS

Thr.	Pitcher	G.	W.	L.	ERA
R	Waite Hoyt	36	22	7	2.64
R	Wilcy Moore	50	19	7	2.28
L	Herb Pennock	34	19	8	3.00
R	Urban Shocker	31	18	6	2.84
L	Dutch Ruether	27	13	6	3.38
R	George Pipgras	29	10	3	4.12

OTHER CONTRIBUTORS (20+ Games): Myles Thomas.

Number 2

Yankees Fuel Bats With M&M Power

In 1961, Roger Maris (left) and Mickey Mantle formed the most prolific one-season home run combination in baseball history.

In the summer of 1955, a 20-year-old outfielder with the Reading Indians of the Class A Eastern League attracted the attention of a New York Yankees scout, who notified headquarters that the prospect hit with power, possessed an excellent arm, ran the bases with considerable know-how and had adequate speed.

In the Yankees' executive offices on Fifth Avenue, General Manager George Weiss took note of the promising player. Inquiry disclosed that the kid was unavailable for purchase from the Cleveland organization, but Weiss was undeterred. Thorough as he was in all his operations, the coldly efficient overseer of baseball's most successful empire dispatched a representative to Fargo, N.D., the player's home town, to check on his pedigree, character and work ethic.

All the reports were favorable. Accordingly, Weiss concluded that the budding slugger would fit perfectly into the Yankee scheme. He envisioned the lefthanded hitter driving baseballs into the right-field seats at Yankee Stadium. Shades of Babe Ruth, Lou Gehrig, Bill Dickey, Yogi Berra and the switch-hitting Mickey Mantle.

Two years later, after the player had been promoted to the Cleveland roster, Weiss mentioned casually to Kansas City Athletics Owner Arnold Johnson that if the A's ever acquired title to the 6-foot, 197-pounder, the Yankees would be interested in dealing for his services.

As if he had programmed the sequence of events, Weiss learned in June 1958 that the Athletics had obtained the outfielder in a multi-player trade. His interest was revived, but it wasn't until after the 1959 season that the Yankees and A's negotiated a deal. It was a seven-player swap, with four players going to Kansas City and three to New York, including the prize whom Weiss had craved for more than four years, Roger Eugene Maris.

Because Maris' vast potential elicited considerable awe throughout baseball circles, the trade perpetuated the feeling that the powerful Yankees were "jobbing" the also-ran A's in quantity-for-quality swaps. (From March 1955 through June 1961, the teams made 17 deals involving 64 players—and many of the trades, in the view of observers, seemed to connote a Yankees-A's "farm system" arrangement that benefited the New Yorkers.) Still, not everyone associated with the Yanks was thrilled over the transaction.

"I don't like it," said New York second baseman Bobby Richardson, who expressed regret over the departure of one player in particular. "I know Maris is a good player, but I hated to see Norm Siebern leave us. He was a good player, too, who wasn't given much of a chance with us. He has the ability at the plate and in the outfield in my book."

While Siebern was only 26 years old and had bat-

ted .300 for the Yankees in 1958, the Yanks thought they had something special in Maris.

A three-sport star in high school, Maris had been offered a football scholarship to the University of Oklahoma. He declined the opportunity for Sooner gridiron glory to play baseball professionally and almost immediately questioned the decision. Roger tried out with the Chicago Cubs, only to be told that he was "too small." Considering Maris' fit-for-football physique, there is substantial reason to question the visual acuity of the Cubs' official who passed judgment on the strapping young man.

Roger later accepted a modest bonus to sign with Cleveland and made his way to the Indians after four seasons in the minor leagues.

Weiss' confidence in Maris as a home run hitter was justified instantly. After hitting 16 home runs for Kansas City in 1959, Maris smashed 39 for the Yankees in 1960. His runs-batted-in figure also shot up dramatically, from 72 to 112. These statistics, added to his exceptional defense that earned him a Gold Glove, won Maris acclaim as the American League's Most Valuable Player in '60. Manifestly, George Weiss had made no mistake in his acquisition of Roger Maris. Weiss, in fact, seldom erred on decisions involving player personnel.

In the '60 World Series, Maris cracked two home runs as the Yankees bowed to the Pittsburgh Pirates in seven games. Other than the Bombers' failure to win the Series championship, it was a fulfilling season for the crewcut blond, one that presaged even richer rewards in 1961.

The Yankee club as a whole was seeking greater riches in '61, having spent a long, cold winter trying to cope with the Series defeat. The Yanks had lambasted the Pirates by scores of 16-3, 10-0 and 12-0 and outscored the Bucs 55-27 overall, but somehow managed to lose four games to their upstart opponents.

While most teams don't regroup after a pennant-winning season, the Yankees made some major noise after the '60 season. Casey Stengel, who had directed the club to 10 American League championships and seven World Series titles in 12 years, was dismissed as manager and Weiss was replaced as general manager. Stepping into the breach were Ralph Houk, a longtime reserve catcher for the Yanks and a coach on Stengel's staff since 1958, and Roy Hamey, who had been New York's assistant general manager.

"I am not Casey Stengel," Houk said after succeeding a baseball legend. "I am Ralph Houk, and the fans and writers will have to accept me, as best they can, for what I am as a manager and not as an imitation and the left-over from a previous regime."

Houk, a World War II hero and a noted battler in a baseball uniform as well, had three years of managerial experience on his resume, having pilot-

The big bat of Roger Maris shocked the country as he threatened Babe Ruth's home run record.

ed the Yankees' Denver affiliate from 1955 through 1957. In '57, he led the Class AAA Bears to the Junior World Series championship.

Houk's rapport with his players and his knack of never getting down on himself proved particularly crucial to his success at Denver.

"Unquestionably, Houk's greatest characteristic as a manager is his player relationship and the ability to get the very best out of the players," a Denver sportswriter reported. ". . . He never second-guesses them to writers or at any time where the public is apt to hear about it. Such matters are strictly clubhouse secrets, usually in the privacy of his own dressing room."

As for mentally replaying a Denver game and decisions made therein, Houk said: "I don't do things without a reason. So, if it doesn't pan out, why should I second-guess myself? I do something

because I think it is the best thing I can do under the circumstances."

Houk learned his lessons well as a minor league skipper, further molded his philosophies in his three years as a Stengel aide and was ready to step in when Stengel stepped—er, was shoved—out.

Houk, no one would argue, was walking into an attractive situation. The Yankees had won pennants in five of the last six seasons, and the 1960 club was a typically well-rounded unit. Mickey Mantle had led the league in home runs with 40, Maris was No. 1 in RBIs and Bill Skowron and Yogi Berra provided additional thump. The defense, featuring the wizardry of young third baseman Clete Boyer and the skilled keystone combination of Richardson and Tony Kubek, was solid. And the pitching staff boasted the American League's best team earned-run average.

The 1961 Yankees looked much the same as the previous year's aggregation, with the principal changes coming on the pitching staff. Key newcomers were righthanders Rollie Sheldon and Bill Stafford.

"That Sheldon was in Class D in 1960 must not 'react' against him," Houk said of the tall youngster who compiled a 15-1 record in the New York-Pennsylvania League. "We need another pitcher, and possibly he is the man. I am going to act in the belief that he is ready for the American League until, and if, he proves that he should be optioned out.

"As for Billy Stafford, who came to us last August (from New York's Richmond farm club), he is set and ready," said Houk, continuing his springtime analysis. "He is a remarkable young man and, unless I am all wrong, will have an important part (in the Yanks' quest for another pennant)."

While Houk liked his kid pitchers—Sheldon was 24 years old, Stafford 22—there was little doubt about the manager's opening-day mound selection. It would be 32-year-old Edward Charles (Whitey) Ford, possessor of a dazzling 133-59 (.693) lifetime record in the big leagues.

Ford, who had won 19 games for the Yankees in 1956 and twice had fashioned 18-victory seasons in the majors, had been a poised pitcher since day one in the big leagues. Literally, from day one.

Called up from Class AAA Kansas City, Ford made his major league debut on July 1, 1950, at Boston's Fenway Park. Fenway's cozy confines— particularly its enticingly close left-field wall— struck terror into the hearts of most pitchers, but the ball park's layout didn't faze the precocious Ford.

"It didn't bother me," said Ford, who nevertheless was rocked in a 4⅔-inning relief stint against the Red Sox. "Nervous? Not me. I was tired. I didn't get too much sleep on the train last night and I wasn't sharp. But I wasn't nervous. Why should I be? The pitcher's always got the edge on the hitter, hasn't he?"

Ford surely didn't have the edge that day, but the lefthander proceeded to run up a 9-0 record before losing his final decision of the year. Then, after two years of military service, the native New Yorker compiled marks of 18-6, 16-8, 18-7 and 19-6 before posting more modest numbers of 11-5, 14-7, 16-10 and 12-9.

The 1961 season opener would pit the stylish and cunning Ford against the Minnesota Twins, the old-line Washington Senators who were about to begin play under their new banner after leaving the nation's capital after the 1960 season. The Twins, behind the three-hit pitching of Pedro Ramos, ruined Houk's major league managerial debut by beating Ford, 6-0.

Through the first two weeks of the season, only one-half of the Yankees' M&M power show was producing. Entering an April 26 game at Detroit, Mantle had five home runs and Maris zero. That day, in New York's 11th game of the year (excluding a tie contest ended by rain), Mantle cracked two more homers—one tying the game in the eighth inning and the other winning it in the 10th—and Maris belted his first of the season as the Yankees outscored the Tigers, 13-11.

For the muscular Mantle, considered a threat to break Babe Ruth's single-season homer record of 60 since he broke into the majors a decade earlier, just maybe this was the year to relegate the Bambino to second-place status. Mantle had made a run at Ruth's mark in 1956, a year in which the Oklahoman entered September with 47 home runs. Mantle cooled off in the last month of the '56 campaign, though, and wound up hitting 52. He had earned a nice consolation prize, however: the Triple Crown. Mantle, in his sixth big-league season, had shredded American League pitching for a .353 batting average and 130 RBIs.

The 5-11½, 195-pound Mantle first attracted nationwide attention when, as a 19-year-old non-roster player up from Class C ball, he bashed baseballs to distant places in the Yankees' 1951 spring-training camp in Arizona. Besides his awe-inspiring strength, young Mickey also ran like a deer. The combination of power and speed made Mantle a rare find, and he parlayed those attributes to a place

on New York's opening-day roster.

After a frustrating '51 campaign, in which he found himself back in the minors for a month at midseason and later suffered a severe knee injury in the World Series (an ailment that, combined with other physical problems, would rob Mantle of much of his speed), Mickey was a full-fledged regular in 1952. By then, Stengel was saying "no switch-

Ralph Houk, manager of the '61 Yankees.

The center of the '61 Yankees' outstanding infield was manned by second baseman Bobby Richardson (left) and shortstop Tony Kubek.

hitter ever hit 'em as far as Mantle." Teammate Eddie Lopat, a veteran pitching standout, took the praise a step beyond. "I'll tell you something," Lopat said, "as long as I've been in baseball, I've never seen anybody who could hit a ball as far as Mantle . . . I mean, I've never seen any righthanded hitter hit 'em as far as Mantle does righthanded and I've never seen any lefthanded hitter hit 'em as far as he does lefthanded."

Hardly needing a Herculean feat to give lore status to his strongboy image, Mickey Charles Mantle supplied one anyway. On April 17, 1953, at Washington's Griffith Stadium, he poled a 565-foot home run off Senators lefthander Chuck Stobbs.

"No doubt about it, that was the longest home run ever hit in the history of baseball," said an admiring Clark Griffith, 83-year-old president of the Senators and a man whose major league experience dated to 1893.

Dickey, a Yankees coach and onetime teammate of Ruth and Gehrig, said: "I saw Babe and Lou hit balls out of parks all over the country. Also, I was catching when fellows like Jimmie Foxx were blasting pitches a good country mile. Frankly, I never thought I'd see their like again, but now I've changed my mind."

Mantle captured his first American League homer crown in 1955 and was a four-time titlist when the '61 season got under way. And, once more, he was off and running.

It took Maris and most of the other Yankees a while longer to get up a head of steam. But once they got going, they moved with extraordinary force. Through May 27, Maris had eight homers; after games of June 22, he had 27. Three weeks into May, New York was in third place with a 17-15 record and 5½ games behind league-leading Detroit; three weeks into July, the Yankees were 60-32 and in first place by one game over the Tigers.

While Maris' homer binge—he connected 19 times in 29 games—ignited the Yanks' surge, the Yankees also were getting plenty of sock from Man-

Third base was in the capable hands of flashy-fielding youngster Clete Boyer.

Yanks (left to right) Elston Howard, Bill Skowron, Luis Arroyo and Yogi Berra celebrate a September win over Detroit that moved them closer to the 1961 A.L. pennant.

tle, first baseman Skowron and catcher Elston Howard. Mantle had 22 home runs through June 22, Skowron had 14 homers and Howard was hitting .363. Plus, Ford had gone into high gear. After dropping the season opener, he had won 12 of 13 decisions.

Skowron, a former Purdue University football player, was in his eighth season with the Yankees. While he could muscle up—as his 26 homers and 91 RBIs in 1960 would attest—Moose foremost was a pure hitter. Going into the '61 season, the Chicago product owned a .304 lifetime batting average in the majors.

After hitting .340 for New York in part-time duty during his rookie year of 1954, Skowron drew raves from Kansas City A's coach Burleigh Grimes early in the '55 season.

"This boy Skowron, he's going to be the best righthanded hitter the Yankees ever had," praised Grimes, a longtime National League pitching star. "He's not the finished hitter that (Joe) DiMaggio was yet, but he will be. He's hard to fool right now and he can hit to all fields. And when he pulls the ball with all that strength of his—crack!—it's like the bat meeting a rotten egg . . . . "

Skowron failed to live up to Grimes' billing, to be

sure. Recurring injuries contributed to Moose's inability to rise to another plane of excellence. But he nevertheless was an integral member of great Yankee teams for almost a decade.

Howard, the first black player in Yankees history, was having a rousing season in his seventh year in pin stripes. An outfielder at the outset of his professional career, he was converted into a catcher in 1954. The position switch drew criticism from some observers, who believed the Yankees—one of the last of the established big-league clubs to integrate—were giving Ellie the run-around. After all, Howard now faced the sizable task of trying to unseat Yogi Berra behind the plate and Berra, nearing only his 29th birthday, wasn't exactly ready to be phased out.

"Why can't they leave me alone?" asked Howard, who was furious over a reporter's claim in the spring of '54 that Elston's conversion had racial overtones. ". . . I told him I was satisfied with the change. Told him I liked catching. Told him I was getting a real good shake, good treatment from everybody, then he writes . . . . "

Stengel, also irritated by the article, focused on Howard's potential.

"He (Howard) can become one of the great catch-

A few weeks later, Skowron (left) and Howard (right) were celebrating with Whitey Ford after the pitcher's two-hit victory over Cincinnati in Game 1 of the World Series.

ers," Stengel said. "He's got the size. He doesn't scare from runners or when he's hitting. He's got a great arm. The only thing he hasn't got is experience. He's got to learn how to handle that glove and handle the pitchers. He's got to learn how to think like a catcher. That'll come only with experience."

Howard accepted the challenge. "I hear the Yankees have been looking for a good righthanded-hitting catcher for a long time. Hope I'm the one," said Howard, who went on to catch in 97 of 138 games for Class AAA Toronto in '54. He batted .330 for the Maple Leafs.

Howard made the Yankees' varsity in 1955 and was a major contributor for the New Yorkers through 1959 as an outfielder, first baseman and catcher. It wasn't until 1960, however, that Howard caught more games than Berra.

"I realized from the start that I was second-string to a man who was a cinch to be elected to the Hall of Fame someday," Howard said. "When I broke in, Yogi and (Brooklyn's Roy) Campanella were the best there were. Thank God, I was able to play more than one position. That's what kept me going, the ability to fill in at first base and in the outfield . . . ."

Howard was behind the plate in 91 games in '60, a season in which he continued to learn the intricacies of the catching craft but batted only .245. Now, in 1961, he was doing it all—hitting mightily and catching masterfully.

As for Berra, the three-time Most Valuable Player in the American League found himself sharing left field with Hector Lopez. Berra had glittering career statistics, figures that included 20 or more home runs in 10 consecutive years and 100-plus RBI totals in five seasons. In baseball parlance, Yogi went up there hacking.

Addressing his penchant for going after pitches out of the strike zone, Berra once cracked, "I hit the bad ones so good that I don't see why I should wait for the good ones."

A 5-8, 190-pounder with a face never mistaken for Clark Gable's, the squat Berra didn't worry about his physical appearance. Nor did his superiors.

"In this racket, all you got to do is hit the ball, and I ain't never seen anybody hit it with his face," explained the ever-quotable Yogi.

"Why, he doesn't even look like a Yankee," a reporter suggested in Berra's early days with New York.

"He'll hit like one," shot back Bucky Harris, the

Yanks' manager at the time.

And hit he did. When the '61 season got under way, Berra had a .287 career batting average in the majors and 318 homers.

The Yankees slipped out of first place on July 23, but regained the top spot July 25 and never let go of it. Playing the Chicago White Sox in a doubleheader at Yankee Stadium, New York got two home runs in each game from Maris—bringing his season total to a staggering 40—and swept the Sox, 5-1 and 12-0. In the opener, Mantle also belted a homer, his 38th, and Ford, with relief help from Luis Arroyo (acquired from the minors in 1960), ran his record to 18-2 with his 12th straight victory. Stafford hurled a six-hitter and boosted his mark to 9-4 in the nightcap, a game in which the Yanks also got two homers from third baseman Boyer and one by Howard.

Boyer, outstanding defensively and showing flashes of promise at the plate, came to the Yanks' organization in a 1957 swap with the Athletics after signing two years earlier as a bonus baby. Brother of St. Louis Cardinals star Ken Boyer and former big-league pitcher Cloyd Boyer, Clete made his debut with the Yankees in 1959 and saw extensive duty as a regular in 1960.

"He is the best I have seen in this league," Yankees outfielder Bob Cerv said. "Did you ever see anybody play third base so close in as Boyer does at times? He dares 'em to hit it by him, and they can't. It must be great to be a pitcher with a man like that behind you snapping up two-base hits."

Frankie Crosetti, a longtime Yankee as both a player and coach, marveled at Boyer's diving stops and perfect throws (often made while he was clambering to his knees). "I came up too late for Joe Dugan (the third baseman for the 1927 Yankees)," Crosetti said, "but I have seen everybody who played third base for this club since 1932, and this man is the best. What can't he do?"

Boyer had company in the slick-fielding department. Kubek and Richardson, Houk's shortstop-second base combination at Denver in 1956, were manning their positions with consummate skill and proving steady at bat.

"We just seemed to click right from the start," Richardson said of his diamond relationship with Kubek. "We made mistakes, but we could feel each other getting better. I think that's because we worked hard at improving our techniques. We talked a lot about the plays we had made. After a game, we'd hardly talk of anything else. It was almost a case of eating, sleeping and drinking baseball. And to us, that meant going over the problems on the field as well as discussing maybe new ways of improving ourselves. Those talks led to renewed efforts the next day. We just lived our jobs."

Richardson and Kubek also lived lives perceived as considerably different from the average professional athlete. Recalling an incident in 1958 when an investigator was hired to check on possible late-night carousing among the Yankees, Richardson said he, Kubek and two other players led their pursuer to a YMCA building, where the foursome engaged in "a few hot games of Ping-Pong." Then, Richardson said, the detective "might have had something on our breaking training at that. We stopped in an ice-cream parlor and really loaded up on the stuff."

Wholesomeness aside, these guys could flat-out play.

In addition to his shortstop duties, Kubek saw action in the outfield and at the other three infield positions for the Stengel-led Yankees.

"I like to be handy," Kubek said. "I want to be able to move in and help in many places. But above everything else, I want to be the best shortstop in the American League." Houk obviously saw merit in Kubek's objective. He put the Milwaukee native at shortstop at the start of the '61 season and left him there.

Richardson, perhaps best known for his remarkably quick release of the ball while completing double plays, had captured headlines offensively in the 1960 World Series when he whacked a bases-loaded home run and set fall-classic records with six RBIs in one game and 12 overall. Kubek, who had managed a total of only 11 homers in the 1957, 1958 and 1959 seasons, poked 14 in '60 and then hit .333 against the Pirates in the Series before being forced out of Game 7 after being struck in the throat by a bad-hop ground ball (a play that helped Pittsburgh mount a key rally).

Catcher/outfielder John Blanchard, a heralded minor league slugger who before 1961 had failed to put up major league numbers rivaling even those of Kubek and Richardson, found himself cast in a different light under Houk. After finding playing time a precious commodity under Stengel, Blanchard saw significantly greater service in '61 and responded in a big way. The day after Maris' four-homer performance in the twin bill against Chicago, Blanchard smacked two homers against the Sox in support of Sheldon's four-hit pitching. The drives gave Blanchard four homers in as many at-bats over three games. New York won, 5-2, as Mantle (No. 39) and Boyer also homered.

Righthander Ralph Terry, originally a Yankee before being traded to Kansas City in 1957 and then dealt back to the Yankees in 1959, pushed his pitching record to 6-1—at one juncture of the season he would be 11-1—by beating the White Sox in the series finale.

While the first-place Yankees never really opened a comfortable lead until after Labor Day, national attention focused on the home run derby. Would

Maris break Ruth's homer record? Would Mantle? Would both surpass it?

With Ruth's celebrated mark in clear danger, Commissioner Ford Frick addressed a controversial point in late July. The 1961 American League season featured the addition of two expansion teams and the introduction of a 162-game schedule. Ruth, of course, had walloped his 60 homers in a 154-game schedule. Would Ruth's mark fall if one of the Yankee strong men bashed No. 61 in one of the extra eight games?

"Babe Ruth's mark of 60 home runs, made in a schedule of 154 games in 1927, cannot be broken unless some batter hits 61 or more within his club's first 154 games," Frick said. He later said he meant 154 games played to a decision (like the '61 Yankees, the '27 club played one tie game).

Further amplifying his position, Frick said that 61 homers struck with expanded-schedule help would enter the books as a record for 162 games but would not be accepted as having displaced the Ruth achievement. Never did Frick suggest using an asterisk in dealing with the situation.

Fans across the country got caught up in the Maris/Mantle/Ruth hubbub. The younger element, to whom George Herman Ruth was only a history-book character, cheered heartily for the pretenders. Older generations, to whom the Bambino remained a vibrant personality, rooted just as ardently for the preservation of the record.

Among Yankee fans, one sentiment grew increasingly apparent. Most preferred that Mantle, not Maris, be the one to break Ruth's record if indeed the standard were to be eclipsed. Mantle was perceived to be a "true" Yankee, based on his long-proven superstar skills that put him in the class of Ruth, Gehrig and DiMaggio. Personal popularity and years of service with the club also made Mantle the favorite. Maris, on the other hand, was seen as something of an intruder—a Johnny-come-lately—to all this tradition. He had worn a Yankee uniform for only a year and a half.

Maris and Mantle continued to slug away, with Maris finding it increasingly difficult to handle the media attention and Mantle oblivious to most of the clamor. Mickey, after all, had been in the spotlight during his entire career.

Churning inside over the pressure of facing reporters and microphones day in and day out and being bombarded with repetitive questions, Maris kept up his furious long-ball pace. In six games

played from August 11 through August 16, Roger rifled seven home runs. One of those homers came on August 15 in support of Ford, who nevertheless saw his 14-game winning streak stopped in a 2-1 loss to Chicago. Five days earlier, Whitey had become a 20-game winner for the first time in his career.

"Don't ask me about that damn record," Maris would say as the frenzy mounted surrounding his pursuit of the Babe. With patches of his hair falling out, Maris would plead, "I just want to be left alone."

On the morning of September 1, Maris had 51 homers and Mantle 48. Ruth had 43 on the same date 34 years earlier. Two weeks later, the numbers read: Maris, 56; Mantle, 53. And time was running out—particularly for Mantle, who gave way to illness, but also for Maris, who was a frazzled warrior.

Maris socked No. 57 off Detroit's Frank Lary and No. 58 against the Tigers' Terry Fox. Now, with the Yankees invading Baltimore, Maris had three games in which to tie or break the Babe's record.

In a September 19 doubleheader against the Orioles, Roger reaped only one infield hit in eight at-bats. On September 20, in the Yankees' 154th game played to a decision and their 155th game overall, Maris clubbed No. 59 off Milt Pappas, connecting in the third inning. He was foiled the rest of the night, however, and the great home run chase was over. So, too, was the pennant chase. New York won, 4-2, that night, clinching its 26th American

Manager Ralph Houk celebrates the Yankees' five-game World Series victory.

League pennant.

"I tried hard all night," Maris assured everyone. "Now that it's over, I'm happy with what I got . . . If what I can do from now on cannot count toward an official record, there's no sense in yapping. I had my chance, and I didn't quite make it."

Regardless of the Frick ruling, "60" remained a magic number. And Maris reached that figure on September 26, against the Orioles' Jack Fisher, in New York's 159th game overall. Then, in the season finale played October 1, Maris rocked Boston's Tracy Stallard for No. 61, the homer accounting for the only run of the game. It was a dramatic finish to a season of great theater.

Finally, Maris could go back to being himself. If he overreacted to living in a fishbowl and being harassed with often-inane questions, so be it. Roger was a private man of simple tastes—and proud of it. And he handled matters as best he could.

"I always try to be honest with myself," Maris said. "As far back as I can remember, I've never kidded myself, and so if I feel one way, I can't act any other way . . . .

"I am Roger Maris. I like playing ball and I try to play to win. I love my family. There's nothing complicated about that."

The Yankees made quick work of Cincinnati in the World Series, dispatching the Reds in five games and enabling Houk to win it all in his first season as a big-league manager. Maris struggled in the Series, going 2 for 19, but one of his hits was a ninth-inning homer that won Game 3. Mantle, bothered by a hip injury, had only six at-bats against the National League champions. Lopez, another acquisition from Kansas City, and Blanchard picked up the offensive slack. They combined for seven hits in 19 at-bats and totaled 10 RBIs. Lopez collected seven RBIs despite having only nine official trips to the plate.

Ford won two games against the Reds and he, not Maris, turned out to be the man who broke Ruth's record in 1961. Crafty Whitey pitched 14 consecutive scoreless innings, stretching his Series shutout streak to 32 innings and thereby erasing Ruth's previous fall-classic mark of 29 straight scoreless frames (which the Bambino established while hurling for the Boston Red Sox).

The World Series seldom could be called an anticlimax to any season. But just maybe such was the case in 1961, a most extraordinary year in baseball annals.

Maris wound up with a league-leading 142 runs batted in for the Yankees, who compiled a 109-53 record and outdistanced the runner-up Tigers by eight games. Mantle finished with 54 homers and 128 RBIs. The Yankees set a major league record with 240 homers, with Maris and Mantle establishing a two-man mark of 115 and Skowron contributing 28, Berra 22, Howard 21 and Blanchard 21 (in

only 243 at-bats). Howard hit .348 and Mantle batted .317. Ford fashioned a 25-4 record and his rescue man, lefthander Arroyo, went 15-5 in 65 appearances. Terry won 16 of 19 decisions, Stafford and Sheldon justified Houk's spring assessment of their talents with 14 and 11 victories, respectively, and righthander Jim Coates also won 11 times. And lefthander Bud Daley notched eight triumphs after being obtained in June from—you guessed it—Kansas City.

The crown jewel of this talent-laden team was, of course, Maris. Performing on one of baseball's most fearsome clubs, Maris had risen above all his gifted teammates. And the quiet man from North Dakota had done so in the maelstrom that is New York.

After the 1961 season, Maris, the league's MVP for the second consecutive year, received the baseball he had belted for homer No. 61. After the ceremony, he gave a wheelchair-bound youngster an autographed ball. The boy smiled, thanked Maris and then said: "Next time you come here, bring Mickey Mantle with you."

Even with youngsters, respect for Maris came grudgingly.

Fortunately for the New York Yankees, the scout who had seen Maris perform for Reading in 1955 had no such problem in judging the skill and respecting the talent of Roger Eugene Maris.

1961
FINAL STANDING

Club	W.	L.	Pct.	GB.
New York	109	53	.673	——
Detroit	101	61	.623	8

BATTERS

Pos.	Player	G.	HR.	RBI.	B.A.
1B	Moose Skowron	150	28	89	.267
2B	Bobby Richardson	162	3	49	.261
SS	Tony Kubek	153	8	46	.276
3B	Clete Boyer	148	11	55	.224
OF	Yogi Berra	119	22	61	.271
	Hector Lopez	93	3	22	.222
	Mickey Mantle	153	54	128	.317
	Roger Maris	161	61	142	.269
C	Elston Howard	129	21	77	.348
UT	Johnny Blanchard (c)	93	21	54	.305

OTHER CONTRIBUTORS (20+ Games): Bob Cerv, Joe DeMaestri, Billy Gardner, Jack Reed, Earl Torgeson.

PITCHERS

Thr.	Pitcher	G.	W.	L.	ERA
L	Whitey Ford	39	25	4	3.21
R	Ralph Terry	31	16	3	3.16
L	Luis Arroyo	65	15	5	2.19
R	Bill Stafford	36	14	9	2.68
R	Jim Coates	43	11	5	3.45
R	Rollie Sheldon	35	11	5	3.59

OTHER CONTRIBUTORS (20+ Games): Tex Clevenger, Bud Daley, Hal Reniff.

The Great Revival, Philadelphia-Style

Built by the legendary Connie Mack, the 1929-30-31 Philadelphia Athletics had a solid pitching foundation with bullet-fast hurlers Lefty Grove (left) and George Earnshaw.

With the legendary Connie Mack at the helm, the Philadelphia Athletics either soared with angels or wasted away under the fallout of the rest of the American League.

Never has a team suffered through a darker age than that which gripped the Athletics from 1915 through 1921. For seven uninterrupted seasons, Mack's "White Elephants" languished in last place, a major league record. Only three other franchises, however, have equaled the three straight A.L. pennants Philadelphia won in the 1929, 1930 and 1931 seasons. And while one of the teams to do it, the 1926-28 New York Yankees, has been acclaimed baseball's greatest team and "Murderers' Row" on the merits of a thundering 1927 season, the fact remains that the 1929-31 Athletics were their executioners.

It was no coincidence that Cornelius McGilli-cuddy's teams could be baseball's princes several years running and its paupers the next. When it came to business, the skinny grandmaster from East Brookfield, Mass., was, arguably, a greater tactician off the field than he was as an orchestrator in the dugout. As part-owner of the club he helped found in 1901, Mack mastered the art of exchanging a little cash for talent and selling it off after success was served. Even if it meant starting over.

Above all, Mack's greatest success stories were the fruition of his sagacious scouting. He built the Athletics' early powerhouse teams by plucking talent off college campuses or from the minor leagues for little more than trainfare. The Tall Tactician's commitment to the undiscovered yielded such warriors as Eddie Plank and Rube Waddell, the pitching mainstays of Philadelphia's first two pennant teams in 1902 and 1905; Eddie Collins, John (Stuffy) McInnis, Frank (Home Run) Baker and Jack Barry, the "100,000 Infield" that, after the A's won the flag in 1910, reigned over baseball while the Athletics romped to three more pennants in the next four seasons; and "Chief" Bender, Herb Pennock, Jack Coombs and "Bullet Joe" Bush, other pitching marvels on those early pennant winners.

But after stampeding all over the American League, the Philadelphia juggernaut was disassembled. With the outbreak of World War I in 1914, Mack foresaw lean years ahead. And what ultimately proved detrimental to the Athletics' fortunes was the rise of the Federal League that year and the "long green" the new league's clubs waved under the noses of Mack's players. "I knew that the 'wonder team' was engaged in a civil war, fighting one another" over remaining loyal to the American League and jumping to the Federal, Mack said in his autobiography, "My 66 Years in the Big Leagues."

After the divided Athletics lost the 1914 World Series in four straight games to the Boston Braves, several players jumped ship, including Bender and Plank. "If the players were going to cash in and leave me to hold the bag, there was nothing for me to do but to cash in, too," Mack said. And he sold his greatest stars.

As the 1920s roared upon a country eager to welcome back prosperous times, Mack decided it was time to rebuild. Just after he finished, a depression had returned to prey upon the nation. And the Philadelphia Athletics were laying waste to the American League.

The Athletics had first served notice they were returning to the demolition business in 1928, when they nearly upended the powerful Yankees. Philadelphia overcame a 51-18 getaway by New York and slipped into first place for a day in September, but the Yanks recovered and the A's finished 2½ lengths back at 98-55. Over the next three seasons, however, the Athletics punished their competition. This bunch bore down with everything they had. They were fierce and they were frightening. And they were just what Philadelphia needed after an unwelcome fling with futility.

Even while the Athletics were resigned to labor in last place, Mack had fit together the first pieces of his powerhouse.

Near the end of the 1916 season, Jimmie Dykes showed up already talking at an Athletics' workout, bringing with him the protruding tailgate that earned him the nickname "Little Round Man" in some circles. At 5-foot-9 and 190 pounds, Dykes could whistle the ball around the infield and he showed enough hitting potential that Mack signed the chatterbox to a contract the following spring. After a stint in the service and some necessary minor league seasoning—"I'm afraid if you sit on the bench up here you'll swell up and explode," Mack told Dykes—the righthanded-hitting infielder cracked the Athletics' regular lineup in 1920. In 1924 he batted .312, his first of five .300 seasons for the A's, and was making the plays at second base, third and shortstop.

One of the top pitchers of the 1920s bloomed right along with Dykes—but not without some anxious moments. Eddie Rommel, a successful spitball pitcher with Newark in the International League, had the *misfortune* of being purchased by Mack before the 1920 campaign—the same season the spitter was banned for all but 17 veterans already throwing it. But on the advice of a friend, semipro first baseman Cutter Drury, Rommel banked his chances on a knuckleball he learned before going to camp. As a rookie, he split even in 14 decisions; in 1922, he cashed in with 27 victories, nearly half of the seventh-place Athletics' 65 wins.

Early the next season, Mack brought a strapping lefthander who, in the pitcher's own words, "was born on a farm on the frontier of a new land and ran away from home when 13 years old." The son

The talented Lefty Grove was the centerpiece of impressive staffs that also included
(inset left) Rube Walberg and (inset right) Eddie Rommel.

of a Swedish immigrant, he roamed the timber country of the Great Northwest, working as a fur trapper and lumberjack until he toured Japan with a barnstorming semipro team in 1921. And when the New York Giants returned the big blond hurler to Portland in the Pacific Coast League after a one-month trial in 1923, Mack snapped up George (Rube) Walberg.

Walberg, however, was farmed out to Milwaukee in the American Association the next season with this parting admonition: "Don't come back until you have a curveball." Rube was back with eight victories in 1925. Over the following three seasons he won 12, 16 and 17 games due largely to one weapon—perhaps the league's best curve.

After the 1923 season, Mack purchased a slick-fielding second baseman who had toiled for six seasons with the Baltimore Orioles in the International League. Max Bishop let his fielding speak for itself, for he seldom uttered a word. In 1926, when he played 53 consecutive errorless games at second, Bishop boasted nary a time. "He is merely a name in a lineup, a workman on a job," one reporter wrote. "Bland, blond, phlegmatic and no more responsive to the glamor of his game than a dead man to an indictment."

"He plays for payday, not because he enjoys the game," Mack said. "I never can understand how fellows can come along every now and again who can play a game so well with so little liking for it."

When Bishop joined the team in 1924, Mack converted him into a leadoff hitter. And after Mack ordered him to lay off the bad balls, Bishop became one of the greatest leadoff men in the game, not for his .271 lifetime average, but for his ability to work *any* pitcher for a free pass. In 12 major league seasons, Bishop coaxed more than 100 walks seven times.

"Max had one of the greatest batting eyes in the game," Dykes said. "If he didn't swing at a pitch, the umpires just assumed that it didn't catch the plate and called it a ball."

By 1924, the Athletics could gulp the heady atmosphere of fifth place, thanks largely to the hitting of a 22-year-old rookie who had been purchased from Milwaukee. He had been christened Aloysius Harry Szymanski but, to the relief of everyone, changed his name to Al Simmons after he saw the name on a hardware company's billboards. To the wisecracking veterans, however, the righthanded-swinging left fielder became known as "Bucketfoot" for plopping his left foot toward the third-base dugout with each cut. Never mind the ringing line drives. The stance was all *wrong.*

"It's hits we want, not beauty," Mack reminded a coach eager to tamper with Simmons. "Let him alone. I look for this fellow Simmons to make good right off the reel."

Simmons exploded as if a modern weapon in medieval warfare. He attacked each pitch with a vengeance and hacked with power from corner to corner. Simmons followed a .308 rookie season with a league-leading 253 hits and a .384 average in 1925. He hit .343 in 1926, .392 in 1927 and .351 in 1928. "A fellow's got to hit the way that comes naturally to him," he explained. "Hitters are born, not made."

That was a polite way of explaining his real work ethic: "I hate pitchers. Those guys are trying to take the meat and potatoes right off my plate, the bread and butter out of my mouth."

And the loving care that he provided for dear old mom.

"The fundamental factor of my success," Simmons said, "is my determination to care for my mother. As a boy, my natural love of baseball prompted me to seek a career in the field of professional sport. Always ahead of me as a goal was the house which, when a little boy, I had promised to buy my mother. In the days of failure, when I was being kicked about the minor leagues as an awkward misfit, the mental picture of that house was a shining beacon that led me on."

Robert Moses Grove was driven to win. Period. And pity his teammates if Grove didn't succeed. His personality was as rough and wild as the Maryland mountainsides on which he was raised. And when he lost, Grove tore through the clubhouse like a torrential mountain rapid.

"It burned me worse than a fever to get beat," he said. "I just couldn't stand to lose."

"On the day he was pitching, it was suicide for a photographer to try to take his picture," Dykes said. "He'd throw the ball right through the lens."

Perhaps the only thing more feared than Grove's temper was his exploding fastball. That was his big pitch; that was all he needed. It brought the left-hander notoriety as he won at least 25 games in three of his four full seasons with Baltimore. After the 1924 campaign, Mack hurried to meet with Orioles Owner Jack Dunn and laid down an eye-popping $100,600 to land the 24-year-old hurler.

At the price, "Lefty" Grove was a steal. The humorless 6-foot-3 mountaineer was 10-12 as a rookie but fanned 116 batters to earn his first of seven straight strikeout crowns. After notching 13 victories in 1926, Grove won at least 20 games in each of the next seven seasons.

"All things considered," Mack said, "Grove is the best lefthander that ever walked on a pitcher's slab. He surpasses everybody I have ever seen."

Grove's flair for fight couldn't be topped; but in Gordon (Mickey) Cochrane, Lefty met his emotional equal.

"Much has been written about the way Caesar cried," teammate Bing Miller said, "but he had nothing on Mickey. When we'd lose, he'd weep and

The Philadelphia Athletics' version of Murderers' Row was (left to right) Mickey Cochrane, Al Simmons, Mule Haas and Jimmie Foxx.

stomp and pull his hair and butt his head against the wall. He was the fiercest, scrappiest and cryingest guy I ever saw."

He was "Black Mike" to a legion of admirers, "Ty Cobb wearing a mask" to Mack, and the uncontested field general to his teammates.

Although Cochrane had learned the catcher's trade only in 1923—a move that helped him make the Dover, Del., club in the Eastern Shore League—Mack purchased the bulldog Irishman from Portland after the 1924 season.

"I spent a little money for Cochrane," Mack said, "and for a little while in 1925, I was afraid someone had taken advantage of my trust. The boy was full of energy and all that, but my goodness, he wasn't a catcher. But there was something in the way he tried that made me think we could do something with him. Besides, he could hit and run, and he had the strength to work all day.

"So we taught him a few things about catching

and he came on so fast that it wasn't long until I had to take (Cy) Perkins out and use a better man."

Cochrane batted .331 as a rookie, then stroked away to five more .300 seasons in his nine years in Philadelphia. In 1928, he was recognized as the A.L. Most Valuable Player.

"There is no one quite like him," umpire George Moriarty said. "When he fields a bunted ball in front of the plate, it is like a steam shovel operating because he also comes up with half of the infield soil. Baserunners idle in great fear of his throwing arm . . . and wisely save steals for another day and another catcher. Many star catchers are weaklings in blocking off runners at the plate, but the big, bad wolf usually bounds off Cochrane's shinguards like a schoolboy off a banana peeling."

Like Cochrane and Grove, James Emory Foxx broke into the Philadelphia box scores in 1925; unlike his peers, he did so with far less frequency and fire. The 5-11, 180-pound Foxx was a cordial Maryland farm boy with a gentle smile—and he became known to everyone as "The Beast." No monicker was more fitting for the vicious-swinging slugger with the python arms who pounded titanic home runs farther than, yes, even the Bambino.

Foxx actually joined the Athletics in 1924 at the tender age of 16 after Home Run Baker, his manager at Easton in the Eastern Shore League, called Mack that August. "Please, take him," Baker said. "He can hit with more power than any hitter I've ever seen, including Ruth. You'll find a place for him somewhere."

"When Mack saw me," Foxx recalled, "he said, 'Now I'll be accused of robbing the cradle.' "

Foxx, a righthanded-hitting catcher, watched how the big leaguers operated from the bench. In 1925, he watched Cochrane blossom and appeared in only 10 games. "I didn't play much (26 games) in '26, either," Foxx said. "Most of the time I sat on Mr. Mack's knee, so to speak, and learned a few things."

But Mack could afford to sacrifice his bat to education only so long. After shuffling Foxx between catcher, first base and third, Mack designated "Double X" his regular first baseman in 1929.

In 1927, Mack turned his attention to shortstop, where light-hitting Chick Galloway had been the regular since the 1921 season. Mack called on Dunn to acquire Joe Boley, a slick fielder and clutch hitter who had helped lead Baltimore to seven straight championships in the International League.

A product of the Pennsylvania coal mines, Boley hit .311 as a 29-year-old rookie in 1927. And although he never again hit .300 for the Athletics, the gritty shortstop made his mark with great range, quick hands, and guts in the line of duty.

"To a man toughened by labor in the mines, baseball accidents are unimportant," he said in reference to his fortitude. "I dislocated my shoulder once. My legs are scarred all over with spike wounds. I played through three games of one Little World Series with two broken fingers on my throwing hand. Of course you get minor knocks and bruises, but they don't amount to much."

The 1928 race was barely under way when Mack was back in touch with Dunn. The Athletics' favorite supplier was harboring a former three-sport star at Swarthmore College who had been raised in an environment that merited his family's place in social registers from London to New York. But George Livingston Earnshaw was anything but polite on the mound. His fastball ticked at frightening speeds and he had little regard for control. By the time he joined the Athletics, Earnshaw was 28 and had won 78 games in just over three seasons with the Orioles.

"People tell me that I'm a smart pitcher and use my head," said the 6-4 righthander known as "Moose." "I try to appreciate the compliment and certainly I'm too polite to argue the question. But I must admit it leaves me cold. . . .

"Why should a pitcher be called smart when all he is trying to do is bear down hard and shoot the ball over the plate with so much stuff on it that the batter can't even get a good hold of it? I'm not always sure of getting the ball over the plate, but that doesn't worry me particularly."

Earnshaw was 7-7 for Mack as a rookie, a performance satisfactory enough for a manager who was carefully studying his outfield. Aging greats Ty Cobb, acquired in 1927, and Tris Speaker, signed the following February, were both a steadying influence during the flag chase of 1928, but Mack could see that two other solid-hitting outfielders— Bing Miller and Mule Haas—would be the keys to the future.

Edmund John Miller had always been held in high regard by Mack—even while the Tall Tactician was trading him to the St. Louis Browns midway through the 1926 season. Mack, however, parted with Miller only to acquire veteran pitcher Howard Ehmke in a three-team deal. Mack brought the aggressive righthanded hitter back into the fold for 1928, and Miller announced his return with a .329 mark and 85 runs batted in, proof that he had lost none of the flair that marked his three .300 seasons during his first tour with Philadelphia. And few pitchers ever slipped a third strike past Miller. "Connie used to tell us, 'You're born with two strikes against you so don't take a third one on your own,' " Miller explained.

George William Haas didn't consider his job prospects too promising when he came to camp in 1928. After kicking around the minors for the previous five seasons—with time out for three at-bats with the Pittsburgh Pirates in 1925—Haas had stiff competition among Simmons, Speaker, Cobb, Miller and Walter French. Haas impressed Mack, however, by stinging the ball in the manner that earned him his nickname a few years earlier.

"This sportswriter said my bat packed the kick of a mule," Haas explained.

Mule, a lefthanded hitter who choked up and punched the ball around, batted .280 in 1928 and entered the '29 season as the A's starting center fielder.

As the Athletics departed camp that spring, Mack maintained a cautious optimism. Boley was suffering from a sore arm, and the Yankees were overwhelming favorites to capture their fourth straight pennant. Said Martine Corum in The Sporting News' preseason poll of the Baseball Writers' Association of America:

"We come to the problem of finding somebody to beat (the Yankees). The Athletics? I hardly think so. The Athletics are a great ball team with a screw

Good gloves all, three-quarters of the A's infield featured (left to right) third baseman Jimmie Dykes, second baseman Max Bishop and shortstop Joe Boley.

loose somewhere. We must remember, too, that the Ruppert Rifles always have had the Indian sign on Mr. Mack's mournful men. That's bad. . . ."

Bad, indeed. Despite posing a heavy threat to New York in 1928, the Athletics had lost 16 of 22 games to the Yankees. And Miller Huggins, the Yankees' little giant of a leader, was expecting his pitching staff to rebound from an average year—by Yankee standards.

"I am counting on Pennock being all right again," Huggins said, alluding to the sore arm that sidelined his 17-6 pitcher in the World Series. "That will be a big thing. Hank Johnson and (George) Pipgras are sure to win more games than they did in 1928 (14 and 24, respectively)."

And then there was Ruth, Gehrig, Meusel, Lazerri, Combs and Dickey.

"Now don't quote me as saying that the Yanks will cop another pennant," Huggins cautioned. "What I say is that they seem to have pennant power. I have confidence in them, like their spirit and see no signs of any ominous cracks in the morale, which is most important to be kept intact in a team that has repeatedly tasted the pleasures of victory."

True to Huggins' word, the Yankees assumed their customary spot at the top of the standings on May 7. And one week later, on May 14, the Athletics shot past the New Yorkers and bid them farewell.

Even without Boley, who except for three starts in mid-May and one game at third on June 7, was out until June 10, the Philadelphia grinding machine was an awesome sight to behold. Three days after pushing past New York, the Athletics began an 11-game winning streak and romped through May with a 22-5 record. Once they took over first place, the Athletics only pulled farther ahead until, at season's end, their 104-46 record placed them 18 games ahead of the second-place Yankees. Since the inception of the league in 1901, only the '27 Yanks had won by a bigger margin (19 games).

While the A's rout certainly can be traced back to May, that stampede was triggered by the return of one man, Al Simmons, who was missing from the starting lineup for the first five games with rheumatism complications. He was back for the sixth game, quite unmistakably, with a triple, single and three runs batted in as the A's pounded the Washington Senators, 9-4.

Reporting in The Sporting News, Philadelphia correspondent James Isaminger noted the signifi-

Bing Miller (above) rounded out a solid outfield that also included Al Simmons and Mule Haas.

cance of the day:

"The return of Simmons had the biggest kind of moral effect on the team. (It) transformed all the players into fighters and they showed the same irresistible spirit that marked them in midseason last year when they succeeded in passing the Yankees."

To the rest of the league, Simmons was an unwelcome malady. Once again, he finished second in the A.L. batting race—with a .365 average—but knocked in a league-leading 157 runs, six of which came in a 24-6 romp over the Boston Red Sox on May 1. Batting cleanup, Simmons ranked third in the league with 34 home runs, tied for the lead in fielding among outfielders and was voted the A.L. Most Valuable Player in a Sporting News poll of baseball

writers.

And as The Sporting News noted, "The steady and spectacular blasts of Foxx (were) making him a national figure in the fast set." Although only 21 years old, Foxx finished fourth in the league in home runs (33), tied for fourth in batting (.354) and drove in 117 runs as the A's No. 5 hitter. If the one-two punch of Ruth and Gehrig gave cause for alarm, the righthanded onslaught of Simmons and Foxx was spreading panic.

As a team, the Athletics ranked second to the Detroit Tigers with a .296 batting average. Bishop hit only .232 in the leadoff slot but walked almost once per game (a league-leading 128 passes in 129 contests). Haas, the No. 2 hitter, batted a hearty .313 in his first season as a regular. Cochrane batted .331, 38 points higher than in his MVP season of 1928, and posted 95 RBIs. Miller batted .335 with 16 triples and 93 RBIs in the No. 6 slot. His 28-game hitting streak from May 30 through June 27 was the longest in the league. Dykes enjoyed career highs with 79 RBIs and a .327 average as the seventh-spot hitter.

All the big numbers added up to one thing—you couldn't pitch around the Athletics' hitters.

As for pitching, the A's only topped the league in virtually every department. Grove led everyone with 170 strikeouts and a 2.81 earned-run average. After a 17-2 showing through July, he finished 20-6. Earnshaw, after a 2-2 start, won 13 of his next 15 decisions on the way to a league-leading 24 victories. Walberg, the No. 3 starter, won 18 games, while Rommel—"the greatest finishing pitcher in the league today," Cochrane declared—was 12-2 with a 2.84 ERA. He was one of only three pitchers in the league to finish with an ERA under 3.00.

But it was the veteran Ehmke who was Mack's pitching hero in 1929, not for his 7-2 record in 11 games during the regular season, but for his World Series masterpiece that Mack ranked as one of his greatest thrills ever. Mack had picked the spots for Ehmke throughout the season but none proved so shocking or clever as his decision to start the 35-year-old righthander in the first game of the Series:

"The Chicago Cubs, the National League pennant winners, feared Grove, Earnshaw and Walberg because of their masterful work in winning the pennant," Mack explained in his autobiography. "I knew that if they could lick one of these star pitchers, they could break the spell and ride on to victory. A major surprise at the offset would break their spirit, so my strategy was to nullify the Chicago plan of campaign at the start."

Ten minutes before the Series began, with reporters and fans alike still buzzing over who among the A's Big Three would start Game 1, Ehmke removed his warmup jacket and began to limber up on the Wrigley Field sidelines. As he did, untrammeled shock swept through more than 50,000 spectators and one Al Simmons.

"Is he going to work?" Simmons gasped as he shot off the bench.

"Yes," Mack replied cooly. "Have you any objections?"

"No," Simmons mumbled, trying to conceal his consternation. "If you think he can win, it's good enough for me."

Thoroughly prepared after scouting the Cubs' feared righthanded hitters—notably Rogers Hornsby, Hack Wilson, Kiki Cuyler and Riggs Stephenson—Ehmke baffled Chicago with his overhand, sidearm and submarine deliveries. In nine brilliant innings he struck out a Series-record 13 batters and the Athletics prevailed, 3-1.

Four days later in Game 4, the Athletics set a Series record of even more astonishing proportions.

Leading 8-0, the Cubs appeared destined for their second victory as Philadelphia batted in the bottom of the seventh inning. Ten hits, 10 runs (both Series marks for one inning) and three outs later, the Cubs were effectively deflated. They were blown away by Grove in the final two innings, then blew a 2-0 lead in the ninth inning of Game 5, when Haas' two-run homer and Miller's game-winning double to center field gave the Athletics their first World Series title since 1913.

The championship was extra special for the 66-year-old Mack, who claimed his fourth Series championship and seventh A.L. pennant, both records at the time. There was, however, a sad footnote to the achievement. The man with whom he had shared the previous marks, Miller Huggins, died September 25 in a New York City hospital.

Given their powerful blend of hitting, pitching and fielding, the Athletics rated heavy favorites to repeat in 1930. But with a livelier baseball being whacked about—and out of—major league parks at terrifying velocities, a darkhorse, the Washington Senators, stepped forward to engage the Athletics in the A.L. baseball wars.

Walter Johnson's club won seven straight from Philadelphia after dropping their first meeting with the A's, 9-0. While that burst explained the Nats' lofty heights through June, the Athletics' 23-9 pace in July—and a seven-game streak of their own against Washington—provided the momentum for a strong second half and a 102-52 first-place finish for the Mackmen.

Simmons, once again, was the Athletics' hitting star. And while he closed the season with a .381 average and his first batting championship, Sim had announced his intentions with an opening-day extravaganza that couldn't be matched for flair. Just the night before the season inaugural, Mack announced that he had not agreed to a contract with his left fielder. Reporting in The Sporting News,

The hard-hitting Simmons piled up 92 home runs and 450 RBIs for the high-flying 1929-30-31 A's.

Isaminger described the scene the following day:

"The Athletics were going through their batting practice at 1:20 when Simmons burst out of Mack's private office and told newspaper writers that he had signed for 1930.

"At that early hour, more than half the stands were already filled. When Al emerged from the tunnel clad in a new white uniform, the fans knew at once that he had signed and the roar that swept over Shibe Park could be heard for blocks. Simmons never received a more tumultuous reception in his career. True to form, he stepped before the batting cage and quickly drove two into the left-field stands and another over the right-field wall.

"Al had a cartridge left for the real thing, however. In the first inning, with one on base, the heavy hitter caught one of Pipgras' pitches on the seam and rammed it over the right-field wall for a homer. That wallop lifted the A's right into the lead at the start and was a blow from which Pipgras and the Yankees never recovered."

True, the Yankees would finish a distant third, 16 games behind the Athletics, despite the sharp attack of Ruth (49 home runs, 153 RBIs) and Gehrig (41 homers, 174 RBIs).

And if the Yankees felt lasting effects from Simmons' opening-day shot, the Senators never really recovered from his Memorial Day spectacular.

In the first game of the holiday twin bill, Simmons slammed a game-tying three-run homer with two out in the ninth inning. In the 13th, he stroked a one-out double, then scored the winning run despite suffering a broken blood vessel in his right knee while diving into third during a rundown. When the knee swelled to twice its normal size after the game, the club physician decided to examine Simmons at a hospital—after the second contest.

"I came out here to see a doubleheader and I'm going to see it," he said. "You can put him back in a uniform and let him sit on the bench. He can't run, but he might come in handy as a pinch-hitter . . . but he'll have to hit the ball out of the ball park.

With Simmons resting on the bench, the A's loaded the bases in the fourth inning. "Suddenly, I saw Connie look down the line and crook that finger at me," Simmons said.

"Looks like this is the time and the place," Mack said. "This is what Dr. Carnett meant. You know what he said. Walk around the bases if you can."

Simmons limped to the plate and whaled the first pitch into the left-field stands for a grand slam.

"I hobbled around the bases and got back to the bench and Connie was sitting up straight, his eyes bright like a bird's, and he said, 'My, that was fine, Al.' "

The home run helped propel the Athletics to a four-game sweep of the Senators and into first place by a game.

Simmons finished the season with 36 homers and 165 RBIs, both career highs, and scored a league-leading 152 runs. But just as in 1929, he was only one gun in a menacing arsenal. Miller (.303, 100 RBIs) and Haas (.299) both wielded hot bats to round out the robust-hitting outfield. At first base, Foxx pounded 37 home runs, batted .335 and notched 156 RBIs. At the other corner, Dykes checked in at .301. Up the middle, Boley led the league's shortstops in fielding and batted .276, while Bishop drew 128 walks for the second straight year. Cochrane, once again, improved his average—to .357.

While the Athletics' hitters created considerable carnage, Grove stood out as the major league's premier hurler. In the year of the hitter, Grove posed

an incredible 28-5 record, 209 strikeouts and a 2.54 ERA, all league-leading totals. With a league-high 50 appearances, he teamed with Earnshaw (22-13, 49 games) to give Philadelphia the most effective and hardest-working pitching tandem in the league.

Heading into the 1930 World Series, the Athletics faced a torrid-hitting St. Louis Cardinals lineup that boasted a .300-hitter in every slot. Unfazed, Grove and Earnshaw subdued the Redbirds in six games, working all but eight innings in the autumn classic. Earnshaw posted a spectacular 0.72 ERA in 25 innings—which included 22 consecutive scoreless frames—and earned victories in the second and sixth games. Grove was only slightly less dominating with a 1.42 ERA and 2-1 record in 19 innings. He won the Series opener and Game 5, in relief of Earnshaw.

Opening play in 1931, the Athletics looked like anything but champions as they stumbled to a 2-5 start. But, perhaps after recalling what a merry month May had been in 1929, the A's steamrolled the pack with a 17-game winning streak that began May 5. Philadelphia was 23-4 in May, 20-9 in June and 26-7 in July as it charged toward a franchise-record 107 victories and a 13½-game advantage over the runner-up Yankees.

The Athletics' .704 winning percentage was only the second above .700 in A.L. history and second only to the 1927 Yankees' .714 mark. But in claiming their ninth pennant, the A's became the first team in major league history to win 100 games in three consecutive seasons. Their 313 victories over that span also established an A.L. record.

Three words explained the Athletics' 1931 romp: Earnshaw, Walberg, Grove.

After losing his first two decisions, Earnshaw won his next 12 on the way to a 21-7 season. Walberg was at his busiest—and most productive—pitching 291 innings on the way to a career-high 20 victories.

Grove was virtually invincible as the league's MVP. He finished 31-4 to boost his record to 79-15 over the Athletics' three-year reign. Grove struck out a league-leading 175 batters and topped the circuit in ERA—for the third straight year—with a 2.06 mark. But perhaps his most outstanding achievements were two incredible winning streaks.

Grove began the year by winning nine of his first 10 decisions. "He lost his 11th and ripped the locker room apart," Dykes recalled. "He was so mad he didn't talk to anyone. He got in his Pierce Arrow and drove to his home in Lonaconing, Maryland. He didn't show up at the park for days.

"He came back on the (third) day, didn't say a word to anybody and started another winning streak. He won 16 in a row (to equal the A.L. record). He lost the 17th (1-0 to the St. Louis Browns on August 23) because Jim Moore misjudged a fly

A's Manager Connie Mack and Cubs Manager Joe McCarthy at the 1929 World Series.

ball in left field. Moore was substituting for Al Simmons. . . . When Simmons asked Mr. Mack for a few days vacation (to rest a bad left ankle), the old man let him take off.

"When we got into the clubhouse after that game, Lefty never said a word to Jim Moore. But you should have heard the things he said about the vacationing Mr. Simmons."

Simmons shook off the pain in his left ankle to pace the A's hitters and win his second straight batting crown, thanks to the inspiration of Mack. "Connie said to me, 'Al, a champion is never a real

champion until he repeats.' " The Duke of Milwaukee batted .390 with 22 homers and 128 RBIs.

Besides Mack, only one other man—John McGraw of the New York Giants—had earned the chance to win three straight World Series titles. And it was one man, the St. Louis Cardinals' John (Pepper) Martin, who saw to it that Mack would fall short, just as McGraw had.

Showing quite clearly why he was known as the "Wild Horse of the Osage," Martin jolted the A's like a bolt of prairie lightning, batting a resounding .500 with five stolen bases as the Cardinals prevailed in seven games.

Mack hailed Martin as "an excellent specimen of manhood," congratulated the Cardinals as a "team of gentlemen" and looked ahead to 1932.

"I am contemplating no upheaval," Mack said. "I see no reason why, even though we lost the World Series, there should be any drastic shakeup in the present team.

"If our club was composed largely of aged players who were past their primes and were on the down grade, the situation would be different. But with only one or two exceptions, we have a comparatively young team. It ought to have a lot more years left in it."

To be specific, it had two. After finishing in second place in 1932 and third in 1933, the Athletics suffered through 13 consecutive losing seasons—and only Foxx and Miller were around for the beginning of the decline. Never again would they climb higher than fourth place.

As the 1932 campaign got under way, Boley was released on waivers. Simmons, Haas and Dykes were sold to the White Sox at the end of the season. In 1933, Rommel turned to coaching while Grove, Walberg and Bishop played out their last season for Mack; he traded them to the Boston Red Sox in December for the likes of infielder Harold Warstler, pitcher Bob Kline and cash. Cochrane met a similar fate that month, going to Detroit for $100,000 and catcher John Pasek, whom Mack sent

to the White Sox with one George Earnshaw for catcher Charlie Berry and $20,000. And by 1936, Miller and Foxx both were with the Red Sox.

"Another great era had come and gone," Mack said. "The big Depression was on. Attendances at ball games were dropping down. Another crisis loomed ahead.

"The law of diminishing returns is unrelenting."

But for three memorable seasons, the Philadelphia Athletics had shown baseball what "unrelenting" was all about.

1930
FINAL STANDING

Club	W.	L.	Pct.	GB.
Philadelphia	102	52	.662	——
Washington	94	60	.610	8

BATTERS

Pos.	Player	G.	HR.	RBI.	B.A.
1B	Jimmie Foxx	153	37	156	.335
2B	Max Bishop	130	10	38	.252
SS	Joe Boley	121	4	55	.276
3B	Jimmie Dykes	125	6	73	.301
OF	Al Simmons	138	36	165	.381
	Mule Haas	132	2	68	.299
	Bing Miller	154	9	100	.303
C	Mickey Cochrane	130	10	85	.357
UT	Eric McNair (inf)	78	0	34	.266

OTHER CONTRIBUTORS (20+ Games): Doc Cramer, Spence Harris, Cy Perkins, Wally Schang, Homer Summa, Dib Williams.

PITCHERS

Thr.	Pitcher	G.	W.	L.	ERA
L	Lefty Grove	50	28	5	2.54
R	George Earnshaw	49	22	13	4.44
L	Rube Walberg	38	13	12	4.70
R	Bill Shores	31	12	4	4.19

OTHER CONTRIBUTORS (20+ Games): Roy Mahaffey, Jack Quinn, Eddie Rommel.

1931
FINAL STANDING

Club	W.	L.	Pct.	GB.
Philadelphia	107	45	.704	——
New York	94	59	.614	13½

BATTERS

Pos.	Player	G.	HR.	RBI.	B.A.
1B	Jimmie Foxx	139	30	120	.291
2B	Max Bishop	130	5	37	.294
SS	Dib Williams	86	6	40	.269
3B	Jimmie Dykes	101	3	46	.273
OF	Al Simmons	128	22	128	.390
	Mule Haas	102	8	56	.323
	Bing Miller	137	8	77	.281
C	Mickey Cochrane	122	17	89	.349
UT	Eric McNair (3b)	79	5	33	.271

OTHER CONTRIBUTORS (20+ Games): Joe Boley, Doc Cramer, John Heving, Jim Moore, Phil Todt.

PITCHERS

Thr.	Pitcher	G.	W.	L.	ERA
L	Lefty Grove	41	31	4	2.06
R	George Earnshaw	43	21	7	3.67
L	Rube Walberg	44	20	12	3.74
R	Roy Mahaffey	30	15	4	4.22
R	Waite Hoyt	16	10	5	4.22

OTHER CONTRIBUTORS (20+ Games): Eddie Rommel.

1929
FINAL STANDING

Club	W.	L.	Pct.	GB.
Philadelphia	104	46	.693	——
New York	88	66	.571	18

BATTERS

Pos.	Player	G.	HR.	RBI.	B.A.
1B	Jimmie Foxx	149	33	117	.354
2B	Max Bishop	129	3	36	.232
SS	Joe Boley	91	2	47	.251
3B	Jimmie Dykes	119	13	79	.327
	Sammy Hale	101	1	40	.277
OF	Al Simmons	143	34	157	.365
	Mule Haas	139	16	82	.313
	Bing Miller	147	8	93	.335
C	Mickey Cochrane	135	7	95	.331

OTHER CONTRIBUTORS (20+ Games): George Burns, Jim Cronin, Walt French, Ossie Orwoll, Cy Perkins, Homer Summa.

PITCHERS

Thr.	Pitcher	G.	W.	L.	ERA
R	George Earnshaw	44	24	8	3.28
L	Lefty Grove	42	20	6	2.81
L	Rube Walberg	40	18	11	3.59
R	Eddie Rommel	32	12	2	2.84
R	Jack Quinn	35	11	9	3.88
R	Bill Shores	39	11	6	3.59
R	Howard Ehmke	11	7	2	3.27

Number 4

Chicago's Cubs Slay the Giants

The 1906 National League champion Chicago Cubs were able to grin and bear their good fortune.

Those who knew him best stoutly maintained that John Joseph Evers, upon retiring to his hotel room during his playing days, took with him several daily newspapers, some candy bars, the latest issue of The Sporting News and a baseball guide that containd the playing rules.

Furthermore, contemporaries contended, Evers digested the contents of the journals, consumed the confections and then fell asleep while studying the playing code of the game.

Evers read and reread the rules until he had committed them to memory. He knew them as well as any umpire and better than many. Having learned them, he delighted in discussing them, debating them and then devising stratagems to circumvent them while still abiding by the word of the law.

Through most of Evers' primal years as an outstanding second baseman, Hank O'Day was a National League umpire. O'Day had been a pitcher in the game's formative years before lending his dour disposition to the art of umpiring. On the field, Evers and O'Day were the cobra and the mongoose of baseball, constantly bickering over rules interpretations or unpopular calls by the arbiter.

Hugh Fullerton, a Chicago newspaperman who traveled with the Cubs during Evers' heyday, related one confrontation between the two men. At issue was the infield fly rule.

On a day when baserunner Evers was perched on second base and a teammate was on first with fewer than two men out, a batter lifted a high pop fly.

"What is it?" Evers yelled to O'Day.

"Infield fly," bellowed the consummate autocrat.

With that, Evers set sail for third base. He was standing there triumphantly when the ball was caught and O'Day called him out with an imperious wave of the hand.

"Wait a minute," screamed Evers, his jut jaw at a defiant angle. "Wasn't the ball technically caught when you declared it an infield fly? Isn't that the rule?"

The umpire conceded the point.

"Well, it's the rule, too," Evers said, "that a runner can advance after a fly ball is caught, isn't it?

The early-century Cubs' infield trio immortalized by newspaperman Franklin P.
Adams was made up of (left to right) Joe Tinker, Johnny Evers and Frank Chance.

Technically, it was caught; so I went to third. How can you call me out?"

O'Day was flabbergasted by the player's logic, but only momentarily. Regaining his composure, O'Day answered his tormentor. "To hell with them technicalities," the umpire shot back. "I say you're out—and you're out."

The incident typified Evers' approach to the game. He was ever in search of an advantage, whether in the playing rules or in the heat of combat. To some folks, he was "The Crab" because of his pugnacious attitude. To others, he was "The Trojan" because of his association with Troy, N.Y.

To everyone, he was known as a fierce competitor.

Evers was born in Troy on March 21, 1883. When he entered professional baseball with his hometown team in the New York League in 1902, the 5-foot-9 infielder reportedly weighed little more than 100 pounds.

Despite his unimpressive physical stature, Evers was a major leaguer before the season was over. He was sold to the Chicago Cubs for a reported $250 and joined his new teammates in Philadelphia in time for a Labor Day doubleheader. Manager Frank Selee installed the newcomer at shortstop.

Within a few days, Evers was shifted to second

The missing link on the Cubs' famous infield was third baseman Harry Steinfeldt.

perman Franklin P. Adams. After their defensive wizardry had snuffed out repeated scoring threats by the Giants, Adams composed "Baseball's Sad Lexicon," a bit of doggerel that eventually helped the threesome win election to the Hall of Fame:

These are the saddest of possible words,
Tinker to Evers to Chance.
Trio of bear Cubs and fleeter than birds,
Tinker to Evers to Chance.
Thoughtlessly pricking our gonfalon bubble,
Making a Giant hit into a double,
Words that are weighty with nothing but trouble,
Tinker to Evers to Chance.

Chance was the first of the three to join the Cubs. Originally a catcher, he had attended Washington College in Irvington, Calif., and at age 20 became a Cub in 1898 without benefit of minor league experience. He was a 6-foot, 190-pounder and thereby answered to the nickname of "Husk." Later, as he attained renown as manager of the team, he was known familiarly as "The Peerless Leader."

In the opinion of Chicago newsman Oscar Reichow, Chance was "fearless . . . aggressive . . . tactful and diplomatic . . . beloved by all the players . . . (and) never took undue advantage of anyone."

Chance was partially deaf in his left ear, the result of frequent beanings. On many occasions, he remarked that he would have preferred faulty hearing in his right ear so that he would not be subjected to the incessant chatter of the voluble Evers.

Tinker, a native of Muscotah, Kan., donned a Chicago uniform for the first time at the start of the 1902 campaign. He had been acquired from Portland of the Pacific Northwest League and won instant employment with the Cubs.

"Tinker played a deep short, far back on the grass, as his deadly arm enabled him to throw out runners from any position," baseball historian Fred Lieb wrote more than three decades after the double-play unit's halcyon days. "A mental telepathy seemed to connect Tinker and Evers; each always seemed to sense exactly what the other would do under all circumstances. An oddity of this perfect understanding on the ball field is that off the field the two men were not friendly. There was a . . . period in which they did not speak to each other off the field . . . Joe and Johnny made up in later years, but it was typical of the scrappy nature of both of these players that they carried their feuds into their own clubhouse."

Tinker, according to longtime New York reporter Dan Daniel, "was the jolly man of the great Chicago trio. He had a keen sense of humor and roared his way through the passing seasons. Joe could undress you out at second with a loud guffaw. He went

base and Joe Tinker, who had been playing third, was switched to shortstop. Frank Chance, who went to the sidelines because of an injury shortly after Evers arrived, returned to first base on September 13 and, on that day, the Tinker-Evers-Chance trio appeared in its famous alignment for the first time. Two days later, the first Tinker-to-Evers-to-Chance double play was executed at the Cubs' home park, West Side Grounds, in a game against Cincinnati.

In time, the shortstop, second baseman and first baseman were immortalized by New York newspa-

right on through life that way . . . ."

Evers, of course, approached baseball and life in a considerably more intense manner. New York Giants pitching star Christy Mathewson, his tongue apparently *not* planted in his cheek, once even claimed that "Evers cannot keep a watch going because his body is so full of electricity. This may sound ridiculous on the face of it, but it is absolutely true. Evers has been presented with several fine watches and they will not keep accurate time when he carries them because of something in his physical makeup which prevents every timepiece from doing its job properly."

While the 1902 Cubs boasted other skilled players besides Chance, Tinker and late-comer Evers—in particular, outfielder Jimmy Slagle and catcher Johnny Kling—and had a steady pitching staff as well, Selee's charges lacked the top-to-bottom strength to be a factor in the pennant race and wound up in fifth place. The Chicagoans climbed to third in 1903 and second in 1904 before slipping back to third in 1905, a season during which Chance supplanted an ailing Selee as the Cubs' manager.

All the while, the Cubs were improving their roster and fine-tuning the talent on hand. The pitching had been bolstered by the addition of Mordecai

Brown in 1904 and Ed Reulbach in 1905 and would be further strengthened by the arrival of Western League recruit Jack Pfiester in 1906 and the in-season acquisitions of Orval Overall and Jack Taylor. Still on hand from the '02 club was Carl Lundgren.

Changes weren't limited to the mound crew. Frank Schulte, who had made his major league debut in a stint with the Cubs in 1904 after finishing up the last of his three minor league seasons with Syracuse, moved into regular outfield duty in 1905 and he and Slagle would be joined in 1906 by Jimmy Sheckard, obtained from Brooklyn in December 1905.

Finding little reason to be content with the exploits of only three-fourths of their infield, the Cubs swung a deal before the start of the '06 season to put third base in hands just as capable—if not as well-known—as those performing wondrous deeds elsewhere in the team's inner defense. Acquired was Harry Steinfeldt, a member of the Cincinnati club since 1898 and a one-time minstrel man who had

The hard-hitting and hard-charging manager of the Cubs was first baseman Frank Chance.

deserted his troupe in Texas to help out a local team and never returned to the stage.

Kling remained the main man at catcher. Pat Moran, purchased from Boston's National League entry, was ticketed for a backup role behind the plate.

While the Cubs no doubt had improved themselves significantly and had pennant ambitions, John McGraw and his swashbuckling Giants were reigning National League and World Series champions. Dethroning the New Yorkers would take a monumental effort. The Giants had won 211 games in the last two seasons—they also captured the N.L. flag in 1904—and, among a bevy of talented players, laid claim to the game's No. 1 pitcher in Mathewson, who in 1905 had chalked up 30 or more victories for the third successive season.

Almost from the start of spring training, though, the 1906 Giants encountered trouble. If it wasn't poor weather, it was Mathewson being hounded by illness, Mike Donlin reportedly being guilty of alcoholic indulgences or the team being beset by other misadventures. The correspondent of The Sporting News informed readers in March that "since the McGraw bunch reached Memphis (the Giants' training site), there has been nothing but trouble. Rain and cold weather! Mathewson in bed at the hotel with the doctors saying that he has had diphtheria although McGraw denies it! Mike Donlin putting away the old stuff and suspended! Then begs McGraw's pardon and is reinstated though all the time Michael not drawing salary! Pool rooms nearby putting Giants on the blink . . . Up to this writing Giants have had no beneficial practice to speak of . . . ."

Nor was that all. Catcher Roger Bresnahan lost several teeth when struck by an errant bat, first baseman Dan McGann was the focal point of a training-room row, pitcher Joe McGinnity was confined to bed because of illness and, McGraw's insistence to the contrary, Mathewson did suffer from diphtheria and wouldn't pitch in the regular season until May 5.

Despite their various misfortunes, the Giants got off to a 14-3 regular-season start. And, after games of May 27, McGraw's club was atop the N.L. standings (25-12 record, .676 winning percentage) but clinging to the narrowest of leads over the runner-up Cubs (27-13, .675).

On May 28, Chicago—no stranger to the top spot in the early going—slipped back into first place as the Giants lost to St. Louis and the Cubs beat Boston. Brown was a 4-2 winner against the Braves, getting the edge he needed when Schulte cracked a late-inning home run.

Brown, a 29-year-old righthander, was en route to a marvelous season in what would prove a memorable career. It was a remarkable rise to fame for a

man who, as a curious youngster, had thrust his hand into a feed cutter on the family farm and suffered the loss of part of his right index finger. Not only did the mishap fail to deter the Indianan, it seemingly gave a boost to his baseball career. The finger stub, it turned out, imparted an unusual spin to Brown's pitches, which dipped sharply as they approached the plate.

"It was a great ball, that down-curve of his," Ty Cobb would say after batting against Brown in future World Series competition. "I can't talk about all of baseball, but I can say this: It was the most deceiving, the most devastating pitch I ever faced."

In 1903, his first year in the major leagues, "Three Finger" Brown won nine games for St. Louis' National League club before being traded to the Cubs after the season. He proceeded to win 15 games for Chicago in 1904 and 18 in 1905.

The man who also was known as "Miner"—he labored in the Indiana coal fields before entering professional baseball—wasn't so sure that his handicap was a blessing in disguise.

"Few know the excruciating pain I suffered when

Chatterbox catcher Johnny Kling had a lot to do with the Cubs' pitching success.

I had to grip the ball in certain ways," said Brown, reflecting on his career in later life. "I always felt if I had had a normal hand, I would have been a greater pitcher."

As it was, Brown was the essence of greatness. The 1906 season was the first of six straight years in which he won 20 or more games. And in four of those campaigns, he won 25 or more contests.

Schulte, a 23-year-old lefthanded hitter, was a free spirit who loved to win but could deal with losing. And he dealt with defeat in unusual ways— by breaking into a monologue, or verse, or song.

"Mr. Schulte careth not whether he has an audience," Ring Lardner once wrote. "When he is in the mood to talk, he will talk and talk loud, and he isn't particular whom he criticizes nor who is listening to his monologue. Mr. Schulte is best after the Cubs have lost a hard game. He likes to win, all right, but he doesn't see why defeats should be the cause of tears or post-mortems.

"Aboard the sleeper, after one of those defeats for which two or three slips were responsible, there are gathered various little knots of athletes telling each other how it happened, how the beating could have been avoided, and mourning and wailing over the unkindness of fate. In his seat, all alone or with a willing listener, sits Mr. Schulte.

"'The boys seem to forget there'll be a game tomorrow to play,'" Lardner quoted Schulte as saying. "'They act as if this is the last one they ever were going to get into . . . .'"

One day, as teammates replayed—and agonized over—a tough setback, Schulte surveyed the situation and sang softly:

"Kidney stew and fried pig's feet—
That's the grub I love to eat."

Whether the occasionally irreverent Schulte could or couldn't carry a tune was of no concern to the Cubs or their fans, who simply asked that the fleet-yet-powerful right fielder carry a potent bat. And "Wildfire" Schulte did just that. Schulte tied for the league lead in triples in 1906, shared the N.L. home run crown four years later and then really muscled up in 1911 when he won the league homer title outright with a figure of 21, the highest total in the major leagues thus far in the century (and a mark that included four bases-loaded homers, a big-league season record at the time).

The May 28 move of the Cubs into the league lead was not a mere "blip" on another banner season for the New York Giants. Indeed, the Chicagoans never relinquished their grip on first place. And as well as Chance's men had been playing, they soon began performing on an even higher plane. And then higher yet.

That the Cubs were intent on stealing away with the Giants' crown was never more evident than in an early-June series at the Polo Grounds. Brown outpitched McGinnity in the opener, 6-0, allowing only three hits. Overall, obtained less than a week earlier in a trade with Cincinnati, won the second game, 11-3, backed by a 19-hit bombardment that featured five hits by Schulte and four by Tinker.

McGraw attempted to avoid further pounding— not to mention humiliation—by sending Mathewson to the mound in game three. Matty, still in a debilitated condition from his bout with diphtheria, retired only one batter as the Cubs went on an 11-run spree in the first inning. Disbelieving New Yorkers watched in horror as Chicago buried the Giants under a 22-hit barrage and won, 19-0. Slagle and Steinfeldt each collected four hits.

The acquisition of Overall proved a coup for the Cubs, as did a subsequent deal for righthander Jack Taylor.

Overall, a 6-2, 215-pounder and a former baseball and football star at the University of California, had merited advancement to the Cincinnati club on the basis of a 32-victory season in the Pacific Coast League in 1904. After working 318 innings and posting an 18-23 record for the Reds in 1905, Big Orvie was 4-5 in 1906 for Ned Hanlon's Ohioans when he was traded to Chicago on June 1. He won 12 of 15 decisions for the Cubs.

Taylor, a Cubs pitching standout in 1902 and 1903 before being dispatched to St. Louis in the trade that sent Brown to Chicago, was obtained in early July and proceeded to match Overall's 12-3 ledger as a Cub and produced 20 total victories (including eight with St. Louis).

Although the Giants rebounded from the 19-0 debacle and salvaged the series finale against the Cubs, they weren't spared by acerbic newspaperman Joe Vila. Writing in The Sporting News, Vila summed up what he had witnessed: "Hoots, jeers and catcalls for the world's champions! . . . It all came about when the Chicago Cubs beat the champions three straight, the last tumble for the Hoodlums (Giants) being a 19-to-0 pitfall. This game was a disgrace to the National League and an insult to the local fans who paid good money to see a real article of ball. The Cubs were not to blame, but the Giants, beaten at their own game—outplayed, outgeneraled and outbluffed—turned the struggle into a farce until the people in the stands treated the former Swelled Heads to an awful roast."

The National League pennant was destined for farce status, too. The Cubs, who compiled a gaudy 39-18 record (.684) in their first 57 games, fashioned an incredible 77-18 mark (.811) in their final 95 games and established a still-standing major league season record of 116 victories (against 36 losses). McGraw's New Yorkers won 96 games and finished second, *20* games behind Chicago.

Brown wound up winning 26 games and tossing nine shutouts. Pfiester, the lone lefthander in the

Mainstays of the Cubs' successful pitching staff were (left to right) Three Finger Brown, Ed Reulbach and Orval Overall.

Cubs' rotation, fired four shutouts and won 20 games in his first full season in the majors. Reulbach posted an imposing 19-4 record and blanked the opposition six times.

Reulbach was a many-faceted individual. A native of Detroit, he studied engineering at the University of Notre Dame and medicine at the University of Vermont and at Washington University in St. Louis. In later years, he took courses in industrial management at the University of Rochester and in law at Columbia University. He also delighted in playing under assumed names. In the minor leagues, he first was known as "Lawson" and then as "Sheldon."

Reulbach also carried the well-documented reputation of a practical joker. Frank Shaughnessy, a contemporary at Notre Dame and later president of the International League, once said that Reulbach "upset dignified professors by dropping paper bags of water on their unsuspecting heads. He also daubed keyholes with a mixture that exploded when a key was inserted. He was a big, fun-loving kid who counted a day lost when he didn't put over at least one practical joke."

Reulbach was all business on the mound, however. He won 12 straight decisions in one stretch of the 1906 season, the first of three consecutive years in which he topped N.L. pitchers in winning percentage.

Once asked to explain how the Cubs ever managed to win 116 games in one season, Reulbach reflected on the team's blend of personnel and smiled. "When I look back," he said, "I wonder how we came to lose 36."

Lundgren, from Marengo, Ill., and a former University of Illinois standout, made his fifth year with the Cubs his best one to date, throwing five shutouts and putting together a 17-6 season.

Considerable credit for the pitching staff's success went to the club's cerebral catcher, Kling, who was a great handler of pitchers, solid mechanically behind the plate, a strong thrower and a steady hitter.

A constant chatterer, Kling derived considerable satisfaction from needling opposing batters and controlling a game from his catching position—hence his nicknames "Noisy Johnny" and "Brainy Johnny."

Kling and Chance once were catching rivals on

the Cubs, and Kling's potential as a receiver no doubt contributed heavily to Chance's conversion into a first baseman.

While Kling provided leadership from his vantage point, Chance did likewise in his role as playing manager.

"Talk about great managers," outfielder Sheckard said, "none of 'em had anything on Frank Chance. He might have been hard to get along with at times, but he was the players' best friend. And he wasn't strict when it came to training rules.

" 'If you want to take a glass of beer, take one,' Frank would tell us. 'If you need two drinks—OK. And if it's three beers you like, that is all right. Go and get drunk if you want—but be sure you come out the next day at the park in condition to play ball.' "

Besides guiding his troops with just the right touch on and off the field in 1906, Chance batted .319—his fourth straight season of hitting .310 or higher—and tied for the league lead in runs scored with 103. Tinker and Evers lent their special brand of grace to the Cubs' league-leading defense, and newcomer Steinfeldt gave the offense added firepower with a .327 batting average (second-best figure in the National League) and an N.L.-high 176 hits.

The Cubs' pennant performance, wrote one reviewer of the campaign, "gave a tremendous impetus to baseball throughout the west. Exactly as the victories of the New York club in the two preceding years had aroused baseball sentiment to the highest pitch in the east, so the Chicagos, by their successful career, brought out the real love of the people for the national game in the west. Never had there been such crowds, such excitement, such loyalty and such warm demonstrations for a club in the great city of Chicago."

Adding to the frenzy in the Windy City was the fact that the town's other big-league entry, the White Sox, had captured the championship of the American League.

That the Cubs, who stormed to the finish line with 48 victories in their last 54 games, couldn't cope with the White Sox's "Hitless Wonders" in the 1906 World Series caused the National League franchise considerable anguish. In one of the biggest Series upsets of all time, the White Sox—.228 hitters collectively in the regular season—knocked off the mighty Cubs, four games to two. The National Leaguers' only victories came on a one-hitter by Reulbach and a two-hitter by Brown.

Still, the talent was in place for a Cubs run of domination that set major league baseball on its ear. With virtually the same cast of players on hand, Chance's men swept to World Series championships in 1907 and 1908. While the 1907 club won the pennant by 17 games, the 1908 team pre-

vailed only after winning an end-of-season makeup contest precipitated by perhaps the most memorable blunder in the history of the game.

In a September 23 Cubs-Giants game, Giants baserunner Fred Merkle failed to touch second base after Al Bridwell delivered an apparent game-winning hit in the bottom of the ninth inning. That ol' rules expert, Evers, called for the ball after seeing a celebration-bent Merkle sprint off the field before reaching second. By the time the Cubs retrieved the ball and eventually forced the 19-year-old Merkle at second, fans had swarmed the field. With order impossible to restore, the game was declared a 1-1 tie. As fate would have it, Chicago and New York wound up with 98-55 records—a situation demanding that the "Merkle game" be made up.

In the October 8 replay, Brown's 8⅓ innings of stellar relief pitching—wildness forced Pfiester out of the game in the first inning—beat Mathewson, 4-2, and made the Cubs N.L. champions for the third consecutive season. The triumph was Brown's ninth straight over Big Six in a stretch of whammy that had begun after Mathewson's no-hitter against Brown and the Cubs in 1905.

The '08 season featured memorable exploits by Brown and Reulbach. Brown won 29 games and became the first N.L. pitcher of the century to toss four consecutive shutouts in one year. Reulbach collected 24 victories and took a cue from Brownie by blanking the opposition four straight times in the late stages of the season. The middle two shutouts in Reulbach's string came on the *same* day— September 26—when Reulbach became the only pitcher in major league history to throw shutouts in both games of a doubleheader. He set down Brooklyn, 5-0, on five hits in the opener and came out a three-hit, 3-0 victor in the nightcap.

The Cubs won the 1907 and 1908 World Series in a total of 10 games, losing one game and tying another against the Detroit Tigers and their young phenom, Cobb. Steinfeldt batted .471 in the 1907 fall classic and Chance hit at a .421 clip in the 1908 Series. Brown and Overall each went 3-0 in those two Series.

The Cubs' 1909 season was clouded by the year-long holdout of Kling, who balked at salary terms offered by Cubs Owner Charles Murphy. Perhaps underscoring Kling's value to the team, the Cubs— despite winning 104 games and getting 14 straight triumphs from Reulbach—endured their only non-pennant year from 1906 through 1910 as the Pittsburgh Pirates won the N.L. flag.

Missing besides Kling in 1909 was pitcher Lundgren, who departed after just two appearances, and veteran center fielder Slagle, whose position was filled by Artie (Circus Solly) Hofman. Hofman had played all four infield spots and seen outfield duty for the Cubs in earlier years before nailing down a full-time outfield job in 1909. A .304 hitter in the 1906 World Series and a .316 batsman in the 1908 Series, the versatile Hofman won Kling's approval as "the greatest asset our great Cub teams had."

The Cubs were little changed in 1910, with names like Chance, Tinker, Evers, Steinfeldt, Schulte, Sheckard and Hofman still dotting the box scores, Kling easing back into duty behind the plate and Brown, Overall and Reulbach continuing to serve 'em up from the mound (with considerable help from rookie righthander King Cole, who went 20-4). At season's end, this smooth-running machine stood 13 games ahead of the second-place Giants.

World Series disappointment ensued for the 1910 Chicago Cubs in the form of a four games-to-one loss to the Philadelphia A's, then came a pennant drought that lasted through 1917.

But what a fabulous run by these Cubs—highlighted, of course, by their record-smashing victory total in 1906 and World Series championships in 1907 and 1908. All told in the five-year blitz that began in '06: four pennants, one second-place finish, 530 regular-season victories and the two Series crowns. It was the kind of domination that drove opposition to cover and one writer to the extreme of penning verse.

. . . Making a Giant hit into a double.
Words that are mighty with nothing but trouble,
Tinker to Evers to Chance.

"I wrote the piece because I wanted to get out to the game and the foreman of the composing room . . . said I needed eight lines to fill," said Adams, a member of the staff of the New York Evening Mail.

Told that no matter what else he wrote, he forever would be known as the man who produced the baseball verse, Adams was of the opinion that the eight lines "weren't much good at that."

Adams knew very well, though, that the Chicago Cubs of the Tinker-Evers-Chance era were very, very good—the kind of team that made everyone, not just sportswriters, hurry out to the ol' ball park.

1906
FINAL STANDING

Club	W.	L.	Pct.	GB.
Chicago	116	36	.763	——
New York	96	56	.632	20

BATTERS

Pos.	Player	G.	HR.	RBI.	B.A.
1B	Frank Chance	136	3	71	.319
2B	Johnny Evers	154	1	51	.255
SS	Joe Tinker	148	1	64	.233
3B	Harry Steinfeldt	151	3	83	.327
OF	Jimmy Sheckard	149	1	45	.262
	Jimmy Slagle	127	0	33	.239
	Wildfire Schulte	146	7	60	.281
C	Johnny Kling	107	2	46	.312

OTHER CONTRIBUTORS (20+ Games): Doc Gessler, Solly Hofman, Pat Moran.

PITCHERS

Thr.	Pitcher	G.	W.	L.	ERA
R	Three Finger Brown	36	26	6	1.04
L	Jack Pfiester	31	20	8	1.56
R	Ed Reulbach	33	19	4	1.65
R	Carl Lundgren	27	17	6	2.21
R	Orval Overall	18	12	3	1.88
R	Jack Taylor	17	12	3	1.84

1907
FINAL STANDING

Club	W.	L.	Pct.	GB.
Chicago	107	45	.704	——
Pittsburgh	91	63	.591	17

BATTERS

Pos.	Player	G.	HR.	RBI.	B.A.
1B	Frank Chance	109	1	49	.293
2B	Johnny Evers	151	2	51	.250
SS	Joe Tinker	113	1	36	.221
3B	Harry Steinfeldt	151	1	70	.267
OF	Jimmy Sheckard	142	1	36	.263
	Jimmy Slagle	135	0	32	.257
	Wildfire Schulte	97	2	32	.287
C	Johnny Kling	104	1	43	.284
UT	Solly Hofman (of-ss)	134	1	36	.268

OTHER CONTRIBUTORS (20+ Games): Del Howard, Pat Moran, Newt Randall.

PITCHERS

Thr.	Pitcher	G.	W.	L.	ERA
R	Orval Overall	36	23	8	1.68
R	Three Finger Brown	34	20	6	1.39
R	Carl Lundgren	28	18	7	1.17
R	Ed Reulbach	27	17	4	1.69
L	Jack Pfiester	30	15	9	1.15

OTHER CONTRIBUTORS (20+ Games): Chick Fraser.

1908
FINAL STANDING

Club	W.	L.	Pct.	GB.
Chicago	99	55	.643	——
New York	98	56	.636	1
Pittsburgh	98	56	.636	1

BATTERS

Pos.	Player	G.	HR.	RBI.	B.A.
1B	Frank Chance	129	2	55	.272
2B	Johnny Evers	126	0	37	.300
SS	Joe Tinker	157	6	68	.266
3B	Harry Steinfeldt	150	1	62	.241
OF	Jimmy Sheckard	115	2	22	.231
	Jimmy Slagle	104	0	26	.222
	Wildfire Schulte	102	1	43	.236
C	Johnny Kling	126	4	59	.276
UT	Solly Hofman (of-1b)	116	2	42	.243
	Del Howard (of)	89	1	26	.279

OTHER CONTRIBUTORS (20+ Games): Pat Moran, Heinie Zimmerman.

PITCHERS

Thr.	Pitcher	G.	W.	L.	ERA
R	Three Finger Brown	44	29	9	1.47
R	Ed Reulbach	46	24	7	2.02
R	Orval Overall	37	15	11	1.92
L	Jack Pfiester	33	12	10	2.00
R	Chick Fraser	26	11	9	2.26

OTHER CONTRIBUTORS (20+ Games): Carl Lundgren.

A Flag Flies In Brooklyn

The 1955 Dodgers were kings of Brooklyn and champions of the world—finally.

Walter Emmons Alston seemed out of his element. But there he was in November 1953, being introduced as manager of the Brooklyn Dodgers at the club's Montague Street office.

Alston's strong point was his acknowledged skill as a gifted teacher of the young, as evidenced by his managerial success in the Dodgers' farm system. But precious little teaching would be required at this level. After all, the Dodgers were a veteran team stocked with mind-set superstars who probably neither needed nor would take kindly to refresher courses in the fundamentals of the game.

Alston, who had appeared in exactly one big-league game during his playing career, was a virtual unknown in the majors. He would be presiding over some of the best-known players in baseball, household names who had made the Dodgers one of the best teams in the big leagues. Ever.

Brooklyn's new field boss was the very antithesis of the man who had held the job the previous three seasons. Charlie Dressen was a fiery, flamboyant, kick-'em-in-the-pants-if-they-don't-respond type of manager. Alston, manager of the Dodgers' Montreal farm club for the last four seasons, was quiet and low-key in his approach.

Dressen had survived the rigors of pressure-packed pennant races in the major leagues—he also had guided the Cincinnati Reds in the 1930s—and led the Dodgers to National League championships in 1952 and 1953. Alston had endured nothing more than the butterflies associated with competing for the top spot in the likes of the Middle Atlantic League, Inter-State League, New England League, Western League, American Association and International League.

But if Alston had yet to experience big-time pressure, he was about to. Whereas managerial appointees often face sizable tasks, Alston encoun-

Dodger Manager Walter Alston (right) finally fulfilled Owner Walter O'Malley's fondest dream.

tered something beyond the obligatory expectation of improvement, or first-division status or even pennant contention. As rookie manager of this talent-rich band of Brooklyn Dodgers, he was expected to win the World Series. The pennant? Brooklyn was a shoo-in for that honor. The Dodgers had won N.L. titles in four of the last seven years and just missed in the Philadelphia Phillies' Whiz Kids season of 1950 and in the New York Giants' Miracle of Coogan's Bluff year of 1951.

No one in the Dodgers' front office ever came right out and said Alston would be counted on to

bring home in his first season what no other manager in club history had been able to deliver (seven times Brooklyn had played for the World Series championship and seven times the Dodgers had lost). From Dodgers President Walter O'Malley on down, though, the October frustration was getting to be just a bit much. And Alston, in the view of almost everyone connected with the club, was in a perfect position to do something about it.

Alston was taking over a team that, while a Series loser to the New York Yankees in six games, had won 105 regular-season contests in 1953 and cap-

Three of the Dodgers' biggest sticks were carried by (left to right) first baseman
Gil Hodges, catcher Roy Campanella and right fielder Carl Furillo.

tured the National League pennant by 13 games. He
had the league's Most Valuable Player in Roy Campanella, its Rookie of the Year in Jim Gilliam, its
batting champion in Carl Furillo, two of its leading
sluggers in Duke Snider and Gil Hodges (who combined for 73 home runs and 248 runs batted in) and
one of its top pitchers in 20-game winner Carl Erskine. Plus, pitching standout Don Newcombe was
due back after two years of military service, and big
Newk had notched 20 victories in his last season
with Brooklyn.

Some juggernaut, this.

The best-laid plans sometimes get waylaid, however. And such was the case with Alston and the
1954 Dodgers. The '54 Bums did not win the World
Series. In fact, the Dodgers couldn't have gotten
into the Series without a ticket. With a hand ailment turning Campanella's season into a night-
mare, Newcombe providing only nine victories and
the pitching staff faltering overall, Brooklyn wound
up closer to third place (three games) than first (five
games). The Giants had dethroned the Dodgers as
N.L. kingpins.

Most of the finger-pointing was aimed at Alston,
who appeared too laid-back for the job. Maybe
Dressen overmanaged, but critics charged the 42-
year-old Alston with benign neglect. Nothing
seemed to stir the professorial Ohioan, and he had
trouble stirring others. Perhaps Alston, after years
of toiling in baseball's bush leagues, couldn't relate
to the likes of Campanella, Furillo, Snider, Hodges,
Newcombe, Pee Wee Reese and Jackie Robinson.

One thing was certain. Teacher Alston had learned a lesson in 1954. Showing a Mr. Nice Guy image
mixed with a no-nonsense approach was fine, but
more was required to get his message across. A firm
hand had to be clearly evident.

Something else was demonstrated in '54. These
Dodgers, as good as they were, needed strong managerial leadership. They couldn't, as some observers
had contended, bash their National League opposition regardless of who was running the show.

Alston, armed with a second one-year contract,
exerted leadership in 1955. And how.

Where he had been tentative a year earlier because, in part, of his unfamiliarity with National
League personnel overall—his advice-seeking sessions with Dodger veterans were viewed as signs of
weakness—Alston showed from the start that he
was in control in '55. On the field and off the field.

After their disappointing '54 season, the Dodgers
weren't the cheeriest of athletes when they gathered
for spring training in Vero Beach, Fla. And all
spring, there were rumblings of discontent among
the troops. Robinson was furious over his lack of
playing time in exhibition games, the usually placid
Campanella was chippy over his eighth-place standing in the batting order and other players voiced
grievances of varying severity. Finally, when the
Dodgers reached Louisville on their exhibition
swing northward, Alston called a clubhouse meeting.

Alston's "forthright comments included a direct
challenge to at least one player," The Sporting News
reported later in an editorial, "and an indirect challenge to any player on the squad who cared to pick

Jackie Robinson (right) was playing third base by 1955 while Jim Gilliam saw action at second base, Robinson's former position.

up the gauntlet Alston flung down.

"When Alston ended his speech, none of his listeners had any further doubt about who was managing the club. There may have been some players who disliked him or his methods, or both, but respect for his authority became mandatory.

"...'It is doubtful,' one observer said later, 'that any ball club except some under John McGraw ever had heard anything quite like it.'"

Robinson, Campanella and anyone else with a complaint got the message, loud and clear.

Although Jackie Robinson no longer was the dominant figure he had been when he pioneered the integration of modern major league baseball eight years earlier, he still showed occasional flashes of the greatness that had earned him Rookie of the Year (1947) and Most Valuable Player (1949) honors in the National League. And on opening day of the 1955 season, Robinson—despite his fears that firebrand Don Hoak would get the starting call over him—was playing third base for Brooklyn.

At age 36, Robinson was nearing the end of a storied career. As the first black player in the

majors in this century, Jackie had endured hardships that would have broken an ordinary man. But Jack Roosevelt Robinson was no ordinary man.

Robinson was a fiercely competitive and proud individual, and it was not in his makeup to take racial abuse—or any kind of abuse, for that matter —without fighting back. But Dodgers General Manager Branch Rickey, in preliminary talks to Robinson's signing in the fall of 1945, assessed the temper of the times and the prevailing social climate and told Robinson: "I want a ball player with guts enough not to fight back. You've got to do this job with base-hits and stolen bases and by fielding ground balls, Jackie. Nothing else."

Whatever might lie ahead—taunts from fans and opponents, rumored player rebellions, segregationist housing policies—Robinson agreed to keep his cool, at least until he had established himself.

While Robinson had been a standout player for the Negro league Kansas City Monarchs, there were those who wondered if Jackie was of major league caliber. Some even questioned his ability to compete successfully in the high minor leagues. Here

The heart and soul of the Dodgers was veteran shortstop Pee Wee Reese.

"Tell you what I'm going to do, Clay," Derringer said before a 1946 spring-training outing, "I'm going to knock him down a couple times and see what makes him tick."

First, Robinson dropped to the ground to avoid a high-and-tight pitch. He then got up and singled. Derringer subsequently sent Jackie sprawling a second time, after which Robinson leaped up and lined a triple.

"He'll do, Clay," Derringer yelled to the Montreal bench.

Robinson collected four hits—including a home run—in his first regular-season game with Montreal and went on to lead the International League in hitting with a .349 average. In 1947, he batted .297 for Brooklyn and topped the National League with 29 stolen bases; two years later, in his MVP season, he hit an N.L.-best .342 and drove in 124 runs.

A baserunning marvel whose derring-do left pitchers' nerves in tatters, Robinson himself was unflappable.

"You can't intimidate this man any more than you could a player like Frank Frisch," said Eddie Dyer, manager of the St. Louis Cardinals during Robinson's first four years in the league.

Robinson entered the '55 season with a lifetime .319 average in the majors.

The surehanded Reese was starting his 13th season as the Dodgers' shortstop, and there was little doubt that the man from Louisville was the heart and soul and leader of the club.

Reese, 35 years old at the start of the season, was the Dodgers' captain and the only team member whose Brooklyn service dated to pre-World War II days. He had supplanted Leo Durocher in the Dodgers' infield in 1940 at the behest of Durocher himself, who at the time was the club's playing manager. At that juncture, Brooklyn had won two National League pennants. In Pee Wee's first wire-to-wire season of regular duty, 1941, the Dodgers won flag No. 3. After Reese returned from three years of military service, Brooklyn won four more N.L. championships.

Once asked to describe Reese, Campanella—hardly given to great public utterances—could hardly contain himself.

"Just a minute," Campy said. "Just a minute. I want to make sure I say everything just right . . . a first-rate baseball player, first-rate . . . a great shortstop. Yes, I said great . . . a tremendous competitor, one of the finest . . . a splendid gentleman."

Robinson recalled a particularly poignant moment involving Reese, his white teammate from the South.

"There was a game in Boston the second year I was up," Robinson said, "when the Braves' bench got on me pretty bad. There were a lot of Southerners on the Braves, I guess. It was pretty rough.

was a man whose main athletic claim to fame had come as a football and basketball star at UCLA. Plus, he would turn 27 years old in January 1946—not exactly the prime age to break into Organized Baseball.

Mississippian Clay Hopper, manager of the International League's Montreal club with whom Robinson was to make his debut in the minors, figured Robinson might have trouble against quality pitching. Paul Derringer, a four-time 20-game winner for the Cincinnati Reds who was headed for a stint with the Indianapolis club of the American Association, volunteered to test Robinson for Hopper's benefit.

"Anyway, just when it got to be the worst, Pee Wee called time out and walked over from short-stop and put his arm around me.

"It made me feel, you know, like I belonged."

Reese himself belonged to Brooklyn, to the point that he was the odds-on favorite to succeed Dressen as Dodgers manager after the '53 season when the volatile skipper was dismissed after demanding a multi-year contract. Reese decided he wasn't ready for the pain and strain of managing (and wondered if he ever would be), and Alston was elevated to the post. Reese went about his playing chores full-bore in '54, hitting a career-high .309 for his new pilot.

Snider also was coming off a banner year, having brightened a dismal Brooklyn season by slugging 40 home runs, knocking in 130 runs and hitting .341.

Edwin Donald Snider, called "Duke" since childhood, had all the "pleasing skills" in Rickey's view. Snider had inspired the Mahatma to rhapsodize further when the 6-foot-2, 180-pound Californian joined the Dodgers in 1947: "What power! And the boy can run and throw, too. Why, he has steel springs in his legs."

While Snider obviously had all the physical talent necessary, there were those who questioned his enthusiasm for the game. "Duke will be a great player when he grows up," former Dodgers Manager Burt Shotton once said of him. "He needs a kick in the pants about every third day."

Late in Snider's Brooklyn days, a reporter cracked: "Duke Snider, as handsome, as talented and as ambitionless as ever, arrived to participate in the Dodgers' first full-scale workout today."

Snider didn't help his image with a national-magazine article entitled "I Play Baseball for Money—Not Fun." But whatever his inspiration, Snider could indeed play. Ranging across center field, he made one spectacular catch after another until even the keenest observers were unable to grade them. Alston watched the Duke execute ballet-like leaps and catches and commented: "I don't think I've ever seen an outfielder go so high to catch a ball while running at full speed. I don't know how he does it. But he catches 'em and doesn't have trouble with the walls."

Snider also hit 'em. Entering the '55 campaign, he had recorded four 100-RBI seasons in the majors and boasted a .306 career batting mark. He had bashed 42 home runs in the 1953 season and smacked four homers in the 1952 World Series.

If the Duke of Flatbush was a bit mercenary in his approach to the game, Campanella went about his ball-playing in just the opposite manner.

"Gosh, I love the game so much—and I wouldn't want Walter O'Malley to know this—that I'd play for nothing," said Campanella, who in 1953 had cracked 41 homers and knocked in an eye-popping 142 runs. "I know there will come a day when I

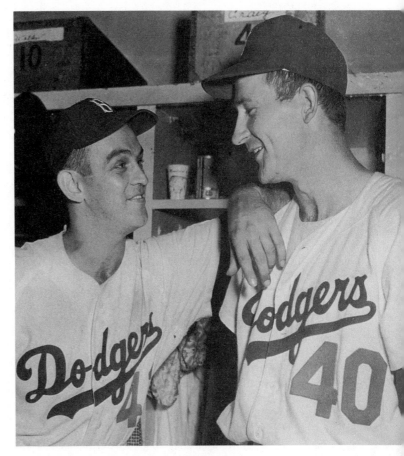

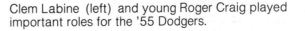
Clem Labine (left) and young Roger Craig played important roles for the '55 Dodgers.

won't be able to play anymore, but I want to remain in uniform. I'll never retire. They'll have to get rid of me."

Campanella, 33, was bent on rebounding from an injury-ruined '54 season in which he batted only .207 with 19 homers and 51 RBIs. Two of the three previous years, he had won Most Valuable Player honors in the National League.

Campanella's emergence as one of the game's most-feared sluggers wasn't taken for granted in the catcher's early days as a Dodger. However, there was no questioning his defensive prowess from day one.

"He can throw as good as any man living," Durocher said in praise of Campanella in the spring of 1948, before Roy had ever played a major league game. "I know he's a good catcher—a great receiver. The only question is his hitting."

"Campanella is the greatest man I ever saw on balls hit around the plate," said International League President Frank Shaughnessy, who had watched the Philadelphian catch for Montreal in 1947. "He is out there on top of them like a cat."

Campy showed the National League he could hit, poling 22 homers in 1949, his first full season in the circuit. In the next four years, he belted 127 homers and drove in 436 runs.

A kindly approach to almost everything in life made Campanella extremely popular with fans, the media and his teammates. Not all of his teammates, though. Campanella, himself a star in the Negro leagues, never quite hit it off with Robinson. While Robinson seethed at injustice, soft-spoken Campy tended to turn the other cheek. "I'm no crusader, I'm a baseball player," he would say.

Alston and Hodges were kindred spirits—strong, silent types and first basemen.

Hodges was reputed to be one of the greatest first basemen in the game's history, quite an accolade considering that Gil wasn't moved to the position until late June of 1948. Stationed at third base when he played one game for Brooklyn as a 19-year-old in 1943, Hodges was converted to a catcher after two years of military duty and was even the Dodgers' opening-day receiver in '48. But when Campanella was recalled from St. Paul, Durocher switched Hodges to first base in an effort to keep his promising bat in the lineup.

Within three years of Hodges' conversion, Dressen saw fit to call the slick-fielding Midwesterner "the best I've ever seen." Cat-like grace, lightning reflexes and quick, big hands helped Hodges play first base with consummate skill.

"He only wears a first baseman's mitt because it's fashionable," Reese cracked.

The down-to-earth Hodges was a particular favorite of Brooklyn fans. Six consecutive 100-RBI seasons and that smooth-as-silk glove provided part of the reason, to be sure. No small factor, though, in the Brooklynites' affection for Gil was that he had become one of 'em. A product of a small town in Indiana, Hodges married a Brooklyn girl and lived in the borough year-round. Residents cheered for Hodges when things were going well (which usually was the case) and prayed for him when they weren't (a classic case being his hitless performance in the seven-game '52 World Series).

Furillo, the Dodgers' right fielder, was stubborn, hardnosed, opinionated and talented. Reared in a grim Depression-era environment in Pennsylvania, he had little time for causes—unless they centered around such issues as winning the National League pennant.

Furillo possessed extraordinary defensive skills. He had a powerful arm (hence his nickname "The Reading Rifle"), great range and a special knack of playing the tricky right-field wall at Brooklyn's Ebbets Field. He also could hit—as a .300 lifetime average would indicate—and was noted for his ability to deliver in the clutch.

Joining Snider and Furillo in the 1955 Dodgers' outfield was 23-year-old Sandy Amoros, a Cuban speedster who had won the International League batting title two years earlier while playing for Alston's Montreal club. In a 79-game stint with Brooklyn in '54, Amoros had shown promise with a .274 average, nine homers and 34 RBIs.

Gilliam manned second base when Brooklyn began the season, having staved off the sophomore jinx in fine fashion. After winning N.L. rookie honors in '53, the Nashville native boosted his average four points to .282 in '54 and increased his home run total from six to 13.

Key reserves were infielders Hoak and Don Zimmer, first baseman Frank Kellert and outfielder/pinch-hitter George Shuba. Hoak and Zimmer had made their major league debuts in '54, Kellert had been obtained in a March trade with the Baltimore Orioles and Shuba was a veteran who had first played for Brooklyn in 1948.

Erskine was Alston's choice as the opening-day pitcher. The slightly built righthander from Anderson, Ind., was a master on the mound, a cerebral hurler who had overcome various arm ailments to build an 89-49 (.645) career mark in the majors through 1954.

"Pitching today is not overpowering the hitter," said Erskine, who possessed a devastating changeup, a great curveball and an effective fastball. "It's outthinking and out-guessing him. The pitcher must rely more than ever on his cunning and finesse." Erskine had out-thought N.L. batters to the tune of 38 victories over the '53 and '54 seasons, and at this juncture of his career he had tossed one no-hitter in the big leagues (against the Chicago Cubs in 1952) and established a World Series strikeout record (14 in one game, against the New York Yankees in 1953).

Newcombe, at 6-4 and 230 pounds, was an imposing specimen of mankind. He could propel a baseball at astonishing speed and, with fair regularity, hit it prodigious distances.

The righthanded pitcher was one of the first blacks to trickle into Organized Baseball after the racial barriers were removed in the late 1940s. From the beginning, he exhibited rare talent. Three superb seasons in the minor leagues took him to Brooklyn in 1949, and Newk was 23 years old that year when he won 17 games for the pennant-winning Dodgers and copped Rookie-of-the-Year honors.

By 1951, Newk was a 20-game winner. He also was a candidate for military service. He spent the next two seasons in the U.S. Army.

When big Don rejoined the Dodgers in 1954, he discovered that Brooklyn's managerial reins were now in the hands of an old friend, Alston, who had been the pilot of Nashua in the New England League when Newcombe and Campanella broke into Organized Baseball with that club in 1946.

In the purlieus of Brooklyn, the return of New-

The jubilant Dodgers celebrate after their pennant-clinching victory over Milwaukee.

combe was viewed as a sure pennant catalyst. Like numerous others before and after him, however, Newcombe discovered that adjustment to a baseball regimen after an extended absence was no simple matter. In his case, a soreness developed in his upper throwing arm. To compensate for the pain, Newk began to throw with a kind of sidearm swipe. He wound up with a 9-8 record and a fat 4.56 earned-run average.

By springtime of 1955, the soreness that had forced Newcombe into an unnatural pitching style was gone from his arm. With the disappearance came the return of his normal pitching motion and the blazing fastball that had been his stock in trade.

Billy Loes, young Johnny Podres and veteran Russ Meyer also figured in the rotation at the beginning of the season. Loes, a righthander, had compiled a 40-21 record in three-plus seasons of big-league pitching. Lefthander Podres, crafty beyond his 22 years, had won 11 games for Brooklyn in 1954 (his second season in the majors). Meyer, a 31-year-old righthander who had pitched for the Phils' Whiz Kids, also was coming off an 11-victory year.

The bullpen was in the hands of Jim Hughes, rookie Ed Roebuck and Clem Labine, all righthanders. Hughes had led the National League in appearances in '54, working in 60 games for Brooklyn and

winning eight of 12 decisions. Roebuck spent '54 primarily as a starter in the International League, winning 18 games for Montreal. Labine had pitched in 47 games for the Dodgers.

Also on hand—but not ready to pitch at the outset of the season because of shoulder problems— was lefthander Karl Spooner, who had burst upon the major league scene in stunning fashion the previous September. Called up by Brooklyn from Class AA Fort Worth late in the '54 season, Spooner struck out a total of 27 batters in his two appearances. He fanned 15 New York Giants in a three-hit, 3-0 triumph and struck out 12 Pittsburgh Pirates in a four-hit, 1-0 victory.

Determined to get off to a good start, the Dodgers opened the season at home on April 13 against the Pittsburgh Pirates. Rain, fog and mid-30s temperatures held the Ebbets Field crowd to a meager 6,999, but a gray day meteorologically turned into a bright one artistically as Brooklyn bounced Manager Fred Haney's team, 6-1. The clubs were in a 1-1 standoff until the seventh when Gilliam ignited a five-run inning with a home run and Furillo capped the outburst with a three-run shot. Erskine tossed a seven-hitter.

The next day, Newcombe clubbed two homers at the Polo Grounds and was the winning pitcher in a 10-8 slugfest with the New York Giants. Campanella and Furillo also connected for Brooklyn.

The Dodgers were off and running. Soon, they would be sprinting.

Alston maneuvered his pitching staff adroitly in the early going and looked on dispassionately as Dodger home runs sailed to distant points. In the first six games of the season, Alston sent six different starting pitchers to the mound. Four of the starters turned in complete-game performances, one went 7⅓ innings and the other hurled eight innings as Brooklyn won all six games. The Dodgers' muscle men did their part, crashing 11 home runs in the first five contests.

As it turned out, the Dodgers were just getting warmed up. They won their first 10 games of the season, a modern major league record at the time, before Marv Grissom, the Giants' peerless fireman, gained a 5-4 decision over Podres at Ebbets Field.

The Dodgers had another winning streak going —this one had reached six games—when trouble flared before a May 5 game against the St. Louis Cardinals. Newcombe, who had blamed a lack of work for his failure to go the distance in any of his three starts, nevertheless refused to pitch batting practice when requested to do so. No amount of persuasion could shake his resolve. Ultimately, he was ordered to remove his uniform and consider himself under indefinite suspension. It was a shocking turn of events for the giant pitcher, on whom so much depended.

The suspension lasted one day, until Newcombe had time to reconsider his impulsive decision and offer an apology to Alston (whose newfound authority was in evidence once more). When the Dodgers arrived in Philadelphia for a game the next evening, Don was with the club and wearing the robes of humility. He was prepared to accept any workload assigned to him. Accordingly, Newk was summoned out of the bullpen in the series opener and pitched two hitless innings in a 6-4, 12-inning Dodger triumph. The victory was Newk's third without a loss, Brooklyn's eighth straight and the Bums' 19th in 21 games.

Four days later, a growling Newcombe escaped the doghouse in a big way with a one-hitter at Chicago. Newk faced only 27 batters—Gene Baker, the Cubs' only baserunner of the day, was thrown out attempting to steal after singling in the fourth inning—and won, 3-0, as Brooklyn notched its 11th consecutive triumph.

The Dodgers were playing at a furious pace. After just 24 games, less than one-sixth of the 154-game schedule, they led their closest pursuers—Durocher's Giants—by an incredible 9½ games. They had won 22 games, good for a winning percentage of .917. And with the season only four weeks old, they had fashioned winning streaks of 10 and 11 games.

Ernie Banks' first bases-loaded home run in the majors contributed heavily to a 10-8 Brooklyn loss to the Cubs the next day, although the Bums showed considerable tenacity in trimming an 8-2 deficit to 8-7 before going down to the two-run setback.

At this point of the season, Snider, Campanella, Furillo, Erskine and Newcombe were sizzling. Snider's 25-game statistics included league-leading totals of nine homers and 31 RBIs. Campanella, who earlier had groused that he "ain't no eighth-place hitter" (his season-opening position in the batting order), was proving his point. Now hitting in the cleanup spot, Campy had 28 RBIs and a .351 average. Furillo had eight homers and 24 RBIs. Erskine was 5-0 with a 1.44 ERA, while Newcombe boasted a 4-0 record.

The Dodgers' grip on first place was loosened by the end of May, to 5½ games, but Brooklyn's lead reached double figures—to stay—a month before the All-Star Game. At the midsummer break, Alston's charges had a 58-26 record and an 11½-game lead. Campanella topped the National League in batting with a .335 mark, Snider already had amassed 28 homers and 89 RBIs and Newcombe, winner of his first 10 decisions, was sporting a 14-1 mark.

Brooklyn persevered despite a wave of physical miseries that struck the pitching staff. Typical of the Dodgers' good fortune was the contribution they received from a couple of newcomers on the first Sunday after the All-Star Game.

With the sore-arm plague spreading (an ailing Hughes was sent to the minors), the Dodgers called up rookies Roger Craig and Don Bessent from Montreal and St. Paul, their Class AAA affiliates, and announced they would make their major league debuts in a doubleheader against Cincinnati. Craig beat the Reds in the opener with a complete-game three-hitter and Bessent worked into the ninth on the way to winning the nightcap.

Also filling in admirably were Zimmer and Hoak. Zimmer took over for a slumping Gilliam at second base at the outset of July and Hoak supplanted an injured Robinson (bad knee) at third base and the Dodgers missed nary a beat.

Brooklyn did suffer through a tough August, winning 13 games and losing 14. Having dropped three straight games and eight out of 11 (but still comfortably ahead in the N.L. race by 10 games), the Dodgers decided to try their luck on August 27 with 19-year-old bonus signee Sandy Koufax. In his second big-league start, Koufax shut out the Reds on two hits and struck out 14 batters. A week later, the Brooklyn native made it two shutouts in a row with a victory over Pittsburgh. The Dodgers were rolling. Again.

In the first game of a Labor Day doubleheader against Philadelphia, Newcombe won his 20th game

For the first time in history, the Dodgers were able to smile after a World Series. Celebrants include Game 7 hero Sandy Amoros and Duke Snider (above), Roy Campanella and Johnny Podres (below left) and Don Newcombe and Snider.

of the year against four losses—at one point he was 18-1—and slashed his seventh home run (a season record for an N.L. pitcher). Brooklyn also won the nightcap, swelling its lead to 15 games. Then, on September 8 in Milwaukee, the Dodgers achieved the earliest pennant-clinching date in league history by pounding the second-place Braves, 10-2, as Spooner—able to make only two appearances in the first eight weeks of the season—flashed his '54 form with nine strikeouts in 5⅔ innings of no-run, no-hit relief. The victory was Brooklyn's eighth straight and 12th in 13 contests, a run of success that had begun with the first of Koufax's successive shutouts.

The Dodgers, having attained a season-high lead of 17 games on clinching day, wound up 13½ games ahead of their nearest challenger, Milwaukee. Alston's team finished with a 98-55 record.

"It was a 25-man job," said Alston, overlooking his own emergence as a strong, assertive leader. "Everybody on the club helped to win this one." Hardly an original quote, but it seemed to fit the situation.

Snider, despite a down period at the plate in which he vented his frustrations by calling Brooklyn hecklers "the worst fans in the league" and a "lousy bunch of front-runners," belted 42 homers and topped the league in RBIs with 136. He also kissed and made up with the good burghers of Brooklyn. Campanella hit .318, whacked 32 homers and knocked in 107 runs (and wound up as the N.L. MVP for the third time in five seasons), while Hodges and Furillo combined for 53 homers and 197 RBIs. And Reese batted .282.

Kellert played only sparingly, but he collected 21 hits and 17 RBIs in his first 53 at-bats. Zimmer, playing what amounted to little more than half a season, drilled 15 homers.

The Dodgers led the National League in home runs (201), yet possessed sufficient speed to top the league in stolen bases (79).

Newcombe not only posted a 20-5 record, but also hit .359 with 23 RBIs. Labine put together a 13-5 season, Erskine won 11 games and Loes was a victor 10 times. Podres was disappointing with a 9-10 record in the regular season, but there was more baseball to be played in 1955. Midseason call-ups Bessent and Craig combined for a 13-4 record, Spooner managed to win eight games after his late start and Roebuck provided help out of the bullpen (as did Bessent, upon his shift there). And don't forget that kid Koufax, either.

Still, there was work to be done. Indeed, the task at hand was one that Alston seemingly had been hired to perform in the first place: Win the World Series.

After six games of the '55 Series, the Dodgers and Yankees were tied at three victories apiece—a fortu-nate turn of events for Brooklyn, considering that the Bums had dropped the first two games in a business-as-usual October performance for the National Leaguers. To the Dodgers' credit, they rebounded from the 2-0 deficit and won all three Series games played at Ebbets Field before dropping the sixth contest.

Alston, who had begun the regular season by using six different starting pitchers in the Dodgers' first six games, was back at it in the Series. He had used six different starters against the Yankees. In Game 7, he would double up—with lefthander Podres, who had celebrated his 23rd birthday with an 8-3 triumph over the Yanks in Game 3.

Given a great lift in the sixth inning when Amoros—inserted into left field by Alston as the Yankees came to bat in that frame—made a marvel-ous catch of Yogi Berra's drive and turned the fielding gem into a double play, Podres set down the Yankees on eight hits and posted a 2-0 victory.

Alston and the Dodgers had meshed. Oh, maybe it occurred a year later than many Brooklyn fans had anticipated. But for fans who had never reveled in the ecstasy of a Series title, this was no time to quibble about the calendar. Not when you've spent a lifetime "waiting until next year."

"Next year," in fact, had come. The 1955 Brooklyn Dodgers, managed by one Walter Emmons Alston, were World Series champions.

1955
FINAL STANDING

Club	W.	L.	Pct.	GB.
Brooklyn	98	55	.641	——
Milwaukee	85	69	.552	13½

BATTERS

Pos.	Player	G.	HR.	RBI.	B.A.
1B	Gil Hodges	150	27	102	.289
2B	Junior Gilliam	147	7	40	.249
SS	Pee Wee Reese	145	10	61	.282
3B	Jackie Robinson	105	8	36	.256
OF	Sandy Amoros	119	10	51	.247
	Duke Snider	148	42	136	.309
	Carl Furillo	140	26	95	.314
C	Roy Campanella	123	32	107	.318
UT	Don Hoak (3b)	94	5	19	.240
	Don Zimmer (2b)	88	15	50	.239

OTHER CONTRIBUTORS (20+ Games): Frank Kellert, George Shuba, Rube Walker.

PITCHERS

Thr.	Pitcher	G.	W.	L.	ERA
R	Don Newcombe	34	20	5	3.19
R	Clem Labine	60	13	5	3.25
R	Carl Erskine	31	11	8	3.78
R	Billy Loes	22	10	4	3.59
L	Johnny Podres	27	9	10	3.96
R	Ed Roebuck	47	5	6	4.71

OTHER CONTRIBUTORS (20+ Games): Don Bessent, Roger Craig, Jim Hughes, Karl Spooner.

Number 6

The Big Red Machine Rolls in Cincinnati

The manager and driving force behind the potent Big Red Machine of the mid-1970s was Sparky Anderson.

Pete Rose, alias Charley Hustle, moved to third base early in the 1975 season and solidified the Reds' talented infield.

They were a dynasty waiting to happen.

"Year in and year out," Cincinnati Reds Manager Sparky Anderson said early in 1974, "we've probably won more games in the last two months of the season than any team in the National League. Any problems we've had usually come in short series— like the playoffs and World Series."

Three times in the 1970s, Anderson had guided the Reds to the N.L. West title. In 1970, they lost the World Series in five games to the Baltimore Orioles. In 1972, they bowed in seven games to the Oakland A's. In 1973, the Reds fell victim to the upstart New York Mets in the N.L. Championship Series.

"We're capable of winning a World Series, you know," Anderson insisted. "We haven't yet, but we will. And when we do, I can see us winning two or three in a row."

Anderson's Reds suffered additional "short series" setbacks in 1974, the most damaging coming in late September. Cincinnati lost two of three games at San Diego and three of four at San Francisco to

fall 4½ lengths behind Los Angeles. Not even a subsequent six-game winning streak could rescue Cincinnati, which wound up 98-64, four games behind the division-winning Dodgers.

Two and a half years later, Anderson was talking World Series again. He remembered the Brooklyn Dodgers, whose 1950s dynasty featured four pennants from 1952 through 1956 and a Series championship in 1955. But now he knew of a more talented lineup, a dream team that had the fortitude to win back-to-back World Series titles, the only N.L. team to do so since the 1921-22 New York Giants. This team combined "speed, power, defense, relief pitching and the best spirit I ever saw." This team was the 1975-76 Cincinnati Reds.

"This club," the 42-year-old skipper said, "has more pride and class than any other club in sports." Even Buzzie Bavasi, general manager of those Brooklyn championship teams, was reminded of his Dodgers when he watched Anderson's Reds.

"If the two clubs hooked up in a World Series, it might have taken them three weeks to decide the championship," Bavasi said. "I hesitate in saying it, but the Reds play the game the Dodger way. They make the game exciting for the public. Maybe that's because Sparky . . . learned the fundamentals of the game growing up in the Dodger organization."

Anderson, indeed, had toiled in the Dodger farm system from 1953 through 1958. His mind-set now, however, was fixed on current events. "At catcher, I'll take Johnny Bench over Roy Campanella in overall ability," Anderson said.

"At first base, it's a tossup between Gil Hodges and Tony Perez. Good as Jackie Robinson was at second base, Joe Morgan is a better offensive player, no question. Dave Concepcion is a better shortstop than Pee Wee Reese, the best I've ever seen. At third base, Billy Cox was better defensively, but Pete Rose has it all offensively.

"I'll take Cesar Geronimo over Duke Snider as a center fielder defensively although Duke had a bigger bat. In right field, Carl Furillo had a great arm, but Ken Griffey has more speed and can do more things. Foster is a better left fielder than anybody the Dodgers had in there in those years. If George played in Ebbets Field, he'd have wrecked the place."

George Arthur Foster, like the Reds themselves, had offered nothing but "tremendous potential" going into the 1974 season. "Foster has all the tools necessary to become a real fine ball player," Anderson had said. "It's our job to exercise patience with him. . . ."

Obtained from the San Francisco Giants three years earlier, Foster was relegated to a platoon role in the Reds' 1974 outfield. He was, however, spared from a "position by committee" strategy that Anderson used at third base, where eight different

Speedy right fielder Ken Griffey (left) had a snappy bat and two .300 seasons for the Big Red Machine. Powerful left fielder George Foster was 'destruction personified.'

Reds proved either offensively or defensively liable. Little did anyone suspect that this glaring weakness would be partly responsible for two World Series titles.

On May 3, 1975, with off-season acquisition John Vukovich batting .218 at the far corner, Anderson shifted left fielder Pete Rose to third base. Not since the 1966 season had Rose played third, and then only for two and a half weeks. "Pete created no problem," Anderson said. "He reacted just the way I knew he would."

To Rose, winning was everything and he'd do anything to get there. When Anderson was appointed manager in 1970, Rose had told him, "I'm the highest paid here and if you want anything done, come to me and I'll do it for you."

When Rose broke into the league as a second baseman in 1963, he was called "Hollywood" for sprinting to first base on walks. Now he was known as "Charley Hustle" for his guts, aggressiveness and energy. "In professional sports, winning is everything as far as I'm concerned—so long as you play clean and don't try to hurt anybody," Rose said.

"I give 110 percent. I don't just give 100 percent because some guy opposite me might be giving that much. If you have a guy equal in ability to me, I'm gonna beat him because I try harder. That guy ain't got a chance."

Since he was voted the N.L. Rookie of the Year, the switch-hitting Rose had batted over .300 nine times, won three batting titles, collected more than 200 hits six times, won the 1973 N.L. Most Valuable Player Award and received two Gold Gloves as an outfielder. And now, on the evening 34-year-old

Key members of the Reds' assault team were (left to right) inspirational second baseman Joe Morgan, first baseman Tony Perez and catcher Johnny Bench.

Pete Rose was to become a third baseman, a pre-game shower welcomed him to Riverfront Stadium.

"Pete though," Anderson related, "made us remove part of the tarpaulin covering the third-base area so he could take some ground balls. That's an example of why he's going to make the Hall of Fame and a lot of players with more natural ability aren't."

With Rose switched to third, into the outfield stepped one 26-year-old George Foster. "If I play Foster for three weeks or a month," Anderson said, "I think you'll see him put the charge on a few baseballs." Three weeks later, on May 20, Foster became the left fielder after stints in right and center. The next day, by no coincidence, the Reds embarked on a torrid streak that netted 41 victories in 50 games.

"The best part of it is that we turned the race around and never did see the Dodgers," said Rose, who had 70 hits during the streak. Foster celebrated with nine home runs, four game-winning RBIs and a .308 batting clip as the Reds went from five games down on May 20 into a 12½-game lead on July 13.

"We needed offense at third base," Anderson ex-

plained after the season. "I knew that George was unhappy not playing. I didn't blame him. But we decided to find out if he was as good a hitter as we thought he might be. As it turned out, having George in left field made the difference in our club winning the World Series."

Foster had a lantern jaw and a 30-inch waist, an affinity for the Bible and a love of karate, a thirst for milkshakes and an appetite for clean living. Most noticeable of all, he had a wicked black Louisville Slugger he wielded to tear up the National League. Batting near the bottom of the order for most of the season, Foster still drove in 78 runs, slammed 23 homers and batted an even .300.

"I call him 'The Destroyer,'" Anderson said. "He is destruction personified." And he personified perfectly the power that surged through this "Big Red Machine."

"I feel we have the perfect lineup—there are no outs in it," Morgan said. It was a lineup that, according to Bench, succeeded by—gasp—thinking "me" before "we".

"When the nine Reds walk onto the field, we successfully pursue our individual goals within a team framework," Bench explained. "I like that idea because it's impossible to remove the individual—the I—no matter how much you talk team.

"With this team, we feed off each other, both on the field and off. Pete Rose lives to get 200 hits a year. It's what motivates him, keeps him going. Well, Pete's so supercharged about it and gets on base so often that he opens up that first-base hole consistently for Morgan and Griffey. In turn, they take advantage of it so well that Tony Perez and myself are always getting RBI opportunities. And, of course, that's what our goal is—RBI.

"I just can't believe that any team has ever had so much talent spread among 25 players."

For power, the Reds had Foster, Bench, Perez and Morgan, a lumber crew that combined for 88 homers in 1975 and 91 in 1976, when Cincinnati's 141 home runs led the National League.

Foster, the league's latest hitting sensation, credited his success to spiritual and physical development. "I figured karate would improve my hand/eye coordination and make me a better hitter," he said. "But I'm more versed in the Bible than in karate. The Bible has helped me understand myself and other people. Karate has helped me keep my concentration longer."

Said Anderson: "I've got to believe that Foster is the cleanest-living athlete in sports." And one of the strongest, too. "He's like Hank Aaron. He doesn't look that strong but he is. He's wiry and long, 6-foot-1 and 195 pounds and not an ounce of fat on him.

"You can turn your back and still know when Foster is hitting in batting practice. There's a different ring when he hits a ball."

Anderson must have been used to the booming drives of Johnny Lee Bench. Two seasons after being voted the 1968 N.L. Rookie of the Year, a 22-year-old Bench hit 45 home runs, drove in 148 (both league-leading totals) and was named the N.L. MVP. In 1972, he was the MVP again with 40 homers and 125 runs batted in, also league-high totals. In his first 10 seasons, he would win 10 Gold Gloves for the receiving skills that earned him the nickname "Little General" among teammates.

"He's the best I've seen," noted distinguished journalist Roger Kahn, "but I only go back to Berra and Campanella."

"He's the best I've seen," said dean Red Smith, "and I go back to Dickey and Cochrane."

Bench wrecked opponents' pitching with his bat, immobilized their running game with his arm and froze their offense with his knowledge. He knew each batter's hitting patterns and preferences, memorized their stances and strides, and called for pitches that no other catcher would dare call for with runners on base.

"The catcher does the pitching on that team," ob-

Cincinnati's shortstop duties were in the capable hands of flashy-fielding Dave Concepcion, a Gold Glover in both 1975 and 1976.

served Casey Stengel in 1971. "The pitcher just throws the ball. He's the best 23-year-old catcher I've seen since Campy—and Campy was 25 years old the first time I saw him.

"Maybe some year he won't hit so good. All they'll have left is a great catcher."

Bench kept ripping, though, and catching, too. He hit at least 25 home runs a season from 1969 through 1975 and knocked in more than 100 runs five times. He caught at least 147 games every season until 1975, when he suffered an injured shoulder in a home-plate collision with San Francisco's Gary Matthews. Still, Bench played in 142 games, postponing surgery until the season ended.

"If any catcher does a better job of blocking the plate than Johnny, I haven't seen him," Anderson said. "He is a wizard back there. Those one-handed tags he makes—and only he can make them—have really become his trademark."

Just as the RBI had become synonymous with Tony Perez. Through 1974, Perez had piled up five 100-RBI seasons and three 90-plus campaigns in his eight seasons as a regular. Seven times the slugging

Cuban had topped the 20-homer mark, setting a career high in 1970 with 40 four-baggers. "Tony is like a mechanical doll," Anderson said. "You wind him up in the spring, turn him loose and wait for his 100 RBIs."

Signed by the Reds' chain as a 17-year-old in 1960, Perez played mostly third base until 1972, when he became the regular Cincinnati first baseman. As a third-sacker, he had led the league in errors from 1968 through 1970. As a first baseman, he never quit trying to improve his skills. "Gotta practice, gotta practice," he would chant as he roamed the clubhouse, digging imaginary throws out of the dirt.

That was the nature of Atanasio Rigal Perez, a dedicated veteran who kept his mind on the game and his emotions under wraps. "He's never up or down," Anderson explained. "He's very gentle to everything but a curveball."

The Reds had an unlikely mauler in Joe Leonard Morgan. At 5-7 and 155 pounds, "Little Joe" wasn't supposed to be a 20-homer man, yet he hammered 26, 22 and 27 circuit shots in three of his first five seasons in Cincinnati. "Judge me on merit, not size," was his only request.

Morgan, however, didn't live for long-ball glory. Joe Morgan lived to do *everything*.

"Morgan might just be the most complete player in the league," Montreal Manager Gene Mauch said in 1975. For combining power, base hits, walks, runs, RBIs and stolen bases, Morgan was, indeed, the league's No. 1 offensive player.

"I learned a lot sitting on the bench and watching games," explained Morgan, recalling his injury-shortened, 10-game season with the Houston Astros in 1968. "I realized that old parks were being replaced by new and larger ball parks, that AstroTurf was fast replacing natural grass. I began to realize larger ball parks would mean fewer home-run hitters, that there was a bright future for the ball players with speed and the ability to make contact.

"You steal a base and a sacrifice bunt isn't needed to put you in scoring position. You can save your club an out. The idea is to score runs. There is little difference between a single to right field and drawing four balls."

After joining the Reds in 1972, Morgan in five seasons: scored no fewer than 107 runs per year; stole no fewer than 58 bases; hit no lower than .290; led the league in walks twice, and became the first player to steal 60 bases and hit 25 homers in one season, 1973, a feat he duplicated in 1976. In the field, he won his first of three straight Gold Gloves in 1973.

"I want to be known as the guy who hits and fields and runs," Morgan said. In 1975 and 1976, Joe Morgan was known as N.L. MVP.

Morgan was, without a doubt, the lead horse of the Big Red Machine, a swift stallion who happened to be paired with two other racehorses, right fielder Ken Griffey and center fielder Cesar Geronimo. They were three of the reasons Cincinnati led the league in steals in both 1975 and 1976. In 1975, the Reds stole 168 bases in 204 attempts, the best success rate in major league history. A year later, they piled up 210 thefts, the club's most since 1914.

That speed, however, wasn't confined to the base-paths. It was evident whenever Morgan sprinted into the hole to backhand a smash up the middle or when Griffey and Geronimo outran drives hit to the farthest reaches of spacious Riverfront Stadium.

Griffey earned a permanent job with the Reds only in 1975, but he quickly fulfilled the glowing forecasts that likened him to Rose and speedy St. Louis Cardinals outfielder Lou Brock. "Anyone could tell that Griffey had tremendous potential," Anderson said in 1976, "but who would have dared predict a couple of years ago that he almost would win the batting title?

"With his legs, he could do it. His speed is going to keep him from having any long slumps."

Batting second or third, Griffey hit .305 in his first full season, then .336 in 1976, when he lost the league batting title to the Chicago Cubs' Bill Madlock on the final day of the season. Once on base, he tallied 36 thefts after swiping a modest 16 bases in 1975. "He's so fast that when he runs, his feet aren't on the ground long enough to make any noise," said Reds reliever Will McEnaney.

Geronimo also awed his teammates with his sprinter's speed. Acquired from Houston along with Morgan after the 1971 season, Geronimo dazzled Rose in his first spring camp with a diving catch of a short fly over second. "Why, the guy must have covered at least 13 feet in his last two steps," Rose exclaimed.

Ray Welsh, a track coach hired that spring, smiled knowingly. "The length of a runner's normal stride is about the same as his height," he explained. "Geronimo (a lanky 6-2) has a 9-foot stride. That's almost unbelievable."

Besides speed and range, Geronimo had a rifle arm that drew comparisons to Roberto Clemente's. To no one's surprise, he won his first of three straight Gold Gloves in 1974.

"Name me a better all-around outfield in the National League than that of Foster, Geronimo and Griffey," challenged Anderson. He conceded that the Cardinals' trio of Brock, Bake McBride and Willie Davis might have matched their speed. "But arms? Forget it."

Few would argue that the Reds had no peers on defense. They led the league in fielding in both championship seasons, committing a league-low 102 errors each year. Up the middle, they had Gold Gloves each season with Bench, Geronimo, Morgan

Righthanders Jack Billingham (left) and Gary Nolan (right) and lefty Don Gullett were key members of the Reds' solid, unspectacular pitching corps.

and shortstop Dave Concepcion.

Anderson had been mildly amused when Concepcion walked into the Reds' training camp as a rookie in 1970. "He was just a baby then . . . 6-2 and only 158 pounds," Sparky recalled. Rose took one look at the Venezuelan native and cracked, "Kid, you may pull a bone, but with that body, there's no way you're going to pull a muscle."

Concepcion added strength and confidence, however, maturing from a .205 and .209 hitter in 1971 and 1972, respectively, to a consistent .280 performer. Working with Morgan, he became a prolific basestealer, swiping a career-high 41 bases in 1974, when he belted 14 homers with 82 RBIs, then following up with 33 and 21 thefts.

Concepcion's most abounding talent, though, was his sparkling glovework that netted Gold Gloves in 1974, 1975 and 1976. Even so, his inferiors thought he should have received a supply of mustard as well.

"Let 'em call David a hotdog," said Sparky. "As for the mustard, I hope he never loses it. It's part of his self-confidence. What's wrong with playing the game with a little flair? Most of the real players do."

With Concepcion as one of the keys, Cincinnati set a major league record by playing 15 consecutive errorless games during their hot streak of 1975.

More important, they made a runaway of the West Division race, clinching the title on September 7, the earliest date an N.L. team had ever won a title. The Reds went on to 108 victories, the third-highest total in N.L. history behind the 1906 Cubs' 116 wins and the 1909 Pittsburgh Pirates' 110 victories.

Fittingly, Foster starred in the division clincher, an 8-4 victory over San Francisco, with four hits and four RBIs. One of four .300 hitters in the line-up, he was second in homers only to Bench, who rapped 28 with 110 RBIs despite battling a sore shoulder racked up in the Matthews collision in April. A foot injury and groin pull that sidelined Bench 10 days in September ruined his chances of becoming only the third National Leaguer to win four RBI championships.

Perez did make RBI history, driving in 109 runs to surpass Frank Robinson as the club's all-time RBI leader, 1,024 to 1,009. Rose also achieved a personal milestone, collecting his 2,500th career hit with a single off Pittsburgh's Bruce Kison on August 17. Unfazed by the switch to third base, Rose posted his 10th .300 season and topped the league in doubles (47) and runs scored (112) for the second consecutive year.

Unquestionably, the biggest success story of 1975 was Joe Morgan. Voted the N.L. MVP and The Sporting News' Major League Player of the Year,

Morgan hit over .300 for the first time in his career, drove in a career-high 94 runs and tied a career-best with 67 stolen bases. He worked pitchers for a club-record 132 walks (breaking his record of 120 in 1974) on the way to a .472 on-base average. Those lofty totals, he explained, were not the fruition of his individual effort. Rather, they were a reflection of the overall might of the Big Red Machine.

"When you win an award like this," he said in reference to the MVP, "it shows you've blended your skills as an individual with those of the 24 other players, your manager and coaches. My award is a reflection of what the others did to help me get it."

Morgan capped his remarkable season by delivering a game-winning ninth-inning single off the Boston Red Sox's Jim Burton in the seventh game of the World Series. After sweeping the Pirates in three games in the N.L. playoffs, Cincinnati overcame a 3-0 deficit in Game 7 of the Series to deliver the city its first world championship since 1940. Perhaps more impressive was the Reds' overcoming an emotionally draining setback in Game 6. After watching their 6-3 lead vanish in the bottom of the eighth inning, the Reds watched Boston's Carlton Fisk hit a 12th-inning homer off the left-field foul pole to give the Sox a 7-6 victory in, arguably, the most dramatic World Series game ever.

Almost remarkably, the Reds became baseball's kingpins and set a club record for victories without having a starter win more than 15 games. They did, however, have three 15-game winners in Don Gullett, Gary Nolan and Jack Billingham. And they didn't go without setting records. The Cincinnati rotation established a major league mark by going 45 games without a complete-game performance, "one record," Anderson admitted, "I'm not too proud of."

Only 24 years old, Donald Edward Gullett already was one of the most feared lefthanders in the major leagues. As a 19-year-old rookie in 1970, he had created a stir by striking out six consecutive batters in relief to tie an N.L. record. "Gullett's fastball comes closer to matching that of Sandy Koufax than any other thrown in recent years," remarked Dodger Manager Walt Alston. "Man," exclaimed Pittsburgh slugger Willie Stargell, "that kid throws nothing but wall-to-wall heat."

Gullett stuck by his fastball but added an effective forkball, slider and curve. He was 16-6 in 1971, his first year as a starter, then bounced back from hepatitis in 1972 to go 18-8 in 1973 and 17-11 in '74. He was 9-3 in 1975 and the best pitcher in the league, according to Anderson, when he suffered a fractured left thumb on June 16.

"Truthfully, I didn't think we'd hold up without Don," the Reds' skipper admitted. But Cincinnati went 43-14 without Gullett, who returned August 18 and topped the league in winning percentage with a 15-4 mark.

Like Gullett, righthander Gary Nolan had been a teen-age phenom, a $65,000 bonus baby signed in 1966. Blessed with a bullet-fast fastball, Nolan was 14-8 with 206 strikeouts as a 19-year-old rookie in 1967. In one game, he fanned 15 Giants in 7⅔ innings, including Willie Mays four times in four at-bats. The next spring, however, Nolan felt the first sharp pains in a troublesome right shoulder that would threaten to end his career.

Nolan had stints in the minors in each of the next two seasons but finally appeared over the hump when he reeled off an 18-7 record in 1970. He sparkled again in 1972, leading the league in winning percentage with a 15-5 mark. Over the next two seasons, he would pitch a total of 10 innings for the Reds.

On May 13, 1974, Nolan yielded to major shoulder surgery. One year later, on May 3, he defeated the Atlanta Braves, 6-1, for his first victory since 1972. Two weeks later, on May 18, he defeated the Montreal Expos by an identical score, only the Reds' second victory in their previous eight games.

"Nolan's winning that game," said Bench, "indicated to everyone that he was going to be a big winner for us. Guys on the club started saying to themselves, 'Hey, I'm not gonna have to do it all by myself for us to win.'"

John Eugene Billingham contributed his fair share, working a team-high 32 starts (tied with Nolan) and winning seven straight decisions before the All-Star break. A distant cousin of Christy Mathewson, Jack had won 19 games in both 1973 and 1974 after arriving from Houston with Morgan and Geronimo (clearly, the best deal ever made by General Manager Bob Howsam). After struggling early in 1975, Billingham, a 6-5 righthander, regained his sharp overhand curve and settled into a 15-victory course. With, of course, a little help from his friends.

"One of our strengths is the bullpen and the starters quickly learn that Sparky likes to use it," he said. "Sometimes I've felt I should have stayed in games I was taken out of, but I've adjusted to the way Sparky manages and I don't argue with the standings."

Last in the league with only 22 complete games, Cincinnati ranked first with 50 saves. And the two most effective stoppers were the two youngest relievers, 24-year-old righthander Rawly Eastwick and 23-year-old lefty Will McEnaney.

Eastwick started the regular season as a minor leaguer but finished it tied for the N.L. lead in saves with 22. In the N.L. Championship Series, he saved the second game and won the third. In the World Series, he won the second and third games and saved the fifth. "Being a reliever is a nice challenge,"

Manager Sparky Anderson (left) and Johnny Bench had reason to celebrate after the Reds had dispatched Boston in the dramatic 1975 World Series.

he said matter-of-factly. "I'm not nervous about coming into tight situations."

It was that cool savvy, a kind of karma built on positive vibes, that helped rocket Eastwick to relief stardom. "I never have a negative thought," he said. "I think this radiates to the hitter. He feels it when you believe you are going to get him out."

McEnaney also was an unflappable sort, a free spirit with an outlook not unlike Eastwick's. "Control and self-confidence, that's me," said McEnaney, who earned enough of Anderson's trust that he pitched in 70 games, second-most in the league. McEnaney had streaks of 17 and 12 consecutive scoreless games and wound up with 15 saves and a 2.47 earned-run average.

Beyond his young hawks, Anderson relied on an old one, Clay "Hawk" Carroll, and Pedro Borbon to round out his bullpen. After his three frontline starters, he employed three starter-relievers to log 33 victories—Fred Norman, a well-traveled left-hander who made the Reds his sixth club; Pat Darcy, a rookie righthander who practiced yoga exercises during pregame warmups and won nine straight decisions, and righthander Clay Kirby, four

times a double-figure winner—and once a 20-game loser, with San Diego in 1969.

"It sometimes bothers us that we don't get a lot of credit," Billingham said, "but we realize that hitting is what makes the Reds. We know it's a lot easier pitching here than it would be with most other teams. We walk to the mound with the feeling that we'll definitely get some runs."

That confidence didn't desert the staff. The Big Red Machine rolled into the Bicentennial year and right over the rest of the major leagues to capture its second straight World Series championship. Batting a composite .280 to lead the league, Cincinnati topped the circuit in virtually every other offensive category as well: hits, runs, total bases, doubles, triples, home runs, RBIs and stolen bases. The Reds boasted five .300 batters, four Gold Gloves and five players voted to starting berths on the N.L. All-Star Game squad—Morgan, Bench, Rose, Concepcion and Foster, who was named the game's MVP with a homer and three RBIs.

By the end of the season, Foster had rapped a team-leading 29 homers and a league-high 121 RBIs to merit selection as The Sporting News' N.L. Player of the Year. "I knew I had to win the Triple Crown to win the MVP," said Foster, whose average dropped from .332 to .306 at season's end. "I started swinging for home runs, pulling everything. That's not me."

Foster wound up second in the MVP voting to Morgan, who became only the second N.L. player to win back-to-back awards (next to Chicago's Ernie Banks in 1958-59). It marked the fifth time in seven years that a Cincinnati player had received the league's highest honor. Morgan, who also was named The Sporting News' Major League Player of the Year again, belted a career-high 27 home runs and drove in 111 runs, second in the league to Foster. In his five seasons as a Red, Morgan had now averaged 22 homers, 85 RBIs, 118 walks, 62 stolen bases and a .303 batting mark.

Rose, meanwhile, scored 130 runs and stroked 42 doubles to become the first N.L. player to lead the league in both categories three consecutive seasons.

There was, indeed, no shortage of offense, which explained why the Reds ran away with their second straight title. After spending most of May behind the Dodgers, the Reds took over first for good on May 29 and rolled to 102 victories, a total they had achieved in 1970 and the second-most in club history. And while the offense exploded in all its glory, the Reds' pitchers went their humble way.

Once again, no pitcher could win more than 15 games, but with seven double-figure winners, Anderson had ample depth. Nolan topped the staff with 15 wins, while two tall-and-talented rookies helped offset the loss of Gullett, who missed much of the season with arm trouble (but still finished 11-3). Pat Zachry, a 6-5 righthander, defeated the Dodgers the first five times he opposed them and was named co-winner (with San Diego Padres pitcher Butch Metzger) of the N.L. Rookie of the Year award with a 14-7 record. Santo Alcala, a 6-6 righty, was moved into the rotation in May and wound up 11-4.

In just his second full season, Eastwick was named The Sporting News' N.L. Fireman of the Year after going 11-5 with a league-leading 26 saves. "I started the year really believing I could win the relief pitching award," he said. "I locked it inside me. It was an overwhelming desire, something I really wanted. The energy from that desire manifested itself physically and good things came about." Wacky Rawley had let his head go to success.

Once in postseason play, the Reds swept the Philadelphia Phillies in three games and, in the first World Series sweep since 1966, the New York Yankees in four contests.

"How can you have a much better team than this one?" asked Morgan as champagne corks popped amid another celebration. "Good power, good base-running, excellent pitching, very aggressive, a great bunch of guys.

"Who could wish for more?"

For George Lee (Sparky) Anderson, World Series title wishes had become a thing of the past.

1975
FINAL STANDING

Club	W.	L.	Pct.	GB.
Cincinnati	108	54	.667	——
Los Angeles	88	74	.543	20

BATTERS

Pos.	Player	G.	HR.	RBI.	B.A.
1B	Tony Perez	137	20	109	.282
2B	Joe Morgan	146	17	94	.327
SS	Dave Concepcion	140	5	49	.274
3B	Pete Rose	162	7	74	.317
OF	George Foster	134	23	78	.300
	Cesar Geronimo	148	6	53	.257
	Ken Griffey	132	4	46	.305
C	Johnny Bench	142	28	110	.283
UT	Merv Rettenmund (of)	93	2	19	.239
	Doug Flynn (inf)	89	1	20	.268
	Dan Driessen (1b)	88	7	38	.281

OTHER CONTRIBUTORS (20+ Games): Ed Armbrister, Darrel Chaney, Terry Crowley, Bill Plummer, John Vukovich.

PITCHERS

Thr.	Pitcher	G.	W.	L.	ERA
L	Don Gullett	22	15	4	2.42
R	Gary Nolan	32	15	9	3.16
R	Jack Billingham	33	15	10	4.11
L	Fred Norman	34	12	4	3.73
R	Pat Darcy	27	11	5	3.57
R	Clay Kirby	26	10	6	4.70
R	Pedro Borbon	67	9	5	2.95
R	Clay Carroll	56	7	5	2.63
L	Will McEnaney	70	5	2	2.47
R	Rawly Eastwick	58	5	3	2.60

1976
FINAL STANDING

Club	W.	L.	Pct.	GB.
Cincinnati	102	60	.630	——
Los Angeles	92	70	.568	10

BATTERS

Pos.	Player	G.	HR.	RBI.	B.A.
1B	Tony Perez	139	19	91	.260
2B	Joe Morgan	141	27	111	.320
SS	Dave Concepcion	152	9	69	.281
3B	Pete Rose	162	10	63	.323
OF	George Foster	144	29	121	.306
	Cesar Geronimo	149	2	49	.307
	Ken Griffey	148	6	74	.336
C	Johnny Bench	135	16	74	.234
UT	Dan Driessen (1b)	98	7	44	.247
	Doug Flynn (inf)	93	1	20	.283
	Mike Lum (of)	84	3	20	.228

OTHER CONTRIBUTORS (20+ Games): Ed Armbrister, Bob Bailey, Bill Plummer, Joel Youngblood.

PITCHERS

Thr.	Pitcher	G.	W.	L.	ERA
R	Gary Nolan	34	15	9	3.46
R	Pat Zachry	38	14	7	2.74
L	Fred Norman	33	12	7	3.10
R	Jack Billingham	34	12	10	4.32
L	Don Gullett	23	11	3	3.00
R	Santo Alcala	30	11	4	4.70
R	Rawly Eastwick	71	11	5	2.08
R	Pedro Borbon	69	4	3	3.35
L	Will McEnaney	55	2	6	4.88

OTHER CONTRIBUTORS (20+ Games): Manny Sarmiento.

Number 7

The Swingin' A's Win Three Straight

Oakland A's Owner Charles O. Finley had a leg up on everyone. Hot Pants Day (above) and the ever-present Charlie O., Finley's Missouri mule, were but two of his many innovations.

They were a belligerent bunch composed of equal parts acrimony and controversy. They sparred with the club owner and swapped punches with one another, just to stay in trim. They flourished on discord, dispelling the notion that harmony was essential to success. And with plenty of anger to burn, the Oakland Athletics thundered forth and beat up on the rest of baseball as world champions of the 1972, 1973 and 1974 seasons.

As if by design, this mod troupe lived by a double-entendre emblazoned on the team insignia: "The Swingin' A's." They let punches fly when provoked in the clubhouse or between the foul lines. And there was no mistaking their stylish self-ex-

pression: shoes of white, hair flowing to shirt collars and beyond, and mustaches above nearly every lip.

By 1972, the club that had moved west from Kansas City before the 1968 season was flourishing as a progressive force amid the conservative American League culture. In 1971, the A's won their first West Division championship for Charles O. Finley, the maverick club owner and general manager who made even the avant-garde appear conventional.

Once described as the "P.T. Barnum of Baseball," Finley overflowed with ideas—many of them ridiculed—to popularize his club. Frequently, he antagonized members of the establishment—magnates,

The successful managers of the swingin' A's were
Dick Williams (above, 1972-73) and Alvin Dark
(1974).

players, the commissioner, and the media—with
what they considered irreverent practices.

Finley introduced multicolored double-knit uniforms that, after the initial criticism subsided, became commonplace in the major leagues. The A's,
most definitely, made a dazzling baseball fashion
statement in their jerseys of Kelly green, California
gold and polar bear white.

The Athletics' team mascot, a Missouri mule, was
a carryover from Finley's years in Kansas City.
Nicknamed Charlie O., the mule was almost always
visible—even in the buffet line at World Series din-
ners. And it perfectly symbolized the stubbornness
of the team owner.

Finley's special promotions delighted the fans.
On Baldheaded Day, he offered all bald men "or,
for that matter, any baldheaded woman" free ad-
mission—and an A's cap to cut down on glare in
the stands. After several players grew mustaches
early in the 1972 season, Finley organized Mustache
Day. Mustachioed fans were admitted free, and
each player received a $300 bonus for
growing a mustache. "It was the greatest special day ever," Finley said. "It
showed young fans that the A's are
with it."

Finley pushed for night World Series
games, the designated hitter and orange
baseballs. "By the end of the century," he
said, "the white baseball will be obsolete."

And for a man who once said, "I have
no expertise in baseball at all," Finley
tried out nine different managers until he

found one worthy—and tolerant—enough to retain at least two full seasons.

Dick Williams, a former infielder-outfielder with five teams—including Kansas City—in the 1950s and early '60s, guided the Athletics to 101 victories and the 1971 West title in his first year at the Oakland helm.

From 1967 through 1969, he had been the strict, tough-talking manager of the Boston Red Sox. "I didn't win any friends, but nobody turned down the World Series checks," said Williams, whose club lost a seven-game showdown with the St. Louis Cardinals in 1967.

But as the field boss of the swingin' A's, Williams was known as a players' manager, a man to whom they related. "I have very few rules and very few meetings," he said. "My players speak their minds and that's all right with me. . . . Today's players do some things differently, but they follow instructions and work hard."

My, how the A's spoke their minds.

Third baseman Sal Bando, commenting on the Oakland experience early in 1973: "In another town, someplace back East, we might be heroes. Here, we're not even something special. . . .

"The Oakland Coliseum is the worst park in baseball. The weather is terrible, there's too much room beyond the foul lines, the ball doesn't travel well, the players lack good parking facilities and the security for our families and ourselves is poor.

"Look how drab this place is. All gray cement. It's so dead, so gray, no fans. The players call the place the Oakland Mausoleum."

Outfielder Reggie Jackson, waxing prophetic that same season: "I can't play here and be happy. Make a mistake and the manager and coaches are on you. Don't drive in a run and the coaches go to the dugout and complain, kick the water cooler, go into the bathroom and holler. They must think they were Babe Ruth or something when they played, that they never made mistakes.

"It's tough to play here with a smile on your face. . . ."

Pitcher Vida Blue, after an upsetting 1972 salary dispute: "Charlie Finley has soured my stomach for baseball. He treated me like a damn colored boy."

Only the year before, in his first full major league season, Blue had won 24 games, struck out 301 batters, notched a league-leading 1.82 earned-run average and received the Most Valuable Player and Cy Young awards. His exploding fastball was something that hadn't been seen since the likes of Sandy Koufax: "It speeds up on you, then disappears," said the New York Yankees' Roy White; "It's in and out, up and down," said the Baltimore Orioles' Brooks Robinson. And heading into 1972, the 22-year-old lefthander expected to be financially rewarded for providing a big return on Finley's

$14,750 contract investment in 1971.

"Vida Blue," President Richard M. Nixon had said, "is the most underpaid superstar in sports. I'd like to be his lawyer when he negotiates his 1972 contract."

But without Nixon on retainer, Blue was offered $50,000, less than half of his original asking price of $115,000. Consequently, he held out, salary negotiations reached an impasse and a news conference was called March 16 in Oakland. Giggling through a prepared statement, Blue announced he was retiring to become a vice president of public relations for a Los Angeles steel products company. "This is a wonderful opportunity for me and one that I feel I should take," he said. "It is with deep regret and sadness I announce my leaving baseball."

On May 2, after Commissioner Bowie Kuhn infuriated Finley by calling the parties together to resolve the salary dispute, a disgruntled Blue signed his contract for $50,000 and $13,000 in bonuses. As the year progressed, his mood became even bluer, something that 6-10 seasons do to pitchers.

Even with Blue out of uniform, Williams had maintained an upbeat attitude as the Athletics departed spring training. "We certainly hate to lose Blue—and that has to be the understatement of the year—but I feel we can win with or without Vida," he said.

The A's, you see, were breaking camp with left-hander Ken Holtzman, owner of two National League no-hitters and a pair of 17-victory seasons for the Chicago Cubs. Holtzman, acquired over the winter for outfielder Rick Monday, was an arrant misfit where major league ball players were concerned. For one thing, he had a college degree. For another, baseball wasn't at the top of his priority list. "I love baseball . . . but there are other things in life, too," he said. He made it clear that he was playing to underwrite his future career in business.

But in 1972, Holtzman came through as the trump card in Williams' pitching deck. With Blue struggling and righthander Chuck Dobson, a 15-game winner in 1971, lost following off-season elbow surgery, Holtzman dealt the Athletics 19 victories. That total was exceeded by only one other Oakland pitcher: James Augustus Hunter, the team's righthanded bellwether.

He was known simply as "Catfish," a born-and-bred country boy from Hertford, N.C. He took his nickname when he ran away from home as a 6-year-old only to be discovered toting a stringer of catfish; he earned his stripes as a competitor by overcoming a high school hunting accident that took off one toe and left 15 shotgun pellets in his right foot.

Without throwing a pitch in the minors, Hunter won eight games for the Athletics as a 19-year-old rookie in 1965. By 1970, he had emerged as the A's pitching mainstay, winning 18 games for John McNamara's second-place club, then 21 for Williams in 1971.

And sticking to pitching fundamentals, Hunter finished 21-7 in 1972 to become the first Athletics pitcher since Lefty Grove to win 20 games in consecutive seasons.

"I haven't got an overpowering fastball like some pitchers have," Hunter explained. "I hold it a certain way and I've got real good control of it. When you've got good control, it doesn't make any difference how fast you throw it. You hit the right spot, they're not going to get real good wood on the ball."

And with John (Blue Moon) Odom healthy again as the third starter, Oakland's opponents did, indeed, fail to measure up many servings.

Odom was a hot-tempered righthander with a wicked sinking fastball that netted 16 victories for the A's in 1968 and 15 in 1969. He reported to camp in 1972 with two .38-caliber bullet wounds he had suffered in a shootout with two burglary suspects. Showing sympathy, Williams asked Odom to do only one thing: regain the fastball he had lost after elbow surgery following the 1970 season—or find other work. Not eager to change careers, Odom won 15 games and helped the A's record the league's second-best ERA (2.58) with a 2.51 mark. It was, however, Odom's last productive season. Phased into the bullpen, Blue Moon won only 10 more games over his last four seasons in the majors.

The Athletics' three frontline starters combined for a 55-24 record in 1972, but Williams' ultimate weapon was a formidable bullpen loaded with three full-fledged stoppers.

"We've got the best bullpen in the league," Williams said. "Why not use it? Why not get a fresh arm in there? We're not paying off on complete games. We're paying for wins."

Righthander Bob Locker, formerly one-third of a great Chicago White Sox bullpen that included Hoyt Wilhelm and Wilbur Wood, finished 6-1 with 10 saves in 56 games. Lefthander Darold Knowles was 5-1 with 11 saves and a 1.36 ERA in 54 appearances. And righthander Rollie Fingers, playing the part of the villain with the handlebar mustache, posted 11 victories and a team-leading 21 saves in 65 games.

"He knows what's going on, he never alibis, he never says no and he can pitch every day," marveled pitching coach Bill Posedel.

Said one teammate: "He has a rubber arm—and a rubber head."

True, Fingers was a master of relief—both pitching and comic. There was the time he remained standing, cap over heart, long after the National Anthem had ended. And although Fingers argued otherwise, his teammates insisted he once strolled to

the plate without a bat. His idol was W.C. Fields—and he was idolized for a superb slider responsible for 17 saves in 1971, when Williams astutely moved a hard-luck starter into the bullpen.

Capitalizing on rock-solid pitching, the Athletics overcame prolonged hitting slumps, injuries and a plethora of personnel changes in 1972 to win their second consecutive division title. And it was the re-hiring of Williams in August that helped settle the A's emotions and fears as they slumped into second place behind the White Sox.

"Smartest move Charlie's ever made," several players said.

"We all worried about him," left fielder Joe Rudi explained. "It eased my mind a lot. I love that man."

After building an 8½-game lead through July 19, Oakland lost 20 of its next 35 games and dropped a game and a half behind Chicago on August 26. With everything slipping away, the A's hurlers surrendered only six runs over five consecutive victories. Oakland regained the lead for good and went on to a 93-62 record, 5½ games ahead of the White Sox.

Forty-seven different players played in at least one game for Williams, but only Rudi could hit .300 among the regulars. First baseman Mike Epstein (26 home runs), Jackson (25), catcher Dave Duncan (19) and Rudi (19) paced the A's to a league-leading 134 homers, but the team's composite .240 batting average ranked only sixth.

Rudi, a 26-year-old native of Modesto, Calif., was a silent-but-deadly force in Oakland's lineup. Cranking out a barrage of line drives, "Gentleman Joe" led the league with 181 hits. He ranked fifth in batting with a .305 mark, second in doubles with 32 and tied for the lead in triples with nine. For the second straight season, he committed only two errors in the field. And he went about his business in the same soft-spoken manner that explained why he had gone virtually unnoticed while hitting .309 in 1970, his first season of extended duty.

"Leo Durocher was wrong," Jackson said. "Nice guys don't always finish last—not when they're Joe Rudi."

But, Williams cautioned, "Joe can be real mean with a bat in his hands. He's a tough hitter—and I mean against *good* pitching.

"I'd take 25 Joe Rudi's. I'm sure one of them could pitch."

Or play second base. Williams used 11 different second basemen during the season, including six in a 15-inning game on September 19 against the White Sox to set a major league record. Steady-fielding Dick Green, a 13-year veteran of the A's organization, suffered a herniated disc in his back in the seventh game of the season. His replacements, Larry Brown and Tim Cullen, also went down with

1972 fashion report: Mod mustaches, big belts. Oakland's hip sluggers included
(left to right) Joe Rudi, Sal Bando, Reggie Jackson and Mike Epstein.

injuries. By the end of August, Williams had begun to substitute pinch-hitters almost every time his second basemen were due to bat.

The A's headed into the A.L. Championship Series against the Detroit Tigers without Knowles, who had suffered a broken left thumb on September 27. And they closed the series without shortstop Bert Campaneris, who had led the league with 52 stolen bases, and Jackson.

Campaneris was fined $500 and suspended for the final three playoff games for throwing his bat at Lerrin LaGrow when the Detroit reliever hit him with a pitch in Game 2. Jackson went down—and out for the World Series—with a pulled hamstring when he crashed into catcher Bill Freehan as he stole home in Game 5.

Through it all, the Athletics endured to win the franchise's first pennant since 1931. They defeated the Tigers in the opening two games, dropped the next two contests in Detroit, then regrouped to turn back the Tigers, 2-1, behind the pitching of Odom and Blue. The two heroes celebrated by shouting angrily at one another in the clubhouse.

"Why didn't you go nine?" Blue screamed at Odom, who had departed after five innings when he couldn't catch his breath.

After tempers cooled, Blue rebuked the A's man-agement for being limited to four relief appear-ances.

"They (Williams and Finley) have no respect for me. Now when I take the field, I don't pitch for Finley and I don't pitch for Williams and I don't pitch for the Oakland A's. I pitch because it's my job, that's all."

With emotions running high, the Athletics scrapped and clawed their way through a dramatic seven-game World Series with Cincinnati's "Big Red Machine." Six games were decided by one run. No starting pitcher could last a full nine innings. Both teams batted a paltry .209. And led by the hitting of utility man Gene Tenace, the Athletics captured the franchise's first world championship since 1930.

Tenace, who had taken over the catching job only after Duncan slumped down the stretch, bombed home runs in his first two World Series at-bats to set a record in Game 1. He batted .348 overall with eight hits, nine runs batted in and a record-tying four homers. His .913 slugging average broke Babe Ruth's .900 mark for a seven-game series. And to cap a season in which he had batted only .225, Ten-ace was named the Series' MVP.

The spotlight was a welcome change for Tenace, who had signed with the A's as a shortstop in 1965. "They took one look at me and moved me to the

outfield before somebody got hurt," he said. Tenace learned to catch in 1967—a smart move with Jackson and Monday crowding the A's outfield picture —and joined the A's to stay in August 1970 to give Duncan competition for the catching job.

"As far as I'm concerned, I've always been a good hitter," said Tenace, who had twice hit 20 homers in the minor leagues. "The problem is I've never really had a shot at playing regularly. Nobody is going to be very consistent if he's in the lineup one day and out the next."

Tenace proved his point in 1973. With Epstein and Duncan gone in trades, Tenace stroked 24 home runs with 84 RBIs as the A's starting first baseman.

"You don't know what a great feeling it is to come to the park every day and know you're going to play," he said. Fury Gene Tenace had arrived. And after a year of comparative mediocrity, Sal Bando and Reggie Jackson returned to the limelight.

They had attended Arizona State University, received their first call to the majors late in 1967 and broke into the starting lineup in 1968. In 1969, their bats boomed in stereo—Jackson slammed 47 home runs with 118 RBIs, Bando rapped 31 homers and drove in 113. They were the most feared hitters in the Oakland lineup, capable of carrying the RBI load even while battling injury or inconsistency: In 1972, Bando topped the team with 77 RBIs despite a disastrous 7-for-70 slump and .236 average; Jackson ranked second with Rudi (75) while hindered by a rib cartilage injury.

But neither slumps nor suffering could keep Salvatore Bando out of the lineup. In his five full major league seasons through 1973, the brawny third baseman with the rifle arm never played fewer than 152 games. In 1971, he had finished second to Blue in the A.L. MVP voting after collecting 24 home runs and 94 RBIs. Respected for his drive and commitment, he was elected the team captain. And, like Rudi, his emotional stability set him apart from most of his teammates. "On this club," summarized Bando, "if you go to bed at night and wake up in the morning, you're considered strange."

While Bando held title to the captain's job, Jackson was the A's unmistakable leading player. In his first five seasons, Jackson had averaged 31 homers and 82 RBIs—and led the league in strikeouts four times. Often, he topped the league in banner headlines for his frank opinions that were tailor-made for the media's image makers.

"I don't care what the news media does," Jackson said. "They made a star out of me, let them write on."

All that mattered to the fleet, powerful right

Featured members of the A's outstanding pitching
staff were (left to right) relief ace Rollie Fingers and
starters Catfish Hunter, Vida Blue, Ken Holtzman
and Blue Moon Odom.

fielder was his record on the
field.

"I want to be known as a leader, a
professional, a tough player, a guy who can beat
you any way he can. It's the pride and respect you
get. I want to be considered a ball player in every
aspect of the word."

And in 1973, Jackson was accorded the three
words that typify the league's consummate athlete:
most valuable player. Jackson, a unanimous choice
for the honor (and The Sporting News' Player of
the Year), hammered 32 homers with 117 RBIs,
both league-leading totals, to set the pace for Oakland's more balanced—and powerful—offensive attack.

The A's scored a league-leading 758 runs (154
more than in 1972), stroked 147 home runs and
raised their composite batting average to .260. Tenace replaced Epstein admirably, Bando bounced
back with 29 homers, 98 RBIs and a league-high
(tie) 32 doubles, and veteran Deron Johnson, acquired from the Philadelphia Phillies in May, collected 19 homers and 81 RBIs in the first year of the

designated hitter. Fellow newcomer Bill North provided a burst of speed, swiping a team-leading 53 bases and batting .285 as he took over the leadoff duties from Campaneris.

The switch-hitting North, acquired from the Chicago Cubs for Locker, had hit only .181 between trips to the minors in 1972. In Oakland, however, he clicked among kindred spirits.

"He covers more ground in center than anyone we've ever had," Jackson said.

"North's an aggressive ball player," Williams said. "He's a heck of a ball player. Some people say he's a hotdog, but he can play for me anytime."

In May, North charged the mound to waylay Kansas City Royals reliever Doug Bird in retaliation for a beaning—three years earlier in the Midwest League. In August, he tangled with the Royals' Kurt Bevacqua after a shoving match on the basepaths. Weeks later, North squared off with Epstein when the former Athletic applied a vicious tag.

"They can't intimidate me," North said. "There's no one in this game who can intimidate me."

Intimidation, however, was a very real part of Oakland's pitching staff. With Hunter and Holtzman each winning 21 games and Blue posting 20 victories, the 1973 A's became only the 15th team in A.L. history to boast as many as three 20-game winners in one season.

"Catching these three guys over here is like catching three Gaylord Perry's at a time," said catcher Ray Fosse, acquired from the Cleveland Indians for Duncan and outfielder George Hendrick. "Individually, they're all super pitchers.

"To righthanders, Cat has a super slider. Kenny has a real easy delivery—suddenly his ball is right on top of you, eating you up. Vida's ball just explodes."

Fingers (7-8, 22 saves, 1.91 ERA) and Knowles (6-8, nine saves) again headed an effective relief corps, but newcomer Horacio Pina, acquired from the Texas Rangers for Epstein, earned Williams' confidence with a 6-3 record and eight saves in 47 games.

As the 1973 season unfolded, confidence was a scarce commodity in the Oakland clubhouse. The Athletics stuck close to fifth place and didn't climb above .500 until June 10. At the All-Star break, they could have buckled under two potentially disastrous developments.

Five days before the All-Star Game, Williams suffered an appendicitis and underwent emergency surgery. Remarkably, he kept his appointment to manage the A.L. squad in Kansas City. In the second inning, however, he watched in disbelief as Hunter suffered a fractured right thumb when he barehanded a smash off the bat of the Cubs' Billy Williams.

"Heck, it might help me," said Hunter, who was 15-3 at the time. "I need the rest. I'll be strong for

Soon to be "fired," second baseman Mike Andrews laments his second error in the 12th inning of Game 2 of the 1973 Series.

August and September. That's when we're going to need it most."

The Athletics, who had steadily made up ground to lead the division by 2½ games at the break, lost six of their first 10 games after the recess and fell into second place behind Kansas City. By the time Hunter returned on August 19, Blue was enjoying a six-game winning streak, the A's were in the midst of a nine-game run and Oakland was back in the lead for good. At season's end, the A's were 94-68, six games ahead of the Royals.

Once again, however, they entered the A.L. Championship Series without one of their catalysts. North's season ended in Minnesota on September 20 when he tripped over first base and severely sprained his right ankle. But the spunky Campaneris, back in the leadoff slot, helped propel Oakland to a five-game decision over the Orioles with two home runs, including a game-winner in the 11th inning of Game 3, and a team-leading seven hits.

Dagoberto Blanco Campaneris was a 160-pound bucket of scrap who had left his native Cuba in 1962 to join the Athletics' organization. In one game during his first minor league season, the versatile live wire pitched two innings of relief—righthanded to the righthanded hitters and lefthanded to the lefthanded swingers. In his first big league game, he tied a major league record by hitting two home runs. In 1965, he played all nine positions in a September 8 game against the California Angels.

Campy succeeded for his hustle, daring baserunning and never-say-die attitude. He led the league in stolen bases six times from 1965 through 1972 and had steadily improved his fielding after committing at least 30 errors in three of his first four full seasons.

"I think all the time about baseball," Campaneris said. "I think about what I'm going to do the next day. If I do something wrong, I don't do it again. I never forget."

And Oakland may never forget the unsettling episode that took the edge off the A's second straight World Series title. Pulling together against the New York Mets, the Athletics prevailed in a fall classic featuring two victories by Holtzman, appearances in all seven games by Knowles, six RBIs by Jackson and, most notably, Finley's "firing" of second baseman Mike Andrews.

Andrews' dismissal, which came hours after the veteran infielder had let in three Mets runs with errors on consecutive plays in the 12th inning of Game 2, was overturned by Kuhn before Game 3. But Andrews' return to the Oakland roster—while cheered by his teammates—did little to placate the seething Williams, who seemingly was at wits' end over the sideshows in Oakland. In a closed-door meeting before the third game, Williams informed his players he was resigning at the end of the Series, even with two years remaining on his contract.

Once more, the A's had risen above controversy to perform like champions. And with Alvin Dark hired as manager three days before spring training in 1974, the A's, in essence, merly changed set directors for another championship performance—on the field, that is.

Dark, who had managed the A's to a seventh-place finish in 1966 and been fired in the midst of a 10th-place showing in 1967, had his "freedom" explained early.

"The manager and general manager must work together as a team," Finley said. "If I have any suggestions, such as putting Fosse at shortstop, and he doesn't like it, then he'll explain to me why he doesn't. And if I say Fosse is at shortstop, then Fosse is at shortstop."

Dark offered no objections. "If a manager thinks he can run a baseball club without the general man-

Reggie Jackson was the World Series MVP and the king of baseball after leading the A's to their second straight championship.

ager, especially when the general manager is the owner, then the manager is a little foolish."

In the players' eyes, Dark wound up playing the part of the fool. With almost each week, he was embroiled in—or witnessing—some new rift.

• Just 10 days into the season, two reporters observed Finley and Dark meeting between games of a doubleheader. Dark pushed the lineup card across a table. "Here's my second-game lineup, Charlie," he said. "Want to look at it?"

• Dark had two heated meetings with his starters, who suspected they were being pulled early—on Finley's orders. "I knew Alvin Dark was a religious man," Blue said, "but he's worshiping the wrong God—C.O.F."

• Shortly thereafter, North and Jackson squared off in a two-round clubhouse fight that landed Fosse on the disabled list. For his efforts as peacemaker, the innocent catcher suffered a crushed disc in his back. Jackson, meanwhile, "escaped" with a bruised shoulder.

• Two weeks later, Bando stomped into the club-

A's Owner Charlie Finley pours champagne over Gene Tenace's head as Bert Campaneris and Jesus Alou (right) look on during the 1973 victory celebration.

house with an announcement: "He couldn't manage a meat market." The subject, Dark, was standing right behind Bando.

By midseason, Dark had endured enough. "I'm the manager of this ball club," he bellowed to his cast of critics. "If you want to be the manager, phone Charlie and ask for the job. But don't be second-guessing me."

With the message received loud and clear, the A's won six games in a row. More important, Dark won some respect from his team.

Finley, however, had lost a little more among some players this season with his latest innovation —the designated runner. He signed Herb Washington, a world-class sprinter, to serve strictly as a pinch-runner and basestealing specialist. Washington wound up with 29 steals in 45 attempts despite not having played baseball since the 10th grade.

"That's a joke," Tenace said upon Washington's signing. "This is going to cost somebody who should be in the major leagues a job."

Washington, did, however, win the respect of his teammates with his dedication and hard work. Teamed with North (a league-high 54 steals) and Campaneris (34), he helped the A's lead the league with 164 stolen bases.

The Athletics shot into first early in 1974, taking

over the lead for good on May 20 as they galloped to a 90-72 finish, five games ahead of Texas. Once again, the A's combination of power and pitching couldn't be matched. Oakland ranked second in the league with 132 home runs and led the majors with a 2.95 ERA.

Just as in 1973, no Oakland regular hit .300. But just the same, the A's scored often with a powerful lineup led by Jackson (29 homers, 93 RBIs), Bando (22 homers, 103 RBIs), Rudi (22 homers, 99 RBIs) and Tenace (26 homers, 73 RBIs).

Rudi's presence was especially gratifying after injuries kept the left fielder out of 42 games in 1973. "You don't win pennants without a guy like that," Bando said. "Joe not only makes the great plays in left, he makes the routine plays consistently, too." And Rudi was justly rewarded with his first Gold Glove in 1974.

A Cy Young Award season by Hunter and record-setting work by Fingers told the A's pitching story. Hunter tied for the league lead with 25 victories and posted a league-low 2.49 ERA. After an 8-8 start, he won 17 of his final 21 decisions to post his fourth-straight 20-win season. Fingers set a club record with 76 appearances on the way to a 9-5 record and 18 saves.

Pitching also propelled the A's past the Orioles in

the A.L. Championship Series, three games to one. After Oakland dropped the opening game, Holtzman, Blue, Hunter and Fingers surrendered a total of 12 hits over the next three contests to give Dark his first A.L. pennant. Dark, who guided the San Francisco Giants to the N.L. flag in 1962, joined Joe McCarthy and Yogi Berra as the only managers to win pennants in both leagues.

The mood was set for Oakland's World Series showdown with the Los Angeles Dodgers when Odom and Fingers squared off in the clubhouse the day before Game 1. "There's no problem on this team," Holtzman explained. "We get along fine when we aren't beating the hell out of each other."

They took out their aggressions on the Dodgers once they took the field, dispensing with Los Angeles in five games to become only the second franchise (next to the Yankees, of 1936-39 and 1949-53) to win three consecutive World Series titles. They were foiled in their attempt for a fourth when they were swept by the Boston Red Sox in the 1975 Championship Series.

Nevertheless, the angry A's had proved that action between the foul lines was all that mattered. When they were done throwing punches, hurling insults and grabbing negative headlines, the Athletics executed the baseball fundamentals better than 23 other major league teams. They had aroused the passions of fans, players, reporters and even the president of the United States as the top-ranked show in baseball—and the most entertaining sideshow as well.

1973
FINAL STANDING

Club	W.	L.	Pct.	GB.
Oakland	94	68	.580	——
Kansas City	88	74	.543	6

BATTERS

Pos.	Player	G.	HR.	RBI.	B.A.
1B	Gene Tenace	160	24	84	.259
2B	Dick Green	133	3	42	.262
SS	Bert Campaneris	151	4	46	.250
3B	Sal Bando	162	29	98	.287
OF	Joe Rudi	120	12	66	.270
	Billy North	146	5	34	.285
	Reggie Jackson	151	32	117	.293
C	Ray Fosse	143	7	52	.256
DH	Deron Johnson	131	19	81	.246
UT	Ted Kubiak (2b)	106	3	17	.220

OTHER CONTRIBUTORS (20+ Games): Jesus Alou, Pat Bourque, Billy Conigliaro, Vic Davalillo, Mike Hegan, Jay Johnstone, Allen Lewis, Angel Mangual, Gonzalo Marquez, Dal Maxvill, Rich McKinney.

PITCHERS

Thr.	Pitcher	G.	W.	L.	ERA
R	Catfish Hunter	36	21	5	3.34
L	Ken Holtzman	40	21	13	2.97
L	Vida Blue	37	20	9	3.27
R	Rollie Fingers	62	7	8	1.91
R	Horacio Pina	47	6	3	2.76
L	Darold Knowles	52	6	8	3.09
R	Blue Moon Odom	30	5	12	4.50

OTHER CONTRIBUTORS (20+ Games): Paul Lindblad.

1974
FINAL STANDING

Club	W.	L.	Pct.	GB.
Oakland	90	72	.556	——
Texas	84	76	.525	5

BATTERS

Pos.	Player	G.	HR.	RBI.	B.A.
1B	Gene Tenace (c)	158	26	73	.211
2B	Dick Green	100	2	22	.213
SS	Bert Campaneris	134	2	41	.290
3B	Sal Bando	146	22	103	.243
OF	Joe Rudi	158	22	99	.293
	Billy North	149	4	33	.260
	Reggie Jackson	148	29	93	.289
C	Ray Fosse	69	4	23	.196
DH	Deron Johnson	50	7	23	.195
UT	Angel Mangual (of)	115	9	43	.233
	Ted Kubiak (2b)	99	0	18	.209
	Jesus Alou (dh)	96	2	15	.268
	Herb Washington (pr)	92	(0 plate ap.; 29 sb)		

OTHER CONTRIBUTORS (20+ Games): Pat Bourque, Phil Garner, Larry Haney, Jim Holt, Dal Maxvill, Champ Summers, Manny Trillo, Claudell Washington.

PITCHERS

Thr.	Pitcher	G.	W.	L.	ERA
R	Catfish Hunter	41	25	12	2.49
L	Ken Holtzman	39	19	17	3.07
L	Vida Blue	40	17	15	3.26
R	Rollie Fingers	76	9	5	2.65
L	Paul Lindblad	45	4	4	2.05
L	Darold Knowles	45	3	3	4.25

OTHER CONTRIBUTORS (20+ Games): Dave Hamilton, Blue Moon Odom.

1972
FINAL STANDING

Club	W.	L.	Pct.	GB.
Oakland	93	62	.600	——
Chicago	87	67	.565	5½

BATTERS

Pos.	Player	G.	HR.	RBI.	B.A.
1B	Mike Epstein	138	26	70	.270
2B	Tim Cullen	72	0	15	.261
	Ted Kubiak	51	0	8	.181
	Larry Brown	47	0	4	.183
SS	Bert Campaneris	149	8	32	.240
3B	Sal Bando	152	15	77	.236
OF	Joe Rudi	147	19	75	.305
	Reggie Jackson	135	25	75	.265
	Angel Mangual	91	5	32	.246
C	Dave Duncan	121	19	59	.218
UT	Gene Tenace (c)	82	5	32	.225
	Mike Hegan (1b)	98	1	5	.329

OTHER CONTRIBUTORS (20+ Games): Matty Alou, Brant Alyea, Ollie Brown, Dick Green, George Hendrick, Allen Lewis, Gonzalo Marquez, Marty Martinez, Dal Maxvill, Don Mincher, Bill Voss.

PITCHERS

Thr.	Pitcher	G.	W.	L.	ERA
R	Catfish Hunter	38	21	7	2.04
L	Ken Holtzman	39	19	11	2.51
R	Blue Moon Odom	31	15	6	2.51
R	Rollie Fingers	65	11	9	2.51
R	Bob Locker	56	6	1	2.65
L	Vida Blue	25	6	10	2.80
L	Darold Knowles	54	5	1	1.36

OTHER CONTRIBUTORS (20+ Games): Dave Hamilton, Joe Horlen.

Number 8

An Indian Summer To Top All Others

Hank Greenberg shook his head in bewilderment. As a star first baseman and outfielder with the Detroit Tigers, he had seen the pressures of baseball tear at teammate Mickey Cochrane until the catcher suffered a nervous breakdown. As the Cleveland Indians' general manager, Greenberg lived under the stress of trying to find and acquire players who could provide pennants.

Yet the Tribe field boss he had hired before the 1951 season was like someone he had never seen.

"That Lopez," Greenberg said. "He's the eternal optimist . . . .

"Usually, it's the manager who can't see anything but disaster ahead unless he gets a lot of help real quick, and it's the general manager who keeps assuring him that everything's going to be all right. But not us, we gotta be different.

"The patience of Job, that's what he's got."

Patience was clearly a virtue of Al Lopez. Senor Al lived the Golden Rule. Honest, understanding, gentle, always forgiving. As nice guys go, Lopez finished second to no one. Except, as Leo Durocher once philosophized about managing, in pennant races. Since winning the American Association pennant with Indianapolis in 1948, his first season as a manager, Lopez had guided his teams to five straight second-place finishes. And although he managed with the soft touch, Lopez took losing hard.

"Worse than losing," said pitcher Bob Lemon, "is to look at Lopez after the game. Sometimes he'll come in the clubhouse instead of going directly to his office and it kills us to see the look on his face."

Lopez succeeded popular player-manager Lou Boudreau, who had slipped to fourth place in 1950 just two seasons after leading the Tribe over the Boston Braves in the '48 World Series.

Lopez brought Cleveland back into contention in the early 1950's by developing the Indians' confidence, unity and team spirit. That the New York Yankees had won five consecutive World Series championships in no way diminished the Indians' revitalization as the 1954 season approached. Cleveland had won at least 92 games in each of Lopez's first three seasons, boasted perhaps the major leagues' best pitching staff and, most important, possessed a manager who was genuinely liked by his players.

"A player can make a terrible mistake on the field," infielder Hank Majeski said. "Al doesn't get excited or blow up. The only way you can tell if he's perturbed is that the veins in his forehead might stand out a little more."

Lopez's philosophies, formed and entrenched

Manager Al Lopez developed the confidence, unity and team spirit that made the 1954 Indians a winner.

long before his '54 Indians set out to end the Yankees' reign, went like this:

On reprimands: "I decided a long time ago there is no point in getting mad at anybody. You play better when you're relaxed. If I tried to be mean and nasty, it would be an act."

On skull sessions: "Clubhouse meetings are a waste of time.

"I've played for managers who had meetings. While the manager is talking, half the guys are sleeping or thinking about some personal problem."

On slumping hitters: "A slump is mostly a matter of having your timing off. Then you start fighting yourself, then you lose your confidence. It's a simple thing but it can feed on itself, especially if someone is hollering at you to do better. I like to let the boys alone and have them think for themselves."

And on pitching, an area in which Lopez was an acknowledged master after handling some of the game's best in 1,918 major league games as a catcher, a record that stood until 1987: "I feel that a pitcher should be allowed to get himself out of jams he gets into. I got that idea from my days as a catcher. That's why I probably leave my pitchers in longer than some managers."

It didn't hurt that Lopez had the American League's winningest pitchers of the 1950s: the "Big Three" of Bob Lemon, Early Wynn and Mike Garcia.

Lemon had been an ordinary outfielder and third baseman until Boudreau insisted in 1946 that the righthander's powerful arm was best suited for the pitching mound. Lemon won four games, primarily as a reliever that year, and 11 games the next as he became a starter midway through the season. In five of the next six seasons, Lemon was a 20-game winner.

"What a life this would be for managers and coaches if all the players were like Lemon," said Muddy Ruel, an Indians coach from 1948 through 1950.

Lemon's big pitches were a sinking fastball and sharp curve. "But I suppose," he said in 1954, "that the slider is the pitch I've relied on most during these last few years. . . . I didn't even know I had it until the fellows started complaining about the tricks the ball was doing in batting practice."

Burly Early Wynn, had plenty of tricks, too, but the opposition dared not even grumble. "Gus" was a fierce righthander who was twice a 20-game winner after being acquired from the Washington Senators before the 1949 season.

"He's the best," said Yankees Manager Casey Stengel. "He knows how to pitch and set you up for his pitch. He can throw anything—a fastball, slider, curve or knuckler. You guess what's coming."

Wynn credited his success to Cleveland pitching

The cigar-chewing pitchers are Mike Garcia and Art Houtteman, who combined for 34 victories for the '54 Indians.

coach Mel Harder, who taught Early the slider and developed his curve.

"The really successful pitcher is the one who can throw a curve and get it over when he's behind on the count," said Harder, who spun off 223 victories in 20 seasons with the Indians.

"Mel is the best teacher I ever saw," Wynn said. "I don't know of a man in baseball who has more admirers among professional ball players than Harder does."

One thing Harder didn't develop was Wynn's mean streak. The stories about Early's affinity for the brushback grew to such proportions that even his family was considered fair game.

"Why should I worry about hitters?" Wynn said. "Do they worry about me? Do you ever find a hitter crying because he's hit a line drive through the box? . . . I've got a right to knock down anybody holding a bat."

"Suppose it was your mother?" a writer asked.

"Mother was a pretty good curveball hitter," Wynn replied.

"Somebody once said that I knocked my own son

down with a pitch," Wynn said another time, "but that was a gross exaggeration. I just scared the hell out of him."

Just as intimidating for Lopez's Indians was Mike Garcia, a broad-beamed Californian whose sloping shoulders and long arms led to his nickname, "Bear." Had it not been for a frisky quarterhorse, Garcia might have pursued his childhood dream— to become a jockey. A nasty spill prompted a teenage Garcia to seek other endeavors. Regardless, 6-foot, 200-pound mounts were not in demand.

Garcia used his frame to good advantage, whipping a blazing fastball that brought him 20-victory seasons in 1951 and 1952.

"When I warm him up," said bullpen coach Bill Lobe, "he seems right on top of me. I can imagine how he must look to the hitters." Lobe held up a swollen, red left hand. "From catching Mike," he explained. "His fastball stings even through leather and sponge."

The fastball was Garcia's bread and butter, but certainly not his only serving. Credit Harder with turning the Bear into a full-course meal ticket.

The Indians' top firemen, lefty Don Mossi (left) and righthander Ray Narleski, with coach Bill Lobe.

"Even when Feller was at his best, he didn't get by on speed alone," Harder had told Garcia during spring training in 1948. "He had a great curve and, once in a while, he slowed up."

Garcia listened and learned. By the end of the summer, his curve was good enough to help him win 19 games at Oklahoma City in the Texas League. Good enough in 1949 that, employed with his smoker, it helped him to a 14-5 record as a Cleveland rookie.

But even with Garcia, Wynn and Lemon, preseason polls in 1954 accorded the Indians little chance of winning the A.L. pennant. The Sporting News' poll of the Baseball Writers' Association of America established the Yankees as overwhelming favorites to win their sixth consecutive flag. The Chicago White Sox and Indians received only token support to place second and third, respectively.

As the season unfolded, the writers' opinion of the Tribe appeared to be valid. The Indians lost six of seven games after winning their first two and fell to last place. They turned things around briefly, but then lost two of three to the Yankees and dropped to 13-10.

Then, as the Indians were winning 11 straight games and streaking into first place, two things became distinctly evident: Cleveland had developed a solid second line of pitching, and a diligent Greenberg, knocked in the past for an unproductive farm system and trades of Minnie Minoso and Mickey Vernon, had assembled a stronger, deeper team by analyzing the talent the farm would provide and trading for what it would not.

Greenberg's message to the club as it departed spring training had been simple yet direct: "I honestly believe you have the tools to win the pennant. All you have to do is use them."

They made the most of Art Houtteman, a product of the Detroit sandlots who was only 17 years old when he first appeared with the Tigers and only 23 when he won 19 games and led the American League in shutouts in 1950. Art then entered the military, returned to Detroit in 1952 and lost 20 games. He began experimenting with his delivery but succeeded only in eroding his confidence. Traded to the Indians during the '53 season, Houtteman came under the sympathetic counsel of Lopez and Harder. He regained his winning touch and the "Big Three" became a "Big Four."

"Houtteman had all the equipment to win," Lopez said. "All he needed was to regain his confidence, to get back in the groove."

"When I got to Cleveland, Mel Harder, who is a really great pitching coach, was a big help," said the young righthander. "He got me to quit experimenting, to seek my natural delivery. Mr. Lopez also offered constructive, fatherly advice. In fact, they did a complete overhaul on me."

Houtteman lost two of his first three starts in 1954 but twice pitched 10-inning games. On May 23, he hurled 12 innings against the Baltimore Orioles to earn his second victory, then won his next five starts as the Indians took off.

Greenberg also had kept watch on another Detroit sandlot star who had blossomed in the big leagues for the hometown Tigers. But unlike Greenberg, the Detroit brass saw a pitcher at the end of his road when Hal Newhouser was disabled by recurring arm trouble in 1953. Given his unconditional release at midseason, Prince Hal was called immediately by his old friend Hank. The next spring, he was trying out with Cleveland.

Newhouser was a sight to behold under the warm Arizona sun. He not only made the team but would win seven games in relief in 1954 as one of only two lefthanders at the Indians' disposal. No one doubted that Newhouser still could pitch. No one ever doubted his obsession with perfection. One needed only to note his two Most Valuable Player awards and four 20-victory seasons.

But of all the Cleveland pitchers, the biggest sur-

Cleveland coach Bill Lobe (left) poses with pitcher Bob Feller after the veteran righthander had recorded his 250th career victory.

prise were two rookies, one a lefthander, the other a righthander. To some, they were "Cleveland's Double-Barreled Shotgun." To others, they were the "Gold Dust Twins." By either title, they were superb.

They were Don Mossi and Ray Narleski and what they did to American League batters sent tremors through enemy camps. Mossi, a 24-year-old southpaw from California, and Narleski, a 25-year-old from New Jersey, exploded without warning when the pennant race got under way. Their performance in the minor leagues only a season earlier certainly hadn't provided a clue to their potential—Mossi was 12-12 at Tulsa in the Texas League while Narleski finished 6-8 for Indianapolis in the American Association.

Nevertheless, Lopez was captivated by the youngsters at first glance. "I'm a fastball kind of manager," the Senor noted. "Those two kids can throw."

Narleski and Mossi received their major league baptisms in the fourth game of the season. Narleski hurled two hitless innings against the White Sox while Mossi yielded three hits in three innings. Thereafter, Lopez relied constantly on the "Gold Dust Twins." When he wanted Mossi, the skipper cupped his hands to his ears in reference to the reliever's prominent audio equipment. When he wanted Narleski, Lopez drew a huge "N" in the air.

Mossi pitched in 40 games for Lopez, finished 6-1 and had a 1.94 earned-run average, the lowest mark of all A.L. pitchers appearing in at least 10 games. Narleski made 42 appearances, finished 3-3, and had a 2.22 ERA.

"I used to hate to see Lopez come out at me," Wynn said. "He'd stick out his hand for me to give him the ball and I felt like eating it rather than give it to him. I guess you'd call it pride. I wanted to murder anybody who took me out. But now when I hear the balls popping into the catcher's mitt in the bullpen, I know Mossi or Narleski is coming in and somehow I don't feel so bad."

With the success of the two rookies—and with Houtteman entrenched as the fourth starter—the greatest pitcher of his day found himself riding the

Cleveland's 1954 infield featured (left to right) third baseman Al Rosen, shortstop George Strickland, second baseman Bobby Avila and first baseman Vic Wertz.

pine rather than toeing the rubber. But Bob Feller, even at 35 years old, wasn't to be kept down for long.

In his prime, Feller could throw a fastball that exploded like nobody else's. He first served notice of his speed as a 17-year-old country boy taking on the brash St. Louis Cardinals in a 1936 exhibition game.

Frank Frisch, the Cardinals' second baseman and manager, watched Feller fire a stray bullet nearly through the backstop as the youngster took his warmups upon entering the game.

"Have you ever played second base?" Frisch asked outfielder Lynn King.

"Well, you are today," Frisch continued. "The Flash is too old to get killed in the line of duty."

That was the legend that was Feller, frightfully fast with regular bursts of heart-stopping wildness. The flamboyant delivery hinted at the impending rocketry as the arms flailed wide like a windmill's and the left leg kicked high into the air.

Now, 249 career victories later, the former Boy Wonder of baseball started only two games in the

first month of the '54 season. But when the Indians' pitching sagged slightly in June, Lopez tabbed Feller for a start per week. Rapid Robert responded by winning seven straight assignments.

"Of course I'm not as fast as I was 10 years ago," said Feller, whose white heat had produced three no-hitters, 11 one-hitters and nearly 2,500 strikeouts. "But the fastball is still my basic pitch. Now, instead of rearing back and fogging the ball through there, I rely on control. . . ."

Lopez could have been excused for turning slightly pessimistic when his biggest offensive weapons, Bobby Avila and Al Rosen, were sidelined in June, each with a broken finger. At the time, Avila held a slim lead over Rosen for the league lead in hitting.

Rosen had picked up where he left off in 1953, when he led the league in home runs (43) and RBIs (145), finished second in hitting—.337 to .336—to Washington's Mickey Vernon and was the first-ever unanimous choice as a league MVP. Called out in a close play at first base in his final at-bat of the season, Rosen held no grudges even though a hit

The ecstatic Indians cheer their September 16 pennant-clincher over Detroit and the last flag Cleveland would win in a dry spell that stretched beyond 30 years.

would have given him the batting title—and the Triple Crown.

"I missed the bag," Rosen said. "I had to take one extra step and that did it. (Umpire Hank) Soar called it right and I'm glad he did. I don't want any gifts. Why, I wouldn't sleep at night all winter if I won the batting championship on a call I knew was wrong."

Rosen had been confronted by judgment calls early in his career. Though his hitting was never suspect, his fielding was.

"Any resemblance between Al Rosen and a major league third baseman is purely coincidental," wrote Cleveland Press columnist Franklin Lewis.

"He'll help you with his bat," said St. Louis Browns Manager Rogers Hornsby in 1952, "but he'll kill you in the field."

"Those old guys like to knock," Rosen fired back. "They should give credit to a guy who tries to improve . . . . I might get maimed out there trying to

stop everything hit down third, but I'll knock them down or they'll knock me down."

Rosen never committed more than 20 errors in his first four full major league seasons yet twice led the league in assists, in 1950 and 1953. He drove in more than 100 runs and hit at least 24 home runs each year. He had proven his detractors wrong, even the old perfessor Stengel, who had raised Rosen's ire by ignoring the Cleveland rookie for the All-Star squad in 1950. Rosen would lead the league with 37 round-trippers that year.

In 1953, Stengel was singing a new song: "What I like about the fellow is that he has taught himself to hit to all fields. He can shoot 'em from one foul line to another.

"Another thing I noticed. I saw him put on his uniform at the All-Star Game in Cincinnati a couple of weeks ago. Why, that boy is all black and blue. Yet he never misses a game. Must be made of the stuff that was in those old Orioles."

Rosen, most assuredly, had guts. That wasn't lost on Lopez, who pulled his "Big Switch" early to shake up the Indians after they had slipped to 3-6. Rosen was shifted to first base to replace Bill Glynn, who was batting .419, and rookie Rudy Regalado was installed at third. That Rosen could have struggled offensively while adjusting to a new position did not concern Lopez.

"Confidence," said Lopez, explaining Rosen's biggest attribute. "He thoroughly believes in his ability to hit.

"I've seen Al get three-for-three, fly out on his next try and come back to the bench storming at the pitcher. He'll shake his fist at the man in the box and yell, 'I'll get you next time.' "

Bobby Avila was the national hero of his native Mexico and the pepper pot of the Indians' lineup.

A backup at second base in his first two seasons, Avila had yet to make a glowing impression on Greenberg or Lopez when the two brain trusts reviewed the spring training roster in 1951.

"Now Avila," Greenberg said, "he'll field all right, but I'm not sure about his hitting." Joe Gordon, the Tribe's second baseman for the last four seasons, had taken to managing in the Pacific Coast League, however, and Lopez was resigned to give Avila a chance. Bobby hit .305 that season, then .300 the next.

Avila held his ground to sliding runners—"He's death on the double play," said Detroit outfielder Pat Mullin—and created a furor when the tables were turned. When he arrived at a base, Avila was flying high, his spikes cutting the air as he kicked his right foot at the fielder's glove or a foolish barehanded tag.

"He's too rough on the base lines," protested Yankees catcher Yogi Berra.

"I used to be a good soccer player," countered Bobby.

And by 1954, perhaps the American League's best all-around second baseman. "If any modern hitter can hit .400 it'll be Bobby Avila," said Dizzy Dean, the Hall of Fame pitcher turned broadcaster.

"If I ever hit .400, they make me president of Mexico," Avila replied.

He appeared to be a strong candidate heading into June, his average hovering near .390 as he and Rosen battled for the league's batting crown.

"Rosie will be glad to be one-two with me," Avila said. "I be glad to be two-one, with Rosie on top. If we both are high, I think maybe it mean the pennant."

But then came the injuries, and with them, many believed, went the Indians' pennant chances. Cleveland did, in fact, fall into second for four games.

But what followed epitomized the essence of this Indians team. Cleveland dodged a season's worth of miseries as newcomers and reserves played as well as the injured stars they replaced, and timely switches boosted production at key positions.

"When you've got a strong bench, you can't go wrong," Lopez said.

Hank Majeski, whose biggest contribution had been to make roommate Avila "feel at home," stepped in for the injured second baseman and was batting .353 when Bobby returned to full-time duty June 23.

"You go back to bench and rest up," Avila told his friend. "If you keep showing me up, I'll lose my job to you."

For power insurance, Greenberg had obtained veteran outfielder Vic Wertz from the Baltimore Orioles on June 1. "We don't figure on him to play regularly now," Lopez said at the time, "but he's insurance in case something happens to one of our power men."

Days later, Rosen went out and Wertz was at first, a position he had played only once before—in spring training. "The position wasn't as hard to play as I expected," Wertz said, "because our pitchers don't let very many men get on base."

After batting just .202 with the Orioles, Wertz hit a robust .357 in Rosen's cleanup spot.

When Regalado, the new third baseman in the "Big Switch," was injured in his second game in the lineup, second-year sub Al Smith took over third, batted .295 and triggered the "Little Switch" when Regalado returned. Smith, replacing Wally Westlake, became the new left fielder and leadoff batter. Avila moved to second in the order.

"Wally has been doing a good job for us," Senor Al noted, "but Smith has great speed, makes us more dangerous on the bases and I like the way he stands up there against the toughest pitchers. He makes them work."

Westlake, "Old Reliable" among his teammates, became the swing man in the outfield behind right fielder Dave Philley and center fielder Larry Doby. "I'm always ready," said Westlake, a .272 hitter in six National League seasons before coming to the Indians late in the 1952 campaign.

Greenberg had traded for Philley just before spring training in 1954. Coming off a career-high .303 season with the Philadelphia Athletics, Philley was shipped to Cleveland for two minor league pitchers when he demanded a hefty raise. The 33-year-old switch-hitter had topped Greenberg's shopping list but became a .226 hitter in a Cleveland uniform. Still, Senor Al applauded the acquisition.

"He's proof," said Lopez, "that statistics should be thrown into the waste basket. I go on performance, not on figures. Anyone who watches Philley day after day would realize how much he helps us. He has saved several games with spectacular catches, he runs hard on the bases and he has knocked in many important runs."

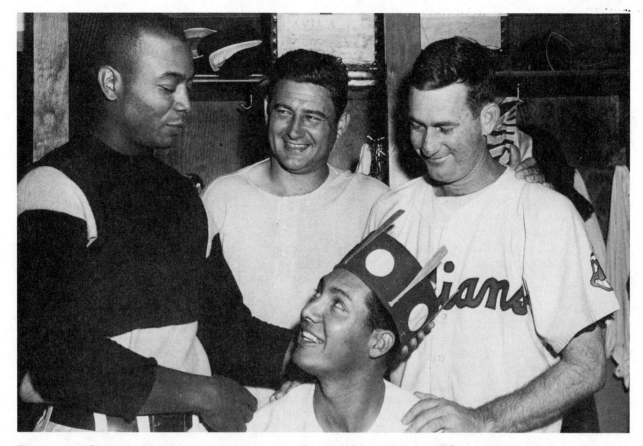

The toast of Cleveland's champagne season were (back, left to right) A.L. RBI-champ Larry Doby, victory leaders Early Wynn and Bob Lemon and (front) batting king Bobby Avila.

If Philley suffered a particularly rough spell, as he did when he carried an 0-for-20 streak into early August, Lopez could bring rookie Dave Pope off the bench and move Smith to right field. Pope, a .300 hitter in four minor league seasons, provided reserve punch along with Dale Mitchell, whom Smith had also bumped to the bench despite the veteran's six .300 seasons with Cleveland.

Reserve infielder Sam Dente's contributions were the most inspiring. Though contending with his own injuries, Dente rescued the Indians when shortstop George Strickland suffered a broken jaw July 23 and missed a month and a half. "Win plenty with Dente" became the good-humored infielder's personal battle cry as he batted a steady .266 for the season, even while playing the final six weeks with a broken finger.

Catcher Jim Hegan was one of the few Indians who was healthier than in years past. Plagued by a bad back, Hegan still had caught 100 or more games for seven straight seasons. The pain disappeared, however, as 1954 approached, and Hegan quarterbacked with a vigor that belied his 34 years. He caught 137 games for the Indians, getting occasional rest with rookie Hal Naragon available.

With so many injuries, the responsibility of car-

rying the offense rested on the broad shoulders of Larry Doby.

Since entering the majors in 1947, Doby had failed to reach the level of excellence that many had expected from the American League's first black player. That he hit .301 as a rookie in 1948, had five 20-home run seasons and three with more than 100 RBIs never seemed to satisfy Doby, who waged a war of self-persecution.

"I spoke to Al Rosen about Larry," Brooklyn Dodgers catcher Roy Campanella related in spring training. "I asked him what was wrong with (Larry) because I knew Larry should be a better ball player than he had shown. Rosen told me that Doby felt the world was against him. He had it in his head that nobody wanted him, including his own teammates."

Doby's smile months later showed he had been convinced otherwise. Larry was joking in the clubhouse and clicking at the plate. His strikeouts dropped as his RBI-count soared. For most of the season, Doby would contend for the league lead in both home runs and RBIs.

Doby would also hit his first home run in six All-Star games in front of almost 70,000 hometown fans. But Doby had to settle for a supporting role in this particular game, for it was Rosen who stood above the game's greatest stars in a July 13 midsummer slugfest that topped all others.

Still pained by his injured finger, Rosen bombed two consecutive homers and drove in five runs to tie All-Star Game records as the American League defeated the Nationals, 11-9. Avila, starting at second, contributed three hits in three at-bats. Altogether, the three Indians combined for seven hits and eight RBIs.

Cleveland's stars continued to shine when the regular-season resumed. In the first six games after the break, Rosen and Avila collected nine hits apiece while Rosen drove in 12 runs. Rosen, who had shifted back to third at the end of June, felt at home again. "I am 100 percent more comfortable at third," he said.

And Lopez was more comfortable with his second-half lineup employing Wertz as the regular first baseman. The team whose lead had shrunk to half a game at the July break won nine of 11 road games immediately afterward and 32 of 39 games overall to pull 5½ lengths ahead on August 22.

If the Yankees still had entertained thoughts of catching the Indians, their hopes were dashed September 12 when Lemon and Wynn led Cleveland to a doubleheader sweep of the New Yorkers before 84,587 fans at Cleveland Stadium, the largest crowd ever to watch a twin bill. The sweep gave the Tribe an 8½-game lead.

"So we're the choke-up champs," crowed Newhouser as he led the jubilant Indians in a victory celebration.

"Yeah! We choked up! Yeah!" the Indians chanted to newsmen. "Tell the world we choked up!"

"This was the way we wanted it," Lopez said. "We wanted to beat the Yanks ourselves. This was the way we wanted to win the pennant."

Three games later, they did, beating Detroit, 3-2.

"Wasn't it wonderful the way Dale Mitchell, the forgotten man, stepped up as a pinch-hitter and hit a two-run homer?" Greenberg said. "It typified the job our bench has done."

On the next-to-last day of the season, Wynn pitched a two-hitter for his 23rd victory as Cleveland routed the Tigers, 11-1. The win was the Indians' 111th of the year, wiping out the A.L. record of 110 set by the 1927 Yankees. Avila, who paced the Indians' offense with two singles and a double, finished the season with a .341 batting average to win the A.L. crown. Doby added two hits and his 126th RBI, tops in the league. Doby also won his second home-run title by clouting 32.

As a team, the Indians hit a league-leading 156 homers. Rosen, despite a finger that never completely healed, finished with 24, followed by Avila with 15, Wertz 14 (for Cleveland), Philley 12, and Smith, Hegan and Westlake, 11 each.

"Our game was to hold the other side with our good pitching and wait for somebody to sock one out," Lopez said.

And Cleveland's staff provided some of the best pitching ever witnessed: Lemon and Wynn led the league in victories with 23 each while posting identical 2.72 ERAs; Garcia captured the ERA title with a 2.64 mark and won 19 games; Houtteman contributed 15 wins, his most since 1950; and Feller finished 13-3, correcting everyone who said he was washed-up.

As remarkable as their regular season was, the Indians lost the World Series in four straight games to the underdog New York Giants.

A harbinger of the Indians' fate occurred in the eighth inning of the first game. With the score tied 2-2, Giants center fielder Willie Mays made an incredible over-the-shoulder catch of Wertz's 460-foot drive to the farthest reaches of the Polo Grounds. The Giants won the game in the 10th on pinch-hitter Dusty Rhodes' three-run homer.

From their giddy pinnacle, the Indians fell to second place in both 1955 and 1956. From there, they faded into the pack. But for one glorious year, when Lopez made all the right decisions, when the "Big Three" won 65 games and everyone hit with timely effect, there has never been a season to equal that of the 1954 Cleveland Indians.

1954
FINAL STANDING

Club	W.	L.	Pct.	GB.
Cleveland	111	43	.721	——
New York	103	51	.669	8

BATTERS

Pos.	Player	G.	HR.	RBI.	B.A.
1B	Vic Wertz	94	14	48	.275
2B	Bobby Avila	143	15	67	.341
SS	George Strickland	112	6	37	.213
3B	Al Rosen	137	24	102	.300
OF	Al Smith	131	11	50	.281
	Larry Doby	153	32	126	.272
	Dave Philley	133	12	60	.226
C	Jim Hegan	139	11	40	.234
UT	Billy Glynn (1b)	111	5	18	.251
	Wally Westlake (of)	85	11	42	.263

OTHER CONTRIBUTORS (20+ Games): Sam Dente, Hank Majeski, Dale Mitchell, Hal Naragon, Dave Pope, Rudy Regalado.

PITCHERS

Thr.	Pitcher	G.	W.	L.	ERA
R	Bob Lemon	36	23	7	2.72
R	Early Wynn	40	23	11	2.72
R	Mike Garcia	45	19	8	2.64
R	Art Houtteman	32	15	7	3.35
R	Bob Feller	19	13	3	3.09
L	Don Mossi	40	6	1	1.94
R	Ray Narleski	42	3	3	2.22

OTHER CONTRIBUTORS (20+ Games): Hal Newhouser.

Number 9

The Orioles Fly High For Earl of Baltimore

The often-bellicose Earl Weaver arrived in Baltimore and lit a fire under the Orioles and major league umpires.

In height and girth, Earl Sidney Weaver bore a striking resemblance to John Joseph McGraw, the legendary manager of the New York Giants of yesteryear. There also was a marked similarity in their approaches to their profession. Both were intense, dedicated and knowledgeable, both supremely confident and bellicose as major league pilots. Both could turn an opposing player or an umpire into blind fury with syllables borrowed from a longshoreman's vocabulary. Neither was a stranger to fines and suspensions.

Both had been infielders in their younger years. Both began their big-league managerial careers in Baltimore, and they enjoyed inordinate success many years apart. For Earl Weaver, there could have been no finer compliment than to be linked with the Little Napoleon as masters of their craft. Unlike McGraw, Weaver was undistinguished as a player. One year, after he had become a playing manager in the minor leagues, the stumpy second baseman batted .294 in a Class D league. It was Weaver's highest average as a professional, although strictly as a player he had progressed to Class AA on the baseball ladder and even had gone to spring training with the 1952 St. Louis Cardinals.

As a manager, Weaver carried the unmistakable stamp of success. Beginning at Knoxville, Tenn., in 1956 and proceeding through Fitzgerald and Dublin, Ga., Aberdeen, S.D., Fox Cities, Wis., and Elmira and Rochester, N.Y., the St. Louis native demonstrated an unqualified gift for leadership. Nobody doubted that sometime and somewhere, leather-faced Earl would direct the fortunes of a major league team.

That moment arrived in 1968. Serving his first season as a coach with the Orioles after having guided Baltimore farm clubs to two first-place finishes and four runner-up spots in the preceding six years, Weaver was lounging by the pool at his home during the All-Star Game break when he received a phone call from Orioles General Manager Harry Dalton telling of the im-

minent dismissal of Manager Hank Bauer. Was Earl interested in the job? Could he bring himself to relinquish his cushy, no-worry role as a subaltern for the headaches, anxieties and sleepless nights of a manager? The reply was instant and emphatic. He grabbed the offer. A major league manager's portfolio had been his goal since he accepted $2,000 to sign with the St. Louis Cardinals' organization two decades before.

Weaver's acceptance of Dalton's offer signaled

Weaver's first order of business in Baltimore was fine-tuning what he believed to be a strong Orioles team.

the birth of a bright new era in Baltimore baseball. Under Bauer, the club that had won the 1966 American League pennant and swept the Los Angeles Dodgers in the World Series fell to a sixth-place tie the next year and was in third place, 10½ games out of first, when Dalton decided to make a change of command.

At the outset, Weaver maintained that he "had inherited a good club," one "that could improve. . . with a change here and there."

On the night that he took charge of the struggling Orioles, Weaver implemented two changes that he had envisioned. First, he elevated Mark Belanger from eighth place to second in the batting order to utilize the shortstop's bunting and base-stealing talents. Next, he installed handyman Don Buford in the outfield on a permanent basis. That stratagem paid immediate dividends. In the first inning of Weaver's first game as pilot, Buford, a former University of Southern California football player, walked and scored a run against Washington. In the fifth inning, he rapped a home run, helping Dave McNally to a 2-0 victory.

At his first press conference, Weaver mentioned that "by scrambling more, maybe we can produce one or two more runs a game, bunt for a hit. It'll take pressure off our pitchers."

The "scrambling" practice became quickly apparent. In Weaver's managerial debut, spectators were pleasantly shocked to see Boog Powell, Baltimore's 6-foot-4½, 245-pound first baseman, steal a base. In the Orioles' second game under Earl's direction, fans were equally startled to see Frank Robinson, not known for risky baserunning, dive headlong across the plate with the winning run.

Baltimore won its first six games with Weaver at the controls. By the close of the 162-game schedule, the new skipper showed a record of 48-34 as the Orioles rallied for a second-place finish with a 91-71 mark. Still, the Birds were 12 games behind the pennant-winning Detroit Tigers.

Weaver was convinced that his Orioles merely needed some fine-tuning—not a major overhaul—to return to the glory days. That assessment was shared by the Baltimore front office and other baseball people, most of whom viewed the Birds' roster—from top to bottom—as downright frightening.

The team had top-of-the-line sluggers in first baseman Powell and right fielder Frank Robinson, sensational defensive players in third baseman Brooks Robinson and center fielder Paul Blair, a potentially outstanding glove man in shortstop Belanger, steady performers in second baseman Dave Johnson and catchers Andy Etchebarren and Elrod Hendricks, and a quality pitching staff headed by McNally, Jim Hardin and Tom Phoebus.

While strong pitching had been a Baltimore trademark since the beginning of the decade and

was evident again in 1968, Weaver sought reinforcements for his talented—but not overly deep—mound staff. Perhaps most of all, he sought a comeback from righthander Jim Palmer, who at age 20 had won 15 regular-season games for the World Series-champion Orioles of 1966 before encountering physical miseries. Beset by arm, shoulder and back ailments, Palmer worked only 37 innings—all in the minor leagues—during the 1968 season and appeared in only nine games for Baltimore the previous year.

Not willing to bank on a Palmer recovery, the Orioles went to the swap mart two months after the conclusion of the '68 season. In a multi-player trade, Baltimore gave up a front-line player, outfielder Curt Blefary, to the Houston Astros in a transaction that sent 31-year-old pitcher Mike Cuellar to the Orioles.

Blefary, former Rookie of the Year in the American League, never quite emerged as the power hitter that the Orioles had projected and slumped to a .200 batting average in '68. And, considering Weaver's fondness for Buford, Blefary was deemed expendable.

Cuellar was the not-so-strong, silent type. At 5-11 and 167 pounds, the Cuban-born lefthander hardly was an imposing figure on the mound. Until he starting serving up his vast assortment of pitches, that is. Fastball, curveball, slider, changeup and screwball. You name it, Cuellar let it fly.

Cuellar's repertoire with the English language wasn't as extensive. In fact, Mike had a difficult time communicating with members of the media. Monosyllabic answers to reporters' queries were the rule, not the exception. Truly, Cuellar's actions spoke louder than his words.

"Mike can pitch," Astros pitcher Don Wilson said of Cuellar, who won a total of 36 games for Houston from 1966 through 1968, years in which the Astros weren't exactly the scourge of the National League. "He's just one of those fellows who knows how to pitch."

"Frankly, we don't know Mike," Grady Hatton said of the communications gap that existed while Hatton was managing the Houston club. "We don't know what makes him tick. But we go out of our way to let him know we appreciate him. He likes to be kidded, and we kid him a lot."

Mastering the finer points of hurling didn't come easily for longtime minor leaguer Cuellar, the kind of player Houston coach Jim Busby described as a "10-year prospect." Entering the 1966 season, Cuellar's major league experience consisted of a two-game stint with Cincinnati (1959) and 3½-month stays with the St. Louis Cardinals (1964) and Houston (1965). Then, in one of those baseball mysteries that defies explanation, it all came together for Cuellar, who posted the second-best earned-run average in the National League in '66 and then won 16 games the following season.

"I think he feels he belongs on this team," said Busby, striving to pinpoint a reason for Cuellar's emergence after the slender pitcher had fashioned a 2.22 ERA for the Astros in 1966. "It makes a big difference when a player believes he belongs."

Now, Cuellar belonged to the Baltimore Orioles.

The Birds' incumbent starters—McNally, Hardin and Phoebus—were coming off strong seasons as they girded for 1969.

McNally, a 26-year-old Montanan with a blazing fastball and an outstanding curve, had blossomed in his sixth full year with the Orioles. A bonus signee in 1960, McNally had compiled a lifetime 48-38 record in the majors entering the '68 season and then proceeded to put together a 22-10 mark that featured a 1.95 ERA, a 12-game winning streak and five shutouts.

"I remember in 1966, when I won 13, my older brother asked me, 'Think you'll ever win 20?' I said no," McNally recalled. " 'Why?' he asked. I said because I needed another pitch."

McNally found that pitch—actually, he rediscovered it—in spring training of '68. Working in the bullpen, the lefthander regained the ability to throw an effective slider, a pitch he had used with great success in the minors.

Righthanders Hardin and Phoebus combined for 33 victories in '68. Hardin, drafted out of the New York Mets' organization in 1965, won 18 games in his first full season in the big leagues and Phoebus notched 15 victories. Phoebus, who made headlines in 1966 when he broke into the majors with back-to-back shutouts, re-entered the spotlight in the first month of the '68 season when he tossed a no-hitter against the Boston Red Sox.

Weaver and the Orioles started the 1969 season with high expectations, the club having been fortified by the addition of Cuellar and boosted by the return of Palmer, who showed flashes of his former brilliance in the spring. Opening day was no great shakes, however, as the Orioles suffered a 5-4, 12-inning defeat to the Red Sox. Little else went badly for Baltimore over the next six months, though.

Beginning with their fourth game of the season, the Orioles got three consecutive shutouts. All came against the Washington Senators, with McNally, Palmer and Phoebus delivering the pitching gems (the latter two coming in a doubleheader). The Baltimore faithful was cheered most, of course, by Palmer's effort, a five-hit, 2-0 triumph that came in his first regular-season appearance in the majors since September 19, 1967.

"Back in 1966, when I was 20, I didn't know how

The acknowledged leader of the 1969-70-71 Orioles was slugging outfielder Frank Robinson, one of the team's top guns.

to pitch," Palmer said. "I didn't even think about it. All I thought about was going out there every fourth or fifth day and gunning it by people.

"Then, if I got my curve over, I had a good game. If I didn't, I had a fair game. Before the sore arm, I never pitched with bad stuff. I mean, really bad stuff. It was just there.

"One night I pitched to one extra batter in a one-hitter and, believe me, I had nothing. This is when it dawned on me how easy pitching can be sometimes."

Until, of course, myriad maladies began cropping up. Stung by charges that he lacked toughness and was a hypochondriac or a malingerer, Palmer unloaded on his critics.

The Orioles' other Robinson, third baseman Brooks, dazzled with his spectacular defense and fast-improving bat.

"They have to be kidding," he said. "For two years, I had shots, oh, did I have shots, straight into the shoulder with my arm at my side. Dr. (Robert) Kerlan found the spot where it hurt, had me hold my arm in the position where it hurt the most (almost straight up) and injected that way . . . ."

Buoyed by Palmer's April 13 performance, the Orioles moved into first place three days later. And they stayed there for the rest of the season.

Clearly, the Birds came out smokin' in 1969. When the April portion of the American League schedule ended, Baltimore boasted a 16-7 record and a 3½-game lead atop the American League East. Frank Robinson had clubbed 10 home runs in the 23 games, while Palmer and Phoebus each had pitched two shutouts. McNally had a 4-0 record, and he was just getting warmed up.

For Frank Robinson, the fast start was particularly rewarding. The menacing slugger had hit only 15 homers in all of 1968, a year in which he had vision and arm problems and even the mumps. Now, he was back in his old form, and what form that was.

After drilling 324 homers in 10 years for the Cincinnati Reds, Robinson was traded to Baltimore in a stunning deal following the 1965 season. Angered that the Reds considered him an "old 30," Robinson set out to prove his former club wrong. He did just that, immediately and with a vengeance. Frank won the Triple Crown in 1966, topping the American

League with a .316 batting average, 49 homers and 122 runs batted in, and sparked the Orioles to their first Series championship in his initial year with the club. He then had a 30-homer, 94-RBI season in 1967, a year in which he batted .311.

Robinson's leadership qualities were apparent on and off the field. Besides hammering American League pitching, Robinson, sullen and combative in his early days in the majors, helped to develop team camaraderie by holding forth as judge of the Orioles' Kangaroo Court, which was called into session to review various misdemeanors perpetrated by the players.

Nearing age 34, Robinson, the only man in major league history to be selected the Most Valuable Player in both leagues (National League in 1961, American League in 1966), was thinking beyond his days as one-man wrecking crew and court jester. He had taken his first fling at managing after the 1968 season, guiding a winter-league club in Puerto Rico.

"Respect is everything," said Robinson, analyzing his debut as a pilot. "OK, so a guy doesn't have to like you, but if he respects you, he'll run through a wall for you. I didn't go around forcing help on anyone. If a player came to me, I did what I could to help, but he had to ask."

As Robinson slugged away and at the same time pondered a managerial future, Phoebus continued to pitch well—he ran his record to 7-1 at one point

—and Palmer built a 9-2 mark before suffering a recurrence of back problems that forced him to a spot on the disabled list. McNally, meanwhile, was putting up staggering numbers. Tossing shutouts in consecutive starts on June 15 and June 19, he lifted his record to 10-0 as the Orioles savored an eight-game lead over second-place Boston. Admittedly benefiting from considerable good luck (he pitched poorly in a number of no-decision contests), McNally nevertheless pushed his ledger to an astonishing 13-0 by the All-Star Game break, at which time Baltimore held an 11-game lead.

Powell, too, was on a tear. After a slow start, he had slugged 22 home runs in a little more than two months and had 24 homers and 86 RBIs at the break. Both totals exceeded his season-long figures for 1967 and 1968.

A hulk of a man, Powell was always fighting the battle of the bulge—and not always winning. Lee MacPhail, former Orioles' president, once said that only two things could keep Boog from becoming a great hitter—a knife and a fork. Forthrightness, usually an admirable trait, may have posed a threat, too. Asked his weakness at the plate, and knowing the answer surely would find its way into print, Powell responded thusly: "Good hard stuff anywhere inside from my chest to my knees. But there's only about a three-inch area the pitcher has to play with. If he gets it outside that narrow space, then the ball is on the sweet spot of my bat. . . ."

The ball was finding that sweet spot in 1969, just as it had in 1966 (when Powell crushed 34 homers and knocked in 109 runs) and in 1963 and 1964 (seasons in which Boog totaled 64 homers and 181 RBIs).

Not exactly nimble, Powell was surprisingly good defensively.

"I'm not saying this because I play with the guy," Belanger said, "but the guy is nothing but great. He has a fantastic pair of hands."

"You know," Brooks Robinson said one year, "I can't remember him missing a scoop this season. He might have, but I don't remember it.

"I'll tell you what I think is the biggest advantage having him on first. Not only his hands, but his size. You know if you get it (a throw) anywhere in the general area, he's going to get it."

McNally's '69 winning streak reached 15 games—thus tying an American League record for consecutive victories from the beginning of the season—when he beat the Kansas City Royals, a first-year expansion club, on July 30. In his next start, against Minnesota, McNally saw his string come to an end when the Twins' Rich Reese cracked a bases-loaded homer.

While McNally no longer was the center of attention, Palmer soon was. Less than a week after coming off the disabled list, he spun a no-hitter against

The biggest man, literally, in the Baltimore lineup was first baseman Boog Powell, who contributed 94 home runs to the Orioles' three-year total.

Oakland. Before the August 13 Orioles-A's game, Palmer had stood in front of his locker and proclaimed that his arm—given a six-inning test four days earlier—didn't "feel live." Pondering his observation, Palmer was quick to add: "Of course, I felt the same way after my first appearance in Puerto Rican ball last winter. Then I went out and pitched a no-hitter in my second (game)."

Palmer's ability to give the opposition trouble was perhaps equaled only by his tendency to give Weaver fits. Or was it the other way around?

Over the years, Palmer and Weaver developed a love-hate relationship. After trading insults, some of which were plain nasty, they always managed to negotiate a truce.

"They're two of the same kind of people," said Belanger. "Earl feels he should win every game, that every move he makes is the right one. He has such intensity, he'll be old before his time. Jim's a perfectionist. He thinks he can go the whole nine innings without making a bad pitch."

During their manager/player relationship, which stretched into the 1980s, Weaver liked to mention how many games Palmer had won in the majors. Earl's total would fall noticeably short of the actual number, and Jim would correct him. "I'm only counting the ones you won since I've been here," Weaver would say. "The others don't count."

Palmer had a rejoinder: "I can only repeat what Dave McNally once said about Earl. That is, the only thing he knows about pitching is that he couldn't hit it."

The "feud" was the kind in which Weaver would joke about Palmer's many physical problems— "The Chinese tell time by the Year of the Dragon and the Year of the Horse, I tell time by Palmer... the Year of the Shoulder, the Year of the Elbow, the Year of the Ulna Nerve"—and then lend support to his righthander during salary squabbles.

At the time of Palmer's 1969 no-hitter, Baltimore led the East Division by 14½ games, and the margin would grow to 17 in a few days. It was a cakewalk for Weaver and his Orioles, who got a stellar performance from Cuellar in the final two months of the season and defensive excellence from virtually everyone.

Cuellar, possessor of a 10-9 record at the All-Star break, won 13 of his first 14 decisions following the midsummer respite. "He's an artist," longtime Orioles scout Jim Russo said of Cuellar. "He throws all kinds of pitches and gets them all over the plate."

On those instances when opposing batsmen made contact against Cuellar and company, chances were good that the offensive players would suffer severe cases of frustration. "Trying to hit a ball through the Baltimore infield," Detroit Manager Mayo Smith said, "is like trying to throw hamburgers through a brick wall."

Trying to get the ball into the outfield gaps was just as difficult, considering that Blair was patrolling center field and running down everything in sight. Weaver was fond of saying that with the opposing team at bat in a clutch situation, he was supremely confident when the ball was hit to either of two places: to center field, or to the left side of the infield.

Blair was just as confident. Once, after hitting a triple to the deepest part of Detroit's Tiger Stadium, he was told in jest that perhaps center fielder Mickey Stanley should have gotten to the ball. "Listen," Blair cracked, "only one man could have got that ball ... and he hit it."

Blair, who had connected for only seven home runs in 1968 and previously had a big-league high of 11 in one season, gave the Orioles an unexpected power lift in '69 by smashing 26 homers. Baltimore's other defensive wonders, Brooks Robinson and Belanger, also made major offensive contributions. Robinson, despite a paltry .234 batting mark, supplied 23 homers and 84 RBIs and Belanger, a career .198 hitter in the majors entering the season, came through with a surprising .287 average. Robinson and Belanger weren't being paid for their of-

fense, however.

A Gold Glove-winning third baseman for the 10th consecutive year in 1969, Robinson constantly was being thrown verbal bouquets—and from the highest sources.

"I've been around a long time," Casey Stengel said in the early '60s, "but I've never seen anyone make the plays he does. I saw (Pittsburgh's Pie) Traynor—and he was the best. Robinson is almost up there with him."

"He has exceptional reflexes, and the strongest pull hitters in the game can't seem to get the ball by him," Traynor himself said. "Sure, he'll miss now and then, but it's an accident when he does."

Ed Hurley, an American League umpire for almost two decades, said: "That Robinson plays third base like he came down from a higher league."

Robinson's stature with the glove would reach even new heights in the years ahead, as mind-boggling as that would appear. Brooks' value to his team—as exemplified by his all-around skills and competitive fire—needed no embellishing. While dazzling observers with his glove from the outset of his major league career, Robinson made himself into a first-rate hitter. In 1964, he belted 28 homers, drove in a league-leading 118 runs and made off with the American League's Most Valuable Player Award. Two years later, he knocked in 100 runs. Twice he had batted above .300, and he was in the .290s on two other occasions. And, all the while, he played with ultimate zeal.

One day, in Detroit, he chased a ball toward the stands and wound up crashing into a concrete ledge. His lower jaw was cut open and teeth were broken off. "Call an ambulance," the trainer cried. Brooks struggled to his feet and pleaded his case: "Didn't you ever see anyone shaken up before?" he asked. "Give me my glove and let's go on with this ball game."

Belanger, a much-ballyhooed minor league player, had suffered through a dreadful 1968 season after he supplanted gifted shortstop Luis Aparicio, who had been traded away. Promoted as being in the mold of Marty Marion, the rangy star shortstop of the 1940s St. Louis Cardinals, the 6-2 Belanger endured futility at the plate and a surprising number of gaffes afield. In 1969, it was a different story.

"Most of it has to be a year's experience," said Weaver, analyzing a season in which Belanger performed the defensive magic expected of him and also showed remarkable improvement at the plate. "I knew he could play this type of ball because I managed him in the minors when he did, and I expected him to play it up here. He's sure of himself now."

Baltimore sportswriter John Steadman, after watching Belanger over an extended part of his career, was moved to write:

The Orioles' superb pitching was epitomized in 1971 when (left to right) Jim Palmer, Dave McNally, Mike Cuellar and Pat Dobson all won 20 or more games.

Belanger is not exactly a symphony in motion. There's nothing of the high-wire aerialist or the ballerina in how he plays shortstop. . .just an expertise that is thorough and dependable.

. . .Belanger does it with a professionalism that becomes him. The grandstand play isn't in his makeup. He knows what it is, sees it all the time but couldn't deal in such bogus activity.

. . .Belanger doesn't have a tag like "Rabbit" or "Slats". . .but he covers shortstop with a dexterity that is almost deceitful.

There's no show to the performance Belanger sets out to give, merely (a desire) to surround ground balls, swallow up line drives and run down the left-field foul line to catch pop flies with a thoroughness that leaves nothing undone.

He'll cut off the ball in the hole, brace himself and get something on the throw, not one of those rainbow trajectories delivered with a jumping-jack act and a synthetic touch of the spectacular.

On the topped grounder that has to be charged or feeding the double-play ball or making the relay from short center field, the play is handled with a quiet kind of perfection. . . .

It was easy to rhapsodize about these Orioles, who wound up with a 109-53 record while winning the 1969 East Division race by 19 games, and considerable prose spewed forth at the end of the regular season. Much of it focused on how Weaver's mighty

charges would make quick work of the West champion Minnesota Twins in the American League's inaugural Championship Series—a World Series-qualifying round resulting from the adoption of two-division league alignments—and then beat up on either the Atlanta Braves or the upstart New York Mets, the National League's postseason combatants, in the fall classic. After all, this was a team with sledgehammer power, as evidenced by Powell's 37 home runs and 121 RBIs and Frank Robinson's 32 homers and 100 RBIs; superb pitching, as demonstrated by the 23-11, 20-7 and 16-4 records hung up by Cuellar, McNally, and Palmer, respectively; and airtight defense, as numbers couldn't quite convey but the artistry of Brooks Robinson, Belanger and Blair could.

The Twins fell, all right. In a sweep. The National League champion Mets didn't. Getting marvelous pitching and slightly incredible defense, the Mets stunned the Orioles in the World Series. In five games.

The defeat was crushing to the Orioles, and no one took it harder than the supreme battler, Brooks Robinson. Instead of pouting, though, Brooks set out on a mission. His destination was clear; in fact, he even inscribed it on a suitcase identification tag as the Orioles embarked on their first road trip of the following season: "Brooks Robinson, Baltimore Orioles, 1970 World Champions."

Brooks and company got there, and they made it using the same formula that had worked so well—but not quite well enough—in 1969. The long ball. Masterful pitching. Suffocating defense.

"Strategy in baseball is overrated," Weaver

The honorable Frank Robinson was presiding judge over the Orioles' Kangaroo
Court, which meted out fines for various player indiscretions.

would say later in his career. "People say, 'That
Weaver, he plays for the long ball too much.' You
bet I do. Hit 'em out. Then I got no worry about
somebody lousing up a bunt, I got no worry about
the hit-and-run—and that's *really* overrated—I got
no worry about baserunning errors. And I can't
screw it up myself. Just instant runs. You bet Weaver likes the long ball. . . ."

The Orioles' manager took particular delight in
power baseball in 1970, a year in which eight Baltimore players posted double-figure home run totals.
Powell led the way with 35 homers in what proved
a Most Valuable Player season for the big guy.
Frank Robinson walloped 25 and outfield mates
Buford, Blair and Merv Rettenmund, a reserve who
saw extensive duty because of injuries and his own
hot bat, combined for 53.

Cuellar and McNally again entered the 20-victory
circle, being joined this time in the select class by a
healthy Palmer. The two lefthanders each won 24
games, while Palmer finished with exactly 20 triumphs.

Righthanders Eddie Watt and Dick Hall and lefthander Pete Richert, who in 1969 had ERAs of 1.65,
1.91 and 2.21 as Baltimore's bullpen triumvirate,
weren't quite as stingy in 1970 but nevertheless
combined for 24 victories.

The defense was typically surehanded, with second baseman Dave Johnson stealing the statistical

thunder by sporting a .990 fielding percentage and
playing errorless ball in his last 43 games of the
season.

All of this added up to a 108-54 record and a
15-game romp over the New York Yankees in the
American League East race, after which Baltimore
again dispatched Minnesota in three games in the
Championship Series before preparing for a World
Series meeting against the Cincinnati Reds. The prototype of Cincinnati's vaunted Big Red Machine of
the 1970s was no match for a revenge-bent band of
proud Orioles, still smarting from their '69 Series
loss to the Mets.

Fittingly, Brooks Robinson saw to it that the Orioles' mission was accomplished. In one of the most
incredible fielding displays in any setting, Brooks
foiled the heavy-hitting Cincinnati club time and
again with awe-inspiring defensive plays. Plus, he
batted .429 with two home runs and six RBIs.

"That guy can field a ball with a pair of pliers,"
marveled Reds right fielder Pete Rose.

"The only way to beat him is to hit it over his
head," Cincinnati catcher Johnny Bench said.

"Robinson beat us," Reds Manager Sparky Anderson said succinctly. Never had great defensive
play been so universally appreciated and widely
written about.

Robinson had a little help in sending the Reds
packing after five games. Powell and Frank Robin-

Four Orioles, (left to right) Brooks Robinson, Mark Belanger, Dave Johnson and
Paul Blair, were 1971 Gold Glove winners.

son also hit two homers apiece, Blair batted .474
and Baltimore's crack pitching staff turned the Big
Red Machine into a sputtering heap.

As the Orioles enjoyed a winter of contentment,
team officials weren't willing to rest on their laurels. Accordingly, they went to the trade mart. And
what do you get for a club that has everything, including three 20-game winners? More pitching,
that's what.

Hardin, winner of a total of only 12 games in the
last two seasons as he divided his time between
starting and relieving, no longer figured prominently in Baltimore's plans. Someone else did, however,
and that certain someone had worn a National
League uniform in 1970.

In a December 1, 1970, deal, the Orioles traded
four players—including Phoebus, who had
slumped to a 5-5 season after going 14-7 in 1969—to
the San Diego Padres for starting pitcher Pat Dobson and reliever Tom Dukes. Dobson had won 14
games for the '70 Padres, a team that finished last in
the National League West, and his acquisition was
considered a major coup. And it turned out to be
just that.

Dobson, in fact, did exactly what the most ardent
of Baltimore fans expected him to do: He gave the
Orioles a *fourth* 20-game winner. It seemed a bit

much to ask Cuellar, McNally and Palmer to repeat
their 20-victory accomplishments of 1970, let alone
ask Dobson—a man with a 25-35 career record in
the majors—to join in the fun. For the 1971 Baltimore Orioles, though, it was a case of let the good
times roll.

McNally racked up 21 victories for the '71 Orioles, while Cuellar, Palmer and, yes, Dobson all
won exactly 20. An amazing 8-0 record in July fueled Dobson's drive to the coveted figure. No major
league team had boasted four 20-game winners in
one season since the Chicago White Sox achieved
the feat in 1920.

A wrist fracture incurred by Powell slowed the
Baltimore offense, but Frank Robinson, Brooks
Robinson and big Boog still slammed a total of 70
homers and drove in 283 runs overall and helped
power the club to a 101-57 record and its third consecutive divisional championship. Rettenmund, inserted into the lineup in right field when Powell
went down (Frank Robinson moved to first base),
followed up his .322 hitting of 1970 with a .318
mark. Buford, proving an ideal leadoff man (he
coaxed a total of 205 bases on balls in the previous
two seasons), scored 99 runs for the third straight
year and even won a place among the heavy-hitter
brigade with 19 homers. And, for the third consecu-

tive campaign, Hendricks and Etchebarren contributed significantly offensively (a total of 18 and 71 RBIs in '71) while handling the pitching staff with aplomb.

Weaver's athletes swept through the Championship Series once more, bouncing the up-and-coming Oakland A's this time, but lost to the Pittsburgh Pirates in a stirring World Series, which went seven games and was decided by a 2-1 finale.

What a wondrous three seasons, however, for Earl Weaver and the Baltimore Orioles. A cumulative 318 regular-season victories. Divisional titles by margins of 19, 15 and 12 games. A 9-0 record in Championship Series competition. One World Series crown and, of course, the three pennants.

Other numbers were telling. Powell socked 94 home runs and drove in 327 runs in the three years, Frank Robinson belted 85 homers and knocked in 277 runs and Brooks Robinson had 61 homers and 270 RBIs. Cuellar won 67 games, McNally posted 65 victories and Palmer won 56 times.

From the biggest star to the last man on the bench, consistency was a trademark of these Orioles. Second baseman Johnson epitomized it, batting .280 in 1969, .281 in 1970 and .282 in 1971.

"There's no way a man can be a champion manager without a championship team," philosophized Weaver in a statement that the likes of John McGraw would have found difficult to dispute.

"Usually, if his team is winning, the manager is doing a good job. That doesn't necessarily mean he's a good manager. It might just be that his team is playing well under his type of managing. . . ."

Weaver, surely too modest in assessing his impact on the club, clearly exhibited a style of managing that suited his personnel perfectly. Without question, the Baltimore Orioles of 1969, 1970 and 1971 played the game of baseball uncommonly well.

1970
FINAL STANDING

Club	W.	L.	Pct.	GB.
Baltimore	108	54	.667	——
New York	93	69	.574	15

BATTERS

Pos.	Player	G.	HR.	RBI.	B.A.
1B	Boog Powell	154	35	114	.297
2B	Dave Johnson	149	10	53	.281
SS	Mark Belanger	145	1	36	.218
3B	Brooks Robinson	158	18	94	.276
OF	Don Buford	144	17	66	.272
	Paul Blair	133	18	65	.267
	Frank Robinson	132	25	78	.306
C	Elrod Hendricks	106	12	41	.242
	Andy Etchebarren	78	4	28	.243
UT	Merv Rettenmund (of)	106	18	58	.322
	Terry Crowley (of-1b)	83	5	20	.257

OTHER CONTRIBUTORS (20+ Games): Bobby Grich, Dave May, Curt Motton, Chico Salmon.

PITCHERS

Thr.	Pitcher	G.	W.	L.	ERA
L	Mike Cuellar	40	24	8	3.47
L	Dave McNally	40	24	9	3.22
R	Jim Palmer	39	20	10	2.71
R	Dick Hall	32	10	5	3.10
L	Pete Richert	50	7	2	1.96
R	Eddie Watt	53	7	7	3.27
R	Tom Phoebus	27	5	5	3.07

OTHER CONTRIBUTORS (20+ Games): Moe Drabowsky, Jim Hardin, Dave Leonhard, Marcelino Lopez.

1971
FINAL STANDING

Club	W.	L.	Pct.	GB.
Baltimore	101	57	.639	——
Detroit	91	71	.562	12

BATTERS

Pos.	Player	G.	HR.	RBI.	B.A.
1B	Boog Powell	128	22	92	.256
2B	Dave Johnson	142	18	72	.282
SS	Mark Belanger	150	0	35	.266
3B	Brooks Robinson	156	20	92	.272
OF	Don Buford	122	19	54	.290
	Paul Blair	141	10	44	.262
	Frank Robinson	133	28	99	.281
C	Elrod Hendricks	101	9	42	.250
	Andy Etchebarren	70	9	29	.270
UT	Merv Rettenmund (of)	141	11	75	.318

OTHER CONTRIBUTORS (20+ Games): Clay Dalrymple, Jerry DaVanon, Curt Motton, Chico Salmon, Tom Shopay.

PITCHERS

Thr.	Pitcher	G.	W.	L.	ERA
L	Dave McNally	30	21	5	2.89
R	Pat Dobson	38	20	8	2.90
L	Mike Cuellar	38	20	9	3.08
R	Jim Palmer	37	20	9	2.68

OTHER CONTRIBUTORS (20+ Games): Tom Dukes, Dick Hall, Grant Jackson, Pete Richert, Eddie Watt.

1969
FINAL STANDING

Club	W.	L.	Pct.	GB.
Baltimore	109	53	.673	——
Detroit	90	72	.556	19

BATTERS

Pos.	Player	G.	HR.	RBI.	B.A.
1B	Boog Powell	152	37	121	.304
2B	Dave Johnson	142	7	57	.280
SS	Mark Belanger	150	2	50	.287
3B	Brooks Robinson	156	23	84	.234
OF	Don Buford	144	11	64	.291
	Paul Blair	150	26	76	.285
	Frank Robinson	148	32	100	.308
C	Elrod Hendricks	105	12	38	.244
	Andy Etchebarren	73	3	26	.249
UT	Merv Rettenmund (of)	95	4	25	.247

OTHER CONTRIBUTORS (20+ Games): Clay Dalrymple, Bobby Floyd, Dave May, Curt Motton, Chico Salmon.

PITCHERS

Thr.	Pitcher	G.	W.	L.	ERA
L	Mike Cuellar	39	23	11	2.38
L	Dave McNally	41	20	7	3.21
R	Jim Palmer	26	16	4	2.34
R	Tom Phoebus	35	14	7	3.52
L	Pete Richert	44	7	4	2.21
R	Eddie Watt	56	5	2	1.65

OTHER CONTRIBUTORS (20+ Games): Dick Hall, Jim Hardin, Dave Leonhard, Marcelino Lopez.

Number 10

DiMaggio Begins New Yankee Era

A young and enthusiastic Joe DiMaggio (right) gets a New York welcome from Yankee Owner Jacob Ruppert (left) and Manager Joe McCarthy.

There is little doubt that one of the most widely publicized and eagerly awaited rookies in more than a century of major league baseball was the son of a California fisherman who had hit safely in 61 consecutive games before he was 19 years old.

The baseball world was first alerted to Joseph Paul DiMaggio in 1933. He was a brilliant, young outfielder with San Francisco of the Pacific Coast League, a well-proportioned athlete with 190 pounds on a 6-foot, 2-inch frame. Style was his trademark. Whether gliding effortlessly after long fly balls, throwing accurately to the bases and cut-off men, or ripping line drives from a model bat-

ting stance, he was picture-perfect in every aspect of the game.

Major league scouts were camped on the young-ster's trail and the bidding for his services was expected to be high. Without exception, he was viewed as the ultimate prize, a can't-miss superstar who could bring happiness and success to a lucky franchise.

Interest in the talented prodigy still was building early in 1934 when it suddenly came to a screeching stop. Young DiMaggio had suffered a most unusual knee injury that raised serious doubts about his future. The once-drooling scouts abruptly directed their attention elsewhere.

The phenom had played a doubleheader at Seals Stadium and then hopped into a cab for a ride to his sister's home for dinner. Sitting awkwardly on the back seat, the youngster was unaware that his leg had fallen asleep. When he alighted at curbside, he placed all his weight on his left foot. "I went down like I'd been shot," he said later. "There was no twisting, just four sharp cracks at the knee. I couldn't straighten out my leg. The pain was terrific, like a whole set of aching teeth in my knee."

A doctor was consulted. Sprained tendons was the verdict. Go home and apply an epsom-salt solution and hot towels, the player was told.

The next day, DiMaggio reported to Seals Stadium. He informed his manager, Ike Caveney, of the mishap, but insisted he could play. Caveney took one look at the limping teen-ager and wisely held him out of the lineup. When he relented in a late inning, however, and let the youngster go to the plate as a pinch-hitter, DiMaggio hit a home run and literally walked around the bases.

Two days later, he pinch-hit again. This time he doubled and hobbled into second base. Quite clearly, DiMaggio was making no progress toward recovery from his "sprained tendons." He was instructed to visit the team physician, who diagnosed the injury as torn cartilage. For the next three weeks, the youngster wore an aluminum splint from ankle to thigh. After finally rejoining the Seals, DiMaggio complicated matters by slipping in the dugout. His leg collapsed again and he was finished for the season.

As other major league scouts shied away, however, one remained confident of the youngster's future. He was Bill Essick of the New York Yankees. Essick expressed his confidence to Edward G. Barrow, the architect of the New York empire. "You can get him cheap," he told the general manager.

Acting on that advice, Barrow opened negotiations with Charley Graham, owner of the Seals. The asking price was $40,000. Barrow offered $20,000. Eventually, they settled on $25,000, five fringe players and one provision—DiMaggio would have to submit to an examination by a doctor of the Yankees' choice. Graham agreed.

Joe visited an orthopedic specialist in Los Angeles. His opinion removed all doubts. At DiMaggio's age, said the doctor, he should make a complete recovery.

With that encouragement, Barrow informed Graham that they had a deal. Now it was the Seals owner's turn to make a request. Because of the player's youth, Graham asked that DiMaggio be allowed to remain with the club for one season to gain the experience necessary to prepare him for the Yankees. Barrow and his manager, Joe McCarthy, talked it over and consented. Both believed that the

Yankees were sufficiently stocked to win the 1935 pennant.

The Yankees fell short of that expectation, finishing second for the third year in a row, but Joe DiMaggio enjoyed a superlative season. The 20-year-old phenom batted .398, hit 34 home runs and drove in 154 runs. He also registered 32 assists from his center-field position. In all respects, his numbers were impressive. He was ready. He was well qualified to join fellow Italians and San Franciscans Tony Lazzeri and Frank Crosetti, as well as such other Yankee luminaries as Lou Gehrig, Bill Dickey, Red Rolfe, Ben Chapman, George Selkirk, Red Ruffing and Lefty Gomez.

The much-ballyhooed rookie was set to make the long, arduous transcontinental train ride from San Francisco to the Yankees' training camp in St. Petersburg, Fla., when he received a phone call from Lazzeri. "I have a new car and plan to drive to St. Pete," advised the veteran second baseman. "How about riding along with Crosetti and me?" Joe jumped at the offer. When departure day arrived, he relaxed on the back seat as Lazzeri wheeled his new vehicle across the highways and byways of America. After several hours, Crosetti slipped into the driver's seat. Four or five hours later, DiMaggio was informed that it was his turn to drive.

"Sorry," he said with a grin, "I don't know how to drive."

Lazzeri glowered at his passenger and then glanced at Crosetti. "How do you like that. We ought to leave the bum here," he growled.

The remainder of the trip was made in near silence, not because of DiMaggio's inability to share in the piloting chores, but because none of the travelers was given to verbosity. All, in fact, preferred quiet contemplation, willingly consigning the right of idle talk to others.

The three were so frugal with words, in fact, that a sportswriter was moved once to describe the trio sitting in a hotel lobby:

> . . . the three of them were sitting there, watching the guests coming and going. I bought a paper and sat down near them, and after awhile became aware of the fact that none of them had a word to say to the others. Just for fun I timed them to see how long they would maintain their silence. Believe it or not, they didn't speak for one hour and 20 minutes. At the end of that time DiMaggio cleared his throat. Crosetti looked at him and said, "What did you say?"
>
> And Lazzeri said, "Shut up. He didn't say nothing."
>
> They lapsed into silence and at the end of 10 minutes I got up and left. I couldn't stand it anymore.

Spring training 1936 featured a little of the old, Yankee veteran Lou Gehrig, and a little of the new, rookie Joe DiMaggio (right).

The Yanks' 1936 Italian keystone combination featured shortstop Frank Crosetti (left) and second baseman Tony Lazzeri.

As the senior member of the three-man troupe, Lazzeri escorted DiMaggio into the Yankee clubhouse at St. Petersburg and introduced him to his new teammates. Gehrig was among the first to greet the rookie. The durable captain and first baseman extended a friendly welcome and the pair moved on to Ruffing.

DiMaggio offered his hand to the rawboned hurler, who ignored it and slowly looked over the young newcomer. "So you're the great DiMaggio, hey?" he said. "I've been reading all about you. Hit .400 out there on the Coast. Well, you ought to hit .800 here because we don't have any lights and we use a nice shiny ball for almost every pitch."

Many weeks elapsed before Joe learned that Ruffing was a master needler. In time, a close friendship developed.

DiMaggio's final introduction was to McCarthy. The one-time minor league second baseman was in his sixth season as manager of the Bronx Bombers. Before coming to New York, Marse Joe had piloted the Cubs for five years. The no-nonsense Irishman had been discharged for failing to duplicate his pennant-winning performance of 1929.

When DiMaggio emerged from that interview, he was met by a band of reporters and the interrogation began.

"What did McCarthy say?"

"Not much."

"Did he tell you where you would play?"

"No."

"Did you express any preference?"

"No. Wherever he wants me to play is all right with me."

"Left field is the sun field at Yankee Stadium. Did you ever play the sun field?"

"No."

"Babe Ruth never would play it."

"I'll play it if Mr. McCarthy wants me to."

"More likely he'll play you in center field."

"That's all right with me."

The inquisition finally ended and DiMaggio was free to mingle with his teammates. But that wasn't an easy chore for the youngster, who was as confident and cocky on the baseball field as he was shy off it. He naturally stuck close to Lazzeri and Crosetti, his traveling companions, as he prepared to face the mountain of expectations that had been heaped upon him.

Lazzeri was beginning his 11th season with the Yankees and provided a convenient role model for a youngster unschooled in the social graces. Lazzeri, too, had arrived upon the major league scene amid much fanfare after hitting 60 home runs in 1925 for Salt Lake City of the Pacific Coast League. That, of course, proved to be a mirage for Yankee fans who were expecting a power-hitting slugger of similar stature to Babe Ruth or Gehrig.

What they got was a 5-10, 160-pound square-shouldered Italian kid who covered second base like a blanket and whistled line drives to all corners of the ball park—if not consistently over the fences. Five times before 1936 the righthanded hitter had batted over .300 and six times he had driven in more than 100 runs. The son of an Italian blacksmith and iron worker, Lazzeri displayed amazing strength while maintaining an almost fearful, businesslike demeanor. Opponents who slid into second base spikes high knew that "Poosh 'em Up Tony" was not given to idle threats and his voice, on those occasions that he chose to speak, always carried an angry tone.

Crosetti, Lazzeri's friend, protege, roommate and keystone partner, had a more slender build and opposite temperament. As the Yankee shortstop since claiming the job in 1932, the light-hitting Crosetti relied on cleverness and a quick wit while maintaining a cool, even temper.

Crosetti was not without his idiosyncrasies. He always went to bed by 9 or 10 o'clock at night and never attended a public function. Not that he was anti-social; he simply saw no value in such events.

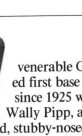

Red Rolfe, whose consistent glove and steady bat made him a fixture at third base, was known as one of the top competitors in the game.

This was the Italian connection that formed the nucleus of the Yankee defense as the 1936 season approached and there was no denying that the talent was impressive. Crosetti was coming off an injury-plagued 1935 season (he was limited to 87 games because of a bad knee) and Lazzeri was entering the twilight of his career. But DiMaggio was destined for stardom and there was a common, unspoken thread that forever linked the threesome.

The other infield jobs were held down by the venerable Gehrig, who had played first base without interruption since 1925 when he took over for Wally Pipp, and Rolfe, the freckle-faced, stubby-nosed third baseman.

The son of German immigrants, Gehrig was New York-born and bred. As a schoolboy, he gained city-wide notoriety for hitting a home run at Chicago's Wrigley Field in an inter-city contest. Later, while a student at Columbia University, he earned additional fame for his herculean clouts.

After joining the Yankees to stay in 1925, the Iron Horse became a model of offensive consistency as he teamed with Ruth to form the most potent power combination in baseball history. Entering the '36 campaign, Gehrig had hit .300 or better and driven in 100 or more runs 10 straight years. He was the heart of the Yankees. He had batted .379 with 41 homers and 174 RBIs in 1930, but had captured the American League triple crown four years later when he batted .363 with 49 homers and 165 RBIs.

Now approaching age 33, the big lefthanded hitter was laying plans to extend his consecutive-game playing streak that already had passed the 1,600 mark.

On the opposite corner of the infield, Rolfe performed efficiently, if not dramatically. According to McCarthy, Rolfe was one of the two most dependable third basemen he ever managed. Stan Hack of the Cubs was the other.

"They're both alike," said Marse Joe. "The other clubs never knew what they were doing, but when the ball game was over they knew who had beaten them."

Rolfe, christened Robert Abial, was a genuine Yankee, a native of Penacook, N. H. He was 6-foot tall and red of hair and face, with deep-set, piercing blue eyes. He was signed by the Yankee organization out of Dartmouth College in 1931 and spent three years in the minors, one with Albany and two as a shortstop at Newark. In 1933 at Newark, the youngster was named the International League's most valuable player.

Rolfe joined the Yankees in 1934 and immediately was pegged as the shortstop of the future. Crosetti held his ground, however, and Rolfe was shifted to third, where he took to the new position like a duck to water.

The lefthanded hitter batted .287 in 89 games in '34 and posted a .300 mark in '35, his first campaign as the Yankee regular third sacker. It didn't take long for the youngster's reputation as a gamer to spread through the league.

"He's the greatest team player in the game," Philadelphia A's Manager Connie Mack once proclaimed. "Half the time when you'd be playing the Yankees, you didn't know he was in the park. He'd

Jake Powell (left) took over Yankee center-field duties after his midseason trade from Washington and later moved to left field, while George Selkirk was solid in right.

go 0 for 3 in a tight game and then suddenly he'd make a great bunt, get a hit or do something to beat you. If a manager had nine Rolfes, he could go fishing every day until the World Series."

McCarthy envisioned the Yankees' 1936 outfield as Ben Chapman in center with DiMaggio and Selkirk patrolling the flanks. Roy Johnson and Myril Hoag would fill in as circumstances dictated.

Chapman, born in Nashville, Tenn., on Christmas Day 1908, had grown up reading about the base-stealing exploits of Ty Cobb and Max Carey. As it turned out, he was cut from the same mold. Exceptionally fast, Chapman arrived in New York as a third baseman in 1930 and was promptly switched to the outfield when McCarthy arrived a year later.

That proved to be a master stroke. After a .316 rookie season, the righthanded-hitting Chapman batted .315 in 1931 for McCarthy and established his credentials as an outstanding baserunner (he collected 61 steals) and a fine defensive outfielder.

By 1936, Chapman was seemingly established as a

Yankee fixture in center field and carried a .300-plus major league average. But he did have one major problem. His quick temper and biting sarcasm had been taking a toll on McCarthy for the past six seasons.

Selkirk's personality was diametrically opposite Chapman's. A native of Huntsville, Ont., "Twinkletoes" took over in right field after the exodus of Babe Ruth in 1935 and performed admirably in the face of unusual pressure. Playing in the Babe's shadow and wearing the Bambino's famous uniform No. 3 in 1935, the lefthanded-hitting Selkirk batted .312 with 94 RBIs. He hit the non-Ruthian total of 11 home runs, however, but still won over skeptical Yankee fans.

Like DiMaggio, Roy Johnson was a newcomer to the Yankees, although a veteran of seven major league campaigns. The 32-year-old Oklahoman was acquired the previous winter after hitting .315 for the Red Sox.

Hoag apprenticed with Sacramento of the Pacific Coast League. He joined the Yankees in 1931, carrying with him a $75,000 price tag and an unusual reputation. He was said to have the smallest feet in the game, one size 4 and the other 4½.

If Gehrig was the heart of the mid-1930s Yankees, Bill Dickey was the soul. The tall, gangly catcher, Gehrig's roommate, bridge-playing partner and close friend, was well established as one of the most efficient catchers in baseball history.

The 20-year-old Dickey had arrived on the major league scene late in the 1928 season, quickly impressing the mighty Yankees, who were about to crush the St. Louis Cardinals for their second straight World Series title. The youngster had arrived too late and was ineligible to participate in the four-game bombardment.

"I would let Bill catch in the Series if he were eligible," said Yankee Manager Miller Huggins, "as he's my best catcher."

Yankee opponents soon discovered that Huggins was not just blowing smoke. For the next six seasons Dickey established himself as one of the steadiest defensive catchers and smartest signal-callers in the game while raising eyebrows with his blazing bat. He batted .324 in 1929 and followed that with seasons of .339, .327, .310, .318 and .322. When he surprisingly stumbled to .279 in 1935, Yankee followers knew that American League pitchers would be paying a stiff price in '36.

But Dickey's biggest contributions to the Yankees transcended his abilities with glove and bat. He was a manager's ball player and a positive influence on teammates, especially pitchers. Like Gehrig, he was lacking in showmanship and flair, but he gave the team backbone and character.

Despite his 6-2 frame, Dickey was extremely agile in handling the deliveries of Lefty Gomez, Red Ruffing, Monte Pearson, Bump Hadley, Pat Malone, Johnny Broaca and Johnny Murphy, the team's premier reliever. And he knew opposing hitters inside and out.

"Dickey never has bothered me, never has shaken me off," said Ruffing. "He just lets me pitch my game."

Ruffing, a righthander, formed an impressive 1-2 punch with the lefthanded Gomez, known throughout the baseball community as "Goofy" because of his off-the-wall antics.

Ruffing was a man's man, big, broad and blunt. He had come out of the coal mines at Nokomis, Ill., to twice lead the American League in defeats while hurling for the lowly Boston Red Sox. He was acquired by the Yanks early in the 1930 season and instantly became a winner.

He posted seasons of 16, 18, 19 and 16 victories after joining the Yankees, but couldn't seem to reach the elusive 20-win plateau. Every time he got close, he would fall back the next year. His 19-11 1934 campaign was followed by a three-victory

drop in '35 and his chances to shake the jinx in '36 appeared slim when he chose to hold out in the spring.

The holdout was based on a $3,000 raise Ruffing sought as compensation for his hitting prowess. The burly righthanded hitter, who turned to pitching in his youth after a mining accident had resulted in the amputation of four toes on his left foot, was regarded as the best hitting pitcher in the game and often helped his own cause with an important hit. By the end of his career in 1947, Ruffing had hit 36 home runs.

But when the Yankees began their 1936 workouts in St. Petersburg, there was Ruffing sitting in the stands as an interested observer. The Yankees were stubborn. The pitcher was stubborn. After losing 24 days of training, however, Ruffing finally acceded and reported—a month behind and badly out of shape.

There was no holding out for Gomez, the tall, skinny lefthander who was as adept at throwing one-liners as his hopping fastball. The fun-loving Gomez had slumped to 12-15 in 1935 after winning more than 20 games in three of the previous four seasons and was intent on correcting that problem.

Whatever Gomez was destined to do in 1936, you could bet that he would do it with flair. And you could bet that he'd do it at the expense of several gray hairs on McCarthy's head.

When he wasn't pitching, Gomez couldn't sit still. He'd pace up and down the length of the dugout. He'd fidget. He'd twist. He'd turn. He'd pitch every ball and slide with every runner. He'd sit and tap a bat on the dugout floor, then jump up and walk across everyone's vision to get a drink of water. No matter how big the Yankee lead, Gomez was a nervous wreck.

One afternoon McCarthy couldn't stand it anymore. There was Gomez, chinning himself on the dugout roof. "Get out of here. Beat it. Go back to the clubhouse," McCarthy ordered.

Lefty shuffled his way out of the dugout, but returned a few minutes later and tapped his manager on the shoulder. "Please Joe, let me stay in the dugout," Lefty pleaded. "I won't move. But don't send me to the clubhouse all alone. I'll drive myself crazy."

Most of the time Gomez was driving his teammates crazy. Such as the time when he fielded a grounder in a double-play situation, ignored Crosetti covering second and threw to Lazzeri, who was backing up the play.

"Why did you do that?" demanded the amazed Lazzeri after running to the mound.

"Because I'd been reading about how smart you were and I wanted to see what you'd do with the ball," Gomez replied.

Despite his clowning, sharp wit and distracted

manner, Gomez was respected and well liked by everybody on the team. He kept the team in high spirits, sometimes with a gag, sometimes with one of his many funny stories. But there was a different side to the man. He was a fierce competitor who hated to lose.

"Nobody ever hated to lose worse than I do," Lefty said. "But when I lose I can't see any reason for making everybody else feel miserable just because I do. I never could holler at the other fellows or tear up my uniform or throw my stuff across the clubhouse."

And when it came to a big game, Gomez was usually exceptional. In the pinch, there would be more hop on his fastball, his nervousness would disappear and the Yankees would win.

Ruffing and Gomez had an outstanding supporting cast.

Pearson was a 26-year-old righthander from Oakland who had been obtained from Cleveland the previous winter in a hotly disputed deal that sent righthander Johnny Allen to the Indians. The temperamental Allen had compiled a 13-6 mark for the Yankees in 1935 while Pearson was slumping to 8-13 for the Indians. The criticism abated after Allen changed deliveries and started producing victories.

Hadley, like Pearson a well-respected curveballer, also was obtained in January of 1936. The 31-year-old chunky righthander, a Massachusetts product by way of Brown University, was coming off a pair of 10-win seasons for the St. Louis Browns and Washington Senators, respectively. The veteran proved to be a worthy addition to the Yankee staff.

So, too, did Perce Lay Malone, the son of a railroad brakeman in Altoona, Pa., who was named for a hard-shelled, two-fisted friend of his father. He lived up to that name. Malone lived hard and loved to have fun, a quality that made him a perfect road roommate for Gomez.

McCarthy was well aware of Malone's penchant for the night life when he signed the big righthander in 1935. He remembered his days as Cubs manager when Malone and Hack Wilson made his life difficult with their carousing. But he also remembered Malone as a two-time 20-game winner who might have lost his fastball, but still knew how to win. He only did that three times in 1935, but was poised for bigger things in '36 out of the Yankee bullpen.

Even with the likes of Malone and Gomez, however, the craziest of the Yankees might well have been John Joseph Broaca, a 24-year-old, bespectacled righthander. Broaca, a native of Lawrence, Mass., had signed with the Yankees organization

Lefty Gomez (above), the self-appointed clubhouse comedian, and Red Ruffing, the durable, steady righthander, were the aces of the Yankees' 1936 staff.

after graduation from Yale and joined the Bombers in 1934, brimful of cockiness with a blinding fast-ball and outstanding curve. He won a three-hitter and a one-hitter against St. Louis in 1934 and high praise from Dickey when he won 15 times in '35. Johnny has "more natural stuff than anyone I've seen in a long time," Dickey said.

Broaca also possessed a strange outlook on life. After winning 12 games by early September in 1936, he disappeared, reportedly to become a boxer. He never returned to the team, thereby gaining recognition, according to Damon Runyon, as "the first fugitive from a World Series." The hurler forfeited a $6,000 paycheck.

The ace of the Yankee bullpen was righthander Murphy, a native New Yorker, a graduate of Fordham University and a profound student of pitching. Teammates called him "Grandma," apparently because he was "sedate and reserved . . . with the kindly eye and smile" of a grandmother. Opposing batters used less-complimentary names.

The Yankee starting pitchers called him indispensable.

Once when Gomez was asked how he felt before a game, he answered, "How I feel isn't important. The important thing is how Murphy feels."

Like tourists, Murphy and his teammates were eager to catch a glimpse of DiMaggio when training camp opened at St. Petersburg in 1936. Could any 21-year-old kid be as proficient as this youngster was pronounced to be?

DiMaggio quickly turned speculation into applause. He was on fire for the Yankees' first five exhibition games and, without exception, was adjudged the genuine article. But then disaster struck. DiMaggio injured his left foot.

As it turned out, it was only a minor bruise. The club trainer prescribed a few days rest and some diathermy treatment to make him good as new.

Forty-eight hours later, Joe was relaxing under a heat lamp when the situation was complicated. Before anyone was aware of the situation, the rookie's left foot had turned a ghastly red. A doctor was called in. One glimpse of the burned extremity was enough. "This man will not be able to play for two or three weeks at least," he announced.

When the Yankees embarked on their exhibition tour northward, DiMaggio entrained for New York, hobbling on crutches and with his injured foot encased in a carpet slipper. There he waited until the team physician pronounced him fit to make his major league debut.

That occurred May 3 on a rainy Sunday afternoon before 25,530 customers. The soon-to-be-called Yankee Clipper signaled his arrival by smashing a triple and two singles and scoring three times as the Yankees mauled the St. Louis Browns, 14-5.

Righthander Monte Pearson recorded 19 victories in 1936 while fashioning an impressive 3.71 earned-run average.

DiMaggio made his auspicious debut in the Yanks' 18th game, when they trailed the Red Sox by one-half length. One week later on May 10, the Bombers charged into first place—a spot they never would relinquish in their 130 remaining games.

DiMaggio was instrumental in that victory, too. In the first inning he drove a pitch from Philadelphia's George Turbeville over the fence at Yankee Stadium for his first major league home run. The Yanks won the game, 7-2.

That five-run margin represented more compassion than the Yankees usually showed Connie Mack's struggling A's.

On May 23, for example, the Bronx Bombers crushed the last-place A's, 12-6 and 15-1, as Lazzeri cracked three home runs at Shibe Park. But that brutalization was only a prologue for the savagery to be visited upon the hapless Mackmen the next day.

Again Turbeville was on the mound. The 21-year-old righthander from Turbeville, S.C., was the only Philadelphia hurler who had not seen action in the preceding day's holocaust. He would have been better off calling in sick. The youngster exited with one out in the second inning, the victim of his own

John Broaca (left), the 12-game winner who disappeared from the team late in the 1936 season, discusses signals with veteran catcher Bill Dickey.

wildness and one solitary hit.

That hit was a home run by Lazzeri. Turbeville had walked the bases full and tried to slip a 3-and-1 pitch past the Yankee veteran. When last seen, the ball was soaring over the right-field fence.

When Lazzeri came to bat in the fifth inning, Red Bullock, a 23-year-old lefthander from Biloxi, Miss., was pitching for the A's and the bases again were full, courtesy of the rookie's wildness. Lazzeri again drove a pitch into the seats.

Lazzeri led off the seventh and worked the count to 2 and 2 against lefthander Woody Upchurch. The next pitch was sent bouncing off the roof of the left-field stands as Lazzeri circled the bases. The RBI was Tony's ninth of the game, tying the American League record held by Jimmie Foxx.

Upchurch still was taking his lumps when Lazzeri batted again in the eighth, this time with only two men on base. Upchurch scored a victory of sorts—he kept the ball in the park. Lazzeri boomed a long drive that struck the top of the outfield wall. A faster runner might have legged it out for a fourth home run, but Lazzeri had to settle for a triple. When the 2-hour, 34-minute bombardment came to a merciful conclusion, the Yankees owned a 25-2 victory and Lazzeri owned an American League record (11 RBIs) that endured for more than 50 years.

Terrible Tony was abetted in the Philadelphia massacre by his fellow townsmen, Crosetti and Di-Maggio. Crosetti hit two homers and drove in three runs while young Joe contributed a homer, double, single and three RBIs. Chapman, in seven plate ap-

pearances, whacked two doubles and walked five times.

The Yankees, in fact, received 16 bases on balls. Additional data included: 52 runs in three games and 40 in two; 13 home runs in three games and 11 in two; 49 hits for 107 total bases in three games and 19 hits for 46 bases in the 25-2 conquest.

The Quaker City atrocity spelled out emphatically that the Yankees were on a mission and mercy was not listed among their qualities. The A's weren't the only team to be treated barbarically. On one occasion the Yankes scored 19 runs against Detroit; twice they scored 18, once in a shutout over Cleveland, and once in an 18-11 trouncing of Chicago in which DiMaggio highlighted a 10-run inning with a pair of homers. The Jolter rapped four hits during that slugfest, as did Gehrig and Dickey.

It was that type of season for the newest edition of "Murderers' Row" as it thundered its way to a team batting average of .300 and league-leading totals in homers, runs, total bases, slugging percentage and fewest runs allowed.

As the Yankees pulled steadily away from the field in late May and early June, McCarthy engineered a deal that was calculated to bolster his outfield. Tiring of Chapman's quarrelsome nature and his sudden rash of charley horses, Marse Joe swapped the six-year veteran to Washington for Jake Powell, a few months older than Chappie and a .312 hitter as a rookie in 1935.

On the surface, Powell hardly seemed like McCarthy's type of player. But Joe liked his aggressive, reckless, pugilistic, all-out approach to the game and his willingness to take orders without complaint. Such attributes were more important to McCarthy than Jake's well-documented reputation as a late-hour carouser and all-round bad boy.

Inadvertently, Jake had aided the Yankees cause early in the campaign while playing for the Senators. During a game against Detroit, he made one of his patented mad charges down the first-base line and crashed into big Hank Greenberg, who was reaching for an inside throw. The slugger, who had driven in 170 runs the previous year, suffered a wrist fracture that idled him the remainder of the year and severely hampered the Tigers' bid to repeat as league champions.

The speedy Powell took over in center field, with DiMaggio and Selkirk alternating between left and right as McCarthy saw fit. It wasn't until August that DiMaggio was moved to center, where he played the balance of his career.

As the season marched on, so did the Yankees—relentlessly toward the A.L. pennant. And often, the Bronx Bombers found unexpected heroes.

On August 28, for instance, when they smothered the Tigers, 14-5 and 19-4, the surprise was supplied by Johnny Murphy, the reliever-supreme who was making one of his infrequent starts in the second game. Grandma was an unchained tiger at the plate. In five at-bats he lashed as many singles, two of them in the second inning when the Yanks scored 11 runs. That accounted for five of his 13 hits for the season. Mercifully for the Tigers, darkness halted the game in the seventh inning.

The pennant that had been conceded to the Yankees for many weeks was clinched in Cleveland on September 9, the earliest date for that accomplishment in league history. To Pearson, the former Indian, went the honor of nailing down the flag. After McCarthy's crew also captured the nightcap, 12-9, behind Gehrig's 44th homer and seven RBIs, the manager told the troops, "This is my biggest thrill in baseball. I have been on pennant-winning clubs before, but I never got a kick out of winning a championship as much as I did this one. And I want to thank all of you fellows for the fine spirit and the fine hustle you have shown all year. You are real champions. Now let's plan to win the World Series in four straight games."

When the Yanks clinched the flag, they led their closest pursuers by 18 games. When they closed the campaign with a loss in Washington, they led second-place Detroit by a record 19½ games.

Gehrig enjoyed another superlative season. The Iron Horse won his second Most Valuable Player Award with a .354 batting average, 49 home runs and 152 RBIs. Dickey led the club with a .362 average and drove in a career-high 107 runs while hitting 22 homers. DiMaggio, the incandescent rookie, batted .323 with 206 hits, 29 homers and 125 RBIs. Rolfe and Selkirk also were .300 hitters, while Powell narrowly missed at .299, although he hit .306 as a Yankee. Both Selkirk (107) and Lazzeri (109) were 100-RBI men while Crosetti chipped in with a career-high .288 average.

Ruffing finally broke his 20-win jinx by compiling a 20-12 mark, while Pearson checked in with 19 victories. Gomez finished 13-7 for the 102-51 New Yorkers.

McCarthy's request for a four-game sweep in the World Series did not materialize, however. In a resumption of the "Subway Series," which had last been held in 1923, the Bombers defeated the Giants in six games.

Carl Hubbell, the Giants' meal ticket who closed out the National League season with 16 straight wins and a 26-6 record, scattered seven hits to capture a 6-1 decision in the opening game at the Polo Grounds. King Carl handled all the Yanks with relative ease except Powell, who collected three hits, and Selkirk, who homered.

The second game was more to the Yankees' liking. Gomez spaced six hits and coasted to an 18-4 triumph behind a 17-hit attack that included three safeties apiece by Crosetti and DiMaggio and a

grand-slam homer by Lazzeri, only the second ever hit in World Series competition.

Though tagged for 10 hits—compared to four by the Yankees off Fred Fitzsimmons—Hadley gained credit for a 2-1 victory in Game 3 at Yankee Stadium. Half of the winners' hits were strung together in the eighth inning when Selkirk singled, Powell walked and Crosetti singled home the deciding run.

Gehrig, who had homered in the second inning of Game 3 against Fitzsimmons, hit another homer the next day as the Yankees, now on a roll, defeated Hubbell, 5-2.

The Giants stayed alive in Game 5 as Hal Schumacher won a 10-inning, 5-4 squeaker over Ruffing and Pat Malone, but the Bronx Bombers resumed their double-digit demolition in Game 6 to close out the Series at the Polo Grounds. Seven runs in the ninth inning blew open the Yanks' 13-5 victory and clinched the club's fifth world championship.

The closing chapter in this remarkable season was a personal triumph for Powell. Just a few months after being the "bad boy" of Washington, Jake was "bad news" to the Giants. He batted .455 with 10 hits. Rolfe posted a .400 average, also with 10 hits, while Gehrig and Lazzeri drove in seven runs apiece.

But the season also marked the opening chapter in another sense. The Yankees were on the threshold of a baseball dynasty.

1936
FINAL STANDING

Club	W.	L.	Pct.	GB.
New York	102	51	.667	——
Detroit	83	71	.539	19 ½
Chicago	81	70	.536	20
Washington	82	71	.536	20

BATTERS

Pos.	Player	G.	HR.	RBI.	B.A.
1B	Lou Gehrig	155	49	152	.354
2B	Tony Lazzeri	150	14	109	.287
SS	Frankie Crosetti	151	15	78	.288
3B	Red Rolfe	135	10	70	.319
OF	Jake Powell	87	7	48	.306
	Joe DiMaggio	138	29	125	.323
	George Selkirk	137	18	107	.308
C	Bill Dickey	112	22	107	.362

OTHER CONTRIBUTORS (20+ Games): Ben Chapman, Joe Glenn, Myril Hoag, Roy Johnson, Art Jorgens, Jack Saltzgaver.

PITCHERS

Thr.	Pitcher	G.	W.	L.	ERA
R	Red Ruffing	33	20	12	3.85
R	Monte Pearson	33	19	7	3.71
R	Bump Hadley	31	14	4	4.34
L	Lefty Gomez	31	13	7	4.38
R	Pat Malone	35	12	4	3.80
R	Johnny Broaca	37	12	7	4.24

OTHER CONTRIBUTORS (20+ Games): Jumbo Brown, Johnny Murphy.

Something Worth Fighting For

The 1904-05 New York Giants may have been the most thoroughly detested champions of their era. Indubitably, this irrepressible club was one of the greatest to ever grace the diamond.

John McGraw had no reservations about the team's ranking in his own sphere of experience. Of the 10 pennant-winning teams he managed in New York, the Little Napoleon emphatically rated his 1905 World Series champions the very best.

"The 1905 Giants were the best that I ever managed," McGraw asserted in his autobiography, "My Thirty Years in Baseball." "I say this, too, in due regard for the fact that I have handled other clubs that were greater hitters or greater baserunners. I hand the laurels to the 1905 team for its smartness. We did not have a really slow-thinking ball player on the club.

"That team was not so fast, but what it lacked in speed of feet it made up in speed of thought. In addition, we had two of the greatest pitchers the game has ever seen—Mathewson and McGinnity."

Christy Mathewson was McGraw's type of player. The handsome blond from Factoryville, Pa., and Bucknell University was a remarkable physical specimen blessed with a sharp mind and phenomenal memory. "I never had to tell Mathewson anything a second time," McGraw related. "Once he learned what they (opposing batters) could hit and couldn't hit, he never forgot."

To McGraw, Mathewson was more than an outstanding pitcher. He was a companion, an intellectual equal and the idol and ideal of American youth. "Matty not only was the greatest pitcher the game has produced—smart and with perfect control—but he was the finest character that ever came into the game," he said. "He never caused a manager a moment's trouble. His heart was in the game and with the players."

When McGraw took over the reins of the last-place Giants in July 1902, he found Mathewson filling in at first base and in the outfield. Only the year before, in his first full major league season, the big righthander had won 20 games and pitched a no-hitter for a seventh-place Giant club. Matty was promptly returned to the mound, where he baffled batters for more than a decade with his famed fadeaway pitch.

"Nobody else ever came up with a pitch quite like it," said catcher Roger Bresnahan. "The secret of the fadeaway was due to its change in speeds. Matty threw it overhand, just like a fastball. He let it go shoulder high with plenty on it, but just before it reached the plate the ball lost all its zip and just floated down over the dish. He was more effective against southpaw hitters . . . because the pitch broke away from them."

Mathewson handcuffed the enemy with much more, however, drawing upon his knowledge of each hitter's quirks and weaknesses and his pinpoint control to pick the spots for his fadeaway, smoking fastball and vicious curve that dropped off a table.

Explained McGraw: "Mathewson wasn't a strikeout pitcher. His sole object was to win the ball game for you. He seldom showed opposing hitters all his stuff until they had men on bases in position to score."

The strikeouts did, however, come easily for Christy Mathewson. After finishing 14-17 with 162 strikeouts in 1902, Mathewson fanned 267 batters in 1903 to win the first of six career strikeout crowns. On October 3, 1904, he mowed down 16 St. Louis batters to set a Giants record. As for winning ball games, Matty won 30 in 1903 for the second-place Giants, then 33 in 1904, when New York halted the Pittsburgh Pirates' three-year reign as National League champions.

Incredibly, one other Giant pitcher was more successful that 1904 season. At 5-foot-11 and 205 pounds, the barrel-chested righthander was an inch and a half shorter and 10 pounds heavier than the virile Mathewson. At 33, he also was nine years older. But Joseph Jerome McGinnity was at the peak of his pitching prowess as he carved up the National League en route to a 35-8 record.

He was dubbed "Iron Man" when writers learned he had toiled in an iron foundry in the off-season, but McGinnity redefined that moniker once he displayed his incredible durability. In August 1903, he pitched—and won—both games of a doubleheader —three times. He pitched 434 innings that season, a modern N.L. record, and won a league-high 31 games. In 1904, he worked 408 innings in 51 games while accounting for nearly a third of the Giants'

106 victories.

McGinnity pitched a baffling up-curve he had developed in semipro ball, a nice complement to his wicked roundhouse curve that was unleashed near his knees, rose several feet, then plunged into the dirt at the plate. In 1899, his first season in the major leagues, he won 28 games with McGraw's Baltimore Orioles in the National League. When the circuit reduced to eight teams for 1900—leaving Baltimore without a franchise—McGinnity notched 29 victories for the Brooklyn Superbas. The next season, with a new Oriole club breaking ground in the fledgling American League, McGinnity won 26 decisions for the team's playing manager and part owner: McGraw. And when the Little Napoleon jumped to New York in 1902, he made sure Iron Joe was in tow.

McGraw had endured a long-running feud with A.L. President Ban Johnson, who was desperately trying to get his new league on solid footing. McGraw's rough and rowdy Orioles were the antithesis of Johnson's "clean ball" platform. And if McGraw was, indeed, rightfully suspected of "crimes" for entertaining overtures from the rival National League, he unhesitatingly confirmed Johnson's allegation by signing to manage the Giants on July 16, 1902.

When McGraw took charge, he promptly released nine of the 23 players he inherited. Club Owner Andrew Freedman, wealthy and powerful in Tammany Hall, bristled. "You can't let those men go," he fumed. "They cost me $14,000."

"That's little enough—and more than they are worth," McGraw retorted. "If you keep them, they'll cost you more. You're in last place, aren't you? I've brought real ball players with me and I'll get some more."

Morosely, Freedman backed down. He was a five-star intimidator—"ruthless, vain, coarse and arrogant" wrote one reporter—but he learned that McGraw would run the Giants his own way, brooking no interference from anyone or any owner. That winter, much to the delight of Giants fans, Freedman sold the club to John T. Brush, a Giants stockholder who had taken over as managing director of the club after selling the Cincinnati Reds that August.

McGraw brought more than his best Oriole players to New York. He exported the Oriole temperament as well, a dynamic, often violent approach that became known as "McGraw rowdyism." He was a paragon of aggressive, yet fair, leadership and backed down from no one. He had been a hellcat as a third baseman; as a manager, he was a lion.

"I had been brought up in a fighting baseball school," McGraw said, "a school that had for its creed the earnest conviction that a ball game—any ball game—was something to fight for."

A Sporting News correspondent once submitted a Giant player's vivid portrait of McGraw:

"We don't work for McGraw. We slave to the crack of a lash and the lash is the tongue of McGraw. He seldom curses a player but his bitter, biting, stinging sarcasm is worse than profanity. He cuts deep, waits a minute and then rubs in the salt. He calls us nitwits, lunkheads and dumbskulls with such regularity that, in time, we come to believe that he is speaking the truth. . . .

"He's a hard master, a slave driver, a modern Simon Legree and a terrible tyrant and we all hate him. But we love him, too, for we know his knowledge of baseball is best and we do win games."

Part of the winning nucleus was installed when the Giants raided the Baltimore roster for McGinnity, catcher Roger Bresnahan and first baseman Dan McGann.

Bresnahan broke into the professional ranks as a pitcher for Washington in 1897 but evolved into

The venerable John McGraw watches from the coaching box as his 1905 Giants go about the business of recording another victory.

perhaps the game's top catcher in the early 1900s. Bresnahan, who would pioneer the regular use of shinguards, had speed, agility, a strong arm and a dangerous bat. In his first full season in New York, he batted a career-high .350. Moreover, he was versatile enough to play the infield or outfield whenever the occasion demanded.

Like Mathewson, Bresnahan possessed a steel-trap memory. "Once we discovered a weak spot in the opposition and had discussed a plan for attacking it," McGraw said, "I could depend absolutely on

Christy Mathewson 'seldom showed opposing hitters all his stuff' and had back-to-back 30-victory seasons.

Bresnahan to carry it out."

In McGraw's estimation, the Toledo, Ohio, native rated a special spot among catchers. "Did you ever know of another catcher who was a smart enough hitter and baserunner to lead off the batting order?" McGraw offered. "Did you ever know of another catcher who, in addition to his backstop work, could hit over .300 and steal bases?"

McGann was cast in a similar competitive mold. The big switch-hitting son of Shelbyville, Ky., could run like the wind, field his position brilliantly and inflict heavy damage with his long-ball hitting. From 1903 through 1906, McGann would lead the league's first basemen in fielding and average more than 30 stolen bases per season.

With keen perception and conviction, McGraw remolded the Giants along his well-defined precepts. Shortly after his arrival in New York, McGraw welcomed outfielder George Browne to the Polo Grounds. One of the fastest men in the game, Browne had been batting only .260 for the Philadelphia Phillies in his first tour of regular major league duty. Turned loose in New York, Browne hit .319 over 53 games that season, a stirring exhibition that scored as a positive harbinger.

Once the 1902 campaign ended (with the last-place Giants 53½ games behind the N.L. champion Pirates) McGraw enlisted a second baseman—Billy Gilbert, his rangy shortstop in Baltimore that season—and a left fielder—hard-hitting Sam Mertes. A formidable RBI threat, Mertes had starred as both an infielder and outfielder for the Chicago Nationals and, more recently, their A.L. counterparts, consistently hitting near .290 in a time of comparatively few .300 hitters. In 1903, his first season under McGraw, the muscle-packed San Franciscan drove in a league-leading 104 runs and the Giants climbed into second place.

Now at a genesis of eminence the New York club hadn't enjoyed since winning pennants in 1888 and 1889, McGraw completed deals for third baseman Art Devlin and shortstop Bill Dahlen.

Devlin, a native of Washington, D.C., and graduate of Georgetown University, was a hard-bitten third-sacker in the McGraw vein. As much as anyone, he was responsible for the Giants' reputation for two-fisted orneriness, often driven to action by taunts of being "McGraw's college boy."

Purchased from Newark, N.J., of the Eastern League, Devlin was blessed with uncommon speed for a 6-footer. Twice he swiped more than 50 bases for the Giants. In the field, he streaked in to pounce on bunts and weak grounders, gunning out batters with room to spare. "He can throw them out standing on his elbow," players marveled.

The deal for "Bad Bill" Dahlen puzzled many observers. Dahlen, a veteran of 13 N.L. campaigns, made his mark as one of the game's great hitters, most notably for batting .362 with 15 homers and a 42-game hitting streak in 1894. On the day the streak was snapped, his Chicago teammates pounded out 17 hits, including five apiece by the batters immediately ahead of and behind Dahlen. The next day, Bad Bill began a 28-game streak.

Now, however, Dahlen was hardly more than a .260 hitter in the twilight of a brilliant career. Or so the critics thought. When Dahlen's fiery temper flared, his competitive juices flowed—much to McGraw's liking. He was a staunch disciple of McGraw's smart baseball—the squeeze play, the double steal and the hit-and-run. "There's more to the game than just trying to knock the cover off the ball," Dahlen would spit.

Another key member of McGraw's emerging powerhouse was catcher Frank Bowerman, a Giant since 1900. Bowerman, a renowned handler of pitchers, split time with John Warner in 1904 and Bresnahan in 1905 but was Mathewson's favorite receiver. He also was respected for his extraordinary strength. Once, while walking to the Polo Grounds, he was knocked down by a huge dray, whose massive steel wheel rolled over his chest. Regaining his feet, Bowerman continued to the ball park and caught the entire game without mentioning the mishap.

Even with Mathewson and McGinnity, McGraw had ensured the Giants' pitching was deep enough to challenge the Pirates.

Luther (Dummy) Taylor, a deaf-mute righthander from Oskaloosa, Kan., was one of the hardest-working and most animated Giants. Taylor frequently dressed down the umpires with sign language and disdainful looks. After one such incident, he was astonished to see an arbiter gesture back—with orders to leave the game. The umpire, it so happened, knew the language, too.

Taylor was 18-27 in 45 games for New York in 1901, his first full season in the majors, but jumped to Cleveland in 1902. "They sent Frank Bowerman, my old buddy, over to Cleveland to talk me into coming back," Taylor related. "Frank sat in the grandstand and every time I walked out to the pitching mound and back to the bench, he kept talking to me with his fingers. I kept shaking my head 'no' and Frank kept boosting the money. Soon, I nodded my head 'yes' and that night I was on my way back to New York with Frank."

That next season, Leon (Red) Ames made his major league debut in fine fashion, pitching a five-inning no-hitter against St. Louis on September 14. The fireballing righthander with the fiery thatch racked up strikeouts with proficiency in nine full seasons with the Giants. He would set a modern major league record with 30 wild pitches in 1905, but his intimidating speed induced McGraw to install the 21-year-old in the rotation that same season.

George (Hooks) Wiltse arrived from Troy of the New York League in 1904 and promptly won his first 12 decisions, a major league record. A 6-foot lefthander, Wiltse remained with the Giants for 11 seasons. Along the way, he pitched a 10-inning no-hitter against Philadelphia in 1908 and struck out seven straight Cincinnati batters on May 15, 1906—three in the fourth inning and four in the fifth, due to a dropped third strike.

As the Giants galloped toward the 1904 pennant,

Iron Man Joe McGinnity won 35 games for John McGraw's 1904 New York Giants and recorded 21 more victories in 1905.

Third baseman Art Devlin (left) was fast with his fists and a glove; second baseman Billy Gilbert was a recruit from the hard-bitten Baltimore Orioles.

McGraw's search for a slugger turned up another old Oriole. McGraw hadn't forgotten Michael Joseph Donlin after the strutting outfielder batted .341 for the Orioles in 1901. Then again, few people ever forgot "Turkey Mike," who starred under a hot sun by day and under city lights by night. Eventually, he would quit baseball to pursue the spotlight on the Broadway stage.

"He had color and swagger," wrote one who knew him. "He was rough, tough and profane—likable. He wore his cap at a belligerent angle over one ear, and there was always a prodigious plug of tobacco stuck away in a corner of his jaw. He was the most picturesque player of his time. . . ."

Few hitters could match the consistent slugging of Donlin, who had batted better than .325 in four of his first five major league seasons. And few mortal men could indulge in after-hours escapades with as much vigor. Donlin drank lustily, entertained the fairer sex with frequency and slept only when necessary. That lifestyle sometimes led to trouble. In 1902, Donlin was fined $250 and sentenced to six months in prison for assaulting a couple on the streets of Baltimore. That attack came two days be-

fore he beat up a streetcar conductor. In 1906, Donlin was accused of holding a gun to the head of a train porter.

Nevertheless, Donlin, acquired from Cincinnati in August 1904, became one of the idols of Manhattan for his crafty stickwork that added a mighty dimension to the Giants. Donlin finished the season with a .329 average, best overall among the Giants, who had caught fire with an 18-game winning streak in June and early July to steamroll to a major league record 106 victories and the pennant.

Mathewson and McGinnity formed the most formidable pitching pairing of all time, combining for a modern major league record 68 victories in 99 appearances. When they rested, the Giants lost nothing with Taylor (21 wins) and Wiltse (13).

The jack rabbit New York offense succeeded on speed and timely hitting, leading the league in runs scored (744), team batting (.262) and stolen bases (283). McGann, Bresnahan, Browne and Devlin all hit better than .280 while Dahlen, Mertes and McGann led the club in runs batted in.

Even while the Giants coasted down the stretch, New York crackled with pennant excitement. The

New York Highlanders (formerly the Oriole franchise) were locked in a tight struggle with Boston for the A.L. flag. On the final weekend of the season, they headed into a decisive five-game showdown with the Pilgrims. Any prospects of a subway World Series, however, died because of politics and grudges. In the days leading up to season's end, Brush clarified the Giants' postseason intentions in a statement that mirrored his resentment of Johnson's establishing a rival club in New York.

"The club that wins from the clubs that represent the cities of Boston, Brooklyn, New York, Philadelphia, Pittsburgh, Cincinnati, Chicago and St. Louis, the eight largest and most important cities in America, in a series of 154 games is satisfied to the honor of champions of the United States without being called upon to contend with or recognize clubs from minor league towns. Neither the players nor the manager of the Giants nor myself desires any greater glory than to win the pennant of the National League. This is the greatest honor that can be obtained in baseball."

On the final day of the season, McGraw announced that he, not Brush, was responsible for the club's decision to ignore the precedent that had been set for a world championship series by Pittsburgh and Boston in 1903.

"I know the American League and its methods," McGraw said. "I ought to, for I paid for my knowledge. They induced me to join them when they raided the National League and as a souvenir of my experience they still have my money.

"I have not forgotten its boast when it entered New York last year. It promised to put the National League club in this city out of business by June. That was the American League idea of sportsmanship then.

"Never while I am manager of the New York club and while this club holds the pennant will I consent to enter into a haphazard box-office game with Ban Johnson and company. No one, not even my bitterest enemy, ever accused me of being a fool, and I am not going to give them a chance to say now that I am a candidate for Bloomingdale."

To add injury to insult, the Highlanders lost three of their final four games to Boston and finished second, 1½ games back. More significantly, baseball's World Series suffered its only interruption in what would have been its second year.

The Giants' 1905 season began on a successful (a 6-1 start) but combative note. On April 22 at Philadelphia, the Giants' 10-2 victory was marred by ugly scenes during and after the game. Trouble boiled over when McGann, trying to score from second base on a base hit, was thrown out as catcher Fred Abbott blocked off the plate. McGann reacted by punching Abbott in the stomach, which prompted a riotous scene that was reported in The Sporting

Dan McGann, one of the smoothest-fielding first basemen in the business, averaged more than 30 stolen bases for the 1904-05 Giants.

News:

Abbott threw the ball at the big tough and hit him hard on the back. McGann turned around and squared off at Abbott, who was there ready to defend himself. Umpire (George) Bausewine jumped between the pair and ordered both out of the game. McGraw helped to irritate the 22,000 spectators by running out to argue with Bausewine.

Mathewson, just to show that his association with the old Baltimore crowd had also made a hoodlum out of him, hit and knocked down a little lemonade boy passing in front of the New York players' bench, splitting the boy's lips and loosening several teeth for him. (The boy had hit Mathewson in the face with his tray before being ejected from the grounds by a policeman.) All this was done in full view of the spectators, who became wildly excited over the ruffianly conduct of the visiting players.

The result was that several thousand blea-

cherites mobbed the New York players in their carriages after the game, throwing stones and missiles at them, and a hundred police officers had great difficulty in quelling the riot and rescuing McGraw and his team of ruffians.

After the next day's game, reports indicated, Bresnahan jumped out of his carriage to smack a "hooting small boy" as the Giants returned to their hotel. The players ran from an angry mob, holing up in a store until police arrived to rescue Bresnahan.

The melees were the first in a season-long series of incidents that soured the rest of the league on McGraw and his rowdy tactics. The New York players attracted howling hordes virtually everywhere they went. This was particularly true in Pittsburgh, where the glimpse of a Giant uniform (the players dressed in their hotel rooms) was sure to draw curbstone demons, all laden with overripe produce and equipped with accurate throwing arms.

In his rabble-rousing way, McGraw took on the great and not-so-great. During Pittsburgh's first visit to New York, McGraw chose pitcher Mike Lynch and Pirates Owner Barney Dreyfuss as his targets for invective.

Lynch was struggling on the hill Saturday, May 20, when McGraw began taunting the lefthander from the third-base coaching box. "Stay in the game you big quitter and take your beating," McGraw sneered. "You'll get plenty of it."

Pittsburgh Manager Fred Clarke accosted Muggsy, a nickname McGraw despised, and a fist fight appeared imminent until Umpire Jim Johnstone intervened and ordered both managers off the field.

McGraw had torn into Dreyfuss a day earlier, berating him as he watched the game with friends and suggesting that he umpire the rest of the series. At least that's what the Pittsburgh executive charged. That allegation and a more serious one involving a second verbal assault Saturday were filed with N.L. President Harry Pulliam, demanding that McGraw "be put on the rack for his conduct." Dreyfuss wrote:

"On Saturday, May 20, I was standing at the main entrance to the Polo Grounds, watching the game and talking quietly to some friends when McGraw, who had been put off the field for using bad language (in the Lynch affair), appeared on the balcony of the New York clubhouse and shouted, 'Hey Barney.'

"I did not answer to that familiar greeting, nor did I respond to any of his several attempts to attract my attention. He then urged me to make a wager and was so insistent that I finally told him I would not have anything to do with him. With that he accused me of being crooked, of controlling the umpires and made other false and malicious statements."

When Pulliam moved to make the charges public, he incurred the wrath of McGraw. "Why that is the most one-sided case I ever heard of," McGraw bellowed. "Why didn't Pulliam keep the charges to himself until I had a chance to answer them? Cannot Pulliam forget that he was once the paid secretary of Barney Dreyfuss when the latter was the owner of the Louisville club and also of the Pittsburgh club?"

Pulliam fined McGraw $150 and suspended him for 15 days for his first assault on Dreyfuss, but the N.L. Board of Directors convened in a special session to act upon the "Hey Barney" incident. After the evidence was heard, McGraw was exonerated, Dreyfuss was blasted for engaging in an "undignified" public altercation with a manager, and Pulliam was commended for "the courageous action he has taken to safeguard the good name of professional baseball."

With that, Brush and McGraw adjourned to the Superior Court of Massachusetts, where they obtained an injunction restraining Pulliam's fine and suspension for "lack of proper proof."

On the front page of The Sporting News, a correspondent reacted with considerable rage: "The Hoodlums will win the championship again in a walk, but instead of playing baseball in a dignified, skillful and clean manner, they will continue to resort to bulldozing, obscenity and terrorism to their own satisfaction...."

The weeks rolled on, and so did the Giants. Donlin, Bresnahan, McGann and Browne soared amid the gaudy heights of the league's batting leaders. Sammy Strang clicked above .300 as an invaluable utility player. Taylor won eight straight decisions and Ames won nine before losing. Mathewson held to a 30-victory gait.

On June 13 in Chicago, Matty hurled his second career no-hitter to best Mordecai Brown, 1-0. Only two Chicago batters reached base—both on infield errors—but the Giants had little more success against Brown. He surrendered only one hit until the ninth inning, when the Giants stroked four consecutive singles to pull out the victory.

The Giants cantered through July with a 20-6 record to pull nine games ahead of the Pirates, but tumult walked hand in hand with New York into August. On August 5 in Pittsburgh, the Giants staged one of their most turbulent demonstrations against authority—according to the local Pittsburgh press.

With the teams deadlocked, 5-5, in the last of the ninth, Claude Ritchey touched Mathewson for a leadoff double to deep center field. George Gibson, attempting to sacrifice, tapped back to the mound, where Matty fired the ball to third trying to nip

Ritchey. Bausewine, who had run down the line from his umpire's position behind the plate, called the runner safe—according to Pittsburgh accounts—and the Giants swarmed the arbiter like iron filings to a magnet. In the press box, a reporter wrote:

The whole team flocked around Bausewine and tried to scare him, but his training as a Quaker City policeman had hardened him to bluffers and he paid no attention to them. Then the quitters approached Umpire Emslie, who was officiating on the bases. They tried to get him to make a decision, but Robert hadn't seen the play and wisely kept silence.

The Giants refused to play and Umpire Bausewine finally warned them that unless they played ball within one minute, he would forfeit the game. They still refused to play and the game was given to Pittsburgh.

The Giants continued to argue after this and Arthur Devlin . . . paid particular attention to Mr. Emslie. He made some insulting remarks and the result was that the umpire's good, strong right arm swung out and his fist collided with Devlin's physiognomy. It was a stunning blow and Devlin staggered back. Quitter again, he wandered away from Emslie and hid behind burly Dan McGann.

The race swept past Labor Day with little doubt about the outcome. Except for a late spurt by Pittsburgh that pulled the Pirates within five games of the lead for much of early and mid-September, New York continued rolling over the outclassed competition. The Giants finished the campaign with an edge in every season series, a 105-48 record and their second straight N.L. pennant. The triumph was more overwhelming than final numbers conveyed, but those figures certainly were indicative. The Giants' success was a season-long experience, a collage of intimidation, vicious hitting, deerlike speed, masterly pitching and diamond savvy.

"We have the standard team now," Brush remarked, "and we can afford to sit back and watch the other clubs trying to build up to our strength."

Explained the architect McGraw: "Why did we win the championship? Because we had a good team, we played good baseball, we had good pitchers, we took advantage of opportunities and we attended strictly to business, every one of us, from the time the first game was played...."

The Giants' offense succeeded for its proficiency, pushing across runs via the base hit, stolen base and long ball. Donlin paced the attack with 216 hits (second only to Cincinnati's Cy Seymour) and a career-high .356 average, third-best in the league. The hit parade included Bresnahan, McGann and Browne, who each hit better than .290 to help the club post a league-best .273 composite mark. The Giants held a

Mike Donlin (left) loved to hit, lived to party. Lefthander Hooks Wiltse was young, steady and a combined 28-9 in 1904-05.

decisive edge in home runs (39 to runner-up Brooklyn's 29) and ran rampant with 291 stolen bases. Altogether, seven Giants stole more than 20 bases apiece: Devlin (a league-leading 59), Mertes (52), Dahlen (37), Donlin (33), Browne (26), Strang (23) and McGann (22).

Mathewson was the toast of the circuit with a 31-9 performance, his third straight 30-victory season. Matty pitched nine shutouts and fanned 206 batters, both league-leading totals, to lead a staff that, for the second straight season, boasted three hurlers with 20 or more wins. One of those pitchers, McGinnity, wasn't himself with only a 22-15 mark, but the young colt Ames compensated for that with a 22-8 season. And with Taylor and Wiltse combining for 30 victories, McGraw could swagger into his first World Series predicting a title "in easy fashion."

Pitching, however, also was the strong suit of a crack Philadelphia Athletics outfit managed by a mild-mannered former catcher named Connie Mack. The A's catered to no one with a starting four of Rube Waddell, Eddie Plank, Andy Coakley and Chief Bender, big winners all. But with the 26-game winner Waddell lost for the Series with a shoulder injury, Philadelphia went into battle with a major chink in its armor.

Only a year after rejecting competition with "minor league teams," the Giants were playing a championship series governed by rules drawn up by none other than John T. Brush. The code, which would give the Series stability forever after, provided for a best-of-seven matchup and the division of the players' share of the gate receipts: 75 percent to the victors, 25 percent to the vanquished. Philadelphia Owner Ben Shibe won a coin flip and was awarded the host role for the Series opener on October 9. It was among the last triumphs scored by the A's in 1905.

The spirit of friendly strife and civic pride permeated the City of Brotherly Love as the gladiators girded for combat. As a public service, the Philadelphia North American newspaper erected a mammoth gong downtown so that mid-city fans could thrill to extra-base hits by their Athletic heroes. One peal of the gong signified a double, two indicated a triple and three a home run. In two Series games at Columbia Park, it would peal only three times.

McGraw's N.L. champions dressed the part with dramatic new black flannel uniforms, boxlike caps and a hugh "NY" emblazoned across the shirt front. "I will never forget the impression created in Philadelphia," recalled McGraw, "and the thrill that I got personally when the Giants suddenly trotted out from their dugout."

And baseball will never forget the artistry exhibited by the great Christy Mathewson.

Dueling against Plank in the opener, Mathewson shut out Philadelphia, 3-0, on four hits. Two games later, after the 21-year-old Bender matched his four-hitter in a 3-0 decision over McGinnity, Mathewson cuffed the Athletics, 9-0, with a second four-hitter.

Giant rooters were still buzzing over Matty's incredible hurling when the teams returned to New York, but McGinnity and Plank briefly stole the spotlight with a stellar confrontation in Game 4. McGinnity scattered five hits, Plank only four. The Iron Man fanned four batters, Plank struck out six. McGinnity walked three men, Plank only two. But two errors proved to be Plank's undoing as the Giants scored the game's lone run on miscues by Monte and Lave Cross, the left side of the A's infield.

One more victory and Muggsy McGraw would be enthroned as King John. The call, not surprisingly, went out to Mathewson. Pitching with a day of rest, Matty yielded six hits in a 2-0 whitewashing of Philadelphia, his third shutout in six days.

Wild celebration enveloped the Polo Grounds. After five brilliant games, five shutouts, the Giants could irrefutably claim the championship of professional baseball. Donlin (.316), Bresnahan (.313)

and McGann (four RBIs) stood out as stars of the scrappy New York offense. Led by Mathewson, New York's record-setting pitching proved to be the most invincible in Series history with a 0.00 earned-run average.

Mathewson's wizardry stood the test of time. He established records for most starts, complete games and victories in a five-game Series (three); most strikeouts in a five-game Series (18); fewest hits allowed, three consecutive complete games (14) and most shutouts in any Series (three).

He was, McGraw said, "pretty much the perfect type of pitching machine." Those Giants were a pretty good machine themselves. The perfect type of fighting machine.

1904
FINAL STANDING

Club	W.	L.	Pct.	GB.
New York	106	47	.693	——
Chicago	93	60	.608	13

BATTERS

Pos.	Player	G.	HR.	RBI.	B.A.
1B	Dan McGann	141	6	71	.286
2B	Billy Gilbert	146	1	54	.253
SS	Bill Dahlen	145	2	80	.268
3B	Art Devlin	130	1	66	.281
OF	Sam Mertes	148	4	78	.276
	Roger Bresnahan	109	5	33	.284
	George Browne	150	4	39	.284
C	John Warner	86	1	15	.199
	Frank Bowerman	93	2	27	.232

OTHER CONTRIBUTORS (20+ Games): Mike Donlin, Jack Dunn, Moose McCormick.

PITCHERS

Thr.	Pitcher	G.	W.	L.	ERA
R	Joe McGinnity	51	35	8	1.61
R	Christy Mathewson	48	33	12	2.03
R	Dummy Taylor	37	21	15	2.34
L	Hooks Wiltse	24	13	3	2.84

1905
FINAL STANDING

Club	W.	L.	Pct.	GB.
New York	105	48	.686	——
Pittsburgh	96	57	.627	9

BATTERS

Pos.	Player	G.	HR.	RBI.	B.A.
1B	Dan McGann	136	5	75	.299
2B	Billy Gilbert	115	0	24	.247
SS	Bill Dahlen	148	7	81	.242
3B	Art Devlin	153	2	61	.246
OF	Sam Mertes	150	5	108	.279
	Mike Donlin	150	7	80	.356
	George Browne	127	4	43	.293
C	Roger Bresnahan	104	0	46	.302
	Frank Bowerman	98	3	41	.269
UT	Sammy Strang (2b-of)	111	3	29	.259

OTHER CONTRIBUTORS (20+ Games): Boileryard Clarke.

PITCHERS

Thr.	Pitcher	G.	W.	L.	ERA
R	Christy Mathewson	43	31	9	1.27
R	Red Ames	34	22	8	2.74
R	Joe McGinnity	46	21	15	2.87
L	Hooks Wiltse	32	15	6	2.47
R	Dummy Taylor	32	15	9	2.66

The Team That Made Milwaukee Famous

The telephone lines between Milwaukee and New York hummed with animated conversation on June 15, 1957. At opposite ends of the wire, executives of the Braves and Giants attempted to negotiate a player deal before the major leagues' midnight trading deadline.

Braves General Manager John Quinn was angling for the Giants' second baseman, a 34-year-old veteran of 12 National League seasons and an eight-time All-Star Game performer. In exchange, Quinn offered Danny O'Connell, a second baseman for whom Milwaukee had given up six players and an estimated $75,000 to the Pittsburgh Pirates 3½ years earlier; Ray Crone, a righthanded pitcher with con-

siderable promise, and outfielder Bobby Thomson, the former Giant whose dramatic home run against Brooklyn in the 1951 N.L. playoff had stamped him with indelible fame.

The Giants liked O'Connell and Crone, but they hesitated on Thomson, who had lost much of his speed because of an ankle fracture he suffered in the spring of 1954. In his stead, the Giants asked for a young outfielder playing with Milwaukee's Class AAA Wichita farm club in the American Association. Negotiations stalled on that issue, but in the last hours of the day the New York team accepted the O'Connell-Crone-Thomson package. By that decision, Albert (Red) Schoendienst was dispatched to the Braves and Wes Covington, the highly coveted Wichita player, was saved for future service in Milwaukee.

The heaviest artillery in Milwaukee's hard-hitting lineup belonged to third baseman Eddie Mathews (left) and outfielder Henry Aaron.

Milwaukee's 1957 acquisition of veteran second baseman Red Schoendienst provided a shot in the arm the Braves needed.

Through games of the previous night, the Braves led the tightly congested National League race by one-half game over the Cincinnati Reds. Only 2½ games separated Milwaukee from the fifth-place St. Louis Cardinals. But when news of the Schoendienst swap was announced, there was no mistaking the tremors.

"I know I'm hurting our own chances," said Cardinals General Manager Frank Lane, weighing the potential psychological impact of his words, " ... but Schoendienst can win the pennant" for the Braves.

Bobby Bragan, manager of the seventh-place Pirates, called the transaction a masterstroke for Milwaukee.

"The Braves outjockeyed the rest of the clubs in making that deal at the last minute," Bragan said. "They put the others on the spot after it was too late to do anything about it. Everybody was talking about trading just before the deadline, but the Braves were the only ones who did themselves any good. If they had made the deal a few hours earlier, I'm sure other trades would have been made, too."

Milwaukee's need for a quality second baseman turned from desirable to urgent in the first two months of the 1957 season. O'Connell had hit .239 and .225 in the previous two years and hopes that he would return to the .288 level of his first three big-league campaigns was waning. Now, one-third of the way through the '57 race, O'Connell was batting in the .230s and proving unreliable defensively. Schoendienst, a lifetime .290 major league hitter entering the '57 season, was batting above .300 and fielding superbly as usual.

Covington, a North Carolinian who had declined football scholarship offers from several major universities to sign a professional baseball contract, had hit .283 for the Braves in limited duty in 1956 after winning the South Atlantic League batting championship a year earlier. He was regarded as the leading candidate for the left-field job in 1957, but played erratically in the spring and was benched by Manager Fred Haney in favor of Thomson. The demotion embittered Covington, but he held his tongue until Thomson was in turn replaced by Chuck Tanner, at which time Wes uttered some caustic comments and was handed transportation papers to Wichita.

Although out of sight in the minor leagues, the outspoken Covington was never out of Quinn's mind. With Tanner having been released on waivers to the Chicago Cubs a week before the Schoendienst deal and Thomson now out of the picture, Quinn dispatched a message to Wichita: "Send us Covington."

In the Milwaukee outfield, Covington teamed with two Alabamians, center fielder Bill Bruton, a 27-year-old speedster from Panola, and right fielder Henry Aaron, a 23-year-old native of Mobile who was developing into one of the game's pre-eminent sluggers.

With second base and left field secured, Haney was satisfied that the team was capable of making a concerted bid for the pennant that had eluded the Braves on the final weekend of the 1956 season.

Haney's contentment lasted about a week. During the Braves' June 23 doubleheader sweep of the Philadelphia Phillies, slugging first baseman Joe Adcock fell awkwardly while sliding into second base and snapped the fibula in his right leg. Doctors pronounced glumly that Adcock would be sidelined at least two months. Frank Torre, a superior fielder but lacking Adcock's power, would take over at first.

Elsewhere, the lineup that Haney presented in 1957, his first full season as Milwaukee manager, remained unchanged from the Braves' cast of a year earlier. Johnny Logan, a 30-year-old scrapper from Endicott, N.Y., was in his sixth year as the Braves' No. 1 shortstop (having taken over the job on a permanent basis in 1952, the team's last season in

Boston before shifting to Wisconsin). Eddie Mathews, only 25 but already an established slugger with speed and an excellent arm, was in his sixth season as the regular third baseman. Del Crandall, like Mathews a Californian, was entrenched behind the plate. Crandall had broken in with the Braves in 1949 as a 19-year-old.

Haney's premier pitcher was 36-year-old lefthander Warren Spahn, who had won 81 games in the last four years and recorded seven 20-victory seasons over a 10-year span. His No. 2 and 3 starters were righthanders Lew Burdette and Bob Buhl.

Burdette was New York Yankees property and pitching for San Francisco of the Pacific Coast League in 1951 when the Yanks purchased Johnny Sain from the Braves. As part of the deal, the Braves were offered their choice of Burdette or fellow minor league pitcher Wally Hood.

"Take Burdette," scouts advised the front office. "He's a low-ball pitcher with . . . plenty of competitive spirit."

That wasn't all Burdette possessed. He had an advanced case of the fidgets the moment he stepped on the mound, tugging endlessly at his uniform and shaking continually between pitches. When he did get around to throwing the ball, batters frequently accused him of applying moisture to it—an allegation that Lew addressed with indignation.

Burdette, a 30-year-old native of Nitro, W.Va., had won 19 games in 1956 and topped the National League in earned-run average with a 2.71 figure.

Buhl, who entered the big leagues with the Braves the same year the club moved to Milwaukee, had posted 18 victories in '56. Buhl was 28 and from Saginaw, Mich.

Among other Milwaukee hurlers, Gene Conley was the most conspicuous, if only for his 6-foot-8, 227-pound frame. A product of Washington State University, Conley had once kept trim in the winter months by playing professional basketball (a practice he would resume in another year and a half).

Righthanders Ernie Johnson and Bob Trowbridge and lefthander Juan Pizarro also saw frequent duty, as did Don McMahon after his call-up from Wichita in late June. McMahon, a sturdy righthander and a native of Brooklyn, proved a tireless worker.

The lineup that appeared set after the arrival of Schoendienst, the recall of Covington and Torre's replacement of Adcock got another jolt July 11

Another key Milwaukee move in 1957 was the promotion of young Wes Covington to fill the Braves' void in left field.

when Bruton tore knee ligaments in a collision with teammate Felix Mantilla during a game against Pittsburgh. Doctors advised Haney that Bruton would miss the rest of the season.

Milwaukee had fallen out of first place by this time, bouncing between second and third place but still within reach of the top. But with Bruton joining Adcock on the sidelines, things were turning decidedly bleak.

What to do?

Aaron, Haney and Quinn determined, could play center field. That left Andy Pafko to patrol right field. But Pafko, at 36, could not play every day. With Covington a lefthanded hitter and Aaron and Pafko righthanded batsmen, the Braves set their sights on acquiring another lefthanded batter and eventually looked—where else?—to Wichita.

Milwaukee's top farm club had two outfielders who might qualify—Ray Shearer, who was batting in the .330s with 20 home runs and more than 70 runs batted in, and Bob Hazle, who had hit above .360 in the last month to lift his average from .230 to .279. Hazle had 12 homers and 58 RBIs. Based strictly on performance, Shearer was the likely call-

When big first baseman Joe Adcock (right) left the Braves' lineup with a broken leg, smooth-fielding Frank Torre stepped in and filled the void.

up prospect. Shearer was a righthanded batter, though, while Hazle hit from the left side. And Hazle was hot.

Hazle it was.

Hazle had broken into professional baseball with the Cincinnati Reds organization in 1950. While he earned a late-1955 promotion to the Reds based on his long-ball show that season for Class AA Nashville (a league-leading 29 homers, plus 92 RBIs and a .314 batting mark), Hazle really wasn't a power hitter. Having hit only 12 homers in his first four minor league seasons (405 games overall), he had benefited greatly from the cozy right-field porch at the Nashville ball park.

The South Carolinian was playing for Cincinnati in exhibition competition in the spring of 1956 when he was traded to Milwaukee in a deal that sent first baseman George Crowe to the Reds. Hazle was expendable because, among other reasons, the Reds had a rookie phenom in a 20-year-old slugger named Frank Robinson.

Without so much as a glance from his new club, Hazle was assigned to Wichita. He didn't exactly tear up the American Association in '56, hitting .285 with 13 homers and 46 RBIs. Furthermore, he suffered a troublesome knee injury during the not-so-stellar season.

Milwaukee left Hazle unprotected in the subsequent major league draft, but none of the other 15 clubs in the majors considered him worth a $10,000 gamble, so Hazle remained with the Wichita club until his July 28, 1957, summoning to Milwaukee.

When Hazle made his debut with the Braves on July 29, the club held a half-game lead in the N.L.

pennant chase. By the conclusion of games of August 15, Milwaukee was up by 8½ and boasting a 10-game winning streak—thanks in large part to Robert Sidney Hazle. In the 11 games he had played for the Braves to that juncture, the 26-year-old Hazle had hammered out 18 hits in 33 at-bats for a .545 average. He had two home runs and 11 RBIs. Red-hot when he left Wichita, he was now white-hot.

While there were those who considered Hazle's success a fluke, Pafko wasn't one of them.

"The kid can really rip the ball," Pafko marveled during the height of Hazle's bashing. "Next to Henry Aaron, he's got the strongest wrists in baseball. And he doesn't swing at too many bad balls, either. That's rare for a rookie."

Included in Hazle's early spree were consecutive games in which he went 4 for 5 and 3 for 4 with a total of five RBIs (August 9-10) and back-to-back contests in which he went 3 for 4 each night (August 14-15).

"I'm not doin' anything different than I did before," Hazle said. "I'm just up there swingin', that's all."

As base hits exploded off his bat, the newcomer was christened "Hurricane Hazle" after the violent storm (hurricane Hazel) that had lashed the Eastern Seaboard earlier in the decade. But like the meteorological phenomenon, baseball's "Hurricane" was expected to die down. But Hurricane Hazle raged on, unabated.

In his next nine games, which extended through August 26, Hazle banged out 14 hits in 28 at-bats. Highlighting his latest onslaught was a six-RBI performance against Philadelphia in an August 25 game in which Hazle went 3 for 3 and slugged two home runs.

"It doesn't seem possible that anyone can keep up such a pace," Schoendienst said of Hazle's heroics. "But right now, the kid is Stan Musial, Mickey Mantle and Ted Williams all wrapped in one."

Contacted one morning via telephone during the Braves' end-of-August visit to New York, Hazle admonished a reporter, "Why did you wake me? I was having such sweet dreams." He later expanded upon his greeting: "You know," Hazle explained, "it's easy to have sweet dreams when you're hitting around .500, have a full belly and sleep in air-conditioned hotel rooms."

It's also easy to be rolling merrily along in a pennant race when, in addition to a sizzling rookie, you have a catalyst like Schoendienst, sluggers like Aaron and Mathews, a defensive wizard like Crandall and pitching stalwarts like Spahn, Burdette and Buhl. And rolling the Braves were. Ahead of second-place St. Louis by 6½ games entering Labor Day action, Milwaukee increased its lead to a comfortable 8½ games by day's end as the result of a doubleheader sweep over the Cubs and two Cardinal losses to Cincinnati. And now only 24 contests remained on the Braves' schedule.

Schoendienst's role in the Braves' ability to build a fat lead was unmistakable.

"He's been the guy baseball people said we needed," Crandall said in the heat of the pennant drive. "He's the take-charge guy out there. When he says something, we know it comes from a fellow who's been around a long time and the players listen. It's not someone just popping off.

"For instance, he seems instinctively to know just the proper time to come in and say something to a pitcher which will help him get out of a particular situation."

Pafko, a major leaguer since 1943 and a World Series participant with the Cubs in 1945 and the Brooklyn Dodgers in 1952, was effusive in his praise of Schoendienst.

"Why, he's all over the place," Pafko said. "He talks to the pitchers when they're in a jam and steadies them down, sees that the infielders and the outfielders are in their right spots. As long as I've been in the majors, he even moves me around on certain occasions. And believe me, I respect his judgment."

Schoendienst, a member of the Cardinals from 1945 to June 1956 when Lane riled the St. Louis populace by swapping him to the Giants, also was receiving high marks from Haney.

"Since we gave up a lot to get him, we expected a lot," Haney said. "But he's really exceeded all of our expectations.

"His biggest value to the club is the way he has taken charge on the field—that was the big reason

One of the big stories of the Braves' run to the 1957 pennant was Bob (Hurricane) Hazle, who banged out an incredible .403 average in 41 games.

we wanted him in the first place. The boys listen to Schoendienst . . . By his very experience and personality, he commands respect."

After Milwaukee's twin-bill sweep of Chicago on Labor Day, Schoendienst sported a .316 batting average and led the league's second basemen in fielding percentage. Five times earlier in his career, he had topped the National League in fielding at his position.

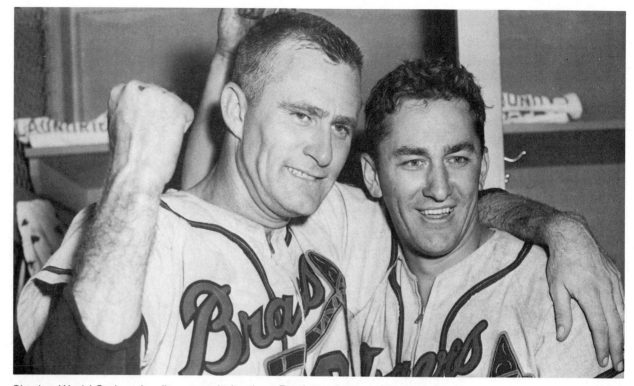

Sharing World Series plaudits were pitcher Lew Burdette (above left) and shortstop Johnny Logan, and pitcher Warren Spahn (below left) and catcher Del Crandall.

Aaron, who in 1956 had won the National League batting championship in only his third big-league season, was exhibiting another facet of his multi-talented game in 1957: the ability to hit with power. Oh, the youngster had driven in more than 100 runs in 1955 and had totaled 53 homers in '55 and '56. But he was rising to another level in '57. Through Labor Day (September 2), Aaron had cracked 38 homers and knocked in 114 runs.

Not overly selective at the plate at this point in his career—"I just grab a bat and go to the plate looking for one thing, and that's the baseball, and if it's near the plate, I'm going to swing at it"—Aaron was proving that his philosophy worked.

"You don't try to change a hitter like Aaron," Bragan said. "In my book, he's a better hitter than Willie Mays. He's going to get better, too. He'll be the one to beat for the batting championship for 10 years, maybe more."

St. Louis' Stan Musial, en route to his seventh and last N.L. batting crown in '57, said Aaron "thinks there's nothing he can't hit. He'll have to learn there are some pitches no hitter can afford to go for. He still has something to learn about the strike zone."

Aaron obviously was—and would continue to be —a quick study in the art of hitting. There seemed no limit to what this young man might accomplish in his big-league career, which had begun in 1954 when Aaron—as a 20-year-old non-roster player— leaped from the Class A South Atlantic League to

Celebrating the Braves' second straight N.L. pennant in 1958 were (left to right) Manager Fred Haney, Owner Lou Perini, Warren Spahn, Don McMahon and Henry Aaron.

the Braves as a replacement for spring-training in-jury victim Thomson, who had just been obtained from the Giants.

Mathews, while a little off the power standards he had established since leading the National League in home runs in the Braves' first season in Milwaukee, was continuing to hone all aspects of his play and was working particularly hard on his defense. Also, he seemed to be mellowing as a young veteran after exhibiting impetuousness and moodiness while dealing with adulation-related pressures early in his career.

"I've always worked hard on my fielding," Math-ews would say by the end of the season. "But I made more improvement (in 1957) than I ever had be-fore.

"For the first time, I gained confidence in my ability to make the tough play in a tough spot."

Whereas he formerly reacted with bitterness to the antics of boo-birds, Mathews now went with the flow. "I know they (the Milwaukee fans) got down on me when I was in a slump," said Mathews, shrugging off the situation, "but fans are like that." Later in his Milwaukee years, Mathews indulged in some self-analysis and commented: "I think I've changed—I should have changed, and I hope it's for

the better."

Mathews' slumps didn't occur with enough fre-quency to suit Braves' opponents. After breaking into the majors with a 25-homer season for the Bos-ton Braves in 1952, Mathews drew Ruthian com-parisons in 1953 when he whacked 47 homers—43 by the end of August—and knocked in 135 runs. In 1954 and 1955, he belted a total of 81 homers and collected 204 RBIs. In 1956, Mathews fell off to numbers of 37 and 95—figures that most sluggers would gladly accept. Now, with less than a month remaining in the '57 season, the lefthanded-hitting third baseman boasted 29 homers and 82 RBIs.

Crandall was doing his usual superb job behind the plate, handling pitchers with aplomb, waylay-ing baserunners and running the show overall. And although he had batted under .245 in each of the last three seasons and was hovering around that mark in the stretch run of the '57 race, Crandall was providing some occasional thump with the bat.

"Del is a receiver first, last and always," Spahn said of the man who made only two errors in 112 games in 1956. "I don't mean he isn't a good hitter. I mean he is incapable of letting a batting slump affect his catching. He feels his first responsibility is to help the team by helping the pitcher. He would consider it disloyal and selfish to look at it any other way."

Still, Crandall was contributing offensively, as evidenced by his 14 home runs. Two years earlier, he had cracked 26 homers for Milwaukee.

"He's a great receiver and handler of pitchers. He has a wonderful arm and he's a clutch hitter," Haney summarized.

Spahn, the only active member of the '57 club who had played for the Braves' losing World Series entry of 1948, was simply getting better with age. With 17 victories already tucked away, he was on target for his eighth 20-victory season in the majors and also was headed toward his seventh sub-3.00 ERA.

"Spahn was able to change over from being a power pitcher," former Boston teammate Johnny Sain said. "He was completely thorough. He hit well enough to stay in a close game. He fielded extremely well. He ran the bases well and his move to first base was superb. I can remember that he picked off Jackie Robinson twice in one vital game during a Labor Day doubleheader at Boston in '48.

"Spahn became great because of these things and because he's one of the smartest men ever to play the game. He came up with a screwball to help when his fastball began to fade and then he added the slider."

"Every pitch Warren throws has an idea behind it," said Whitlow Wyatt, a Phillies coach in 1957 before joining the Braves in a similar capacity in 1958. Usually, it was a better idea.

Burdette had been a steady performer for the Braves in their Milwaukee years, going 15-5 in 1953 and following that mark with victory totals of 15, 13 and 19. With the Braves sitting pretty two days into September of '57, Burdette was 14-7. Buhl, meanwhile, was 16-6.

The privilege of managing such thoroughbreds was not lost on the 59-year-old Haney, who had joined the Braves' coaching staff in 1956 and found himself elevated to manager two months into the '56 season when the club dismissed Charley Grimm. From 1953 through 1955, Haney had managed the woeful Pirates to 299 losses and three last-place finishes.

Haney had reason to be in particularly good spirits on the morning of September 3. Not only had his Braves swept a doubleheader the previous day and boosted their N.L. lead by two games in the process, they had shown just how overwhelming they could be. In the opener at Wrigley Field, the Braves flattened the Cubs, 23-10, as Aaron and Covington each drove in six runs and Hazle and Torre each collected four hits to highlight a 26-hit assault. In the nightcap, Trowbridge tossed a three-hitter and struck out nine batters in a 4-0 triumph. Haney's men could out-hit you and out-pitch you.

And in game three of the series, Haney would be going with his ace, the stylish Spahn.

With Aaron blasting a three-run homer and notching four RBIs overall and Spahn baffling the Cubs on six hits, Milwaukee breezed to an 8-0 victory. The fact the runner-up Cardinals won that night in Cincinnati seemed of little consequence. After all, with 23 games left on their schedule, the Braves were still up by 8½.

St. Louis had considerable making up to do and precious little time to do it. But Manager Fred Hutchinson's Cardinals proceeded to whittle Milwaukee's lead by six games over the next 11 contests, posting a 9-2 record (a surge that began with two straight victories over the Braves) while Haney's club went 3-8. Suddenly, the ball team that was making Milwaukee famous also was making Milwaukee nervous.

Now faced with the task of protecting a 2½-game lead in the final two weeks of the season, Haney sent Buhl to the mound against the Phillies on the night of September 16 in hopes of reversing matters. Buhl, a recent returnee to action (he missed more than three weeks because of shoulder problems), didn't disappoint, ringing up a 5-1 victory. The next night, Adcock, back from the disabled list, and Aaron each went 3 for 4 and cracked homers as Trowbridge set down the Giants, 3-1. Burdette followed with a victory over the New Yorkers and then Spahn won his 20th game of the season by subduing the Cubs. The Braves had regained their mastery just as quickly as they had lost it.

Buhl won his ninth straight decision in a September 21 game against Chicago, a contest in which Adcock drilled two more homers. The next day, Hazle, having slipped under the .400 mark, soared back over the figure as Milwaukee stretched its winning streak to six games. Hazle's final hit in a 4-for-5 day against the Cubs was a game-winning homer in the 10th inning.

The Cardinals weren't keeping pace. Over the same September 16-22 stretch, St. Louis won three times, lost twice and fell five games off the pace. Only six games remained in the season, and up next was a Braves-Cardinals series at Milwaukee's County Stadium. One Braves triumph over the Cards would bring an N.L. pennant to a city that only five years earlier was plying its baseball trade as a member of the Class AAA American Association.

More than 40,000 fans turned out for the opening game of the series. No surprise here. The Braves had been an incredible box-office success since relocating in Milwaukee. After drawing 281,278 fans in 1952, their last season in Boston, the Braves attracted an N.L.-record 1,826,397 fans through the County Stadium turnstiles in 1953. In 1954, 1955 and 1956, the yearly gate surpassed 2 million. Now, the club was headed for another N.L.-record figure (of

The Braves' 1958 season was opened in grand fashion with the raising of the 1957 championship pennant over Milwaukee's County Stadium.

2,215,404). It was a fans-players love affair gone mad.

The County Stadium crowd on the night of September 23 saw what it had come to see. In the bottom of the 11th inning of a 2-2 game, Aaron launched a two-run homer over the center-field fence. Bedlam. The Braves were National League titlists.

"We had the team we had to beat out there tonight—and we beat them," Haney said. "My biggest thrill? You know the answer to that. It's the biggest thrill for every player in this clubhouse."

"It took us nine years to win this pennant," said Braves Owner Lou Perini, reflecting on only the third N.L. flag in franchise history (the others coming in '48 and 1914). "It won't take us that long again."

For good measure, the Braves topped out their winning streak at eight games the next night as Aaron walloped a bases-loaded home run, the first grand slam of his big-league career.

Milwaukee wound up the 1957 season with a 95-59 record and an eight-game bulge over the Cardinals. Aaron, who finished among the top five in the N.L. batting race with a .322 average, further demonstrated that he was destined for greatness by compiling league-leading figures of 44 homers and 132 RBIs. Schoendienst collected an N.L.-high 200 hits, Mathews clubbed 32 homers, Spahn topped the league in victories with 21, Buhl won 18 games for the second straight year and Burdette was a 17-game winner.

Hazle, Covington and McMahon assembled some eye-popping figures, too. Hazle cooled off, to be sure. All the way to a .403 batting mark. Covington smashed 21 homers and drove in 65 runs in only 96 games. McMahon proved a bear out of the bullpen, fashioning a 1.53 ERA in 32 appearances. Conley and Trowbridge divided their time between starting and relieving and combined for 16 victories. And Johnson won seven of 10 decisions coming out of the bullpen.

Aaron's star rose even higher in the World Series, competition in which the young outfielder pounded three homers, drove in seven runs and hit .393 against the Yankees. But Aaron was overshadowed in the fall classic by the fidgety one, Burdette, who pitched three complete-game victories (two of them shutouts, including a 5-0 triumph in the climactic seventh game). Mathews also was in the spotlight, winning Game 4 with an electrifying homer in the 10th inning and fielding superbly throughout the classic. Eddie, in fact, ended the Series for the champion Braves when, with the bases loaded and two out, he made a brilliant play on Bill Skowron's hard smash down the third-base line.

Despite a wave of injuries, the Braves scored another eight-length triumph in the 1958 National League pennant race and thereby proved Perini correct in his title-timetable assessment. They did it with basically the same cast of characters, although pitching newcomers Bob Rush and Carlton Willey provided key assists. Rush, obtained in a December 1957 trade with the Cubs, won 10 games and Willey, called up from Wichita in mid-June, proceeded to rack up an N.L.-leading four shutouts on the way to a 9-7 ledger. Spahn entered the 20-game-winner class for the ninth time, while Burdette reached the select circle for the first time.

Offensively, the '58 Braves lacked the thunder of the '57 crew. Still, Aaron was among the league's best batsmen with a .326 mark and he crashed 30 home runs. Mathews hit 31 homers, while the injury-plagued Covington smacked 24 homers, drove home 74 runs and batted .330 in 90 games.

Hurricane Hazle? After batting .179 in 20 games, he was sold to the Detroit Tigers in May.

The Braves muffed a chance to join baseball's elite—the list of those teams repeating as World Series titlists—when they blew a three games-to-one lead to the Yanks in the '58 fall classic. But there was no questioning what the Milwaukee Braves had accomplished in the late 1950s. Nor what they very nearly accomplished.

The record book shows that the Braves copped N.L. pennants in 1957 and 1958 and a World Series championship in '57. Not so quickly discernible is that the Braves finished only one game behind the pennant-winning Brooklyn Dodgers in 1956—and Milwaukee was atop the standings entering the final weekend of the season. Also, the 1959 Braves— minus the services (except for a few late-season appearances) of the tuberculosis-stricken Schoendienst—tied Los Angeles for first place, only to lose the pennant playoff to the transplanted Dodgers. So, the Milwaukee Braves came about as close as possible to winning four consecutive National League crowns.

Adcock, Logan, Mathews, Aaron, Bruton, Covington, Crandall, Spahn, Burdette and Buhl

formed the nucleus of all four of the Braves' late-'50s powerhouses. One familiar name is missing from that list, however, and therein seems to lie a story. When the Braves, despite their wealth of talent, didn't win—in 1956 and 1959—they were without the wily veteran, Red Schoendienst.

Which just goes to show how important Schoendienst was to Milwaukee's pennant success, and just how important that mid-June call to New York in 1957 was in Braves franchise history.

1957
FINAL STANDING

Club	W.	L.	Pct.	GB.
Milwaukee	95	59	.617	——
St. Louis	87	67	.565	8

BATTERS

Pos.	Player	G.	HR.	RBI.	B.A.
1B	Frank Torre	129	5	40	.272
2B	Red Schoendienst	93	6	32	.310
SS	Johnny Logan	129	10	49	.273
3B	Eddie Mathews	148	32	94	.292
OF	Wes Covington	96	21	65	.284
	Billy Bruton	79	5	30	.278
	Hank Aaron	151	44	132	.322
	Bob Hazle	41	7	27	.403
C	Del Crandall	118	15	46	.253
UT	Andy Pafko (of)	83	8	27	.277

OTHER CONTRIBUTORS (20+ Games): Joe Adcock, John DeMerit, Nippy Jones, Felix Mantilla, Danny O'Connell, Del Rice, Carl Sawatski, Chuck Tanner, Bobby Thomson.

PITCHERS

Thr.	Pitcher	G.	W.	L.	ERA
L	Warren Spahn	39	21	11	2.69
R	Bob Buhl	34	18	7	2.74
R	Lew Burdette	37	17	9	3.71

OTHER CONTRIBUTORS (20+ Games): Gene Conley, Ernie Johnson, Dave Jolly, Don McMahon, Taylor Phillips, Juan Pizarro, Bob Trowbridge.

1958
FINAL STANDING

Club	W.	L.	Pct.	GB.
Milwaukee	92	62	.597	——
Pittsburgh	84	70	.545	8

BATTERS

Pos.	Player	G.	HR.	RBI.	B.A.
1B	Frank Torre	138	6	55	.309
2B	Red Schoendienst	106	1	24	.262
SS	Johnny Logan	145	11	53	.226
3B	Eddie Mathews	149	31	77	.251
OF	Wes Covington	90	24	74	.330
	Billy Bruton	100	3	28	.280
	Hank Aaron	153	30	95	.326
C	Del Crandall	131	18	63	.272
UT	Joe Adcock (1b)	105	19	54	.275
	Andy Pafko (of)	95	3	23	.238
	Felix Mantilla (of)	85	7	19	.221

OTHER CONTRIBUTORS (20+ Games): Harry Hanebrink, Bob Hazle, Del Rice, Mel Roach, Casey Wise.

PITCHERS

Thr.	Pitcher	G.	W.	L.	ERA
L	Warren Spahn	38	22	11	3.07
R	Lew Burdette	40	20	10	2.91
R	Bob Rush	28	10	6	3.43

OTHER CONTRIBUTORS (20+ Games): Gene Conley, Don McMahon, Bob Trowbridge, Carl Willey.

Number 13

Yankees Complete
Their Mighty Quest

Yogi Berra (left) and Manager Casey Stengel had reason to be in a playful mood as the 1953 Yankees began the quest for their fifth straight championship.

The 1953 New York Yankees had gotten off to an impressive start in their mighty quest. No major league team had ever won five consecutive pennants, but the Yanks—American League champions in 1949, 1950, 1951 and 1952—were playing as if they intended to rewrite the record books.

After dropping their '53 season opener against Philadelphia, Casey Stengel's Yankees proceeded to win nine of their next 10 games and they boasted a league-leading 23-10 record on the morning of May 25. Not even a 14-10 loss that night against Boston —the Red Sox combed six Yankee pitchers for 20 hits—could put a damper on things. The Bronx Bombers were playing extremely well, and no letup was in sight.

As it turned out, the Yankees themselves were soon out of sight. From the rest of the competition, that is.

Starting with Eddie Lopat's three-hitter against Washington on May 27 and culminating with Vic Raschi's shutout at Cleveland on June 14, New York thundered to an 18-game winning streak and a 10½-game lead in the American League race. No one was doubting the resolve of these Yankees, who appeared hellbent in their bid to find a special niche in baseball history.

There had been doubt in the past regarding Lopat's ability to sustain his pitching success. And, entering the 1953 season, not everyone was certain that young Whitey Ford could pick up where he had left off in 1950.

The notion that the easy-throwing Lopat would sink into mediocrity as a big-league pitcher long had been dispelled, though, and by now military-service returnee Ford had demonstrated that his rookie-year pitching success of 1950 had not been a fluke. Together, the lefthanders fueled the Yankees' long victory string by winning four times each during the stretch.

Lopat, acquired from the Chicago White Sox prior to the 1948 season, never possessed the speed to blow the ball past a batter. Accordingly, some wondered just how long the New York native could get by on guile. They had been wondering for a long time, ever since Lopat had broken into professional baseball in 1937.

"It is bad enough to be beaten," Paul Richards once said while managing the White Sox, "but it is worse when you are beaten by a pitcher who has nothing," The target of Richards' verbal dart was one Edmund Walter Lopatynski, who would turn 35 years old a week after the termination of New York's 18-0 run.

"I was never blazing fast," said the 5-foot-10, 185-pounder, who opted to shorten his surname. "What I mean is, I could never consistently throw it by the hitters. But if a hitter is looking for something else, I'm fast enough to get the fastball by him . . . .

"My main purpose is to make a hitter hit off stride. I couldn't overpower hitters, so I had to operate from a different angle. Being in the minors so long gave me a wider field of knowledge."

Lopat spent seven seasons in the bush leagues (the first as a first baseman), thereby reaching the majors with a working knowledge of the pitching craft.

"If I can get the batters to guess with me, I figure I've got an edge," explained Lopat, a 21-game winner for the Yankees in 1951 before suffering shoulder problems and plummeting to a 10-victory total in 1952. "I've got five or six different deliveries I can throw, so the odds on their guessing the right pitch are against them."

Lopat had the upper hand, all right, as evidenced by his 81-43 career mark with the Yankees entering the 1953 season. As a member of the White Sox from 1944 through 1947, Lopat compiled a 50-49 record.

Now, a little more than one-third of the way through the '53 campaign, the Yankees' "Junk Man" was sporting a 7-0 record. And so, too, was the 24-year-old Ford, who had earned a "phenom" label three years earlier by winning his first nine decisions as a Yankee rookie.

"I had done considerable pitching in the Army," said Ford, who missed all of the 1951 and 1952 baseball seasons and was about 20 pounds overweight when he arrived at New York's spring camp in 1953. "But I wasn't too proud of what I had accomplished there.

". . . Aside from the problem of getting into shape, there were two things wrong with my pitching. First, I did not have too good a change of pace. Second, I was not masking my curveball.

"Jim Turner (Yankees' coach) worked hard with me—still is working. And Ed Lopat has been like an older brother. He keeps coaching me, day after day.

"The other day, a Chicago newspaper ran a big action picture of me, showing me winding up. Lopat cut it out and showed it to me. 'Take a good look at that picture,' he said. 'How can a man deliver a first-class overhand pitch if his right leg is stiff as yours is? Examine this thing and tell me. How?'

"I took the hint and corrected that weakness, and I think I have eliminated a few other points of dispute in my pitching style."

Very little needed correcting. Yet to pitch the equivalent of a full big-league season—he was a midseason call-up in 1950—Ford now possessed a 16-1 career record in the majors.

Johnny Sain, the former Boston Braves ace who had been acquired from the National League club in August 1951, was a three-time winner during the Yankees' streak and Raschi and Ray Scarborough each won twice.

Offensively, the Yankees had numerous standouts as they went undefeated for 2½ weeks. Foremost among them were center fielder Mickey Mantle, catcher Yogi Berra and first baseman Joe Collins.

Five years earlier, Yankees scout Tom Greenwade had caught his first glimpse of the switch-hitting Mantle during a visit to the zinc and lead country of Oklahoma. What the scout saw he never forgot. "I saw him hit one over the fence lefthanded and then turn around and whack one off the other fence from the right side," Greenwade said of the youngster from the small town of Commerce. "And then I saw him run. That was enough for me."

Under prevailing rules, Greenwade was unable to discuss a professional career with the 16-year-old high school student or his parents. All he could do was drool and wait for the day when the kid would grab his diploma and become eligible to sally forth into an adult world. And wait he did.

Mantle, groomed as a switch-hitter from an early age (his father Mutt pitched to him righthanded

and his grandfather served 'em up lefthanded), signed with the Yankees in the spring of 1949 and was dispatched to the Independence, Kan., club of the Class D Kansas-Oklahoma-Missouri League. He batted .313 in 89 games, connected for seven home runs and drove in 63 runs. The next year, Mantle tore up the Class C Western Association, clouting 26 home runs, driving in 136 runs and hitting a cool .383 for Joplin.

While Mantle's muscle and speed made him an offensive wunderkind, his fielding was suspect. At this juncture of his career, the Commerce Comet was playing shortstop—not center field—and doing so with marginal ability, as 102 errors in 226 minor league games would attest. The Yankees reasoned that Mickey had the equipment to play the outfield, and the conversion was made in the Bronx Bombers' 1951 spring camp at Phoenix. The transformation bore quick results.

Joe DiMaggio, the role-model outfielder who was embarking on what would prove his last season in

The strong arms of (left to right) Vic Raschi, Allie Reynolds, Whitey Ford and Ed Lopat accounted for 60 Yankee victories in 1953.

Yankee catcher Yogi Berra is greeted by Irv Noren (25) and Joe Collins after homering in the Yankees' 17th victory in their eventual 18-game win streak.

While Mickey didn't exactly flunk his first big-league test—he batted .261 in 69 games, with seven homers and 45 RBIs—he nevertheless was sent to the American Association team to hone his skills. After 40 games of sharpening (to the tune of a .361 average, 11 homers and 50 RBIs), Mantle was back with the Yankees to stay.

Mantle, who supplanted the retired DiMaggio in center field for the Yankees in 1952 and responded to the challenge with a 23-homer, 87-RBI season punctuated by a .311 batting mark, had captured headlines in the first week of the '53 season. Playing at Washington's venerable Griffith Stadium, the ballpark with the not-so-cozy 405-foot distance to the left-field wall, Mantle left mouths gaping far and wide when, swinging with destructive force from the right side of the plate, he detonated a 565-foot home run to left-center.

Yankees publicist Red Patterson, stunned by the magnitude of what he had just witnessed, dashed out of the press box and across the street to retrieve the ball. Mantle wasn't so excited.

Presented the ball by Patterson after the game, Mantle cracked: "If I send the ball home, I know what will happen to it. My twin brothers will take it out on the lot, like any 20-cent rocket.

"In 1951, I got the ball with which I had hit my first major league home run in Chicago, and I sent it home, autographed and dolled up. The kids belted it out of shape."

In an exhibition game against Pittsburgh eight days earlier, Mantle, batting from the left side, had become only the third major leaguer in history to clear the right-field roof at the Pirates' Forbes Field.

Demonstrating the breadth of his talents, Mantle crossed up the Senators in his final at-bat in the mammoth-homer game. He pushed a bunt past the mound—and into center field, believe it or not—for a single.

That Mantle was becoming a force was clearly evident. The 18-game winning streak offered another showcase, with the Oklahoman contributing three homers and 23 RBIs during that span. He had consecutive four-RBI days June 3-4.

Berra, whose name seemingly will forever be associated with anecdotes and malaprops, was baseball-smart dating to his days as a St. Louis youngster and playmate of another major leaguer-to-be, Joe Garagiola. Berra's skills weren't quite as refined as those of his boyhood pal, however, and it was Garagiola who first signed a professional contract.

"They were both catchers, both lefthanded hitters and it would be foolish to sign two, so we took the one we thought was better," said a St. Louis Cardinals scout, explaining his team's decision to sign Garagiola but not his playground buddy.

Garagiola received a $500 bonus to sign. Berra sat tight—until the Yankees came along and offered

the major leagues, sized up Mantle's all-around talents and volunteered to shift from center field to right as an accommodation to the rookie. The offer was declined with respect and gratitude.

Astonishingly, Mantle made the leap from Class C ball to the majors.

"How do I feel about all this? It just is not true, that's all," said the 19-year-old Mantle as he reclined in an easy chair at Yankee Stadium prior to the New Yorkers' '51 season opener against the Boston Red Sox. " . . . For years I have been reading The Sporting News, with its stories about Joe DiMaggio, Tom Henrich, Ted Williams, Vic Raschi, Bob Feller and all the rest. Now I am playing right field next to DiMaggio, and Henrich (a Yankee coach) is my teacher. I am playing against Williams, Dom DiMaggio and Bobby Doerr.

"I somehow get the feeling that I hadn't ought to be here. That maybe it is a mistake after all, and I am supposed to be in Kansas City (where a Class AAA affiliate of the Yankees was located) . . . ."

Come mid-July, Mantle *was* in Kansas City.

the same kind of inducement. Yogi snapped it up.

"I was real happy for Joey," Berra would say in later years. "He's my buddy . . . I thought if he got money (beyond what a contract stipulated), I should get some, too." For the Yankees, it was a wise investment—one of the best they ever made.

After 188 minor league games (divided over two seasons) and two years of military service, Berra joined the Yankees for the first time late in the 1946 season—shortly before Garagiola starred for the Cardinals in the World Series—and Yogi walloped two home runs in a seven-game stint. Berra spent his first full season in the majors in 1947, a year in which he belted the first pinch-hit homer in World Series history. From 1948 through 1950, Yogi's latent skills surfaced fully as he drove in a total of 313 runs for the Yankees. In 1951, the year Garagiola suffered a career downturn when he was traded to the lowly Pirates, Berra ruled as the American League's Most Valuable Player. And in 1952, Lawrence Peter Berra merely collected 98 RBIs and belted a career-high 30 homers.

Berra got off to a fine start in 1953, and he had one moment in particular to savor during the winning streak. Playing before many of his old friends in St. Louis on June 7, Yogi socked a pinch-hit, bases-loaded homer off the Browns' Satchel Paige. The smash, coming in the seventh inning of the opening game of a doubleheader, helped send the Yanks winging to their 10th consecutive triumph. (Beating the Browns was no great accomplishment for the Yankees, who had posted 17-5, 17-5, 17-5 and 14-8 records against St. Louis in the previous four years and were on their way to another 17-5 edge in '53. Still, victories over the Brownies were satisfying, considering the bad blood that existed between the clubs. In July 1952 and again in April 1953, fisticuffs erupted in Browns-Yankees games, with scrappy St. Louis catcher Clint Courtney being at center stage in both episodes.)

Of all the Yankees, Collins probably was the one least accustomed to the glare of the spotlight. But, now, the Pennsylvanian was grabbing his share of the attention.

Collins figured prominently in the Yanks' victory skein, whacking five home runs during the surge in which New York came within one victory of matching the longest winning streak in American League history (19 games, by the 1906 White Sox and the 1947 Yanks). The longtime minor leaguer enjoyed a particularly eventful night on June 2, hitting two home runs against the White Sox, the second one a two-out smash in the ninth that won the game for New York.

With the exception of two years in the military and two stints with the Yanks totaling 12 games, Collins toiled exclusively in the minor leagues from 1939 through 1949. In 1950 and 1951, he had a com-

bined 467 at-bats for the Yankees—a total usually attained in one full season. Finally, in 1952, Collins had starting stature (122 games, 428 at-bats) and he delivered 18 homers and a .280 batting mark.

Minor league baseball and its poorly lit fields, rock-hard playing surfaces, interminable bus rides and poor pay have sent many prospects packing long before the players ever got close to their dream of getting a call to the majors. Even Collins' own brother, a member of the Boston Red Sox's organization, "couldn't take the minors like I could," Joe said, "and so he quit."

Joe Collins adapted to the minor league regimen, all right. But that didn't mean he wasn't always striving to escape it. The best way out, he figured, was to hit his way out. And if one technique wasn't quite up to snuff, well, why not try another?

"Every time I moved around the minors," Yankees outfielder Gene Woodling said, "up popped Joe. I was either playing against him or with him, and every time we'd meet he'd have another stance."

"I changed to a crouch (in 1952) instead of (standing) straight up," said Collins, responding to Woodling's good-natured claim that Joe was working on the "97th" stance of his career. "That way I don't hit at as many bad balls. I hold the bat closer to my body . . . I seem to have fallen into the crouch naturally. I see the ball better. The averages tell the story."

At last, it seemed, Collins was comfortable both at the plate and with his role with the Yankees. And the Yanks were clearly comfortable with their stranglehold on the American League lead.

That grip seemed certain to tighten. After all, the last 14 of the Yankees' 18 straight triumphs had come on the road and 15 of the streak victories were achieved away from Yankee Stadium. Now, the Yankees were to open a two-week home stand, a sequence of games that would begin with series against the seventh-place Browns and the eighth-place Detroit Tigers.

St. Louis was playing as poorly as the Yankees were playing well. The Browns, in fact, were in the throes of a 14-game losing streak as they took the field before 30,000-plus fans at Yankee Stadium on the night of June 16. Manager Marty Marion's team hadn't won since June 2; Stengel's charges hadn't lost since May 25.

Righthander Duane Pillette drew the starting assignment for the Browns, while Ford was the Yankees' mound selection. Whitey not only was unbeaten thus far in 1953, he had yet to lose a starting assignment in the major leagues. Until this night, that is. With Pillette and 46-year-old reliever Paige throttling the Yanks on six hits and Vic Wertz belting a two-run homer, the Browns scored a 3-1 victory.

The end of the winning streak surely was disappointing for Stengel's team, but the Yankees let it bother them for the briefest of moments. The Yanks, in fact, won five of their next six games, with Lopat featuring the latest run of success with a shutout that pushed his record to 8-0.

After Ford's 6-3 triumph over Detroit in the first game of a June 21 doubleheader, the Yankees' record stood at 46-13. Second-place Cleveland, having lost a single game that day, stood at 33-24.

As dominant as New York had been since Stengel's arrival as manager in 1949, the Yankees actually weren't used to this kind of cushion. En route to equaling the major league record of four consecutive World Series championships established by the Joe McCarthy-era Yanks, Stengel's teams had won American League pennants by margins of only one, three, five and two games. Dominant, yes. Overwhelming, no.

Stengel himself must have been feeling a bit giddy. In his first nine seasons as a major league manager, time spent with the National League's Brooklyn and Boston clubs in the 1930s and 1940s, Stengel never finished higher than fifth place. Now, he was on top of the baseball world.

Stengel, a fun-loving outfielder in a big-league playing career that spanned 14 seasons, developed a "clown" reputation that was difficult to shake. Enjoying minor league success as a pilot after his dismal managerial experiences in the National League, a "reformed" Stengel was tapped to manage the Yankees following the conclusion of the 1948 season.

Conversing in fractured and often-unintelligible language, Stengel nevertheless got his point across. And there was no doubting his insight into the game.

"When he wanted to make sense, he could," Berra said.

Casey, apparently, didn't always strive to be understood.

"There comes a time in every man's life, and I've had plenty of them," Stengel once philosophized, drawing blank stares in the process.

Discussing a player who had just signed a fat contract, Casey offered this analysis: "It's amazing. I remember him when he first came up to the league. He didn't have a dime to rub together."

Focusing on the keys to success, the Old Perfessor said: "The two things that can keep you from winnin' are the spirit of the players and . . . . " End of statement.

Addressing his team's chance of winning five consecutive pennants, Casey said: "If these players are good enough to win four years, they should be good enough to win five unless there's something the matter and if they don't, then you come ask the manager—got the name?—and some of those play-

ers that did so good the year before why they ain't doin' so good now . . . ."

While regaling the media, Stengel occasionally ran afoul with his players by freely criticizing their shortcomings and increasingly turning to platoon-style baseball. The barbs, which often found their way into print, and the reduction in playing time hurt some feelings, but the Yankees cried all the way to the bank under Stengel's astute on-field leadership.

That leadership underwent a wholly unexpected strain beginning with the second game of that June 21 twin bill against the Tigers. The Yankees absorbed a 10-3 pounding in that contest, and they suffered an 11-3 drubbing to the White Sox in their next game. Then came an 8-4 loss to Chicago. On top of that came six more consecutive setbacks. Nine straight defeats. An exasperated Stengel barred reporters from the clubhouse.

As newsmen knocked on the door, so did the Indians and the White Sox. The Yankees' lead, once as high as 11½ games, was down to five (Cleveland) and 5½ games (Chicago).

The next month saw little change in the Yankees' somewhat-precarious hold on first place, with New York's lead reaching a high of 6½ games and a low of four. Then the Yanks went on another of their fabled spurts—a seven-game winning streak, this time—and by August 8 New York had built an eight-game lead. Raschi stole the show in an August 4 game against the Tigers.

Pitcher Raschi went to the plate three times with the bases loaded that night—and collected a hit on each trip. He drove home two runners with a single, cleared the bases with a double and then singled across two more teammates, all of the pyrotechnics coming in the first four innings of the game. Raschi left the contest after six innings with a two-hitter and a 13-0 lead. Besides Raschi's seven runs batted in, the Yanks got four RBIs and a home run from third baseman Gil McDougald and went on to a 15-0 victory.

The 34-year-old Raschi had been a Yankee stalwart even before Stengel took over the club, winning 19 games for the New Yorkers in 1948. The next three years, Raschi won 21 games each season. In 1952, he won 16 of 22 decisions.

Explaining Raschi's ability to win big in the majors posed no problem for Casey.

"He's got it here and here and here," said Stengel, tapping his head, his heart and his right arm. "He's the strongest and best pitcher I've ever had, because nothing scares him. He takes charge. He's the boss. He's toughest when there are men on base. That's why he can win so many 10-hit games or overcome errors behind him. In the clutch, you'll never see him swallow that big chunk of tobacco.

"Hell, you could chill a bottle of beer with that

guy's blood."

Sain, who entered the double-figure victory column with a 6⅓-inning relief stint the day after Raschi's onslaught, had made an impressive comeback since being traded away by the Braves, the team for whom he won 20 or more games four times.

"I had a sore arm when the Braves let me go," the 34-year-old righthander said. "The soreness is all gone now. It started to disappear last year. My arm is stronger now than it has been since 1948, when I had the best season of my career (as Boston, paced by the pitching of Sain and Warren Spahn, copped the National League pennant)."

While the veteran Sain and the crafty Ford made stellar contributions to the Yankees' great run of success in the team's first five seasons under Stengel, the pitching threesome of Lopat, Raschi and Allie Reynolds had carried the load from day one. They combined for 53 victories in 1949, 55 in 1950, 59 in 1951 and 46 in 1952 (a season in which an ailing Lopat made only 20 appearances).

Reynolds, of Indian heritage and nicknamed "Chief," became a Yankee after the 1946 season when he was acquired from Cleveland in a trade that sent second baseman Joe Gordon to the Indians. At the time, Reynolds' competitive fire was questioned. While seemingly possessing above-average talent, as indicated by his minor league statistics and his 18-victory season for Cleveland in 1945 (admittedly, a war year), Reynolds was only four games above the .500 mark (51-47) as a big-league pitcher when he was dealt to New York.

"The truth was that I was a one-pitch thrower (while with Cleveland)," Reynolds said. "I threw nothing but a fastball. I didn't know how to pace myself. I experimented with a curve but could seldom get it over the plate. And I'd fallen into bad pitching habits—such as not concealing my intentions before delivering. It takes more time to correct a fault than to learn something entirely new.

"Now I have five speeds, a curve and a slider that I use in emergencies. And I also know that won-and-lost records are based on the offensive and defensive skill of all nine members of a ball team as well as upon the pitcher's ability."

Stengel's appreciation for the 36-year-old Reynolds was obvious.

"Reynolds is two ways great, which is starting and relieving, which no one can do like him," Casey said. "He is a tremendous competitor and he has guts and his courage is simply tremendous."

Reynolds, a 20-game winner for the Yankees in 1952, emerged as Stengel's "money" pitcher, quite a turnaround for a man whose fortitude had been questioned at one juncture in his career. In September 1951, with the Yankees needing a victory to clinch a first-place tie, Reynolds went out and tossed a no-hitter (his second such performance of

Shortstop Phil Rizzuto was already a veteran of seven pennant-winning Yankee teams when the 1953 season rolled around.

the season). And Allie would wind up pitching in six World Series, posting at least one victory in each of them.

Ever mindful of his supporting cast, Reynolds obviously had an oustanding one.

Besides Collins at first base, the infield was made up of Billy Martin at second base, Phil Rizzuto at shortstop and Gil McDougald at third base. Bobby Brown and Jerry Coleman, key infielders on earlier Yankee championship clubs, were in the military in

Third baseman Gil McDougald (left), first baseman Joe Collins and outfielder Hank Bauer played major roles in the Yanks' 1953 success.

1953. Joining Mantle in the outfield were Gene Woodling and Hank Bauer, with Irv Noren also seeing considerable duty. Berra, of course, held forth behind the plate. Johnny Mize, longtime slugging star for the St. Louis Cardinals and New York Giants, was the club's No. 1 pinch-hitter. Lefthander Bob Kuzava and righthander Tom Gorman were reliable coming out of the bullpen (fellow reliever Scarborough was released in August), and Sain and Reynolds helped immeasurably in relief roles.

The 25-year-old Martin played with a verve that endeared him to Stengel. Billy had been an integral member of Stengel's 1948 Oakland Oaks team, whose Pacific Coast League championship helped vault Casey into consideration for the Yankees' managerial post, and he had played well for New York in 1952. Martin had made perhaps the most memorable play of '52, a lunging catch of a bases-loaded pop fly by Brooklyn's Jackie Robinson in

the final game of the World Series.

"All big-league players are supposed to know baseball and most of them do. But Billy doesn't have to think for two minutes to do the right thing," Stengel said. "He has sense enough to tell other men what to do. He is a spirited fellow who doesn't loaf. He'll make the double play. If you want a bunt, he'll bunt. He can hit singles, doubles, triples and home runs. If you want him to play a new position, he doesn't say, 'No, it will hurt my work.' He will say, 'Yes.' So you understand he is a valuable fellow."

Rizzuto was steeped in Yankee tradition. Entering the '53 season, the Scooter already had played on seven pennant-winning New York clubs (the first before the United States' entry into World War II). The expert fielder, pesky hitter and superb bunter, now nearing his 35th birthday, acknowledged that the Yankees had benefited from superior

The Yankees win again: (Back row, left to right) Billy Martin and Mickey Mantle and (front row, left to right) Gil McDougald, Jim McDonald and Gene Woodling.

talent over the years. But he focused on another factor, too.

"It's such a simple point that you may not believe it," said the American League's MVP of 1950. "The Yankees bear down harder. There's been a lot of talk about how players from other clubs blossom out when they get traded to New York and put on that Yankee uniform. This has often happened, but I don't think it's because there's something magic about the uniform. It's not that they become better ballplayers. It's just that they play harder.

". . . A fellow from a losing club finds that he never knew what it was like to go all out to win every day. He didn't know what it was like always to be trying for that extra step, that extra jump on the ball. On the Yankees, everybody tries that little bit extra, and that's what wins you that extra ball game.

"Casey Stengel tells you, 'Never waste a time at bat.' He tells you that no matter what the score is, you should always go up to the plate as if it meant the ball game.

"And those old Yankees we have coaching the team, Bill Dickey and Jim Turner and Frank Crosetti . . . we can be winning by a big score, and when we come to bat, Dickey and Turner and Crosetti will say, 'Let's get some runs. Don't stop now.'"

The Yankees didn't stop in their August 12 game against Washington. They collected 28 hits and buried the Senators, 22-1. While Martin and Berra led the way with five RBIs apiece, there were standouts galore. Among them were McDougald, who went 3 for 3, and Woodling, who cracked out four

hits.

McDougald stirred considerable reaction when he made his debut with the Yankees in 1951, first with his unusual batting stance and then with his all-around performance. A righthanded batter, McDougald planted his right foot in the extreme inside corner of the batter's box and placed his left foot at exactly the center. Accordingly, he was at an angle almost in perfect alignment with the third-base foul line. Furthermore, he held the bat loosely.

No way to hit, eh? The San Francisco native proceeded to bat .306, with 14 homers and 63 RBIs. A non-roster player in spring training, just like Mantle, it was Gil McDougald—not the Mick—who ran off with Rookie of the Year honors in the American League in 1951. McDougald topped off the memorable year by becoming only the third player in history to slug a bases-loaded home run in World Series competition.

"No one taught me that stance," said McDougald, who altered the style later in his career. "It just felt natural from the start. When I was with Beaumont, Rogers Hornsby (manager of the Texas League team in 1950) looked it over and told me not to change it, and I guess he ought to know. He was the best right-handed batter of all time."

Woodling, who had seen brief service in the majors with Cleveland and Pittsburgh before joining New York, had been a Yankee since being purchased from San Francisco of the Pacific Coast League after the 1948 season. Oakland Manager Stengel no doubt was impressed that year with the play of the hard-hitting outfielder from the rival team across the bay. Woodling had batted .385 for San Francisco.

"I thought I was a good outfielder when I came to the Yankees," Woodling said. "Then I played alongside DiMaggio, and I became very humble. . . ."

Now, though, Woodling was developing into a solid player in his own right. In 1952, he had batted .309 for the Yankees.

The Yankees' man in right field, Bauer, was a decorated Marine in World War II. One biographer said he "had the stamp of Sarge written all over him. The bumpy nose, the strong, aggressive jaw and the sharp, clear eyes that bespeak the man of supreme confidence and self-assurance to handle any situation that may arise."

Bauer's confidence had been tested in the sixth game of the 1951 World Series against the New York Giants. Going to the plate in the sixth inning with a career .132 Series batting mark, Bauer drilled a bases-loaded triple that broke a 1-1 tie. He then made a sensational game-ending and Series-clinching catch on a low line drive in the ninth inning.

Bauer, who first played for the Yankees late in the 1948 season, batted .320, .296 and .293 for the Bronx Bombers from 1950 through 1952.

A native of East St. Louis, Ill., Bauer was a Cardinals fan while growing up and always thought of the Yankees as "the other guys, the team to beat. But now that I'm up here, I know what it was the old Yankee teams had. The old will to win, same as the Cards (of the Gas House Gang era, during which Hank was a youngster)."

After the Labor Day portion of the '53 American League schedule had been completed, New York held a nine-game lead over second-place Cleveland. A week later, the Yankees achieved the heretofore unprecedented feat of winning five consecutive pennants in the majors. An 8-5 triumph over Cleveland wrapped it up, the Yankees rebounding from a 5-0 deficit and seizing the lead on a two-run homer by Berra. Martin drove in four runs for New York.

At the end of the regular season, the Yanks owned a 99-52 record. Their edge over the Indians —as high as 13 games two weeks earlier—wound up at 8½.

Berra finished as the Yanks' top offensive player, leading the club in homers with 27 and in RBIs with 108. Mantle cracked 21 homers and drove in 92 runs. Woodling ended with a team-high .306 batting mark, while Bauer batted .304.

Lopat, who won 16 of 20 decisions, paced the American League in winning percentage at .800 and was No. 1 in earned-run average with a 2.43 mark. Ford was New York's big winner, posting 18 victories. Sain won 14 games, and Raschi and Reynolds each had 13 triumphs. Righthander Jim McDonald contributed nine victories.

Hardly content with their record of five straight league titles, the Yankees went out and shattered their own mark of four consecutive World Series championships (1936 through 1939), beating Brooklyn in six games. Martin, who had thwarted the Dodgers defensively in the 1952 fall classic, did in the Bums with his bat this time. He totaled 12 hits, a record for a six-game Series, and batted .500. Two of his hits were homers. His final hit came in the last of the ninth inning of Game 6 and drove in the Series-deciding run.

"Look, five straight world championships ain't a bad record, at all," Stengel understated. "I would not like to try to do it all over again. It is rough on your brain, on your digestion, on your sleeping habits and on your family.

" . . . Now, when I arrived in New York (in 1949), I knew a lot of jokes and imagine I could have told them and got a lot of laughs. But I had no intention to be a jokester . . . It was deadly serious business for me. It still is, and always will be.

"So, we rebuilt, and while rebuilding we won the pennant and the World Series in 1949. We did it again in 1950, and we have gone right on doing it every year . . . My ball club is made up of pros. They also know on which side of the toast there is butter, and they are not going to let anybody cut in on their stuff."

No one did, for a period unmatched in major league history.

1953
FINAL STANDING

Club	W.	L.	Pct.	GB.
New York	99	52	.656	—
Cleveland	92	62	.597	8½

BATTERS

Pos.	Player	G.	HR.	RBI.	B.A.
1B	Joe Collins	127	17	44	.269
2B	Billy Martin	149	15	75	.257
SS	Phil Rizzuto	134	2	54	.271
3B	Gil McDougald	141	10	83	.285
OF	Gene Woodling	125	10	58	.306
	Mickey Mantle	127	21	92	.295
	Hank Bauer	133	10	57	.304
C	Yogi Berra	137	27	108	.296
UT	Irv Noren (of)	109	6	46	.267
	Johnny Mize (ph)	81	4	27	.250

OTHER CONTRIBUTORS (20+ Games): Don Bollweg, Andy Carey, Willie Miranda, Bill Renna, Charlie Silvera.

PITCHERS

Thr.	Pitcher	G.	W.	L.	ERA
L	Whitey Ford	32	18	6	3.00
L	Ed Lopat	25	16	4	2.43
R	Johnny Sain	40	14	7	3.00
R	Vic Raschi	28	13	6	3.33
R	Allie Reynolds	41	13	7	3.41
R	Tom Gorman	40	4	5	3.39

OTHER CONTRIBUTORS (20+ Games): Bob Kuzava, Jim McDonald, Ray Scarborough.

Number 14

Three Giant Steps Forward

The New York Giants were in the thick of a battle for the 1908 National League pennant when they astonished the national pastime. Weeks before Fred Merkle would enter baseball infamy with a base-running boner that would cost New York the flag, the Giants jolted the baseball public by purchasing an 18-year-old minor league pitcher for $11,000.

Neither players nor fans could conceive of any player being worth such a kingly sum, not even one who had just won 28 games for Indianapolis in the American Association. Not surprisingly, when the skinny lefthander walked into the New York clubhouse that September, he was greeted by shafts of ridicule.

"Who the hell are you?" demanded Cy Seymour, the uninhibited outfielder.

"Marquard," came the meek reply.

"Hey, fellas," shouted Mike Donlin, joining the repartee, "here's the bum that McGraw paid $11,000 for."

Richard William Marquard, better known as Rube, could have expected that he'd buck some rough terrain as an aspiring major leaguer. His father, a city engineer in Cleveland, had despised the game and encouraged Rube to pursue a college education. When his son announced he had signed a minor league contract in 1907 for $200 a month, the elder Marquard was heartbroken.

"When you cross that threshold, don't come back," he said. "I don't ever want to see you again."

"Well, I'm going," the teen-ager replied, thus beginning an eight-year estrangement, "and someday you'll be proud of me."

Hailed as the "$11,000 Beauty," it took only two seasons for Rube Marquard to become the "$11,000 Lemon." He won just five games and lost 13 in 1909, then was 4-4 in only 13 appearances in 1910. The public ridiculed Giants Manager John McGraw for wasting a fortune. It was the Little Napoleon, however, who would have the last laugh. For two years, Giants coach Wilbert Robinson, McGraw's old teammate and right-hand man with the Baltimore Orioles, had been patiently tutoring Marquard, carefully developing the 6-foot-3 southpaw's three-quarter delivery and perfecting his curve. And as the 1911 season dawned, McGraw was anticipating rewarding results.

As the 1911 season approached, New York Giants Manager John McGraw optimistically contemplated his team's prospects.

Gone were the glory days of 1905 and most of the old heroes. Righthander Christy Mathewson, the centerpiece of those World Series champions, had lost nothing at 30 years old. In the past three seasons, Matty had won 37 (an N.L. record), 25 and 27 games and twice led the league in strikeouts. Lefthander Hooks Wiltse had been a 20-game winner in both 1908 and 1909, and Red Ames, still a speedballer, had fashioned 15 victories in the '09 campaign. Given a young, fleet lineup that could execute the daring baserunning that had become the Giants' trademark, McGraw appeared on the verge of renewed success.

The Giant brain trust, coach Wilbert Robinson (left) and Manager John McGraw, along with cerebral righthander Christy Mathewson.

Three days into the season, however, the Giants were reduced to homeless tailenders. After the Philadelphia Phillies trounced McGraw's troops in their first two contests, the Polo Grounds was reduced to ashes during an early-morning fire on April 14. A special dispatch to the sports weekly Sporting Life detailed the disaster:

It was after midnight when a watchman in the elevated road's towers, which lie just outside the grounds, saw tiny tongues of flame shoot into the darkened sky from inside of the grounds. Immediately after, there was a roar as the unchecked flames wrapped themselves about the grandstand, and soon that portion of the structure was a mass of flames. The watchman gave the alarm, but by the time the first piece of apparatus had arrived, the big double-decked stand had been reduced to a pile of smoking ruins, with the steel uprights alone remaining like gloomy sentinels over the heap of debris . . . .

Only the right-field bleachers, a portion of the seats in center field and the players' clubhouse were left standing. By the end of the week, the Giants had temporarily moved to Hilltop Park, home grounds of the American League New York Highlanders, and begun construction plans for a "modern baseball plant," a giant steel-and-concrete stadium.

Despite the loss of their park, the Giants remained upbeat. They stayed almost even with the fast-starting Phillies and got their first taste of the N.L. lead on May 24, when Marquard won his second decision with a two-hit shutout over the Cincinnati Reds. Pitching "the best game of his life," according to news reports, Marquard didn't allow "even a semblance of a hit" after the first inning.

Rube Marquard (right) established himself as a big winner for McGraw's Giants in 1911. A year later, rookie Jeff Tesreau won 17 games.

That the Giants were able to battle the Chicago Cubs for the lead into July was due to the early pitching of Mathewson, not Marquard. Although McGraw avoided pitching Matty out of turn ("a great advantage, for 'Big Six' will be able to go in top form during July and August when the race will be decided," McGraw said), the veteran righthander was the only consistent winner on the New York staff. He accounted for more than a third of the Giants' 41 victories through June with a 14-3 start.

Curiously, it was in July that Marquard suddenly blossomed while Matty, certainly no washout with a 12-10 record after July 1, lost some of his effectiveness and stamina (due, some believed, to his barnstorming through the vaudeville circuit the previous winter). Mathewson had closed out June with a 3-0 collaring of Boston on June 28, the Giants' first game back in the reopened Polo Grounds, then lost his first three starts in July. Marquard, however, suddenly was tabbed as the key to New York's pennant hopes with a remarkable turnabout.

With only a 4-3 record to show for his work

through June 22, Marquard won his next five decisions, including a 10-1 victory against the strong Phillies on July 5 and a 5-2 decision over the Cubs on July 8. "In both of these games," wrote one correspondent, "Marquard pitched brilliant ball. He had speed, curves and perfect control all at his command. In Saturday's game with the Cubs, besides displaying all three qualities, he showed a coolness and effectiveness that won him the admiration of the crowd. He made, in addition, a tremendous home run drive into the right-field seats and was altogether the 'real thing.'

"At present, Marquard's work in the box affords the best hope the Giants have of landing the pennant."

Rube did, indeed, prove to be the pitching key to the flag. Marquard won 20 of his final 24 decisions, including three low-hit games down the stretch. On August 24, Marquard hurled his second two-hitter of the season to defeat Pittsburgh, 2-1, then pitched back-to-back one-hitters in his next two starts, August 28 against St. Louis and September 1 against

Philadelphia. This was, unquestionably, the "$11,000 Beauty," the league-leader in strikeouts (237) and winning percentage with a 24-7 mark.

The Giants took control of their destiny when they arrived at the Polo Grounds for nearly a monthlong homestand beginning August 11. Having fallen behind Chicago in the N.L. race, New York won 19 of its next 25 games (including a three-game road series in Philadelphia September 1-2) to shoot into first place. They took to the road, won 19 times in 23 games and coasted to a 99-54 finish, 7½ games ahead of Chicago.

Next to Marquard's sudden success, the Giants' pennant prospects improved when newcomer Buck Herzog and utility infielder Art Fletcher joined the regular lineup. After the Giants struggled through an 8-8 start in July, McGraw restored speed and batting punch to a sagging infield by reacquiring Herzog from the Boston Braves for shortstop Al Bridwell on July 20. Herzog, 26, took over third base from 31-year-old Art Devlin (a member of the 1904-05 pennant teams) while Fletcher assumed the duties at short.

Charles Lincoln Herzog was the bane of John McGraw's existence—and the one player he could not live without. Three times Buck would be traded by McGraw—and twice reacquired. He had played sparingly for the Giants in 1908 and 1909 before being shipped to Boston, where he became one of the league's fastest-fielding third basemen. In 1911, he was the kind of scrappy, spirited player McGraw needed at third. Never one of the league's best hitters, Herzog batted only .267 upon his return, but he stole 22 bases and played third in the manner that earned him the nickname "Choke 'Em Charley" for his advice to teammates: "When you get 'em down, choke 'em!"

Fletcher was dangerous at bat and on base, built like an inverted pyramid and never adverse to defend McGraw's Fighting School. Sportswriter Sid Mercer fancied that a blow-by-blow account of a typical McGraw rhubarb would read: "McGraw swings at his opponent and misses. Opponent flattens McGraw. Fletcher flattens opponent."

Fletcher's fielding and bullet-fast throws were initially erratic, but McGraw liked the 26-year-old's high-strung diamond personality. "Fletcher will stay in there," McGraw said. "He's the kind of player I want and I'm not going to break his spirit." After two seasons of virtual inactivity, the Collinsville, Ill., native batted .319 and stole 20 bases in 108 games in 1911.

With McGraw's shift completed, the Giants fielded the hardest-hitting and easily the fastest infield in the National League. Given the fastest outfield, too, the 1911 Giants proved to be the most daring band of thieves in baseball history. They swiped a major

Second baseman Larry Doyle became the New York Giants' captain and helped spark the team's success with his torrid hitting.

league record 347 bases and, according to McGraw, "literally stole the pennant."

"The players got the notion that they could steal on anybody and that belief was so strong they went out and did it," McGraw said.

"On one trip West, we arrived in Chicago with the club in rags and tatters. We had to telegraph for new uniforms. Nearly every man on the club had slid the seat out of his uniform pants. We had patched and patched until the principal feature of our pants was safety pins.

"In the first game in Chicago, Josh Devore slid so completely out of his patched-up breeches that a cordon of players had to form around him and escort him off the field."

Devore wound up second in the league with 61 stolen bases, followed by teammates Fred Snodgrass (51), Fred Merkle (49), Red Murray (48) and Herzog (48).

This New York Giant club stood out not only for its speed but for youth as well. It was a team that

Shortstop Art Fletcher was known in baseball circles as a free swinger, whether his target be a ball or an opponent's jaw.

McGraw had begun building only a few seasons earlier, phasing out the veterans who had served him well in 1904 and 1905 and replacing them with youngsters who, "though still lacking in polish, had the goods."

"The first indication that a player is slipping comes from his legs," McGraw maintained. "When I notice that an infielder or an outfielder has lost that quick spring of youth in going for a ball, I immediately begin looking for his successor."

And as the Giants charged toward their first pennant since 1905, McGraw argued his case. "Some of my *friends* repeated again and again the statement that I never have developed a player since I have been a manager and that the only way in which I could win a championship was by buying seasoned material. Now if this present club doesn't come close to being one which I selected and brought up myself, I am willing to get out of baseball. I tried the men out together to play ball my own way...."

In 1907, McGraw purchased two young prospects who would help lead the New York offense during the golden years of 1911-1913. They were "Laughing Larry" Doyle and Fred Merkle, and they were the hard-hitting right side of the Giant infield.

Doyle became McGraw's captain and one of the idols of New York for his exuberance, Irish charm and familiar diamond refrain, "It's great to be young and a Giant." His marginal skills at second base, however, helped inspire another slogan at the Polo Grounds: "If Larry misses one, he'll miss the next two."

To his credit, Doyle surmounted his fielding shortcomings and made amends with his torrid hitting. He rammed a dead ball for 25 triples, 13 home runs and a .310 batting mark in 1911, his third .300 season since he was purchased from Springfield of the Three-I League. In 1908, at the age of 22, Doyle had batted .308 before an injury ended his season in early September. The Giants, subsequently, lost the pennant to Chicago in a replay of a tie game.

Merkle would struggle with memories of 1908 long after his career ended. As a 19-year-old backup first baseman that year, he cost the Giants a key victory when he failed to touch second base in a September 23 game against the Cubs—the tie game that was replayed on October 8 to decide the race. Merkle's baserunning error would create storms of controversy, but McGraw never censured the young player. Merkle actually was regarded as one of the most intelligent players in the game.

"He was the smartest player on our team," recalled catcher Chief Meyers. "McGraw used to ask Merkle what he thought of this strategy or that. He never asked anybody else, Matty or anyone."

McGraw made Merkle his regular first baseman in 1910, a job he held in New York for 6½ seasons. Tall, strong and confident, the righthanded-swinger could hit in the clutch, batting .292 with 70 runs batted in in 1910, then .283 with a team-leading 84 RBIs in 1911. On May 13 against St. Louis, he set a major league record by driving home six runs in the first inning.

McGraw's reconstruction program also provided the Giants a young, ambitious and lightning-fast outfield.

Fred Snodgrass was a self-admitted "headstrong, quick-tempered, 20-year-old kid" when he joined the Giants in 1908 as a third-string catcher. McGraw, however, detected something more when he watched Snodgrass' mad dashes during practice. After a late-season baptism in the Giants' 1909 outfield, Snodgrass became McGraw's starting center fielder midway through 1910 and batted a career-high .321. In 1911, he ripped at a .294 clip.

Right fielder John Joseph (Red) Murray, just turned 25, had been secured from the St. Louis Cardinals in a trade for veteran catcher Roger Bresnahan after the 1908 season. Signed by the Cardinals

Fred Snodgrass took control of his temper and patrolled center field for the 1911-13 Giants.

while a student at Notre Dame, Murray had three distinctive features: a flaming-red thatch, a perpetual smile and an ever-present wad of chewing gum. The burly righthanded hitter led the Giants in RBIs in both 1909 and 1910, then batted a career-best .291 in 1911.

Murray will best be remembered, however, for his "lightning catch" at Pittsburgh's Forbes Field on August 16, 1909. The Giants and Pirates were tied, 2-2, in the bottom of the eighth inning when the darkness of an approaching storm veiled the field to such a degree that Mathewson had to walk toward the plate to see the catcher's signals. With two outs and two runners aboard, Dots Miller sent a drive deep into right-center field, surely a triple. As spectators peered into the dark, a bolt of lightning flashed to reveal Murray making a leaping, barehanded grab for the third out. Moments later, a torrential downpour halted the game.

Left fielder Josh Devore was but another rising young star in the Giant garden. Signed by New York in 1908, Devore spent most of the season at Newark in the Eastern League but was recalled by McGraw in 1909 to serve his learner's apprenticeship on the bench. The following season, Devore, only 22 years old, was thrust into the regular lineup. The 5-foot-6 live wire responded with a .304 batting mark and 43 stolen bases, then came back with a .280 average in 1911 as the club's leadoff hitter.

The redoubtable leading hitter was catcher John T. (Chief) Meyers, who batted .332, .358 and .312 for the 1911-13 Giant champions. Meyers, a full-blooded California Mission Indian, was purchased from

St. Paul of the American Association in 1908.

"I was purchased July 27, when my baseball age was still 26," Meyers recalled. "My birthday was the next day, when I was supposed to be 27, but actually was 29. I've often wondered whether McGraw would have bought me had he known my exact age. Twenty-nine is pretty old for a rookie."

Nevertheless, Meyers caught no fewer than 110 games for McGraw between 1910 and 1915. A shade under 6-foot and a rock-hard 200 pounds, Meyers was a top receiver, handling the big curves of Marquard and Wiltse, the spitballs of young Jeff Tesreau and the famous "fadeaway" of Mathewson. "You could catch Matty sitting in a rocking chair," Meyers said. "He had perfect control and an encyclopedic mind—knew the strengths and weaknesses of every batter."

Mathewson also had a sense of humor, Meyers recalled, and wasn't adverse to having fun at McGraw's expense. "There were times when Matty used to have McGraw sliding up and down the bench, getting madder by the second," Meyers said. "If he had a four- or five-run lead, he'd let up and lay the ball in there. He liked to see the outfielders run."

Mathewson was all business when the Giants marched into the 1911 World Series to oppose the Philadelphia Athletics and their crack pitching staff of Jack Coombs, Eddie Plank and Chief Bender. In 1905, Matty had shut out the A's three times, defeating Bender in the Game 5 finale to give New York its first Series title. Now, he defeated Bender in the 1911 opener, 2-1, with the Giants bedecked in the sinister black uniforms they had unveiled in their 1905 matchup.

Ultimately, the Series was a case of "same scenario, different results." Matty lost the third and fourth games after Marquard lost his only decision in Game 2, and New York bowed out in six contests. Frank Baker, who batted .375 to lead the Philadelphia offense, would forever after be known as "Home Run" Baker for his game-winning home run in the second game and a ninth-inning game-tying shot in Game 3.

Still, Philadelphia Manager Connie Mack was impressed by these young, aggressive New Yorkers, so much that he expected them to repeat easily in 1912. "I don't see how the Giants can be beaten out of the flag," Mack said. "They didn't come up to my expectations in the World Series, but they may have done better in the pennant race. McGraw has two remarkable pitchers in Mathewson and Marquard, a first-class catcher in Meyers and two top-notch infielders in Doyle and Herzog."

Much of the confidence of New York's fandom could be traced to Marquard, who, according to one spring training report, "seems improved even over his wonderful form of 1911."

That became painfully apparent to the rest of the National League. After turning back Brooklyn, 18-3, on opening day, Marquard was invincible for nearly three months. He won a major league record 19 consecutive games, matching the 1888 feat of Tim Keefe, also of the Giants, before finally losing to Chicago, 7-2, on July 8. After defeating Brooklyn, 2-1, on July 3 for his 19th win, Rube stepped on the scales and discovered he had lost 15 pounds since opening day. The Giants, meanwhile, owned a top-heavy record of 54-11 and led the second-place Cubs and Pirates by 16½ games.

Marquard defeated Boston and Philadelphia four times each, Brooklyn three times and every other N.L. team twice during his victory spree. He pitched 16 complete games (two were called due to darkness) and won once in relief. But it was an April 20 relief appearance against Brooklyn that would leave Marquard somewhat disappointed, despite his remarkable feat.

The Giants and rookie Jeff Tesreau were leading Brooklyn, 2-0, when the Dodgers rallied for three quick runs in the top of the ninth. McGraw summoned Marquard, who retired the side and set the stage for backup catcher Art Wilson's game-winning two-run homer in the bottom of the inning. Under scoring rules in vogue at the time, the decision was awarded to Tesreau, the starter.

"If you're put in a spot where you can lose, you must have an equal chance to win," Marquard contended years later. "Had I been credited with the victory that day, I would have collected 20 straight, instead of 19. It was something to tie the former record, of course, but it would have been much nicer to have beaten it."

After his great streak, however, Marquard failed to pitch .500 baseball, notching only a 7-11 mark over the remainder of the season. The Giants suddenly stumbled during July and then August (when Mathewson won only one game), but the stellar work of the rookie Tesreau helped New York stay ahead of the N.L. pack.

Tesreau had been a sensation in spring training and inspired glossy previews in the press. "Big Jeff Tesreau has proved himself of real major league caliber," reported The Sporting News' New York correspondent. "He is a giant in every sense of the word, a fellow equal to win 40 or 50 games if no injury befalls him. . . . Tesreau has wonderful speed, a good change of pace and a crackerjack spitball. It's one of the best spitballs ever seen in the National League, where the salivary delivery is comparatively rare—for the reason of which the big fellow should be all the more effective."

Charles Monroe Tesreau was a 6-3, 230-pound son of the Missouri Ozarks who had been signed but released (due to being claimed by Austin of the Texas League) by both the St. Louis Browns and

Chief Meyers, a full-blooded Indian, was the catcher and leading hitter for the hungry and talented New Yorkers.

Detroit Tigers. Just 23 years old, the hulking right-hander held off disaster with an 11-4 showing in August and September, hurling seven consecutive complete-game victories from August 23 through September 14. Tesreau wound up with a 17-7 record and league-leading 1.96 earned-run average (the first year the statistic was officially kept).

Tesreau's finest effort of the stretch drive occurred at Philadelphia on September 6. Just two days after defeating the Phils, 5-2, Big Jeff beat them again, this time on a "corrected" no-hitter. Dode Paskert led off the Phillies' first inning with a high pop in front of the plate, a ball that dropped safely between Merkle and Wilson. The official scorer awarded Paskert a hit, the only one that was scored in the book over the course of the game. After a postgame conversation with Wilson, who said that Merkle had touched the ball, the scorer changed the hit to an error and Tesreau entered the record book.

For the third straight year, New York received strong relief help from Otis Crandall, "a demon twirler and a horse for work," wrote one reporter. Crandall was christened "Doc" for his ability to take care of "sick" Giant games and convert them into victories. He was a sturdy righthander with powerful, stooped shoulders that allowed him to break off nasty curves and stroke whistling line drives at the plate.

Signed in 1908 after two seasons of Class-B ball, Crandall was 12-12 as a 20-year-old rookie, then a sparkling 17-4 two seasons later, in 1910. As a busy reliever on his first two pennant teams, Doc contributed 15 wins in 1911 and 13 victories in 1912.

The Giants outlasted their dog days of July and August to finish 10 games ahead of the runner-up Pirates. Once again, the New Yorkers profited from speed, stealing a league-leading 319 bases (still the third-highest total ever), but they hit better as a team, posting a league-high .286 composite average. Meyers (.358) finished second to Chicago's Heinie Zimmerman in the league batting race, Murray slashed 20 triples and a team-high 92 RBIs and Merkle batted a career-high .309 with 84 RBIs. Doyle was named the league's Most Valuable Player, the second time such an award had been presented by the Chalmers automobile company. Batting .330 with 10 homers and 90 RBIs, "Laughing Larry" received a Chalmers car, an award that prompted his hiring a chauffeur for $25 a week for his cruises around the big city.

With 103 victories in hand, McGraw desired four more, these over the Boston Red Sox in the World Series. What he got was a loss of the cruelest sort. According to John B. Foster, editor of the 1913 Spalding Baseball Guide:

"It was a Series crammed with thrills and gulps, cheers and gasps, pity and hysteria, dejection and wild exultation, recrimination and adoration, excuse and condemnation, and therefore it was what may cheerfully be called 'ripping good' baseball.

"There were plays on the field which simply lifted the spectators out of their seats in frenzy. There were others which caused them to wish to sink through the hard floor of the stand in humiliation. There were stops in which fielders seemed to stretch like India rubber and others in which they shriveled like parchment which has been dried. There were catches of fly balls which were superhuman and muffs of fly balls which were 'superawful.'"

And it was Snodgrass' muff of a seemingly harmless fly ball that, deservedly or not, would be blamed on the Giants' losing the Series. The miscue became known as the "$30,000 muff," the difference between the winners' and losers' share of the Series purse, and dogged Snodgrass till his death 62 years later.

The Giants had battled back from a three-games-to-one deficit to square the Series and necessitate a decisive eighth game (due to a 6-6 tie in Game 2, called because of darkness). Mathewson, a 23-game winner in the regular season but a loser in Game 5, hooked up in a pitching duel with rookie Hugh Bedient, his nemesis in the fifth game, and Smokey Joe Wood, a 34-game winner during the season and twice a winner in the Series.

The Giants closed to within three outs of their second Series title when they took a 2-1 lead in the top of the 10th inning on Merkle's run-scoring single. Snodgrass explained the ensuing circumstances that would haunt him forever after:

"Clyde Engle was up, batting for Wood. I was in center field and we were scared to death that Matty was going to walk him. Engle hit a towering fly. It was really more in the territory of Murray (in left) than in mine, but as we played it on the Giants, the center fielder got first call. I called for the ball first and Murray yelled, 'Squeeze it, Snod.'

"Now, that was a matter that could have happened one thousand, one million times. It was a fly ball, but because of over-eagerness or over-confidence or carelessness, I dropped it."

What Snodgrass' critics don't mention, however, is the next play. With Engle on second, Snodgrass robbed Harry Hooper of a game-tying extra-base hit with a spectacular one-handed catch of his drive to deep center field. Engle advanced to third after the grab, but Mathewson then walked Steve Yerkes.

"(Tris) Speaker," continued Snodgrass, "hit a towering foul fly and it was a ball that I swear to you must have fallen in the first-base coaching box. Merkle should have caught it—he could have run only 25 feet—but Matty elected to take command. He coached Meyers, who was catching, to go for the ball because Matty . . . thought Meyers was safer. But the Chief never got near the ball. Speaker, given another chance, singled cleanly (to score Engle)."

After another walk, Larry Gardner belted a deep fly ball to Devore in right field, and Yerkes pranced home with the winning run after the catch.

Although he wore the goat horns, Snodgrass was given a $1,000 raise by McGraw the following year. "He told me that I was a good ball player," Snodgrass recalled, "and that he didn't feel too badly, even though you know how McGraw hated to lose any game, let alone the one that decided the World Series. He shook my hand and said that if it weren't for errors there wouldn't be any baseball.

"Then he added real quick, 'But don't make too many of them, do you hear?'"

After a long and rueful winter—Owner John T. Brush, seriously ill for years, died November 26 on a train bound for California—the Giants stumbled out of the gate in 1913. While they drifted in the middle of the pack, they acquired pitcher Art Fromme from Cincinnati on May 23 for Ames, infielder Heinie Groh and Devore, who had been pushed to the bench a year ago by Beals Becker. Devore became expendable due to one George Burns, a 23-year-old former catcher whom McGraw had retained when the club broke spring camp in 1912.

"You sit next to me on the bench and I'll tell you all I can about the way they play ball in the big leagues," McGraw had told the youngster. "I'll stick you in there now and then to give you some experience, but I don't want you to get impatient. Next year, you'll be in there."

Burns played in 150 games, second only to Merkle, and hit .286 with 40 stolen bases. For the next eight seasons, he was a fixture in the Giant outfield.

Fromme, meanwhile, a 19- and 16-game winner in four seasons with the Reds, would contribute 11 wins to the Giant cause. With Mathewson, Marquard and Tesreau—all 20-game winners—combining for 70 victories, and righthander Al Demaree notching 13 wins in his first full season, the Giants reversed their slow start and took control of first place after a 14-game winning streak in late June and early July. Mathewson established an N.L. record by pitching 68 consecutive innings without a walk, while Marquard, only slightly off his 1912 form, won nine straight decisions between June 28 and July 27.

Led by Meyers and Fletcher, the New York offense again topped the league with a .273 batting mark. Six players swiped more than 30 bases as the Giants easily retained their stolen-base crown with 296 thefts. The numbers were robust, but the Giants weren't as they prepared for a rematch with the Athletics in the World Series. Merkle was hobbled by a bad leg and Snodgrass was suffering from a charley horse. After Game 2, Meyers was missing in action due to a broken finger.

The Giants won only the Series' second game behind Mathewson, who lost Game 5 and wound up with a 5-5 lifetime mark in four fall classics—despite a 1.15 ERA over 11 games.

For the third consecutive year, the Giants exited the World Series as losers, a futile mark duplicated only by the 1907-09 Detroit Tigers. New York's

three straight N.L. pennants, however, have been matched only twice since—by the Giants of 1921-24 and the Cardinals of 1942-44.

Nurtured and guided by the masterhand of McGraw, this ambitious band of youngsters had played some fast and frisky baseball, attacking aggressively and never straying from their pennant course. "There may have been greater teams," Fletcher would reminisce years later, "but nobody could raise more dust on the bases."

1912
FINAL STANDING

Club	W.	L.	Pct.	GB.
New York	103	48	.682	—
Pittsburgh	93	58	.616	10
Chicago	91	59	.607	11½

BATTERS

Pos.	Player	G.	HR.	RBI.	B.A.
1B	Fred Merkle	129	11	84	.309
2B	Larry Doyle	143	10	90	.330
SS	Art Fletcher	129	2	57	.282
3B	Buck Herzog	140	2	47	.263
OF	Fred Snodgrass	146	3	69	.269
	Beals Becker	125	6	58	.264
	Red Murray	143	3	92	.277
C	Chief Meyers	126	6	54	.358
UT	Josh Devore (of)	106	2	37	.275
	Tillie Shafer (inf)	78	0	23	.288

OTHER CONTRIBUTORS (20+ Games): George Burns, Heinie Groh, Grover Hartley, Moose McCormick, Art Wilson.

PITCHERS

Thr.	Pitcher	G.	W.	L.	ERA
L	Rube Marquard	43	26	11	2.57
R	Christy Mathewson	43	23	12	2.12
R	Jeff Tesreau	36	17	7	1.96
R	Doc Crandall	37	13	7	3.61
R	Red Ames	33	11	5	2.46

OTHER CONTRIBUTORS (20+ Games): Hooks Wiltse.

1913
FINAL STANDING

Club	W.	L.	Pct.	GB.
New York	101	51	.664	—
Philadelphia	88	63	.583	12½
Chicago	88	65	.575	13½

BATTERS

Pos.	Player	G.	HR.	RBI.	B.A.
1B	Fred Merkle	153	3	69	.261
2B	Larry Doyle	132	5	73	.280
SS	Art Fletcher	136	4	71	.297
3B	Buck Herzog	96	3	31	.286
OF	George Burns	150	2	54	.286
	Fred Snodgrass	141	3	49	.291
	Red Murray	147	2	59	.267
C	Chief Meyers	120	3	47	.312
UT	Tillie Shafer (inf)	138	5	52	.287

OTHER CONTRIBUTORS (20+ Games): Claude Cooper, Eddie Grant, Grover Hartley, Moose McCormick, Larry McLean, Art Wilson.

PITCHERS

Thr.	Pitcher	G.	W.	L.	ERA
R	Christy Mathewson	40	25	11	2.06
L	Rube Marquard	42	23	10	2.50
R	Jeff Tesreau	41	22	13	2.17
R	Al Demaree	31	13	4	2.21
R	Art Fromme	26	11	6	4.01

OTHER CONTRIBUTORS (20+ Games): Doc Crandall.

1911
FINAL STANDING

Club	W.	L.	Pct.	GB.
New York	99	54	.647	—
Chicago	92	62	.597	7½

BATTERS

Pos.	Player	G.	HR.	RBI.	B.A.
1B	Fred Merkle	148	10	84	.283
2B	Larry Doyle	141	13	77	.310
SS	Art Fletcher	108	1	37	.319
3B	Buck Herzog	69	1	26	.267
OF	Josh Devore	149	3	50	.280
	Fred Snodgrass	151	1	77	.294
	Red Murray	131	3	78	.291
C	Chief Meyers	128	1	61	.332
UT	Art Devlin (3b)	95	0	25	.273
	Al Bridwell (ss)	76	0	31	.270
	Beals Becker (of)	88	1	20	.262

OTHER CONTRIBUTORS (20+ Games): Art Wilson.

PITCHERS

Thr.	Pitcher	G.	W.	L.	ERA
R	Christy Mathewson	45	26	13	1.99
L	Rube Marquard	45	24	7	2.49
R	Doc Crandall	41	15	5	2.63
L	Hooks Wiltse	30	12	9	3.28
R	Red Ames	34	11	10	2.68

Number 15

Big Sticks
And a Cloud of Dust

At a time when Theodore Roosevelt was practicing his presidential policy of walking softly while carrying a big stick, the Pittsburgh Pirates of 1902 were wielding big sticks of a different sort while striding none too tenderly through the National League.

The Pirates, in fact, marched with a ponderous tread. From start to finish of the 140-game schedule, they walked all over their opposition. Never before or since has a major league pennant-winner achieved the 27½-game lead over the runner-up team that the 1902 Pirates enjoyed at season's end.

There was no doubting the excellence of the Pittsburgh club, nor the stroke of good fortune the franchise had received after the 1899 season as a result of problems surrounding the National League's unwieldy 12-team membership.

"The (Pittsburgh) team was superior to any club in the country in the matter of pitchers, strong in batting, fast in fielding and master of a superb system of team play which its rivals could not even fathom, let alone break through," wrote baseball chronicler Francis C. Richter, sizing up the Pirates' dominance in a year in which the upstart American League raided the established circuit for proven talent.

Despite what Richter called "universal light hitting" in 1902, the Pirates compiled a team batting average of .286, highest in the National League. Four of their players topped the .300 mark. Three Pittsburgh pitchers won 20 or more games, a fourth accounted for 16 victories and a fifth for 15.

The Pirates were positioned for this wondrous season—they also won the National League pennant in 1901—by events that culminated in the restructuring of the National League into an eight-team circuit before the start of play in 1900. Among the league's troubled entries in the late 1890s was the Louisville franchise, owned by Barney Dreyfuss. Knowing the future appeared bleak for a handful of the National League's teams, Dreyfuss announced his intention to sell the Louisville club after the 1899 campaign.

The multi-talented Honus Wagner was learning the shortstop position and carrying a big stick for the 1902 Pittsburgh Pirates.

Dreyfuss unloaded the club, all right, but he did not get out of baseball. Instead, he bought the Pittsburgh franchise and immediately consummated a deal that would thrust the long-struggling Pirates toward the top of the National League.

As the new man in charge of the Bucs, Dreyfuss, in a coup of monumental proportions, worked out a transaction involving players and cash that enabled his Louisville stars to accompany him to the Steel City. Fellows like Fred Clarke. Honus Wagner. Deacon Phillippe. Tommy Leach. Claude Ritchey. Chief Zimmer.

Now debilitated to the point of being a competitive risk, the already-in-trouble Louisville club was doomed to the scrap heap as the National League pushed for a "workable" eight-team alignment. Also discarded from the N.L. roster of teams before the start of the 1900 season were Washington, Baltimore and Cleveland.

As separate entities, Pittsburgh and Louisville had fielded middling N.L. teams in 1899. Now, as a "combine," the club had the makings of a powerhouse. Pittsburgh, after all, already boasted standouts in Ginger Beaumont, Jesse Tannehill and Sam Leever.

While Patsy Donovan had managed the Pirates for most of the '99 season, outfielder Clarke, Louisville's pilot beginning early in the '97 campaign, was named to direct the fortified Pittsburgh club.

"I am more than pleased with the deal, for I have long desired to play in Pittsburgh," Clarke said. "Other members of the Louisville team who are included in this deal will, I know, be delighted with the announcement that they are to become Pirates.

"Yes, I consider myself most fortunate—in fact, I cannot recall an instance where a manager of a National League club had so much excellent material from which to select a team. I do not anticipate any trouble when it comes to the task of placing the men, and if nothing happens I am satisfied that the Pittsburgh club next season will be one of the strongest ever known in the National League.

"Look at the pitching talent we have at our command; then glance over the list of players for the other positions. I am not going to do any midwinter boasting, but I think any man who knows a thing about baseball will agree with me that Pittsburgh certainly will figure in the pennant race next summer."

Clarke and the Pirates contested for the 1900 National League flag, to be sure. But Pittsburgh fell short, finishing 4½ games behind the champion Brooklyn club. While no pennant was raised at the Pirates' Exposition Park, plenty of hopes were. The Bucs were playing outstanding baseball, and outfielder John Peter (Honus) Wagner was playing even better than that.

Wagner, competing in his third full season in the major leagues and his first in a Pittsburgh uniform, captured his first National League batting championship in 1900 with a .381 average and collected 201 hits in 134 games.

Unquestionably the most talented player on the Pittsburgh roster, Wagner was the "Flying Dutchman" to some, "Hans" to others, "Dutch" to most of his teammates and the best player of his era to many observers. Many years after Honus' glory days, highly respected critics maintained that the son of German immigrants eclipsed even such superstars as Ty Cobb and Babe Ruth as a multi-gifted athlete.

One historian who observed Wagner in his heyday described him as a "bulging, squat giant, with wide, thick chest; legs so bowed you could roll a barrel through them, but not a baseball; awkward-looking big feet; basket-like hands hinged loosely at the end of long, heavily muscled arms; melancholy

Outfielder Fred Clarke directed the 1902 Pirate express that buried the rest of the National League under an avalanche of victories.

face set off with sharp, arched nose—this was . . .
Wagner. Not a graceful-looking figure . . . on the
field, not a boulevardier off. But he was grace personified in handling a grounder or swinging a bat."

A coal miner as a youth in western Pennsylvania,
Wagner was 26 years old when he copped his first
batting crown. In 1901, he batted .353 (among the
top five figures in the league) as the Pirates won
their first National League pennant.

Wagner's emergence as a shortstop, the position
that carried him to all-time eminence, occurred in a
peculiar manner. The sequence of events began during the 1901 season when Dreyfuss linked veteran
shortstop Fred Ely to attempts to recruit talent
from the Pirates for the American League, which
had burst upon the major league scene in 1901. Ely
was a competent infielder, but his apparent disloy-
alty and a feud with Clarke (over Ely's failure to
"play hurt") earned him his traveling papers.
Clarke was faced with the task of finding an adequate replacement.

Previous efforts to convert Wagner into a shortstop had encountered stiff resistance. "I'm an outfielder," maintained Honus, who nonetheless had
been playing third base at the time of Ely's departure and had manned the hot corner off and on
while with Louisville.

Now that Ely was an ex-Pirate, Clarke exerted
renewed pressure on Wagner in hopes he would
agree to move in at shortstop. The Pirates were well
supplied with outfielders, Clarke noted, and despite
Wagner's recent playing time at third base, Tommy
Leach really was the club's No. 1 man at that position. It was imperative that the left side of the infield be strengthened. Would Wagner finally ac-
cede? He would—after a fashion. He was willing to
continue to play third base rather than his normal
right-field spot if Leach would take over Ely's vacat-
ed post.

That wasn't exactly what Clarke had in mind, but
having Wagner at third base was a step in the right
direction. For the final phase of his strategy, Clarke
enlisted Leach's help.

"Clarke got me aside and told me of his plans,"
Leach recalled in later years. "He would let Wagner
play third base for a week (with Leach at shortstop),
and after that I was to work on him. I had to tell
him I couldn't cover short properly on a championship team, and I was sure a big, agile guy
(Honus stood 5-foot-11 and weighed 200 pounds)
with good hands would do a far better job.

"I would shame him by saying, 'Dutch, balls are
going through me that you would gobble up. I'm
only a runt (5-6½, 150 pounds) and belong on third,
a position I know how to play, but you are big and
fast and you'd make a heck of a shortstop. Suppose
I tell Fred Clarke we want to shift . . . .' "

The scheme worked, at least to the point that it

got Wagner broken in at the position at which he
would win everlasting fame. He wound up playing
nearly half of his games at shortstop in 1901 and
almost one-third of his games there in 1902 (when
one-season Pirate Wid Conroy became the principal
shortstop) before settling into the position in 1903.

Besides being noted for conspiring with his manager to transform an excellent outfielder into a superlative shortstop, Leach was quite a player in his
own right. The 1902 season gave powerful evidence
of his skills. Leach, in fact, led the National League
in home runs that year. Yes, the man they called
"Tommy the Wee." He hit a grand total of six
homers, one more than runner-up Jake Beckley of
Cincinnati.

Reflecting on his long-ball hitting after his career
had ended, Leach said: "In those days, it was rare
for anyone to hit the ball out of the park. The outfielders would play well back for hitters such as
Wagner and Clarke, whereas they would play me, a
real little guy, real close. Sometimes, they'd play for
me right in back of the infield. Every so often, I'd
manage to drive a ball between the outfielders and
it would roll to the fence. I was pretty fast, and by
the time they ran the ball down and got it back to
the infield, I'd scooted around the bases. I don't
ever recall getting a home run on a ball that I hit
outside of the park."

Inside or outside the park, Leach's lusty drives
made big news in 1902, a year in which the Pirates
stole headlines throughout.

Pittsburgh gave its opposition a hint of things to
come by winning 15 of its first 17 games of the season. By the end of May, Clarke's Pirates were 30-6
and Pittsburghers were beside themselves. Things
reached a fever pitch on July 4 when the Bucs, now
boasting a 43-12 record and holding an 11-game
lead over second-place Brooklyn, entertained the
runner-up club in a morning/afternoon doubleheader at Exposition Park. Those fans who thought
their Pirate heroes could walk on water very nearly
got to see them do just that on the holiday afternoon.

Exposition Park was located near the Allegheny
River, and it was not unusual for water to back up
through the storm sewers and onto the playing field
after a heavy rain. Showers often soaked the premises to such a degree that gallons of gasoline had to
be burned on the field before a game could be
played.

Prior to the start of the Pittsburgh-Brooklyn
doubleheader, rain fell by the barrels and then by
the buckets and there was the customary effluvium
from the nearby river. Then, as now, officials made
every effort to get in games with particular appeal.
Every effort.

"The excess from the Allegheny River started to
back up through the sewers into the ball park dur-

Honus Wagner (left), 85-RBI man Tommy Leach (center) and Manager Fred Clarke were three big reasons why the 1902 Pirates ran away from the pack.

ing the morning game," one Pirate stockholder said, "and by the time the afternoon contest got under way center field and the greater part of right field were completely submerged and the water was within 30 feet of second base.

"The left fielders, Fred Clarke and Jimmy Sheckard, were on fairly dry ground, but in center field Ginger Beaumont and ... Cozy Dolan ... were in water above their knees, while in right field Lefty Davis (Pittsburgh) and Wee Willie Keeler spent the greater part of the afternoon standing on a little island in the middle of a lagoon.

"After catching Dolan's fly for the final out of the game, Beaumont fell headlong into the center-field lake . . . ."

Aquatic baseball was a hit in Pittsburgh, mainly because the Pirates won both games of the double-header and stretched their league lead to 13 games. Jesse Tannehill spun a two-hitter in the opener and won, 3-0, and Jack Chesbro notched a five-hit, 4-0 triumph in the second game.

The Pirates built a 16-game bulge by the end of July and, overcoming a siege of injuries, extended their record to 83-28 and their margin to a fat 24 games by the conclusion of August. The rest of the 1902 National League race would consist of a jockeying for also-ran positions.

Success was nothing new for Clarke, who at age 29 was in his sixth season as a playing manager in the major leagues. On the way to his second straight

Happy Jack Chesbro, a strong-armed workhorse, was the ace of the Pirate staff and a 28-game winner in 1902.

pennant (the Pirates had won the 1901 N.L. flag by 7½ games), Clarke also was en route to a .321 batting mark. In 1897, his first season as a big-league pilot (he took over as manager one-third of the way into the season), the lefthanded-hitting Midwesterner led his Louisville club by example. He set some example, all right, batting .406 (but, incredibly, he fell 26 points shy of the batting leader, Wee Willie Keeler). And in his first game in the majors, June 30, 1894, Fred collected five hits.

There was a lot of the chameleon in Clarke, who was born in Iowa and spent a great portion of his life in Kansas. On the field, he was a fiery leader, ever ready to defend his rights with a flurry of fists. Fines and suspensions punctuated his remarkable career.

Before the first pitch, however, Clarke was softspoken and mild—even to umpires. One afternoon,

he laid a gentle hand on the shoulder of Bill Klem and informed the arbiter, "Bill, you're a model umpire."

The "Old Arbitrator" acknowledged the tribute. It coincided with his own opinion. That night, Klem's attitude hardened perceptibly. When Clarke presented his lineup the next day, he was summarily kicked off the premises by Klem. In the interim, the umpire had discovered that "model," in Clarke's dictionary, meant a "small imitation of the real thing."

Along with mixing it up physically and verbally, Clarke wasn't above toying with opponents' psyches, either.

"Everybody knows about Ty Cobb filing his spikes, but that was a common practice when I was in Louisville (for whom Clarke first played more than a decade before Cobb's arrival in the majors)," the Pirates' manager said. "When we would visit those dauntless (Baltimore) Orioles for an important series, it was common to see the whole gang of them lined up in the dugout filing their spikes, saying nothing. They looked like a bunch of murderous mechanics.

"We got onto that, and went them one better. We went to Baltimore one time and all our fellows lined up, with pieces of paper which they sliced on their spikes, to show the razor-keenness."

In addition to Clarke, Pittsburgh's 1902 outfield consisted of Ginger Beaumont in center field and Lefty Davis and then Wagner in right.

Beaumont had joined the Pirates in 1899 after only one year of minor league seasoning.

"Manager (Bill) Watkins tried me in left field, which was the sun field," Beaumont said of his first experience with a big-league club. "The balls bounced off my chest, my knees and all over me and I was in and out of the lineup, unable to get going. There was good competition for the outfield positions, too, and I began to worry that I wouldn't make the grade. . . ."

Three months into his rookie season and the day before his 23rd birthday, Beaumont's fretting came to an end. Playing against Philadelphia, Beaumont went on a six-hit spree—although he didn't exactly pulverize the ball.

"Well, that was my biggest day," the lefthanded batter said. "I had made six hits and scored six runs in six times at bat on four bunts and two topped balls . . . I was 'in' with the Pittsburgh team. I got my confidence and went on to hit .351 for the season."

Beaumont's game was in high gear in 1902.

"Beaumont will lead the National League in batting . . . if he continues to bunt," a correspondent for The Sporting News had reported at midseason. "There is no one . . . who can put the ball down on either side of the plate as neatly as the center fielder can, and Willie Keeler is not excepted. When Beaumont is bunting, he adds 25 percent to his strength as a batsman." When the '02 season ground to a halt, the N.L. batting champion was Clarence Howeth Beaumont, possessor of a .357 average.

Lefty Davis, sidelined in July because of a broken ankle, had seen steady duty in right field before the injury and he batted .291 for the '02 Pirates. When Davis, who had been obtained from Brooklyn during the 1901 season, went down, it necessitated the return of Wagner to his old right-field job and the insertion of Wid Conroy into the shortstop slot.

Wagner, who primarily divided his playing time between shortstop, the outfield and first base in 1902 (but even pitched in one game and appeared at second base in another), finished the campaign with a .329 batting average, the same figure he would own as a career mark when his playing days ended in 1917.

Honus' early major league status as an outfielder "meant nothing," according to Clarke.

"He was a player who could do everything, play anywhere and be a star," said Clarke, reflecting later in life on the multi-talents of his prize athlete. "You ought to have seen him play first. Just like Hal Chase, like a cat. Pitch? He threw the blooper ball long before Rip Sewell was old enough to throw. One day . . . Wagner offered to pitch. He . . . had them breaking their backs trying to connect. . . .

"If you got Wagner on base and told him to steal, I never once saw him caught when he had two or three pitches to pick his spot. His hop at the start was the secret. He was going before anybody had an idea.

"Honus made 'em change that rule which let a batter step across the plate to hit. He was a right-hander who could step over and drill an outside pitch over the first baseman's head for a three-bagger."

Effusive in his praise of Wagner, Clarke had just the right cast of characters to complement his superstar.

Conroy, nicknamed "Wid" as a youngster for reasons that he himself could not explain, proved a valuable fill-in after Davis' injury made Wagner an outfielder once more. A member of the American League's Milwaukee club in 1901, Conroy, in a reversal of the ongoing N.L.-to-A.L. flight, jumped to Pittsburgh for the 1902 season.

"I had a good offer from Pittsburgh, so I went there, and it was a good move," Conroy said, "for we won the pennant in a runaway . . . I got a big kick that year for I played about 80 games at shortstop (95, actually), although I couldn't carry Hans' glove."

With Leach, Wagner and Conroy holding down the left side of the infield, the opposite flank was manned by Claude Ritchey and Kitty Bransfield.

Ritchey had made his major league debut in 1897 with Cincinnati, then was acquired by Dreyfuss' organization. Like Leach, he was a mighty mite. The Pirates' 5-6½, 167-pound second baseman was a .275 contributor at the plate for the 1902 Pirates.

Bransfield was a native of Worcester, Mass., a baseball hotbed at the turn of the century. In his youth, the first baseman was known as "Kid" or "Kiddy." When a young reporter mistakenly referred to him as "Kitty," the name stuck. After three professional seasons, the last two of which were spent with his hometown Worcester team, Bransfield joined the Pirates in 1901. In '02, he batted a creditable .308 for Clarke's club.

Clarke divided the catching duties almost equally among Harry Smith, who worked 49 games; Chief Zimmer, who caught in 40 games, and Jack O'Connor, who was behind the plate in 39 games.

A capable receiver, Smith lacked batting punch. He hit under .200 in 1902. O'Connor, a major leaguer as long ago as 1887 when he joined Cincinnati of the American Association, was a competent hitter at age 35, as his .294 average would indicate. Zimmer, 41, was in his 18th big-league season. Most of his career had been spent with Cleveland's National League club, for whom he teamed with Cy Young to form one of the game's most prominent batteries.

Remarkable as the 1902 Pirates were in the leadership of Clarke, the all-around brilliance of Wagner and the outstanding contributions of others, it was the pitching staff, probably more than any other single component, that enabled the team to dominate its contemporaries and roll to 103 victories, a record total in the 27-year history of the National League.

Jack Chesbro clearly was the ace of the staff, tossing eight shutouts and winning 28 games. Jesse Tannehill and Deacon Phillippe each posted 20 victories, while Ed Doheny's 16-4 ledger and Sam Leever's 15-7 mark also stood out. Chesbro, Phillippe and Leever were righthanders, Tannehill and Doheny lefthanders.

Nicknamed Happy Jack because of his ineradicable smile, the 5-9 Chesbro had been acquired by the Pirates midway through the 1899 season from Richmond after compiling a 17-4 record for the minor league team. After posting a 6-10 mark for Pittsburgh in the second half of that year, Chesbro went 14-12 in 1900 and won 21 of 30 decisions in 1901. In 1902, he was on top of his game with a blazing fastball and a devastating spitball, a combination that helped him win 12 consecutive decisions in one stretch.

Tannehill, who had made his major league debut with Cincinnati in 1894, joined the Pirates in 1897 and he won 85 games for the Bucs from 1898 through 1901. Besides being formidable on the mound, he was effective at the plate (as his .291 batting mark in 1902 shows).

Tannehill, another little man in the Pirates' pitching corps at 5-8, completed 23 of the 24 games he started in 1902 and had decisions in all 26 of his mound appearances (he lost six times).

"They handed you a ball," Tannehill said, "and you started and finished a game."

Further reflecting on his baseball career, Tannehill added: "I never had much of anything. I was just lucky enough always to be on good teams." Quite likely, the good teams always were lucky enough to have Tannehill on their side. The Kentuckian fashioned a career winning percentage of .622 in the majors.

Control was a strong suit for Phillippe, who walked only 32 batters in 273 innings in 1902 (and would issue only 29 bases on balls in 288 innings the next year). Particularly pleased if matched against the opposition's No. 1 pitcher, Deacon owned 80 victories in his four big-league seasons when the curtain came down on the '02 campaign.

Leever, known as the "Schoolmaster" because of his off-season occupation, taught big-league hitters a thing or two while pitching masterfully for the Pirates for more than a decade. Before he left the majors after the 1910 season, he had rung up such records as 25-7, 20-5 and 22-7.

Doheny, who had reached the majors with the New York Giants in 1895 and been obtained from the Giants during the 1901 season, had the best year of his career in 1902. Only two years earlier, he had lost 14 of 18 decisions for the New Yorkers.

"I take some credit for Doheny's fine record with us," Clarke said. "At New York, Ed was always wild, and the Giants were willing to sell him to us. Ed was supposed to have one of the best curves a lefty ever had, but he simply could not get it over.

"When we bought him, I watched him pitch in practice. I said, 'Ed, let's pitch my way for a while and see if we cannot control that wildness. Give up the curve and throw only the fastball.'

"That overhand fastball was a beauty, and as I had suspected, Doheny didn't need a curve . . . . "

Doheny, beset with personal problems, saw his major league career end after the 1903 season. He was not yet 29 years old.

In the midst of their widespread prosperity on the diamond, the Pirates were being targeted by subversive forces. Agents of the American League waved princely inducements before Pittsburgh players. Charles Comiskey, owner of the Chicago White Sox, offered to make Honus Wagner the

Righthander Deacon Phillippe was one of three 20-game winners for Pittsburgh's 1902 National League powerhouse.

highest-paid player in the game. The Dutchman turned him down. Others were more easily enticed.

Irresistible lures came from New York. Ban Johnson, energetic president of the American League, made no secret of the fact he planned to locate a franchise in Manhattan in 1903 under the managerial direction of Clark Griffith, the longtime pitching star who was completing his second season as manager of the junior circuit's Chicago club.

Either by accident or design, word leaked out in the closing weeks of the 1902 season that Tannehill, O'Connor and Davis intended to jump to the American League in 1903. Tannehill's role in all this proved especially puzzling to the Pittsburgh correspondent for The Sporting News.

"... It is a mystery to me what spoiled Jesse," the newsman reported. "When he first came to Pittsburgh he was an ambitious young man with a cheerful word for everybody. He floated into town one rainy morning minus an umbrella and with shoes decidedly the worse for wear and was delighted to accept the shelter that a reporter offered him.

"All that he (Barney Dreyfuss) asked Tannehill and the others to do was to come to him with any offers they received from the American League and give him a chance to match the figure. Was that too much to expect of men who were wearing hats he bought as presents and accepted his cigars, theater and railroad tickets and hundreds of dollars of gift money with merely a nod of the head?"

Discord and forthcoming defections notwithstanding, the Pirates had put together an amazing season in 1902. In fact, their 27½-game championship margin has barely been challenged over the years in the major leagues. The 1936 New York Yankees and the 1983 White Sox posed the biggest threats, the Yanks storming to the American League pennant by a 19½-game margin and the White Sox romping to the American League West championship by exactly 20 games.

That the 1903 National League race would be a tougher row to hoe for the Pittsburgh Pirates was a foregone conclusion. Not only had Tannehill, O'Connor and Davis jumped to the American League's New York Highlanders, so, too, had Chesbro and Conroy. (In 1904, Chesbro would set an American League record for victories with 41.)

The '03 Bucs persevered, however. They even prospered, thanks in particular to the play of Wagner, Clarke, Beaumont, Leever and Phillippe. Wagner captured his second National League batting championship with a .355 average, Clarke hit .351 and Beaumont contributed a .341 mark. Leever and Phillippe combined for 49 victories. The result was a third straight pennant for the Pirates, who wound up 6½ games in front of the Giants.

The entire season was conducted under amicable conditions. Before the beginning of the campaign,

the warring leagues had entered into a peace agreement that helped pave the way for the champions of the two circuits to meet in a postseason series even without official sanction.

Details of the best-of-nine showdown were hammered out by Dreyfuss and Henry J. Killilea, president of the Boston Americans. While Pittsburgh won three of the first four games, Boston proceeded to win four straight in what is acknowledged as the first modern World Series.

The triumph by the upstart Boston club failed to tarnish the performance turned in by Phillippe, who pitched five complete Series games in 13 days and notched all three of the Pirates' victories.

The Pirates' accomplishments on a team basis would falter in the years ahead (Pittsburgh would win only one pennant, in 1909, in the next 21 years), but Wagner's presence made the Pittsburgh club a special attraction.

"We traveled not as 'Pittsburgh' but as 'Wagner,'" Clarke said of Honus' peak years in the majors. "Honus got the billing, just as the Yankees went around later with Babe Ruth ...." Which was easy enough to understand, considering that Wagner would win a total of eight N.L. batting titles (seven of them in the 1903-1911 time frame) and then become one of the five original choices for induction into baseball's Hall of Fame.

In 1902, Clarke's National League club was still known as "Pittsburgh," however. The team also was known as the greatest runaway pennant-winner in big-league history—a claim to fame that remained intact more than 80 years later.

1902
FINAL STANDING

Club	W.	L.	Pct.	GB.
Pittsburgh	103	36	.741	——
Brooklyn	75	63	.543	27½
Boston	73	64	.533	29

BATTERS

Pos.	Player	G.	HR.	RBI.	B.A.
1B	Kitty Bransfield	100	0	69	.308
2B	Claude Ritchey	114	2	55	.275
SS	Wid Conroy	95	1	47	.241
3B	Tommy Leach	135	6	85	.280
OF	Fred Clarke	114	2	53	.321
	Ginger Beaumont	131	0	67	.357
	Honus Wagner	137	3	91	.329
C	Harry Smith	49	0	12	.187

OTHER CONTRIBUTORS (20+ Games): Jimmy Burke, Lefty Davis, Jack O'Connor, Chief Zimmer.

PITCHERS

Thr.	Pitcher	G.	W.	L.	ERA
R	Jack Chesbro	34	28	6	2.17
L	Jesse Tannehill	26	20	6	1.95
R	Deacon Phillippe	29	20	9	2.05
L	Ed Doheny	21	16	4	2.54
R	Sam Leever	24	15	7	2.39

Number 16

Yankees Overcome Sadness, Adversity

Three of the biggest names in New York, Joe DiMaggio (left), Lou Gehrig (right) and Mayor Fiorello La Guardia, share a moment during the 1938 World Series.

The year was one of the saddest in New York Yankee history, though the sadness was tempered by the inescapable enthusiasm that resulted from another World Series championship.

It began in mourning as the Yankees and all of New York paid their last respects to Colonel Jacob Ruppert, the longtime owner who had opened his heart to baseball and his wallet to the task of building a legend. When Ruppert died January 13, 1939, at his New York City home, the baseball fans of Gotham and all America bade farewell to the wealthy brewer who had brought the game into a new era with his lavish expenditures for young talent and his astute development of a complex farm system.

Under Ruppert, the Yankees had developed into a powerhouse of the first magnitude. From 1921 through '38, they had captured seven World Series titles in 10 tries. Ruppert's No. 1 gift to baseball was the immortal Babe Ruth, who changed the course of the game with his colorful personality and mighty, home run-producing swings. Two other special gifts were Lou Gehrig and Joe DiMaggio.

So it was with a black cloud hanging over their heads that the Yankees prepared for the 1939 season. The 1938 Bronx Bombers had captured their record-setting third straight Series championship and hopes were high for a fourth. Ruth was long gone from the New York scene, but the talented DiMaggio was entering only his fourth season and the seemingly indestructible Iron Horse, Gehrig, remained as a link to the Yankee powerhouses of the late 1920s.

Gehrig, a human Gibraltar at first base, had been a tireless sentinel at the gateway and his amazing record for durability had reached 2,122 consecutive games played by the close of the '38 campaign. The New York native was rugged of frame and seemingly capable of rambling on into the forseeable future. Gehrig was 35 when the 1939 season got underway; within weeks he was a national symbol of tragedy.

The precise moment when suspicions first arose over the state of Gehrig's health is unrecorded. But it is extremely unlikely that strong apprehensions were expressed in 1938. For an athlete of Lou's age, there could be nothing ominous in statistics that showed 29 home runs, 114 RBIs and a .295 batting average. Sure, the average broke a string of 12 straight .300-plus seasons and the homer total was his first under 30 in nine years. But he did reach the 100-RBI plateau for the 13th straight season and allowances had to be made for advancing years. Muscular coordination does deteriorate. Decline is inescapable, even for Lou Gehrig.

Gehrig's physical condition was among the least of Manager Joe McCarthy's concerns when the Yankees gathered in St. Petersburg for the start of 1939 spring training. More pressing problems confronted Marse Joe as he prepared his team for a run at baseball history. First base, he assured himself, would be handled in the same incomparable fashion it had been handled since 1925—by H.L. Gehrig.

That picture changed abruptly when the exhibition season opened. Observers started shooting quizzical glances at one another. Granted, Gehrig was a notoriously slow starter in Florida, but he never before had appeared so inept. His bat no longer snapped. His fielding was no longer crisp. He remained the same 210-pound Adonis with the familiar No. 4 on his back, but there the resemblance ended.

Lou himself attributed his weak start to poor judgment.

"I spent the off-season riding in a car and sitting in a boat," he explained. "I rode to get a newspaper two blocks away. I should have been jogging and . . . come to camp with my legs fit."

Late in March, the Yankee correspondent for The Sporting News informed his readers: "Joe McCarthy has only one worry and his name is Henry Louis Gehrig. Gehrig never was a very remarkable March performer. He may snap out of it, or he may not. It would be an awful blow to the game and to the Yanks if the great first baseman had to slip out of the lineup. But they all come to the end of the road, don't they?"

When March turned into April, the Yankees turned their footsteps northward for the start of the regular season. Almost daily, McCarthy was pestered by reporters who wanted to know about "the Gehrig situation." Marse Joe was unable to shed light on the matter. He could only express hope that whatever ailed the Iron Horse was temporary.

When the Yankees opened the season with a 2-0 shutout of Boston, Gehrig was at first base. Hopes that a lively home crowd would restore his old vigor were rudely dispelled as he grounded into two double plays. Defensively, he was charged with an error for losing the ball on a tag play.

Optimism over Gehrig's future was rekindled a few days later in a victory over the Philadelphia Athletics. He lined a single to right field "in the old-time Gehrig style" and looped a Texas Leaguer to left. He tried to stretch the second hit into a double but was thrown out standing up.

Gehrig's apparent revival was a cruel hoax. He managed only four singles and was hitting .143. On April 30, when the Yanks lost to the Washington Senators, 3-2, Gehrig went 0 for 4. Twice he had RBI opportunities and failed.

The big first baseman was equally unimpressive in the field. One play in particular sent a message loud and clear to the determined veteran. "Buddy Myer slapped one down to me," he said. "In other years I would have stuck the ball into my back

The man on the spot in early 1939 was first baseman Babe Dahlgren, who was being asked to replace a legend.

pocket. But it was a hard play for me and I tossed to (Johnny) Murphy, who covered the bag.

"When I returned to the bench, the boys said, 'Great play, Lou.' I said to myself, 'Heavens, has it reached that stage?'"

As the Yankees rolled toward Detroit for the initial stop on their first western trip, Gehrig made a momentous decision. Before the game of May 2, he notified McCarthy he was withdrawing from the lineup because he "was no good to the club, myself, the game or the fans."

Marse Joe accepted the verdict with reluctance. "Take a few days off," he counseled. "I'll play Babe Dahlgren, but remember the job is yours."

In his role as team captain, Gehrig continued to carry the lineup card to home plate and discuss ground rules with the umpires. He carried it to the plate at Briggs Stadium on May 2. The Detroit fans gave him a rousing ovation.

Dahlgren later recalled the mood on the club the first day of Lou's idleness.

"When Lou reached the dugout," recounted the Californian, "he headed for the drinking fountain. It was a long time before he looked up, with watery eyes, and the players looked away to yell at the Tigers in this awkward moment. I guess they were all glassy-eyed. Lou wiped his eyes with one of the big fluffy towels while nobody looked, and the

game was on."

Ellsworth Tenney Dahlgren was a man destined to make his mark as the peripheral sidelight to an historic event. The 26-year-old San Francisco native had been the regular first baseman for Boston in 1935 and was traded to the Yanks after the Red Sox obtained Jimmie Foxx from Philadelphia.

This Babe was a superb fielder and mediocre righthanded hitter, lacking in one traditional Yankee characteristic—power. He was a man looking for a chance to play and on this occasion he was in the right place at the right time.

On the day he supplanted Gehrig, Dahlgren stepped out of character, drilling a double and homer and driving in three runs in a 22-2 mauling of the Tigers. As the final-season statistics would later prove, that was an unusual outburst.

For the next six weeks, Gehrig sat quietly in the dugout, pondering his murky future and watching Dahlgren patrol the area that had been exclusively his for more than a decade. He did not return to action until June 12, when he played three innings of an exhibition game at Kansas City. If anyone had expected the protracted rest to provide a cure, he was doomed to disappointment.

Gehrig remained a pathetic figure, exerting enormous effort with minimal results. In his only at-bat, he dribbled a puny roller to the infield. At first base, he let a ground ball elude him and dropped a low throw. That evening, Lou Gehrig bade farewell to his teammates and boarded a flight for Rochester, Minn., where he was scheduled to undergo an intensive examination at the Mayo Clinic.

Through the days of tests and endless waiting, Gehrig retained his cheerfulness. On June 19, his 36th birthday, he received the medical report. "I thought something was greatly wrong," he said when doctors revealed the nature of his illness. Later, he autographed an inexpensive baseball for a youthful admirer at the airport and headed back to New York.

On June 21, Gehrig returned to the familiar surroundings of Yankee Stadium. He handed copies of his medical report to General Manager Edward G. Barrow and McCarthy. According to one witness, "Barrow, a hard-boiled fellow, was shocked as if he had been hit between the eyes. McCarthy's lips tightened and his face froze, as it does when he is affected by trouble."

Before the report was made public, Gehrig entered the clubhouse, where he was greeted warmly. He chatted amiably with teammates and posed willingly for photographers. When game time approached, he carried out his captain's chores at home plate. He then returned to the dugout and watched the Yankees defeat the White Sox.

The Mayo diagnosis sounded a death knell for the Iron Horse. Gehrig, it said, was suffering from amyotrophic lateral sclerosis, a rare disease that affects the motor pathways and cells of the central nervous system. "The nature of this trouble," wrote a Mayo specialist, "makes it such that Mr. Gehrig will be unable to continue his active participation as a baseball player, inasmuch as it is advisable that he conserve his muscular energy. . . ."

Gehrig played no more baseball in 1939—or ever again. He suited up daily and fulfilled his duties as captain. Afterward he sat in the dugout, pondering in stoic calm the misfortune that had struck him without fair warning.

The routine was interrupted July 4 in one of baseball's most poignant moments. It was "Lou Gehrig Day" at Yankee Stadium. Political dignitaries and assorted celebrities assembled on the field between games of a doubleheader to pay tribute to the Yankees' fallen warrior. Of all those present, none delighted Gehrig more than his teammates from the mighty Yankees aggregation of 1927—Waite Hoyt, Bob Meusel, Mark Koenig, Bob Shawkey, Earle Combs, George Pipgras, Benny Bengough, Joe Dugan, Tony Lazzeri, Herb Pennock, Wally Schang and Babe Ruth.

There was special significance in the appearance of Ruth. Some years before, the superstars had become estranged through Babe's public criticism of Lou's determination to play every game. All that bitterness evaporated when Ruth threw a massive arm around Gehrig's neck in a public display of affection as 61,808 fans roared their blessings.

When the last tribute had been paid, Gehrig took the microphone. He expressed his gratitude to those who had helped mold his Hall of Fame career. Then he moistened the eyes of everyone in the Stadium, including his own. "Fans, for the past two weeks you have been reading about a bad break I got. Yet today I consider myself the luckiest man on the face of the earth . . . I have an awful lot to live for."

Within two years, the best first baseman of his age, perhaps all ages, would be gone. The records he left were imperishable, as was the name attached to the disease that had cut him down before his time. As medical science sought a cure for the disease through the next half century, posterity knew it as "Lou Gehrig's disease."

As the Iron Horse slipped from view in 1939, new names and faces leaped into prominence. Youngsters like Dahlgren, Joe Gordon, Charlie Keller, Tommy Henrich, Atley Donald, Steve Sundra and Marius Russo were asked to carry on in the great Yankee tradition. And with the ghost of Jacob Ruppert and the legendary aura of Lou Gehrig inspiring their every move, how could they miss?

To Dahlgren went the toughest assignment: Replace the great Gehrig at first base. It was too much to ask of anybody.

But Dahlgren gave it his best shot. The 6-foot,

One of the highlights of 'Lou Gehrig Day' on July 4 was the hearty greeting Babe Ruth bestowed on his former teammate.

190-pounder had been disappointed before the 1936 season when, assured that he would be Boston's starting first baseman, the Red Sox instead traded for Foxx and forced Dahlgren to spend most of the season with Syracuse of the International League.

When he was acquired by the Yankees in 1937 to back up Gehrig, he looked at the move with mixed emotions. But not as mixed as the day he was told to replace the Iron Horse.

"I sat in front of my locker, checking the leather lace in the web of my glove," Dahlgren said later while describing the circumstances under which he was given the starting nod. "Suddenly, I felt a tap on my shoulder and I looked up into the eyes of Art Fletcher, the greatest coach I ever knew in baseball. He was close to me, real close, close enough to count the whiskers on his chiseled chin as he said softly, 'Babe, you're playing first base today.'

"I was stunned. The only thing this meant to me at that moment was that after 14 uninterrupted years of play and a fantastic total of 2,130 consecutive games, Lou Gehrig was not going to play . . . I was wishing I was not there."

After it became apparent that Gehrig would not be returning, however, Dahlgren settled into the position. His steady defense helped ease the pain of Gehrig's loss and he contributed 18 homers and 89

One of the highlights of the 1939 season was the introduction of slugging rookie Charlie Keller
(left) to a Yankees outfield corps that also included Joe DiMaggio (center) and Tommy Henrich.

RBIs, though he only batted .235.

Next to Dahlgren on the Yankee infield resided Joseph Lowell Gordon, the acrobatic young second baseman who had replaced the popular and productive Tony Lazzeri the year before. That, too, was a tall order that Gordon handled very well.

Besides hitting 25 home runs and driving in 97 runs, the rookie covered second base like few men in baseball history. The 5-10, 180-pounder could stop and start faster than anybody, he jumped like he had springs in his legs and he covered more ground than many thought humanly possible.

Washington Manager Bucky Harris, an outstanding second baseman himself in earlier years, gazed in wonder at the brilliant newcomer. "If the outfielders behind Gordon weren't so great," he said, "Joe would make the darndest catches an infielder ever made. He'd play second base, short center field and part of right field."

Billy Sullivan, former Detroit catcher who moved to the National League, seconded Harris' praise. "You don't know what a pleasure it is to get out of Gordon's league," Sullivan said. "The plays he makes break a batter's heart."

Gordon's acrobatic style was the result of early gymnastic training. The youngster was a natural at almost every sport he tried and also excelled in tap dancing, tumbling and performing on the horizontal bar. But Gordon's talents weren't limited to athletics. At age 14, the Oregon native performed as a violinist with the Portland symphony orchestra.

Gordon was discovered playing shortstop in an industrial league by Bill Essick, the same scout who brought Joe DiMaggio and the Yankees together. After signing with the Yanks, he worked his way up as a second baseman.

One of Gordon's biggest charms was his gay approach to life and business. Nothing was a matter of life or death, which helps explain his calm demeanor and his cavalier approach to hitting.

"Hitting? What is there to it," he once said. "You swing and, if you hit the ball, there it goes. Ah, but fielding. There's rhythm, finesse, teamwork and balance. I love it."

Throughout his career, that attitude would plague him. He always produced home runs and RBIs, but only once did he manage to hit over .300. While that never seemed to bother McCarthy or Gordon's teammates, critics had a field day.

The youngster and his shortstop partner, 28-year-old veteran Frank Crosetti, hit it off instantly. Besides performing as one of the best double-play combinations in the game, they shared the same temperament and formed a fast friendship.

Crosetti, who had batted .263 in '38 while giving his usual consistent performance afield, also had been close to Lazzeri, though the two had completely different personalities.

Crosetti shared the left side of the infield with Red Rolfe, another veteran of the Yankees' three

Tony Lazzeri (left), the former Yankee second baseman-turned-Chicago Cub, poses with his New York successor, Joe Gordon.

straight championship teams. The 30-year-old Rolfe, considered one of the smartest players and top gamers in baseball, was coming off a .311 campaign in which he had scored 132 runs while driving in 80.

Ironically, Crosetti and Rolfe, who had been paired on the left side of the Yankee infield since 1935, were preparing for what would be their last *big* seasons with the Bronx Bombers. Though both would continue to perform beyond the '39 campaign, they would never do it again with the success of past years.

The incomparable DiMaggio was the middle man of the Yankees' solid young outfield. Flanking the Yankee Clipper was George Selkirk, the man who replaced Babe Ruth in 1935, and third-year man Henrich. By early August, a slumping Henrich had given way to Keller, a 22-year-old rookie, in right field.

DiMaggio had proven to all doubters that he was the real thing when he arrived in 1936. By 1939, the 24-year-old already was a veteran of three Yankee championship teams and had checked in each season with exceptional numbers.

In 1936, he hit .323 with 29 homers and 125 RBIs. In '37, he powered his way to a .346 mark with a league-leading 46 home runs and 167 RBIs. His '38 totals were .324, 32 and 140.

He quickly had established his credentials as the best center fielder in baseball and he had showed only one minor weakness—an inability to stay healthy. And that presented a real problem for McCarthy as the '39 campaign began. Gehrig already was showing signs of failing health when DiMaggio tore some leg muscles in late April. Doctors said DiMaggio would miss 10 days. He was out for a month.

Henrich took over in center and Keller began his long reign in right field as the "second coming of Babe Ruth."

Keller, a son of the Maryland soil, was an amazing human specimen. He gazed upon the world from behind thick black, beetling eyebrows and had big, sloping shoulders, a thick neck, muscular and hairy forearms and an arm-swinging, stalking gait. He reminded teammate Lefty Gomez of an anthropoidal creature. When Gomez, the Yanks' resident wit caught his first glimpse of Keller, he uttered one of his best-remembered quips. "Did our scouts sign him or trap him?" he asked.

Gomez also labeled the young slugger "King Kong," a moniker that seemed to fit his appearance and the vicious lefthanded swing that brought fear to many a pitcher. Once, Keller sprained his wrist while taking a cut and he nursed the injury for more than a year. He was so powerful that one teammate alleged that even his sweat had muscles.

But in reality, Keller was a gentle, soft-spoken

The left side of the Yankees' 1939 infield remained in the veteran hands of third baseman Red Rolfe (left) and shortstop Frankie Crosetti.

youngster who had come to be a Yankee through good, old-fashioned hustle. He had compiled gaudy statistics at the University of Maryland and was demolishing pitching in a fast North Carolina semi-pro league in 1936 when the Yankees told scout Paul Krichell to "drop everything and get Keller." That was a pretty tall order because several other scouts already were hot on the youngster's trail.

Krichell, who was in Buffalo at the time of the call, caught a late-night train heading south. En route, he stopped at the Keller home in Middletown, Md. Because Charlie was a minor, his father's signature was necessary to make any contract binding. Krichell obtained the elder Keller's signature and proceeded to Kinston, N.C.

Arriving at 6 a.m., Krichell roused Gene McCann, the Yankee representative on the scene, and insisted on seeing Keller immediately. They went to the youngster's boardinghouse, got him to slip into shoes, pants and shirt, and walked him around the block, telling him the many benefits afforded by the Yankee organization. Keller liked the sales pitch and finally agreed to sign with one stipulation: He wanted to designate the club with which he would make his professional debut. Krichell consented and while all the other scouts slept, he walked off with the prize.

Keller chose to begin with Newark of the International League and proceeded to hit .353 and .365 while driving in 217 runs in 1937 and '38. He was the league batting champion and The Sporting News' Minor League Player of the Year in '37.

That set the stage for his long-awaited debut with the Yankees. But a pulled thigh muscle slowed him during spring training and kept him on the bench as the season got underway. When DiMaggio went down, however, Keller got his chance. The Keller express was sidelined briefly when DiMaggio returned to the lineup at the end of May and Henrich moved back to right, but Keller finally replaced Henrich in August.

That was only a temporary setback for the unflappable Henrich, who throughout his career was the epitome of role players. A talented outfielder with a strong arm, Henrich came to be known as the Yankees' "Old Reliable" because of his penchant for hitting in the clutch. Though his numbers never were overwhelming, Henrich's value to the Yankees was understood.

Henrich, a native of Massillon, O., originally was a member of the Cleveland Indians organization. But when irregularities were discovered in how the youngster was signed, Commissioner Kenesaw M. Landis made him a free agent and the Yankees signed him for a $20,000 bonus. McCarthy showed faith in Henrich in 1938 by making him the regular left fielder for the defending world champs and the youngster responded by pounding 22 homers, including five in a three-game span.

But when Henrich slumped to nine home runs in '39, he eventually relinquished his starting job. He would return.

The other Yankee starters also were old and reliable—by baseball standards. Selkirk still was swinging a mean bat, having moved from right field to left, and the veteran Bill Dickey still was capable of putting on catching clinics while swinging his lethal, productive bat.

At age 31, the lefthanded-hitting Selkirk was in the stretch of a productive, five-year run that began in 1935 when he replaced Ruth. The 31-year-old Dickey, another lefthanded swinger, also was making his stretch run in an outstanding career that by 1940 would begin a steep, downward slide.

But 1939 was to be memorable. These two veterans were to hit .306 and .302, respectively, while contributing 45 homers and 206 RBIs to the Yankee cause.

Entrusted to Dickey's excellent tutelage was a pitching staff that offered a nice blend of youth and experience.

The staff aces were righthander Red Ruffing and Lefty Gomez, who for eight years had formed one of the best 1-2 punches in the American League. Ruffing, was a workhorse who twice had lost 20 games during his early days with the Boston Red Sox. He turned it around with the Yankees, however, and by 1939 was working on extending his string of three straight 20-win seasons.

Ruffing was a bulldog competitor and a master needler, but nothing compared to Gomez, the resident master of the clubhouse quip. He had a tremendous gift for keeping his teammates loose and a powerful left arm that left opponents scratching their heads.

Entering the '39 campaign, Gomez had recorded 39 victories in the last two seasons and boasted four 20-win seasons in his nine-year career. He also was 6-0 in World Series competition and 3-0 in All-Star games.

But Lefty will be remembered as much for his one-liners and funny stories as his pitching success. One such story, about former roommate DiMaggio, was told years after Gomez had retired.

"He (DiMaggio) used to read Superman," Lefty said with a smile. "This is the truth. Know what Joe used to do? We'd stop by the newsstand in any hotel and he'd nudge me and point to a copy of Superman. That meant for me to buy it for him.

"Our great and shining star wouldn't be caught dead buying a comic book, especially Superman. But it was all right for Gomez to tell the clerk that *he* wanted Superman. I asked him about it one day.

" 'They'd recognize me and tell everybody that DiMaggio reads Superman.' was Joe's reply.

" 'How about me?' I asked him.

" 'They won't recognize you,' Joe said. 'Anyway, you look like the type.' "

Joining Ruffing and Gomez in McCarthy's starting rotation were veteran righthanders Bump Hadley and Monte Pearson, both holdovers from the three straight championship teams. Others who saw starting duty were rookies Atley Donald and Marius Russo and Steve Sundra and Oral Hildebrand. Johnny Murphy remained as the Yankee bullpen stopper.

Donald was a 6-1 righthander from Downsville, La., who made baseball history in his first season with the Yankees. The 28-year-old won his first 12 decisions to open the season, breaking the former record of 10 for first-year pitchers.

The flame-throwing Donald had been a student at Louisiana Tech, where he starred in basketball, baseball and as a discus thrower. When a neighbor offered to arrange a tryout with the Red Sox, Donald declined, saying he preferred to cast his lot with the Yankees.

In 1934, Donald quit college and traveled to St. Petersburg, where he worked as a grocery store clerk for several months until the Yankees arrived for spring training. He managed to get a tryout and was signed to a contract in the low minors. By 1937, he had worked his way up to Newark, where he won 19 games in 21 decisions for a team that captured the International League pennant by 25½ games.

A newcomer to the Yankees' veteran 1939 pitching staff was righthander Atley Donald, a 13-game winner.

Like Henrich, the righthanded Sundra had been a Cleveland farmhand. The Luxor, Pa., native was acquired via trade in 1936 and ran off 11 straight wins in 1939 before bowing on the next-to-last day of the season.

Russo was a 24-year-old southpaw when he was plucked off the Newark roster in June 1939. A native New Yorker, he was a student at Long Island University when he signed with the Yankee organization. Russo threw a blistering fastball that often was compared to the blazer thrown by Cleveland's Bob Feller.

It was with this cast of characters that the Yankees opened their 1939 championship defense. And the early picture appeared bleak as first DiMaggio was sidelined with his leg injury and then Gehrig retired to the Yankee bench.

But the Yankee express didn't miss a beat.

The Bronx Bombers took over first place to stay May 11 with a victory over St. Louis. That completed the Yanks' first invasion of the West, on which they won 10 of 12 games, collected 142 hits and scored 104 runs.

DiMaggio still was recuperating when his teammates ran off 12 straight victories. The last link in that chain was a 7-3 victory over Cleveland in which Henrich, Dickey, Rolfe and Gordon hit home runs. The streak was broken when Detroit rookie Dizzy Trout pitched the Tigers to a 6-1 victory.

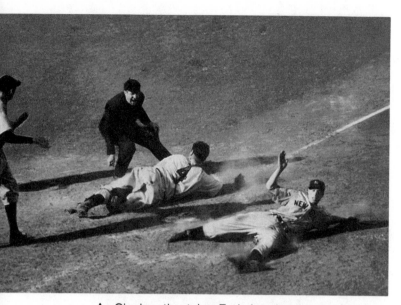

As Cincinnati catcher Ernie Lombardi 'snoozed' in Game 4 of the 1939 World Series, Joe DiMaggio slid safely into home.

By that time, however, the Yanks were well on their way to a 24-4 May record and DiMaggio was ready to return to the lineup. When the Yankee Clipper marked his May 27 return with a two-run pinch double that helped beat the A's, the rest of the American League was in real trouble.

On June 1, the Yanks led the A.L. by 6½ games and were yet to unleash their most withering assault of the season. That came later in the month at Shibe Park, where three years earlier the Yanks had bludgeoned the A's, 25-2.

In some respects, the carnage of June 28, 1939, was even more sanguinary. These truly were Bronx Bombers. Twice they blasted the A's into submission, rapping a record eight home runs in the opener and five more in the nightcap for a record two-game total of 13. The Yanks' 53 total bases in the opener set an A.L. record but missed the major league mark by two.

First-game homers were delivered by DiMaggio (2), Dahlgren (2), Dickey, Selkirk, Henrich and Gordon behind Pearson's seven-hit pitching. The final score—23-2. Nightcap homers were hit by Gordon (2), DiMaggio, Crosetti and Dahlgren. Gomez allowed only three hits in the 10-0 victory.

The St. Louis Browns, who were beaten 19 times in 22 games by the Yankees during the '39 season, felt the sting of the Bomber bats July 26. The Yankees tied a record by hitting safely and scoring in every inning as they throttled the cellar-dwellers, 14-1. Dickey led that charge with three home runs, a single and five RBIs.

The Yanks turned Shibe Park into a shambles again August 13 when they slaughtered the A's, 21-0, in the second game of a doubleheader. The whip-

ping might have been even more horrendous had darkness not halted the game after eight innings. DiMaggio spearheaded the 23-hit assault with four hits, two of them homers, and drove in five runs. Dickey and Ruffing, one of the best-hitting pitchers in baseball history, also chipped in with four hits. Ruffing allowed the A's only three.

Though the Tigers compiled one of the year's better records against the Yankees, it had some ghastly blemishes. On August 27, the Bombers exploded for a 10-run inning en route to a 13-3 victory over the Tigers. More blood flowed the next day. Paced by DiMaggio's two homers, single and eight RBIs, the Yankees pummeled the Tigers, 18-2.

DiMaggio was a terror on the club's final tour of the West. After hammering two triples and a single and driving in six runs at Cleveland on September 1, he showed a batting average of .490 with 26 RBIs for the first 12 games of the 14-game trek.

The Yankees returned east with a lead of 13½ games. They clinched their fourth pennant in as many years September 16 when Russo tamed the Tigers, 8-5. Rolfe struck the key blow with his 200th hit of the season—a base-clearing triple. When all was said and done, the Yanks owned a 106-45 record and a 17-game margin over Boston. The powerful Bombers had spent an amazing 156 of 166 days in sole possession of first place.

Despite missing the first month of the season, DiMaggio finished with a league-leading and career-high .381 average, 30 home runs and 126 RBIs. He was an easy winner over Boston's Foxx in Most Valuable Player balloting.

Three other Yankees topped the 100-RBI mark. Gordon drove in 111 runs while hitting 28 homers, Dickey drove in 105 to go with 24 homers and Selkirk 101 while blasting 21 homers. Keller batted .334 in 111 games while Rolfe finished at .329, Selkirk .306 and Dickey .302.

The Yankees as a team were equally impressive. They finished second to Boston with a .287 season average but led the league in runs (967), total bases (2,388), home runs (166) and RBIs (903). And Yankee pitchers held up their end, posting a league-best 3.31 earned-run average.

Though he couldn't qualify for the league ERA championship, Russo led all A.L. hurlers with a 2.41 mark in 116 innings. Sundra (2.75) finished third, Ruffing (2.94) sixth and Hadley (2.98), in his fourth season as a Yankee, seventh. Ruffing's 21 victories were topped only by Feller's 24. Gomez, who fought arm problems, struggled to a 12-8 record, but Donald finished 13-3 and Sundra 11-1 to pick up the slack.

The Yanks' World Series opponents were the Cincinnati Reds, who had won 97 games and the club's first pennant since 1919 in a heated battle with the Cardinals. Bill McKechnie's N.L. champions ranked second in the N.L. in batting and fielding and boasted two exceptional pitchers in Bucky Walters (27-11) and Paul Derringer (25-7). Frank McCormick, the Reds' 27-year-old first baseman, posted a .331 batting average, the second best in the league, while outfielder Ival Goodman (.323) was only slightly less productive.

When the 36th World Series opened at Yankee Stadium on October 4, a day when national headlines screamed of frenzied efforts to avert war in Europe, pitching assignments went to Ruffing and Derringer. The Yanks thrilled a gathering of 58,541 by winning, 2-1. Keller's triple and Dickey's single produced the deciding run in the ninth and rewarded Ruffing's four-hit effort.

Pearson, a 12-game winner during the regular season, was brilliant the next day. He allowed only two hits and totally handcuffed the Reds, 4-0, before 59,791 screaming fans. A one-out single by Ernie Lombardi in the eighth broke up Pearson's no-hit bid.

A torn side muscle knocked out Lefty Gomez after one inning of Game 3, but Hadley came on to gain credit for a 7-3 victory. Keller hit a pair of homers while DiMaggio and Dickey hit one apiece to make things easy for the veterans.

Game 4 was played at Crosley Field on a hot and sunny Sunday afternoon before 32,794 spectators. At the end of eight innings, things looked brighter for the Reds and electricity engulfed the capacity crowd. Their team led, 4-2, and Walters, pitching in relief of Derringer, had set the Bombers down in order in the eighth.

At that point, wrote a press-box occupant, "the Yankees simply terrified the Reds. Their very appearance was frightening as they came to bat with ruthless determination to make up the ground lost through an error which let the Reds make three unearned runs in the seventh and one that was untainted in the eighth. Under this pressure, the Reds wilted."

Singles by Keller, DiMaggio and Gordon, combined with a misplay by Billy Myers enabled the Yanks to knot the score in the ninth and set the stage for one of the wackiest plays in the history of the classic.

Crosetti opened the extra inning by coaxing a base on balls. He advanced on a sacrifice and took third when Myers committed his second error in as many innings, this time on Keller's ground ball. DiMaggio's single drove in Crosetti and when Goodman misplayed the ball in right field, Keller, running "as though chased by wild beasts," charged toward the plate. Runner and ball arrived simultaneously. Lombardi dropped the ball for the Reds' third miscue of the inning and was instantly knocked down by the onrushing Keller. As Ernie lay dazed behind the plate, with the ball just beyond his fingertips, DiMaggio slid in with the third run of the inning that nailed down a 7-4 win.

The bizarre climax wound up the Yankees' ninth straight victory in World Series competition—one against the Giants in 1937, four against the Cubs in '38 and four against the Reds. The Series championship was the fifth for McCarthy and his fourth in succession, a record.

Marse Joe was the center of attention in the crazy Yankee clubhouse. Everybody wanted to pump the manager's hand, particularly Keller. After the rookie had grasped the skipper's hand for the third time, McCarthy asked, "What do you want me to do, Charlie, kiss you?"

Had the outfielder answered in the affirmative, Marse Joe undoubtedly would have complied. Keller had performed valiantly in bringing the club to its lofty estate. King Kong led all Series regulars in runs (eight), hits (seven), home runs (three), RBIs (six) and batting average (.438).

How good were these Yankees? How did they compare with the "Murderers' Row" gang of 1927 that had won a record 110 games and obliterated the Pirates in a four-game World Series? Why not ask Edward Grant Barrow, the architect of Yankee dynasties in the 1920s and 1930s?

"This Yankee club is better than the much-talked-about 1927 outfit," proclaimed the general manager. "This club has great balance, brilliant youth, speed, pitching, everything."

1939
FINAL STANDING

Club	W.	L.	Pct.	GB.
New York	106	45	.702	—
Boston	89	62	.589	17

BATTERS

Pos.	Player	G.	HR.	RBI.	B.A.
1B	Babe Dahlgren	144	15	89	.235
2B	Joe Gordon	151	28	111	.284
SS	Frankie Crosetti	152	10	56	.233
3B	Red Rolfe	152	14	80	.329
OF	George Selkirk	128	21	101	.306
	Joe DiMaggio	120	30	126	.381
	Charlie Keller	111	11	83	.334
C	Bill Dickey	128	24	105	.302
UT	Tommy Henrich (of)	99	9	57	.277

OTHER CONTRIBUTORS (20+ Games): Jake Powell, Buddy Rosar.

PITCHERS

Thr.	Pitcher	G.	W.	L.	ERA
R	Red Ruffing	28	21	7	2.94
R	Atley Donald	24	13	3	3.71
L	Lefty Gomez	26	12	8	3.41
R	Monte Pearson	22	12	5	4.50
R	Bump Hadley	26	12	6	2.98
R	Steve Sundra	24	11	1	2.75
R	Oral Hildebrand	21	10	4	3.05

OTHER CONTRIBUTORS (20+ Games): Johnny Murphy, Marius Russo.

A Brave
New World

When it became clear that Manager George Stallings and newly acquired second baseman Johnny Evers would get along, the 1914 Boston Braves were on their way to one of the great success stories of baseball history.

George Tweedy Stallings was harsh and profane, gentle and compassionate. He could spit fire and brimstone like an arch demon or portray the cultured Southern planter, which he was in the winter months. He was master of the dictionary—abridged and unabridged. Whether muttering vile imprecations in the dugout or dripping perfumed phrases in the drawing room, he knew all the words.

In short, Stallings was the prototypical Dr. Jekyll and Mr. Hyde.

The handsome son of a former Confederate officer also was superstitious beyond belief. If a wagon load of empty barrels rumbled past the ball park on a day that Stallings' team won a game, the man-

ager arranged for another wagon similarly laden to pass the park the next day—and every day until his club suffered defeat.

Should Stallings be taking a drink of water when his team started a rally, he remained in that hunched-over position until the rally died.

As manager of the Boston Braves, Stallings also was fastidious. If a scrap of paper fluttered to earth near the dugout, someone was dispatched to remove it. If a bird alighted close by, utilityman Oscar Dugey could be counted on to send it aloft again with a well-aimed pebble from the huge supply he always carried in a pocket.

Stallings, whom players called "Chief" and "Big

Daddy," was a recognized strategist. In his unique way, he also was an excellent handler of men. If he fired a volley of invective at a hireling, it was only to goad the player into maximum effort.

Stallings' favorite term of denunciation was "bonehead." Few, indeed, were those who had escaped the label. One afternoon, when he needed a pinch-hitter, Chief called to Hank Gowdy, "Go up there and hit, bonehead." The catcher advanced to the bat rack, only to find it surrounded by teammates, all of whom had grown accustomed to the name.

When a player learned that Stallings harbored no animosity, that the skipper's style was only a means toward motivation, a lasting bond was formed.

Immobility was foreign to Stallings' nature. When a game was in progress, the manager constantly crossed and uncrossed his legs. Also, he would slide up and down the bench. By actual count, he wore out the seat from four pairs of trousers in a single season.

A native of Augusta, Ga., Stallings was a student at the College of Physicians and Surgeons in Baltimore and playing baseball in his idle hours when he was discovered by Harry Wright, star of the old Cincinnati Reds and then manager of the Philadelphia Phillies. Wright advised Stallings, a man of keen intellect, to forget medicine and focus his energies on the diamond. When the advice was accompanied by a contract, the Georgian launched a professional career that augured success from the start.

While still in his 20s, Stallings guided minor league pennant-winners at Augusta and Nashville. He managed Philadelphia of the National League before the turn of the century and piloted Detroit in the American League's maiden season of 1901. He also directed the junior league's New York club in 1909 and most of 1910 before being dismissed despite the fact the Highlanders were bound for second place.

Late in the 1912 season, while managing at Buffalo, Stallings was contacted by James E. Gaffney, a prominent New York politician/contractor who also owned the Boston Braves. George was invited to Gaffney's office in Manhattan, where he was informed that the club owner was weary of last-place performances (the Braves were headed for their fourth consecutive basement finish). Would Big Daddy consent to replace Johnny Kling as manager in 1913? He would. A contract was proffered and signed, whereupon Gaffney and Stallings proceeded to the Polo Grounds to watch the Braves engage the first-place Giants.

As the Braves skidded toward another of their 101 losses for the year, Gaffney inquired, "What do you think about the team?"

"This club is a baseball horror," replied Stallings in his usual straightforward fashion.

"Well, you're the boss," came the response. "Make whatever changes you wish. We want a winner."

"I've been stuck with some terible teams in my time, but this one beats 'em all," concluded the new manager.

Stallings took Gaffney at his do-as-you-please word. Changes were made in droves and when, after a fifth-place finish in 1913, he prepared the Braves for the 1914 campaign, only five players remained from the roster he had inherited. They were Gowdy, shortstop Rabbit Maranville and pitchers George (Lefty) Tyler, Otto Hess and Hub Perdue.

In the spring of 1914, Walter James Vincent Maranville was 22 years old. A native of Springfield, Mass., the 5-foot-5, 155-pounder was in his second full season as Boston's regular shortstop. Reputed more for his fielding than his hitting, Rabbit was renowned most of all for his antics on and off the diamond.

One day, while speeding toward second base, he slid between the legs of umpire Hank O'Day. His dignity severely ruffled, the crusty O'Day held up the action in the belief that a rule had been violated. O'Day consented to resume play only after a careful check of the playing code revealed no infraction had occurred.

Off the field, Maranville was famed for diving fully clothed into a pool in St. Louis and emerging with a fish between his teeth. In Boston, it was reported, he swam the Charles River, again in full attire, because the bridge was a few blocks away and he was in a hurry.

Gowdy was a rawboned product of Columbus, O. Originally a first baseman, the big fellow flunked his first big-league trial, which had come with the Giants. He switched to catching on the advice of John McGraw, but was traded to Boston before switching to the new job.

Tyler, a native of Derry, N.H., joined the Braves in 1910 and, after a shaky start in the majors (which included a 22-loss season in 1912), the lefthander won 16 games in Stallings' first year as pilot. He was 24 years old.

Lefthander Hess, born in Berne, Switzerland, had been a 20-game winner in the American League eight years earlier but now was 35 years old and being used sparingly.

Perdue, a righthander from Gallatin, Tenn., was starting his fourth season with the Braves. While he was coming off a 16-victory year, Perdue's primary claim to fame was his nickname, the "Gallatin Squash," which originated in the fertile brain of Grantland Rice. Sportswriter Rice, it was said, didn't want anyone to confuse ol' Hub with the Hubbard squash.

Before during and after the 1913 season, Stallings

engineered several deals that proved critical in 1914. Outfielder Leslie Mann was purchased from Seattle's minor league club. Then, in an April move, Joe Connolly, another outfielder, was acquired on waivers from Washington. First baseman Charles (Butch) Schmidt and infielder Charlie Deal were obtained late in the 1913 season, Schmidt from Rochester and Deal from Providence. And, after the season, outfielder Larry Gilbert was drafted from Milwaukee and pitcher Dick Crutcher was secured from St. Joseph.

Of that six-man contingent, Schmidt was the most colorful. The Baltimore meatpacker practiced hyperbole to a remarkable degree. When Maranville made a patented vest-pocket catch of a pop fly, the husky Schmidt would shout, "Rab, old boy, you're the greatest shortstop in the world." When a delivery from Rudolph cut the heart of the plate, the hurler could expect to hear, "Dick, old man, you're the greatest pitcher in the world."

At the start of the 1914 pennant race, the left-handed-hitting Schmidt was 26. However, the season would be the next-to-last in the game for the first baseman, who retired after the 1915 campaign to devote his time to his business in Baltimore.

Stallings' prize discoveries were righthanded pitchers Rudolph and Bill James, a 6-foot-3, 212-pound Californian.

James was known as "Big Bill" and "Seattle Bill," the latter because he had won 29 games for Seattle of the Northwestern League before being purchased by the Braves. At age 21, he won six and lost 10 for Boston in 1913.

Rudolph was a graduate of Fordham University. Nicknamed "Baldy," the native of New York City earned a high grade with Stallings in one of his early pitching appearances with the Braves. Relieving with two men on base and two out, Rudolph walked the first batter he faced. He also missed the strike zone on his first three pitches to the next batter. As the Chief squirmed in the dugout, Rudolph whistled a curve across the plate, then a second and finally a third to retire the side.

On the bench, Stallings uncrossed his legs for yet another time, drew a deep breath and said, "Well, at least he has some guts."

One more role remained to be filled for the stirring drama that was about to catapult the 1914 Braves into the ranks of miracle workers. For that spot, Gaffney and Stallings turned to Chicago. There they found Johnny Evers, the middle man in the storied double-play combination—Tinker-to-Evers-to-Chance—that helped make the Cubs indomitable for years.

Evers was 32 and a skinny bundle of bones who weighed about 150 pounds. Some folks called him "The Crab" because of his surly disposition. Others referred to him as "The Trojan" because he hailed from Troy, N.Y. Gaffney and Stallings called him "desirable."

Evers had managed the Cubs in 1913. He was fired at the close of the season after the Bruins lost to the White Sox in the City Series following a third-place showing in the National League race. Boston officials regarded the little fellow with the unconquerable spirit as the player who could transform the Braves into pennant contenders.

On a February morning in 1914, Evers arrived in Boston, there to be greeted in a manner befitting a head of state. A welcoming committee, led by Gaffney, escorted the player to the club offices and Evers proceeded to sign a contract that called for a bonus of $25,000. After endless rounds of hand-shaking and picture-taking, the 600-man party paraded to a nearby hotel. There, following a couple of rounds of drinks, the revelers sat down to more drinks and steak dinners.

Long hours later, the celebrants adjourned. They carried with them the conviction that bright days lay ahead for National League fans in Boston. In the words of one writer, fans "believe that if Evers and Stallings can get along with each other, the Braves actually will be in the hunt for the first time in many, many years."

Manager and player proved perfectly compatible. Spring training confirmed that relationship. But while Stallings found no fault with Evers, he was less than thrilled with his pitching staff. When the Braves arrived in Brooklyn for the start of the season, Stallings lamented, "I've got 16 pitchers and they're all rotten." Schmidt, it appeared, had a little competition in the hyperbole department.

The first three games of the year lent some credence to the Chief's pessimism. In the season inaugural at one-year-old Ebbets Field, Brooklyn battered Tyler, 8-2. The home forces hammered Rudolph, 5-0, in the second game and the Braves then suffered a 5-3 defeat in Philadelphia. Boston won only two of its first nine games and was locked in the basement at the end of April.

Nevertheless, reported the correspondent of The Sporting News, there was at least one encouraging sign. Gowdy, the sportswriter noted, "made a big hit with the fans for the life he put into catching."

The reporter was not impressed as favorably with Evers and Maranville. The second baseman, he observed, "is not covering ground to his left as he used to and, as Schmidt, the heavy-hitting first baseman, is a slow fielder, opposing teams have done a lot of successful hitting to right field, especially on their hit-and-run plays."

The writer charged Maranville's substandard performance to the fact that Rabbit "coined money so rapidly on the stage last winter that his mind is occupied with thoughts of the kind of act he will inflict upon the dear public" next winter. Maran-

Five members of the Miracle Braves were (left to right) Hank Gowdy, 27-game winner Dick Rudolph, George (Lefty) Tyler, Joe Connolly and Oscar Dugey.

ville, it was reported, "spent most of his leisure associating with actors . . . not realizing . . . sufficiently that success on the stage depends on his success on the field."

As the Braves continued to languish in the cellar during May, Stallings displayed confidence in eventual success. He comforted the uneasy public by saying, "Don't think we're a tail-end team. It'll take us a month . . . but then we'll be hard to beat."

One of Stallings' more difficult tasks was to convince Gaffney of brighter days. In June, when the Braves already had lost $40,000 and there was the prospect of a $100,000 deficit for the year, the owner notified the manager that he planned to sell out.

Big Daddy was crushed—but only momentarily. Resorting to his most forceful oratory, he assured the boss that the club would finish among the top three in the National League race.

"I'll take you at your word," replied Gaffney, signaling the passing of another crisis.

A major step toward improvement occurred in late June when the Braves traded Perdue to St. Louis for outfielder Ted Cather and infielder/outfielder George (Possum) Whitted. The deal, along with later swaps for Josh Devore (July, with the Phillies) and Herbie Moran (August, with the Reds), helped Stallings make extended use of a new baseball phenomenon—the platoon system. The manager put together complements of lefthanded-hitting and righthanded-batting outfields, and he thus could pick from Connolly, Gilbert, Devore and Moran against righthanded pitchers and employ Mann, Cather and Whitted against lefthanders.

Platoon baseball was a style of play to which Mann, in particular, grew accustomed. The Nebraska native would wind up playing 15 seasons in the major leagues and averaging about 285 at-bats per year.

"Against a lefthander, I'd rather have Mann up there in the pinch than any other hitter in the National League," said McGraw, who was Mann's pilot when the outfielder ended his big-league career with the Giants. "He knows he can hit them, and they know he hits them."

Along with installing the platoon system, the innovative Stallings incorporated the "tooth sign" into his book of strategy. Anytime a baserunner looked into the Braves' dugout and saw Stallings' pearly whites gleaming against his dark complexion, he knew the steal was on.

Despite Stallings' various stratagems, June passed without noticeable improvement in the Braves' fortunes. When the club dropped a doubleheader to Brooklyn on July 4, its record fell to 26-40. The Braves were 15 games behind the pacesetting Giants, who had a 40-24 mark.

The state of affairs in the Wigwam was indeed

First baseman Butch Schmidt was a Baltimore meatpacker with a lively bat.

woeful. Three days later, matters became particularly bleak when the Braves—embarking on a Western road trip—stopped off in Buffalo for an exhibition game and took a 10-2 lacing at the hands of the local International League team.

The humiliating loss to a minor league club was so distressing that Evers couldn't quite come to terms with it. Years later, when reflecting upon the pratfall, Evers concluded that it had come against a "soap company team."

Buffalo's romp proved an exclamation point to Boston's thus-far sorry season. Soon, though, the experience would be transformed into a turning point.

"Stallings watched us troop into the (train) station," said Maranville of the post-exhibition scene, "and in a tone that dripped with disgust spat out, 'Big-league ball players you call yourselves, eh? You're not even Grade-A sandlotters. I'm ashamed of you all.'

"It was a terrible thing to say to us. The words bit deeply into us. Nobody said anything, but we were

hurt. We vowed then and there we'd show up Stallings. We were still ripping mad when we arrived in Chicago. . . . "

The Braves proceeded to win five of their next six games.

After games of July 18, Boston still lagged in eighth place, but the distance separating the top from the bottom had been reduced to 11 games as a result of nine Braves victories in 12 decisions.

Undoubtedly, some of the surge could be credited to the Chief, whose constant tongue-lashing exhorted the players to superior efforts. On the field, Evers was an extension of Stallings. Nobody loafed in the company of the Trojan. He was everything that Gaffney and Stallings expected him to be. He was the friction primer, the spark that touched off the Boston tinderbox.

Evers and several teammates had extra incentive for superb performances. To reduce the threat of raids from the outlaw Federal League, Gaffney extended the contracts of Evers, Schmidt, Maranville, Rudolph, Gowdy and James through 1917.

The added security was particularly welcomed by James. "Big Bill" had been under attack by the press for inviting a newspaperman to the clubhouse where, one dispatch read, he "proceeded to shower blows upon him." The assault was "unwarranted," according to another writer, who added that "James received no sympathy from his fellow players."

James also was in the news as a member of the Braves' three-man pitching rotation. In early July, Stallings had resolved to stake his prediction of a high finish on James, Rudolph and Tyler. It proved one of his wisest decisions. He rarely deviated from the schedule.

Catcher Gowdy, while contributing to the development of the pitching staff and witnessing its progress from a special vantage point, nevertheless echoed Maranville's sentiments when pinpointing the key moment in the season.

"No big-league club likes to lose ... an exhibition," Gowdy said of the debacle in Buffalo. "Maybe we were in eighth place, but we were still big-leaguers and the pasting we took was galling to our pride. I will always believe that the trouncing ... provided the spark."

The spark became a conflagration. Before other clubs were aware of it, a raging inferno was in their midst. It started in Cincinnati on Sunday, July 19. Three runs in the ninth inning enabled the Braves to overcome the Reds and shed the cellar shackles for good. They climbed over the Pirates into seventh place.

A Boston newspaperman promptly informed his readers: "If nothing else is accomplished, Stallings at least has demonstrated that he knows how to handle a team and how to make it fight."

While Boston's offense never really geared up, Rudolph, James and Tyler were equal to the challenge. They simply curtailed the opposition's ration of runs. When the Braves moved from Cincinnati to Pittsburgh, the "Big Three" registered four shutouts in a five-game series. Tyler opened with a four-hit, 1-0 victory that thrust Boston into sixth place in the closely bunched field. Rudolph blanked the Buccos, 6-0, in the second game and, in the process, Boston leaped two notches into fourth. James went 11 innings before capturing the third game, 1-0, and Tyler emerged a 2-0 winner in the finale.

The pace grew furious. By August 1, the Braves had reached the .500 level for the first time. And when the club reached home several days later, it found the city aroused as it had not been since the 1890s. Thousands roared their greetings to the new heroes, and the groundskeeper at South End Grounds "found a collection of old ropes and stakes, dusty, moldy, rusty and unused for years which he proceeded to implant in the outfield for the proper restraint of a mob of amazed and delighted fans."

Only one position gave Stallings cause for concern as the season pressed on. That was third base, where Deal was adequate defensively but was batting in the low .200s. Accordingly, when the Chief had a chance in early August to acquire J. Carlisle (Red) Smith from Brooklyn, he moved swiftly. Stallings thought so highly of the squatty infielder that he paid $1,500 over the waiver price to get him.

Smith, who had incurred the wrath of Brooklyn management by consorting with Federal League representatives, was greeted warmly in Boston.

"As soon as I reported to Manager Stallings, he began using psychology on me," Smith said. "First, he told me he was raising my salary. Then he put his hand on my shoulder. 'Red,' he told me, 'you're the man we've needed on this club. You're the man who's going to win the pennant for us.'

"After that, I felt like a million dollars. With the Dodgers, I had been hitting .245. For Stallings, I batted .314 . . . . "

James pitched Boston into second place on August 10 when he defeated Cincinnati, 3-1, with the help of three hits by Maranville. Then, in mid-August, the Braves Express thundered into New York for a three-game series and gouged a big divot out of the Giants' lead. Rudolph won the first contest, 5-3; James prevailed in the second contest, 7-3, and Tyler was triumphant against Christy Mathewson in the 10-inning finale, 2-0. New York's lead had been whittled to 3½ games.

"I loaded the bases in the last of the 10th, but we managed to get them out," Tyler said of the drama-filled windup to the Braves-Giants series. "I think beating them three straight in their own park took all the fight out of New York and from then on we just couldn't be stopped."

The importance of Tyler's triumph was underscored in a Boston Globe account of the game.

"Upwards of 35,000 fans turned out to see the game," the Globe story said. "Never except at a world's championship game have there been so many persons at the Polo Grounds and they saw a game that was a game. Three-fourths of them were on hand to see Mathewson check the onward rush of the Braves; to see Stallings' team 'crack,' and then to enjoy watching the Giants make a show of them.

"They did not see any of these things, however. On the contrary, they saw the 'great master' out-pitched by simple Lefty Tyler; they saw their Giants reduced to the size of Lilliputians . . . . "

The Braves' startling ascent to sole possession of first place—they had managed a tie with the Giants on August 23 before dropping back—climaxed on September 2. While the Giants were dropping a single game in Brooklyn, Boston slipped into first place by taking a twin bill in Philadelphia behind Rudolph and James.

Gaffney, who had come from New York to see

Larry Gilbert was part of Manager George Stallings'
lefthanded-hitting platoon outfield for the 1914
Braves.

the games, was deleriously happy. Between whoops
and hollers, he shouted an order: "Throw your
straw hats away, men. I'm buying you all some new
lids when we get back to Boston."

An upset stomach prevented Evers from partici-
pating in the sweep. He returned to the lineup the
next afternoon, only to be thumbed out of the game
by Bill Klem after a first-inning kicking episode. It
is doubtful if Evers' game-long presence would have
materially influenced the outcome. Grover Cleveland Alexander shut out the Braves through eight
innings and won handily, pushing the losers back
into second place.

Entering Labor Day (September 7) action, the
Braves and Giants were deadlocked. They also were
well-primed for a doubleheader that left its imprint
on Boston baseball annals for all time.

The holiday twin bill was played at the Boston
Red Sox's home field, Fenway Park, which had
been offered rent-free to the Braves to accommo-

date the huge crowds that were overflowing obso-
lescent South End Grounds. As a result of the arrangement, approximately 36,000 frenzied New
Englanders were on hand as Stallings' forces scored
two runs in the ninth to boost Rudolph to a 5-4
victory over Christy Mathewson in the morning
game.

Evers' two-run single was the decisive blow in the
contest and it loosed a tidal wave of humanity upon
the field. For approximately 10 minutes, Stallings
was a prisoner in his own dugout, his path to the
clubhouse—as well as that of many players—
blocked by a horde of fans clamoring for the
chance to pump his hand or pound his back.

The afternoon encounter produced as much excitement, although of a different nature, for 40,000
spectators. The Giants romped, 10-1, settling the
issue with four runs in the sixth inning when Fred
Snodgrass precipitated a near riot.

The turmoil started when a Tyler pitch grazed
the sleeve of the New York outfielder. En route to
first base, Snodgrass danced a small jig. And when
he reached the bag, he defiantly thumbed his
nose at the jeering throng.

At the height of the uproar,
Tyler calmed the crowd by turning
comedian. The hurler panto-
mimed Snodgrass' muff of a fly
ball in the same park during the
1912 World Series that helped the
Red Sox to beat the Giants in the seventh game.

The fans' surly mood was reversed, but only
briefly. When Snodgrass returned to his post in
center field, he was greeted by a shower of pop bottles. Now it was Mayor James Curley's turn to exercise his executive powers. Leaping from his box seat,
Curley tried to persuade umpire Bob Emslie and a
police lieutenant to eject Snodgrass. His pleas went
unheeded. Ultimately, the disturbance was brought
under control when McGraw, holding a comfortable lead and acting out of concern for his player's
safety, removed Snodgrass from the game.

Still tied for the lead, the Braves and Giants
clashed again on September 8. James started for
Boston, while McGraw opted for Rube Marquard,
who had lost eight consecutive decisions. The
Braves quickly made it nine straight by hammering
the lefthander, 8-3. The Braves were in undisputed
possession of first place again, this time to stay.

The Giants had battled gamely in the series and
fallen only one game back. Still, the New Yorkers
departed Boston in a poor frame of mind.

"Everybody in the country seemed to be rooting
for the Braves and pulling against McGraw," said
Giants catcher Chief Meyers, reflecting on the
mood.

Legions of Boston rooters had more to applaud
the next day when a virtual unknown pitched the

only no-hit game of the year in the National League. George A. Davis Jr., a law student at Harvard, held the Phillies hitless and managed to keep them scoreless despite issuing five walks and seeing his teammates commit two errors. The Braves won, 7-0, in the second game of a doubleheader. The triumph was one of only seven lifetime victories in the majors for Davis, who had seen brief service in the big leagues in 1912 and 1913.

Boston did not let up. From September 10 through September 28, the Braves won 17 of 19 games (the Giants could muster only 12 victories in 22 contests in that span) and built an eight-game lead. Stallings' upstart crew clinched the pennant on September 29—but, ironically, not behind one of its "Big Three" pitchers. Tom Hughes, a former American League pitcher just up from the minors, put Boston over the top by beating the Cubs, 3-2, on a five-hitter. It proved the only victory of the season for the 30-year-old righthander.

Boston gained momentum as it headed for the wire and wound up 10½ games in front of the Giants. The team that won only 26 of its first 66 games went on to capture 51 of its next 66 contests. James won 19 of his last 20 decisions and finished with a 26-7 record.

Rudolph, a 5-9½, 160-pounder who in one stretch won 12 straight decisions, compiled a 27-10 mark. He fired six of the Braves' 17 post-Independence Day shutouts (Rudolph had not blanked an opponent by July 4 and Boston had managed only one shutout, by Hess, at that juncture).

"Rudolph was one of the smartest pitchers who ever toed a rubber," said Fred Mitchell, Braves coach. "He wasn't fast, but he had a good curve which he mixed up with a spitball and he could almost read a batter's mind. I often sat on the bench with him and heard him tell whether or not the batter would hit or take. He made a real study of his profession.

"While he was good in 1913 (after being acquired early in the season from Toronto), when we were separating the wheat from the chaff and assembling the club for next season, he was positively sensational in '14. He was the bellwether of the pitching staff and, being a little fellow, I believe that his success had much to do with big Bill James and George Tyler putting out that little extra effort to keep pace with the cocky kid from the Bronx."

Tyler contributed 16 victories to the team total of 94.

"During the big drive, we always had the feeling that if we got a couple of runs we'd win," Gowdy said. "Didn't need any more the way Rudolph, James and Tyler were going . . . Bill James had a great fastball, a great spitball. He was a wonderful performer. If he hadn't hurt his arm (James won his last major league game in 1915, at age 23), he would

Big Bill James was a member of Boston's workhorse three-man starting rotation that recorded 69 victories.

have been one of the greatest pitchers of all time. Tyler also was a power pitcher—fastball and a fine curve. Those fellows were also fine fielding pitchers, and not one of them was an automatic out at the plate."

Stallings' crew had only one .300-or-higher batsman, Connolly, among its season-long regulars. Smith, while a .314 hitter for the Braves in 60 games, fashioned a .272 mark overall in 1914.

Smith was unavailable for the World Series. On the closing day of the season, he fractured a leg while sliding in a game at Brooklyn. He was replaced by Deal, the man he had supplanted.

Having achieved one baseball miracle in their stunning rise to the top, the Braves were asked to accomplish another against a team that had won Series championships in 1910, 1911 and 1913 and which, by all criteria, was the most powerful aggregation in the majors. Connie Mack's Philadelphia A's were heavily favored to make it four Series crowns in five years.

Circumstances were ideal for a superb motivator like George Tweedy Stallings. He overlooked no opportunity to laud his players or to denigrate the opposition.

Stallings announced that he would not scout the A's, although one of his assistants did so secretly. He predicted that the Braves would win the Series in four straight. He forbade his players to talk to the Philadelphians except to insult them, and when the Braves arrived in the City of Brotherly Love, the Chief engaged in a telephone shouting match with Connie Mack over the time for the Braves' workout at Shibe Park. When the dispute couldn't be resolved, Stallings took his team to Baker Bowl, home of the Phillies.

Stallings' behavior shocked Mack. "Why, that man called me unsportsmanlike," Connie muttered, "and threatened to punch me on the nose."

The A's were quoted variously as 2-1 and 3-1 favorites to dispatch the Boston club. Detroit Manager Hugh Jennings disagreed. "With Red Smith out," Jennings said, "they should be 10-1."

In the days after the A's clinched the American League pennant, Mack assigned ace pitcher Chief Bender the task of scouting the N.L. champions. Subsequently learning that Bender had not left the city, the manager demanded an explanation.

"We don't need to scout that bush-league outfit," answered Bender, who never had been knocked out of the box in nine Series appearances.

Game 1 of the 1914 World Series featured a Rudolph-vs.-Bender pitching matchup. Bender lasted only into the sixth inning this time around, exiting after Whitted's two-run triple and Schmidt's run-scoring single. Rudolph triumphed, 7-1, as Gowdy paced an 11-hit attack with a single, double and triple.

James held Philadelphia to two hits in the second game and beat Eddie Plank, 1-0. The only run was scored in the ninth inning when Deal got a gift double (on a misplayed drive) and scored on Mann's single.

When the Series shifted to Boston—the Braves continued to play their home games at Fenway—the National League representatives again prevailed in a tight struggle. Gowdy's double in the 12th inning, an intentional walk and a wild throw on an attempted forceout at third base gave Boston a 5-4 victory. James was the winning pitcher, working in relief of Tyler.

Rudolph returned to the mound the next day and brought the Braves' storybook season to a resounding finish by outpitching Bob Shawkey, 3-1. The Braves scored the decisive runs in the fifth when Evers—the Trojan, the Crab and, most of all, the team's spiritual leader—singled home Rudolph and Moran.

Gowdy, who once said that during the 1914 N.L. campaign he "hit the tar out of the ball but it was always at somebody," more than made up for his .243 regular-season batting average in the World Series. He belted three doubles, a triple and a home run in the fall classic and hit .545.

Manager Stallings engaged in little public adulation in the aftermath of the incredible Series sweep of Mack's mighty A's. Instead, the "Miracle Man" beat a hasty retreat to his Georgia plantation, where his cotton crop was waiting for market.

1914
FINAL STANDING

Club	W.	L.	Pct.	GB.
Boston	94	59	.614	——
New York	84	70	.545	10½

BATTERS

Pos.	Player	G.	HR.	RBI.	B.A.
1B	Butch Schmidt	147	1	71	.285
2B	Johnny Evers	139	1	40	.279
SS	Rabbit Maranville	156	4	78	.246
3B	Red Smith	60	3	37	.314
OF	Joe Connolly	120	9	65	.306
	Les Mann	126	4	40	.247
	Larry Gilbert	72	5	25	.268
C	Hank Gowdy	128	3	46	.243
UT	Charlie Deal (3b)	79	0	23	.210

OTHER CONTRIBUTORS (20+ Games): Ted Cather, Wilson Collins, Charlie Deal, Josh Devore, Oscar Dugey, Otto Hess, Jack Martin, Herbie Moran, Jim Murray, Bert Whaling, Possum Whitted.

PITCHERS

Thr.	Pitcher	G.	W.	L.	ERA
R	Dick Rudolph	42	27	10	2.36
R	Bill James	46	26	7	1.90
L	Lefty Tyler	38	16	14	2.69

OTHER CONTRIBUTORS (20+ Games): Dick Crutcher.

Number 18

The Red Sox—
In a Cloud of Smoke

In the unsophisticated days of 1912, when baseball was still in its infancy and intimidating rhetoric was as much a part of the game as conventional equipment, the Washington Senators prepared to meet the Boston Red Sox in a September series at Fenway Park.

The first-place Red Sox already owned a 13½-game lead over the runner-up Nats, yet good crowds were expected for the four-game series. Cunningly, Washington Manager Clark Griffith seized an opportunity to pack the house and inflate his club's share of the gate receipts. Griffith had in his employ one Walter Johnson, the American League's most dominating pitcher and a winner of 16 consecutive games from July 3 through August 23, an A.L. record. With Boston's Joe Wood, already a 28-game winner, threatening Johnson's mark with a 13-game streak of his own, what better way to enflame the Boston partisans, jam the park and perhaps terminate Wood's string than to issue a challenge?

"Tell Wood," the Old Fox announced to the Boston media, "that we will consider him a coward if he doesn't pitch against Johnson.

"The race isn't over yet. Just wait until my team gets through wiping up the floor with the Red Sox and then you'll see we have a chance."

Boston Manager Jake Stahl understood Griffith's motive, yet he had the utmost confidence in the courage of his 22-year-old mound star. "All right," Stahl responded, "Wood will pitch on Friday. I had him down for Saturday, but to accommodate Griff, we will make the change. We intend to beat the Senators with Johnson pitching for them."

Just as Griffith anticipated, Boston fans leaped to his lure. More than 29,000 Red Sox rooters, the largest crowd of the season, jammed the city's new ball park, and at least 5,000 others were turned away. In the outfield, thousands of spectators stood behind ropes. Fans spilled over the dugouts and crowded players warming up on the sidelines. So heavy was the press of the multitude that when umpire Tom Connolly signaled for play to begin, the players occupied chairs along the foul lines.

Jake Stahl, a former football standout at Illinois, left his family's banking business to manage and play first base for the 1912 Red Sox.

For five innings, Johnson and Wood matched wits in a scoreless duel. These were the premier speed kings in baseball, fireballing righthanders who shared a mutual admiration.

"Can I throw harder than Joe Wood?" Johnson mused. "Listen, my friend, there's no man alive that can throw harder than 'Smokey' Joe Wood."

With two outs in the bottom of the sixth inning, Boston broke the drought in this epic confrontation. Tris Speaker, the league's peerless center fielder afield and at bat, sliced a double into the crowd in left field, then streaked home when Duffy Lewis'

Smokey Joe Wood (left) won 34 games for the 1912 Red Sox while Charley Hall (above right) chipped in 15 wins and Ray Collins added 14.

fly ball flicked off the glove of right fielder Danny Moeller. Wood blew away the Senators over the final three frames and Griffith had the answer to his challenge. Two days later, he carried home a sizable check, soothing balm for Washington's three losses.

"Nothing can stop the Boston team now," he conceded.

Wood's streak, however, was halted after his 16th straight victory. Smokey Joe had won his next two starts to tie Johnson's mark, but pressure appeared to get the best of the young pitcher at Detroit on September 20. With two outs in the third inning, he walked four straight batters and the Tigers pushed across three runs on their way to a 6-4 victory. Stahl appeared almost relieved that the streak was broken, noting Wood's gloomy countenance after the game. If any worrying was to be done, Stahl wanted it over with well before the World Series.

The loss was one of only five against a league-leading 34 victories for Wood, whose .872 winning percentage remained an A.L. record until 1931, when Lefty Grove was 31-4 (.886) for the Philadelphia Athletics. Wood pitched 35 complete games and 10 shutouts, both league highs, and struck out 258 batters, second only to Johnson. "Joe Wood in 1912 was the best pitcher I ever saw pitch," Lewis said.

Only the year before, in his third full season, Wood had won 23 games and tossed a no-hitter against the St. Louis Browns. The former Kansas farm boy who once pitched for the barnstorming Bloomer Girls (their wigs were womanly, their whiskers weren't) had a future that glowed by the heat of his burning fastball.

"There is a common expression among ball players in the American League that when you can't see them, you can't hit them," said New York's Hal Chase. "That goes for Walter Johnson and Joe Wood."

Unlike Johnson, Smokey Joe unleashed his fastball with a snap of the wrist that, according to one sportswriter, "looks as if it were breaking bones." That delivery produced curves that exploded like giant firecrackers yet almost always hit their target.

"It is not exaggerating it a bit when I say that at times I have been unable to see Wood's fastball as it sped over the plate," said Cleveland's Nap Lajoie. "He's perfected his curveball so that it's about the quickest breaking ball I've ever tried to hit."

In July 1913, misfortune intervened. Wood slipped and fell on a wet field while fielding a ground ball and broke the thumb on his pitching hand. He was never the same thereafter. "I don't know if I tried to pitch too soon after that or whether something happened to my shoulder at the same time," Wood said years later. "But whatever it was, I never pitched again without a terrific amount of pain in my shoulder."

The mishap eventually ended Wood's career as an overpowering hurler—but not his years as a major leaguer. After pitching with excruciating pain for three seasons, Wood sat out the 1916 campaign. A pitching comeback failed with Cleveland the following year (0-1 in 16 innings), but Wood won a berth in the Indians' 1918 outfield, partly due to the manpower shortage caused by World War I but mainly due to his solid hitting.

"I didn't hit too well when I broke in with Boston," Wood said, "but when my arm went bad and I knew that I had to hit to hold a job, I began to concentrate on hitting." In the five seasons he patrolled the Cleveland outfield, (two years as a regular), Wood batted .298.

In 1912, however, Wood was the major leagues' newest pitching star when everything came up roses on the Boston staff. Three other Red Sox starters—Hugh Bedient, Buck O'Brien and Charley Hall—pitched the best ball of their careers, while another, Ray Collins, recorded 14 victories, a career high through 1912. The Red Sox led the league with 18 shutouts and ranked second to Washington with a 2.76 earned-run average.

Hugh Carpenter Bedient had almost slipped through Boston's fingers. Assigned to Providence in the Eastern League at the close of spring training in 1911, Bedient wound up in Jersey City after the season when the rival Eastern League club purchased his contract. The Red Sox had to surrender five players to reacquire the righthander, who had first attracted attention by striking out 42 batters in a 24-inning semipro game in his hometown of Falconer, N.Y. The 22-year-old Bedient won 20 games as a rookie in 1912—and was released two years later after 15-14 and 8-12 seasons.

Thomas (Buck) O'Brien, a 30-year-old spitballer, was another first-year sensation, an 18-13 pitcher in 1912, his first full season. Picked up late in 1911 after winning 26 games for Denver in the Western League, the Massachusetts native promptly reeled off five victories in six outings. By 1913, his arm was shot. After a disastrous 4-9 start in Boston, Bedient was sold to Chicago. He lost twice in six games for the White Sox and never appeared in the majors again.

With little doubt, Charley Hall was the most conspicuous character on the staff. Born of Mexican-Indian parentage, Hall was christened Carlos Clolo at birth but "Sea Lion" as a major leaguer for his raucous, penetrating voice. The 27-year-old righthander won a career-high 15 games for Boston in 1912, his fourth season with the Red Sox after stints with Cincinnati in 1906 and 1907.

Ray Collins, 25, was a 6-foot-1 lefthander on the rise. The former University of Vermont star joined the Red Sox upon graduation in 1909 and spun off 13 victories in 1910, his first full season. Hampered by an early-season knee injury in 1912, Collins recovered nicely to notch his first of 14 victories on June 22. He remained in top form the next two seasons, winning 19 games in 1913 and 20 decisions in 1914 to lead the Boston staff.

Granted, these Red Sox pitchers sparkled together only for one illustrious season, but there was no doubting that Boston's outfield of Duffy Lewis, Tris Speaker and Harry Hooper was the greatest of its era. It was a hard-hitting, fast-fielding unit that could neutralize entire lineups. Few speed demons dared take an extra base on hits that squirmed through the infield; few power hitters had the muscle to drive a ball beyond or through their picket line.

"Harry and I took our cues from 'Spoke' when in the field," Lewis explained. "We'd watch the way he'd shift for various batters and move accordingly. If he came over in my direction, Hooper would follow about the same distance toward center and I'd move closer to the left-field line. If he went the opposite way, I'd follow him and Hooper would edge closer to the right-field line.

"In this way, we were always pretty well bunched against the batters. Of course, when we shifted in this manner, it left one wide-open hole in the outfield. But we didn't have to worry much about that. Speaker's judgment was uncanny.

"The three of us were really extra infielders whenever a ground ball was hit. If a ball took a bad hop over or a crazy twist past an infielder, we were usually close behind to grab it. Sometimes this protection resulted in an out. We always backed up one another in the outfield. We took nothing for granted. Even if it was just a soft-looking ground ball in Speaker's territory, Hooper and I ran over to cover in case something went wrong.

"We received very little advice and few orders from the bench. It was taken for granted we knew how to play the game and could take care of ourselves out there. If we had any ideas we wanted to try out, we did it without asking anybody's permission."

Always alert and on the move, the three flyhawks combined for 80 assists in 1912, when, for the second time in four seasons, Speaker gunned out an A.L.-record 35 runners.

No center fielder played as shallow as Speaker. And none could retreat as rapidly for an over-the-shoulder catch of a fly ball. Speaker took pickoff throws to catch snoozing runners off second base. In 1918, he completed two unassisted double plays within 11 days by snaring fly balls and outracing the retreating runners to second base.

Strangely, it was a pitcher, the immortal Cy Young, whom Speaker credited with developing his hawkish defense. "Cy was a veteran near the end of his playing career around the time I got my big-league start in Boston," said Speaker, who joined the Red Sox in the closing weeks of the 1908 campaign. "The old fellow took a fancy to me and said he'd help make a slick outfielder out of me. He'd take me out on the practice field and hit fungoes to me by the hour. I got to watching and studying his fungo swing, and by doing that I could start after the ball before he actually hit it."

Speaker hit his stride the next year in just his first full season. He tied Sam Mertes' A.L. record with 35 outfield assists, led the league in putouts and batted .309, his first of 10 consecutive .300 seasons. In his 19 seasons as a regular, Speaker would bat under .300 only once and .380 or better five times.

A lefthanded hitter, Spoke held his bat low,

Right fielder Harry Hooper had a steady bat and a slick sliding catch that enabled him to leap to his feet and throw out aggressive runners.

cocked it in mid-pitch and met the ball with a smooth arcing stroke. Personally, wrote Francis Richter in the 1913 Reach Baseball Guide, he was "a typical Texan with a rough complexion, heavy eyes, a voice like rolling thunder and huge powerful hands. He is a regular Texas cowboy in the saddle and can do as much with a horse as with a baseball bat."

Another scribe said it succinctly: "There is no manlier man than Tris Speaker."

George Edward Lewis, nicknamed "Duffy" for his mother's maiden name, surrendered no quarter as a left fielder. The steep embankment that warned fielders of their proximity to Fenway Park's left-field wall posed no problem to Lewis, who ascended and descended the incline so skillfully that it became known as "Duffy's Cliff." The former student at St. Mary's College joined the Red Sox in 1910 and walloped eight homers, only two fewer than the league leader—his current manager, Stahl. Duffy's steady power earned him cleanup honors for the Red Sox, a position he filled admirably by knocking in 109 runs in 1912.

Like Lewis, Hooper was a California native who had attended St. Mary's. With Boston, he was a do-everything right fielder who made his mark with timely base hits, stolen bases and spectacular fielding. Hooper perfected a sliding catch that enabled

Tris Speaker (right) played the shortest center field around, hit for the highest of averages. Duffy Lewis batted cleanup, scampered up and down 'Duffy's Cliff' in left field at Fenway Park.

him to leap to his feet and quickly unleash power-ful throws that nailed ambitious baserunners. In 17 major league seasons, he would compile 344 assists, steal 375 bases and collect more than 2,400 hits.

Given this formidable outfield combination, Gar-land "Jake" Stahl took over the Red Sox's manage-rial post in 1912 with an added measure of confi-dence. The former football standout at the University of Illinois had played for Boston twice, the New York Highlanders and Washington—where he managed the Senators to seventh-place seasons in 1905 and 1906—before he yielded to do-mestic pressure and entered the family banking business in 1911. When Red Sox President Jimmy McAleer called with an offer to return as player-manager, Stahl eagerly accepted. Some suspected the 33-year-old first baseman was nearing the "has-been" age, but an early report from spring training indicated otherwise. Big Jake was "doing wonder-fully well, as good as he ever did. His fielding is great and he is breaking fences with his bat."

The outlook was favorable for the rest of Stahl's infield as well. Larry Gardner's play promised "to create a sensation" after the third baseman had kept trim by playing hockey all winter. He was, like Col-lins, a product of the University of Vermont and a .280 hitter in each of the previous two seasons. Steve Yerkes was entering his first season as a second

baseman after hitting .279 in 1911 as the Red Sox's shortstop. Heinie Wagner, who played only briefly at second and short in 1911 because of a sore arm, was back at his regular shortstop post. Beginning his sixth full season with Boston, Wagner was, ac-cording to Richter, "the backbone of the club in all departments. His fine fielding, knowledge of the game, timely hitting and the esteem in which the players hold him have made him an invaluable member of the team."

The Red Sox also had a leader in catcher Bill Car-rigan, a former halfback at Holy Cross who was known as "Rough" because of his rugged ways and total dedication to victory. Carrigan could settle a score with his fists and participated in a memorable bout with the Detroit Tigers' George Moriarty. The other players, not wanting to interfere with the heavyweight attraction, let the pair slug it out until the local gendarmes intervened. Carrigan would manage the Red Sox to World Series champion-ships in 1915 and 1916 and urge the club to pur-chase a young lefthanded pitcher named Babe Ruth in 1914.

The 1912 season started on an auspicious note for the Red Sox and their followers. The Sox had a new manager, a new ball park and a look about them that warranted some early attention despite their fifth-place finish the year before.

Catcher Bill (Rough) Carrigan was a team leader and the Red Sox's leading contender for the baseball heavyweight championship.

"We look for big results at Boston," said A.L. President Ban Johnson. "Powerful factors have entered the American League field in that city and it can occasion no great surprise should Jake Stahl and his band of athletes crowd the Athletics and Tigers for first honors."

The Red Sox won four of their first five games on the road and arrived in Boston to open their home schedule at Fenway Park on April 18. Rain, however, washed out the home-opener and a doubleheader the following day. The double rainout cost the club an estimated 60,000 admissions, wrote Tim Murnane, an outfielder-first baseman in the 1870s and 1880s who now served as a correspondent for The Sporting News. Noting that the opener had been canceled two hours before gametime and moments before the sun burst through the clouds, Murnane wrote: "The new covering for the Red Sox ground failed to arrive from Detroit on time and the Boston club was a big financial loser. The time has now come when all the big clubs must have their infields covered, that they may be ready to play games as soon as the rain stops."

The rains ceased on April 20, when the Red Sox overcame a 5-1 New York lead to win their Fenway inaugural, 7-6, but the complaints about the park didn't. Fans in both the bleachers and grandstand growled about being farther away from the diamond than in the old Huntington Avenue Grounds. In the first month, attendances were down 25 per-

cent compared to the same period in 1911. Inclement weather contributed to the poor patronage, but Murnane found some fault with conditions at Fenway:

"The fact that the new park is not as handy to reach and get away from as the old park has hurt some and will until people get accustomed to journeying in the new direction. . . .

"On account of the size of the park and the entrances being on two widely separated ends of the grounds, I find much of the old sociability gone. At the old grounds, you were continually running into old friends as grandstand and bleacher patrons passed through one long runway to be distributed like a lot of mail to the various stations."

After lamenting the long, drawn-out games that were unpopular with out-of-town fans "anxious to reach trains," Murnane spotted a bright note. "I am sure," he wrote, "that with improved weather and everything else connected with the running of the establishment, the old crowds will come back and the fans grow warmed to the new park."

Those brighter days were not long in coming. By May 30, the Red Sox had claimed 15 victories in a 21-game home stand and moved to within two games of the league-leading White Sox. One of their six losses occurred on May 18, when Fenway Park was formally dedicated "amid flag raising, floral presentations and dignitaries from all over the baseball world." The ceremonial first pitch was thrown out by Boston Mayor John "Honey" Fitzgerald, who would have a grandson elected U.S. President 48 years later—John Fitzgerald Kennedy.

Boston took over first place on June 10, when Buck O'Brien defeated the Browns, 3-2, in St. Louis with the help of a triple and two singles by Gardner. Once in possession of first, the Red Sox never relinquished it. They won 21 games in both June and July—and lost a total of only 17—and carried an 8½-game lead through most of August.

"Our team is rounded into a good organization," Stahl said. "We have a catching staff in good shape, five pitchers twirling winning baseball, the best outfield in the country and an infield which is doing all that it is called upon to do. On that we base our expectations of keeping in front in the American League race.

"Of course, Joe Wood has been our mainstay all season, and to him we mainly owe the fact that we are holding the lead we have."

Accolades also were due Stahl himself. No one appreciated the positive influence of the banker-manager more than McAleer: "Jake can mix with the boys and never lose their respect," the onetime outfielder said. "I always figured that Stahl had more baseball brains than given credit for. The boys work their heads off for him and are bound to get results."

Boston's double-play combination featured shortstop Heinie Wagner (left), who some acknowledged as the backbone of the team, and second baseman Steve Yerkes.

The players, The Sporting News reported, were "keeping good hours, sleeping and eating well and not fretting" over their pursuers, the Senators and Athletics. Fans, too, were displaying a positive attitude. "Patrons have finally warmed up to the new ball park," Murnane wrote, "and no finer class of people ever attended the games than is now gracing the grandstand with its presence."

As the Red Sox rolled toward the pennant, the Athletics continued to stumble. The club with the "$100,000 Infield" and brilliant pitching staff confounded fans and experts alike with its lackluster play. They had won World Series titles in 1910 and 1911 and were destined to win the pennant in 1913 and 1914. They would lead the league in hitting and fielding in 1912 and have 20-game winners in Eddie Plank and Jack Coombs. Yet when the race moved into September, it was Washington—another second-division club from 1911—who occupied second place, not the defending champions.

The Red Sox clinched the pennant on September 18, when they were rained out in Cleveland, and continued toward an A.L.-record 105 victories. The club had been a model of consistency throughout the season, winning more games than they lost every month and playing .721 baseball (75-29) after taking over the lead. The Red Sox's longest losing streak of the year was only five games (September 17-20) and they lost three straight only once. They wound up second to the Athletics in team batting

with a .277 mark, principally due to Speaker, who batted near .400 throughout his fourth season.

Speaker failed in his bid to unseat Ty Cobb as the league batting king, finishing third behind the Georgia Peach and Cleveland's Joe Jackson with a .383 mark. Nonetheless, the 24-year-old outfielder was awarded a Chalmers car as the league's Most Valuable Player for his 222 hits (third in the league), 53 doubles (first), nine home runs (second), 52 stolen bases (fourth) and 35 outfield assists (first).

"Wood and Speaker have been our offensive strengths—sort of executioners of our opponents," summarized Stahl, who batted .301 as a "has-been." "But for brainwork, I want to hand the credit to Carrigan and Wagner. Carrigan has been greatly responsible for the development of Wood and the rest of our pitchers, notably Bedient and O'Brien. Wagner has proved himself the most reliable infielder in the league this year and his fighting spirit and great leadership have helped us in every part of the race."

That was borne out by two umpires who, when asked to whom they would award the MVP, responded, "To Heinie Wagner of Boston. If he dropped out, that team would go to pieces in a week."

Wagner remained in the ranks and Boston marched into the World Series for the second time. Victors over the Pittsburgh Pirates in the first-ever championship of major league baseball in 1903, the

Red Sox opposed the New York Giants of John McGraw, who oozed confidence as his team made its third Series appearance.

"It is my opinion that the Red Sox are not as good a team as the Athletics were when we faced them last year," said McGraw, who lost the Series to Philadelphia in six games. "Connie Mack's club was at the very top of its stride in that series, while the Giants had slumped away slightly after the long grind of the National League championship. I feel that I have a better ball club than Stahl, but every man naturally prefers his own product."

With Wood given the ball in the opener, McGraw's fast offense wasn't the same. Smokey Joe struck out 11 Giants on the way to a 4-3 decision over rookie Jeff Tesreau. Two games later, after darkness ended a 6-6 tie in Game 2 and 26-game winner Rube Marquard decisioned O'Brien, 2-1, in the third contest, Wood victimized Tesreau again, scattering nine hits in a 3-1 victory.

The Red Sox moved to within a game of the title behind the arm of their rookie sensation, Bedient, in Game 5. Pitching the first half of the game in a ghostlike fog that almost blotted the field from view, Bedient tossed a three-hitter to defeat Christy Mathewson, 2-1. Given the opportunity to make a quick kill, the Red Sox failed to capitalize.

The Giants unloaded on Boston's pitching in the opening stanzas of the next two contests to square the series at three games apiece. New York roughed up O'Brien for all five of its runs in the first inning of Game 6, then chased Wood from the box after an inning's work in Game 7 by scoring six times. Boston fans had little to applaud in the 11-4 drubbing, save for Speaker's defensive gem in the ninth inning. Playing shallow as usual, Spoke snared Art Fletcher's short fly and beat Art Wilson to second base to complete the only unassisted double play by an outfielder in World Series history.

The Series title that had once appeared so certain seemed out of reach when the Red Sox fell behind, 2-1, in the 10th inning of the decisive eighth game. Wood, pitching in relief, had surrendered a run-scoring single to Fred Merkle in his third inning of work, and Mathewson was pitching magnificently, hungry for his first victory in the Series.

Two costly miscues, however, turned fate against the Giants. Center fielder Fred Snodgrass' "$30,000 muff" of pinch-hitter Clyde Engle's fly ball gave the Red Sox a life to start the inning. After Snodgrass snared Hooper's deep fly and Yerkes walked, Speaker lofted a pop foul near the first-base coach's box, a ball that "any schoolboy first baseman could have caught" wrote one reporter. Speaker, hoping to create confusion, was ready to shout out the call for the Giants' Chief Meyers, knowing full well that the ball was out of the catcher's reach.

"But before I could open my mouth, I heard Matty calling, 'Chief, Chief,'" Speaker said. The ball bounced off the lunging catcher's glove and Speaker had a reprieve.

"You just blew the championship," Spoke yelled to Matty. He spanked the next pitch for a run-scoring single and, after Lewis was walked to load the bases, Gardner belted a sacrifice fly to right field to bring home Yerkes with the title-clinching run.

Jake Stahl's hour of glory was short-lived. Even as he savored an uproarious victory parade that traveled from Boston's Park Square to historic Faneuil Hall, the pillars under his throne had begun to crumble. His downfall had started, one beat writer maintained, days earlier on a train ride from New York to Boston. O'Brien had taken a "healthy wallop" at Wood, "quite a mixup" ensued and the players split into factions. Harmony didn't return the following year when the pitching failed and the offense sputtered. With Stahl and McAleer rumored to be at war, Stahl resigned July 15. Carrigan took over and guided the team to a fourth-place finish.

Only months earlier, Stahl had summed up so neatly the essence of this Red Sox club:

"We have the greatest outfield in the country, (with) wonderful ability on the offensive and defensive. . . . I believe that my pitching staff is the best in the country, with Wood and Collins as headliners. My players are all fast and hard hitters. . . .

"I believe I have the best team in the country today."

All of which was true—at least for one glorious year, 1912.

1912
FINAL STANDING

Club	W.	L.	Pct.	GB.
Boston	105	47	.691	—
Washington	91	61	.599	14
Philadelphia	90	62	.592	15

BATTERS

Pos.	Player	G.	HR.	RBI.	B.A.
1B	Jake Stahl	95	3	60	.301
2B	Steve Yerkes	131	0	42	.252
SS	Heinie Wagner	144	2	68	.274
3B	Larry Gardner	143	3	86	.315
OF	Duffy Lewis	154	6	109	.284
	Tris Speaker	153	9	90	.383
	Harry Hooper	147	2	53	.242
C	Bill Carrigan	87	0	24	.263

OTHER CONTRIBUTORS (20+ Games): Hugh Bradley, Hick Cady, Clyde Engle, Olaf Henriksen, Les Nunamaker.

PITCHERS

Thr.	Pitcher	G.	W.	L.	ERA
R	Joe Wood	43	34	5	1.91
R	Hugh Bedient	41	20	10	2.92
R	Buck O'Brien	37	18	13	2.57
R	Charley Hall	34	15	8	3.02
L	Ray Collins	27	14	8	2.54

Number 19

'We Are El Birdos!'

The man they called "Cha Cha" leaped onto a clubhouse table amid the din of his howling teammates and pumped his fist into the air.

"We are El Birdos!"

"Yeah!"

"We are El Birdos!"

"Yeah!"

"WE ARE EL BIRDOS!"

"YEAH!"

Perhaps never before had a team been swept away by such unrestrained spirit. The animated, fun-loving Orlando Cepeda had unpacked his bags only the year before, and now, in the sizzling midsummer heat of St. Louis, Cha Cha had turned on a team, a town and lifted the Cardinals to the top of the 1967 National League race.

This native of Ponce, Puerto Rico, moved to a percussive beat and set the tempo for these loose-as-a-goose Cardinals. The ever-blaring record player he introduced to the locker room blared louder than ever after thrilling victories. His revved-up spirit covered all corners of the clubhouse as players needled one another and reveled in practical joking. It was just Orlando's way to keep everyone in stitches, to lend humor to even something so serious as a closed-door strategy session.

"Who knows Schroder?" Manager Red Schoendienst asked before one game with the San Francisco Giants. "Orlando, do you know Schroder at all?" he said, trying to gain some insight into the newly recalled infielder's hitting ability.

"Sure I know him," Cepeda replied. "He's a good cat."

Not surprisingly, his teammates erupted. But it was the postgame Cepeda that everyone adored most, Cepeda the cheerleader. For when Orlando was cheering, the Cardinals were winning.

"What really impresses me about Cha Cha," said shortstop Dal Maxvill, "is that even if he's gone 0-for-4 and we win, he gets on the trunk and leads the cheers. If he goes 4-for-4 and we lose, he just quietly undresses. It's easy for superstars to sit back and feel that they've done their job (and not) worry about others on the team. Instead, Orlando is always trying to inspire us."

Cepeda had special cheers and clever salutes, some of them unprintable, particularly those

'We are El Birdos' was the echoing theme of the 1967 and '68 Cardinals, a fun-loving and talented troupe of characters.

directed against San Francisco Manager Herman Franks, a man who nearly broke Cepeda's spirit.

Cepeda had been one of the leading sluggers on the heavy-hitting Giant teams of the early 1960s. In 1958, he had been named the N.L. Rookie of the Year after belting 25 homers, driving in 96 runs and batting .312. The "Baby Bull" averaged 33 home runs and 109 runs batted in over the next six seasons, including league-leading totals of 46 homers and 142 RBIs in 1961. When Franks took over the Giants' reins in 1965, however, Cepeda played in only 33 games, barely able to walk due to an injured right knee that had pained him since 1961.

"I could not move my knee, but Herman thought I was not doing enough to get well," Cepeda said. "He always said I was not doing enough to help his club." Cepeda had endured the same criticism from Alvin Dark, Franks' predecessor, and submitted to knee surgery in December 1965.

"In the spring, I went to Herman and begged him to let me play first base," Cepeda said. "I needed only work, I tell you. I was afraid of losing all my reflexes.

"But Herman, he told me that (Willie) McCovey was a better first baseman than me. He told me that McCovey would break his back for him. He was telling me that I could do nothing for him. I asked him to trade me. He said they tried but that nobody wanted me."

On May 8, 1966, St. Louis General Manager Bob Howsam acquired Cepeda for pitcher Ray Sadecki. By the All-Star break in 1967, the Cardinals had a 3½-game lead on the N.L. pack and Cepeda was leading the league in batting (.356) and second in RBIs (59).

"What made our club click," said catcher Tim McCarver, "can be summed up in one word: Cepeda."

"Here," Orlando said, "Baseball is beautiful."

But no more horrible sight was witnessed in St. Louis than on July 15, four days after the All-Star recess, when Bob Gibson was sent crumpling to the ground by a line drive off the bat of the Pittsburgh Pirates' Roberto Clemente. Gibson, struck on the lower right leg, pitched to another three batters before collapsing again. The leg was broken and Gibson would miss the next seven and a half weeks.

Gibson was the pitching mainstay of the Cardinals and, arguably, the most intense competitor in the National League. Only a select few hitters admired the glowering 6-foot-1 righthander—the rest simply feared him. Every seven seconds or so, batters had to sight in a white blur that buzzed across the plate in excess of 90 mph. Sometimes, the comfortable hitters learned, the strike zone wasn't Gibson's target.

"Bob wasn't just unfriendly when he pitched," said Joe Torre, Gibson's enemy as an Atlanta Brave and, by 1969, his teammate in St. Louis. "I'd say it was more like hateful."

Indeed, Gibson had five intimidating weapons: a fastball that sailed, a fastball that dipped, a snapping slider, a decent curve—and the brushback.

"A great many fans and a few players confuse the knockdown with the brushback," Gibson said. "They think every pitch thrown inside, especially high and inside, is an attempt to deck a man or even hit him. They don't recognize the tactics of the brushback.

"Actually, the brushback is just a fastball inside. The intent is to move back a hitter who crowds the plate and looks for a breaking pitch on the outside.

The always-intense and determined Bob Gibson (above) was a pitching machine in 1968, when he carved out 22 wins and an incredible 1.12 ERA. Nelson Briles rescued the Cardinals in 1967 when he replaced the injured Gibson in the rotation and finished with 14 wins and a team-best 2.44 ERA.

I don't expect to scare anybody or make him hit the dirt when I throw a brushback. I'm only giving the batter something to think about."

Gibson had begun his life 31 years earlier in an Omaha, Neb., ghetto. From there, his unfailing determination carried him on a path to glory, through four years at Creighton University, a tour with the Harlem Globetrotters and into the Cardinals' rotation for good in 1961. In 1964, Gibson helped the Cards win their first pennant and World Series title since 1946, winning 19 games during the regular season and two more over the New York Yankees in the Series. He notched his first 20-victory season the following year, then won 21 games in 1966 despite pitching half the season with a sore elbow. And in 1967, Gibson was 10-6 and on target for his sixth straight 200-plus strikeout season when tragedy struck July 15 at Busch Stadium.

The next week's issue of The Sporting News carried the story and a picture of Gibson, his mouth yanked open by pain, sprawled on the mound moments after Clemente's drive cracked his leg. The story was headlined, "Did Card Flag Dream Go Down With Gibson?" Schoendienst, worried about a young, questionable pitching staff, had just prevailed upon Gibson to pitch with only three days' rest, instead of four.

"We were all set to start on three days between starts with our next series," Schoendienst said.

But it was that suspect pitching staff that rose to the occasion and knocked off the league's top contenders in a one-month surge that broke apart the N.L. race.

On July 24, the Chicago Cubs moved into a first-place tie by defeating the Cardinals, 3-1, in the opener of a crucial series in St. Louis. The next day, El Birdos bounced the Cubs back into second to begin a 22-7 monthlong hot streak that opened up an 11½-game lead. The Cardinals terminated their pursuers with a torrid 19-3 showing against first-division clubs, winning eight of nine from the Cubs, three straight from both the Atlanta Braves and Cincinnati Reds, and five of seven from the Giants. The Cardinals' lead dipped only as low as 9½ games thereafter and they claimed their second pennant in four years with a 101-60 record. Their 10½-game bulge over the runner-up Giants represented the largest winning margin in the league since the 1955 Brooklyn Dodgers' 13½-game spread.

Three pitchers forced to step out of the shadows and shoulder the heaviest burden were the ones who carried the biggest load: Nelson Briles, a 4-15 reliever and spot starter in 1966; Dick Hughes, a 29-year-old rookie, and Steve Carlton, a 22-year-old lefthander with 77 innings of major league experience prior to 1967. In Gibson's absence (July 16 through September 6), Briles and Hughes both posted 7-2 records, Carlton put together a 5-2 mark and

Dick Hughes (left) was a nine-year minor league veteran and Steve Carlton was a budding star when they joined the Cardinal rotation in 1967.

the Cards were 36-19 overall. For the season, the unlikely pitching heroes were a combined 44-20 after a collective 9-19 mark in 1966, a 35-1 difference.

Nelson Kelley Briles was a 24-year-old righthander who was comfortable with the arts—he was bilingual, a guitar picker and a thespian in college—but built like a prizefighter at 5-foot-11, 195 pounds. In 1966, Briles' second season with the Cardinals, he had the unpleasant distinction of losing seven straight decisions to tie Houston's Bob Bruce for the longest losing streak in the league. "Just nothing went right," Briles recalled. "Everything I did was wrong. I didn't want to let it get me down, but I certainly was snakebit."

The Cardinals did, however, fail to score a run for Briles in his final 45 innings, and Nellie settled into the Cardinals' bullpen in 1967 as Schoendienst's No. 1 righthanded reliever. When Gibson was felled, Briles rescued the Cardinals by stepping into his starting slot. After losing two of his first three starts, Briles downed the Reds on August 6 to record his first of nine straight victories, a string that was matched only by the Cubs' Ken Holtzman. Briles closed the season with a 14-5 mark and a team-leading 2.44 earned-run average, crediting his success to a suggestion made by pitching coach Billy Muffett.

"A big help was . . . Muffett getting me to go to

Center fielder Curt Flood combined fearless, superlative defense with a lively bat that produced six .300-plus seasons.

the no-windup delivery," he said. "Pitching coaches have told me that you can throw more strikes by not winding up."

Hughes was another improbable hero, a veteran of nine minor league seasons who had made his first appearance in the majors late in 1966. Like Briles, he switched to a no-windup delivery on Muffett's advice, perfected a hard slider and earned a spot in the Cardinal rotation. "I wouldn't be surprised if he proved to be the second-best pitcher I've got," Schoendienst had remarked as the Cardinals broke camp.

The Redhead wasn't far off—Hughes actually was the Redbirds' winningest pitcher with a 16-6 mark and named The Sporting News' N.L. Rookie Pitcher of the Year. Despite 20-75 vision in one eye and 20-300 in the other, Hughes was a marksman around the plate, surrendering only 6.6 hits and two walks per nine innings. But after a 2-2 start in 1968, torn shoulder muscles ended Hughes' season —and career.

Steven Norman Carlton had won three major league games prior to the 1967 season but already was able to daze hitters with his live fastball and wicked curve. In 1966, Charlie Metro, his manager at Tulsa, had told Carlton, "Get packed, you're going to Cooperstown," after the 6-foot-5 lefthand-

er unfurled a one-hitter in Pacific Coast League action.

"Me? The Hall of Fame already?" Carlton had joked.

The trip to Cooperstown actually was the southpaw's big audition. Pitching against the defending A.L.-champion Minnesota Twins in the annual Hall of Fame game, Carlton struck out 10 batters and pitched a complete game in a 7-5 victory. Four days later, he was called up to the majors to stay.

"I'm sure that game changed the club's mind about when to bring me up," said Carlton, who remembered "all those big guns on the Minnesota club swinging away in a small ball park."

Only two clubs, the Cardinals and Pirates, had pursued Carlton when he was a high school pitcher in North Miami, Fla. Both offered only $5,000 to sign, "but a Cardinal bird dog, John Buik, who was also my Legion baseball coach," Carlton explained, "brainwashed me about the Cardinals and told me they had an old pitching staff."

Carlton signed in 1964 and, surely enough, was a key to a young, rebuilt Cardinal staff in 1967. He was 14-9 in his first full season and nearly shattered Sandy Koufax's single-game major league strikeout record by fanning 16 Philadelphia Phillies—two shy of the mark—on September 20.

"He had a great fastball, a good overhand curve and a good change-up," said Philadelphia's Don Lock. "You say he's only 22? I'd like to trade places with him right now."

Carlton would, of course, become regarded as perhaps the greatest lefthander in baseball history, but in 1967, he was just one of many unsung heroes on this stouthearted staff.

Ray Washburn, a 29-year-old righthander who had torn apart his shoulder—twice—in 1963, finished with a 10-7 record after bouncing back from a midseason thumb fracture. Lefthander Larry Jaster, the 22-year-old rookie phenom of 1966 who set a major league record by shutting out one club, the Los Angeles Dodgers, five consecutive times, contributed nine victories as a starter-reliever in 1967. Al Jackson, acquired from the New York Mets after the 1965 season in a trade for Ken Boyer, also fashioned nine victories, four in a relief role.

Most of the relief burden, however, fell on rookie righthander Ron Willis and lefty Joe Hoerner once Briles left the bullpen. Willis, a product of Kirkwood High School in suburban St. Louis, worked in a team-high 65 games, third-most in the league, and won six times. Hoerner, a veteran of nine minor league seasons (and flings with Houston in 1963 and 1964) chipped in four wins in 57 appearances in his second Cardinal season.

Hoerner may have been the only known pitcher ever relieved due to a heart attack. Pitching for Davenport in the Three-I League in 1958, he collapsed on the mound, gasping for air while his heart pumped wildly. The diagnosis was a heart attack, but tests failed to detect evidence of heart trouble. Doctors concluded that, just possibly, Hoerner's overhand motion had pinched off one of the heart's supply lines. Joe Hoerner suddenly favored a sidearm delivery.

Hoerner admitted that episode left him "scared as hell," much as he left teammates in 1967 after a July 28 game against Atlanta.

The Cardinals had returned to their bus after a 9-1 victory over the Braves and waited impatiently for a driver the charter company was supposed to send. Wisecracks flew in profusion as the wait stretched to half an hour. Suddenly, Hoerner jumped behind the wheel, flicked a few switches and the vehicle lurched forward. As Cepeda shouted, "Go, go, go," Hoerner steered the bus down an expressway and through streams of traffic. "I kept hearing sirens and seeing those flashing red lights on the tops of cars," Hoerner said. Nevertheless, the wayward bus rolled on. Approaching the hotel, the bus demolished an "Exit Only" sign before it screeched to a halt. The door flew open and players

piled out, scattering in all directions "like a bunch of kids after breaking a window."

Much like the bus, El Birdos' pennant express rolled merrily along. On September 7, Gibson returned to the mound and hurled five innings in a 9-2 win over the New York Mets. On September 18, he shut down Philadelphia on three hits and the Cardinals claimed the franchise's 11th pennant. In five starts after his return, Gibby proved he had lost nothing and finished with a 13-7 mark. Had the Cardinals lost Cepeda, they might have been simply finished.

"Without Cepeda, we are down with the Pirates, and look where they are," said third baseman Mike Shannon, noting the sixth-place Pittsburgh club. "It's not just his statistics. It's also what happens in the clubhouse. It's intangible. I can't really explain. Orlando is a prestige player and we have him—the other clubs don't.

"Put it this way: I'm walking down the street and two tough guys coming the other way want to start a fight. Then this friend of mine—a big guy—comes around the corner, and when the two tough guys see him they disappear. Well, my friend the big guy is Cepeda—you can't take him away from me. So I'm going to beat you."

"Cha Cha" was an intimidating strongman and the unanimous choice for the N.L. Most Valuable Player award with 25 home runs, a league-leading 111 RBIs and a .325 batting mark, sixth-best in the league. He wasn't the only tough out in a hard-hitting lineup. These Cardinals were a clutch-hitting, line-drive club capable of erupting anywhere in the order.

Lou Brock backed up Cepeda in the muscle department as the majors' most productive leadoff hitter. Lou pounded a career-high 21 home runs, drove in 76, tied for the league lead with 113 runs scored and ranked second with 206 hits and 12 triples. The Cardinals' left fielder reeled off batting streaks of 20, 17 and 16 games on the way to a .299 average, crediting his offensive firepower to a secret weapon—his wife's lemon cream pies. Those treats didn't slow down the Cardinal comet—he swiped 52 bases to lead the league in thefts for the second straight year.

Since the Chicago Cubs had given up on "Brock, as in Rock" (the Bleacher Bums' harsh salute) and swapped him to St. Louis in a deal for pitcher Ernie Broglio on June 15, 1964, the 28-year-old Brock had become one of the league's most dangerous threats. "Brock wasn't at all relaxed at first in

Cardinal outfielder Lou Brock possessed that sweet combination of power and speed as well as an affinity for his wife's lemon cream pies.

This happy-go-lucky Cardinal threesome possessed plenty of firepower: (left to right) Tim McCarver, Orlando Cepeda and Roger Maris.

Chicago," said Cubs pitcher Larry Jackson. "He'd break out into a big sweat just putting his uniform on. His desire was so intense that he made things tough for himself."

Now, said Jackson, "Lou puts the heat on the defense. He puts the heat on the pitcher and the outfield and the catcher, too, because they know they have to hurry plays when he's on base. . . . It seems that Brock is in on four out of every five Cardinal rallies."

Said Bob Skinner, Brock's teammate in St. Louis from 1964 through 1966 and the Phillies' manager in 1968: "You can't walk Brock because, when you do, it's like a double or triple due to his great speed. He always seems to be creating winning situations, whether by hitting the long ball or bunting or getting on base by making the other team hurry a play."

With Curt Flood or Julian Javier following in the order, Brock was a man on the move. Flood overcame arm and shoulder injuries to bat a career-high .335, fourth-best in the league, while Javier belted 14 home runs, drove in 64 and batted .281 in his best offensive season.

Back in 1960, then-Manager Solly Hemus had told Flood to his face, "You'll never make it," after the undersized (5-foot-9, 160 pounds) outfielder batted .237. The following July, Johnny Keane replaced Hemus and gave Flood the regular job in center field, thus beginning one of the greatest offensive and defensive shows in Cardinal history. Flood batted .322 that year, his first of four .300 seasons prior

to 1967. In center field, he was a human fly, a Gold Glover from 1963 through 1968 for his fearless defense.

"The damned thing about Flood," former Cincinnati Manager Fred Hutchinson had said, "is that he can have his back to the wall and come in and take a soft line drive out of the shortstop's ear." Said famous wall-crasher Pete Reiser: "Curt plays center field just the way you like to see it played."

Flood tied a major league record in 1966 by playing the entire season without committing an error and established an N.L. mark with 226 consecutive errorless games, a streak that stretched from September 3, 1965, through June 2, 1967.

Javier had been a pillar at second base for the Cardinals since 1960, when he was acquired from the Pirates' chain for lefthander Vinegar Bend Mizell. The Dominican native had a pesky bat and catlike speed, but it was his graceful agility around second base that remains a vivid memory for Cardinal fans.

"He's a ghost out there," said Maxvill, his double-play partner. "He gets the ball as fast as anyone and he covers more ground than anyone I've seen. They try to nail him on the double play and he disappears." Gene Mauch called Javier "the greatest I ever saw on getting pop flies and as good as anyone on coming in on a ball."

Surrounding Cepeda in El Birdos' gunners nest were Roger Maris, Tim McCarver and Mike Shannon. At 32, Maris was far removed from the homer-hero days of 1961—and the relentless criti-

Converted outfielder Mike Shannon (left) made the move to third base and played alongside esteemed gloveman Dal Maxvill, the Cardinal shortstop.

cism that marked his final seasons as a Yankee. Acquired before the 1967 season in a trade for Charlie Smith, Maris connected for only nine homers but he helped lead the team with 18 game-winning RBIs and a winning attitude.

"Getting Roger Maris—that's what pulled the team together," McCarver said. "We knew that our pitching would be a question mark, but we just decided that Roger, knowing how to win and what it was like to win, would be the guy who would show us how it was done. We didn't expect too much from him in a physical way, but we knew he could have a great influence on our club, to get our guys to thinking about winning. And he has done exactly that."

To make room for Maris, Schoendienst had moved the strong-armed Shannon from right field to third base. "If I didn't make it at third, that meant I'd end up without a job after having my best season," said Shannon, noting his 16 homers, 64 RBIs and .288 batting mark in 1966. The "great experiment" offered another challenge as well— Shannon, a St. Louis native and star quarterback at local CBC High School, would learn the position in front of family, friends and neighbors.

The big switch paid huge dividends. Shannon drove in 77 runs, second only to Cepeda, and "was a big-league third baseman the last three months," said Maxvill. "They might call him 'Moon Man,' but he's all business once the game starts."

McCarver was another character, a clubhouse cutup who drove teammates to hysterics as a madcap called "Crazy Guggenheim." Nothing was funny about the 25-year-old catcher when he knocked down onrushing baserunners. "He isn't scared of anybody," coach Joe Schultz said of the Memphis native whom Bob Neyland, the former Tennessee football coach, called "the best-blocking lineman I ever saw in high school."

Always one of the toughest batters to strike out, McCarver had been a consistent .280 hitter since becoming a Cardinal regular in 1963. In the 1964 World Series, he batted .478 and tied a seven-game Series record with at least a hit in each contest. He was fast enough to lead the league with 13 triples in 1966 and was a .348 hitter at the All-Star break in 1967 before tailing off to .295. Still, he wound up second to Cepeda in the MVP balloting after rapping 14 homers, driving in a career-high 69 runners and leading the league's catchers with 67 assists.

The slick double-play combination of Julian Javier and Dal Maxvill (above) was always exciting, as was Orlando Cepeda, the wettest Cardinal after the team's 1967 pennant-clinching victory.

Even Maxvill, the Cardinals' No. 8 hitter, got caught up in the hit parade. Though he batted only three points above his .224 career average, Maxie's hits came at opportune times. He picked up the Cardinals with 14 RBIs in the first half of September when Cepeda, McCarver and Maris slumped. And although "Bonesy" weighed only 150 pounds, he was an iron man at shortstop, playing sparkling defense in 152 games. "Maxie and Brooks Robinson should be partners in a vacuum company," reliever Jack Lamabe said of the electrical engineering graduate. "The two suck up everything that's hit."

Once in the World Series, two Cardinals took the Boston Red Sox to the cleaners. As early as the first game, Boston could see its "impossible dream" breaking apart as Gibson fired a six-hitter and struck out 10 batters while Brock went 4-for-4, stole two bases and scored both Cardinal runs in a 2-1 St. Louis victory.

Before Gibson fanned George Scott in the ninth inning of Game 7 to wrap up the Cards' eighth Series title, he and Brock would reorganize the World Series record book. Brock, a .414 hitter over the seven games, tied Series marks for most runs in a seven-game Series (eight), most hits in one game (four) and most stolen bases in one game (three in Game 7, when he swiped two bases in the fifth inning to tie another record). Larcenous Lou's seven stolen bases overall established a World Series record.

"He's murdering us," Boston shortstop Rico Pe-

Cardinal speedster Lou Brock dives safely under the tag of Red Sox catcher Elston Howard in Game 6 of the '67 World Series.

trocelli said amid the slaughter. "Brock's the toughest guy we've ever played against."

"Book on him? There isn't any book on Brock," said Red Sox Manager Dick Williams. "We've thrown him every pitch known to man."

Brock's 12 hits, one shy of Bobby Richardson's record, created chances for Maris and Javier, who compensated for a combined .143 average and five RBIs from Cepeda, Shannon and McCarver. Maris batted .385, his best mark in six career Series, and set a Cardinal Series record with seven RBIs. Javier, a .360 hitter, drove in four runs, three on a home run in the sixth inning of Game 7.

The Red Sox had rallied from a two-game deficit to force the seventh contest and a keenly anticipated duel between Gibson and 22-game winner Jim Lonborg. Lonborg, who had tossed a one-hitter to win 5-0 in Game 2 and a three-hitter to win Game 5, 3-1, was pitching with only two days' rest—and he was opposing the biggest big-game pitcher in baseball.

One day after Scott had predicted Gibson "won't survive five," the Cardinal hurler fired a three-hitter and struck out 10 in a 7-2 victory, capping the win with a solo homer off Lonborg in the fifth inning. Gibson, a 6-0 winner in Game 4, now boasted a 5-1 record in World Series competition with 57 strikeouts in 54 innings. His three complete-game victories against Boston tied a Series mark for most wins and complete games in a seven-game Series.

"The thing that makes Gibson is that he'll never give in, he'll always challenge you," Scott said. "He'll throw the ball across the plate with something on it and say, 'There it is, see if you can hit it.' Other good pitchers will give you the ball when they get in trouble. But not him. He won't give you anything. That's what makes him a winner."

Gibson, however, injected a sobering thought.

"I'm just one guy on this great club. Give the other guys credit."

Briles had sparkled in Game 3, scattering seven hits in a 5-2 victory and had emerged as a force to be reckoned with. "When Gibson was hurt, Briles replaced him so well," Cepeda noted before the 1968 season. "When Gibby came back, we had both of them in the rotation. I think that not only was the turning point for last year but may be for this year, too."

Most convincingly, pitching carried the Cardinals to the 1968 N.L. pennant. In the "Year of the Pitcher," Gibson was *the* pitcher, posting a major league record 1.12 ERA and a career-best 22-9 record as the N.L. MVP and Cy Young Award winner. He led the league with 13 shutouts and 268 strikeouts, and pitched 28 complete games. After a 3-5 start, Gibson won 15 consecutive games and reeled off a streak of 48 consecutive scoreless innings, a string that ended with a wild pitch July 1 in Los Angeles, 10 innings short of the major league record Don Drysdale had established only weeks earlier.

Gibson's worthy constituents combined for another 17 shutouts to help the staff set a franchise record with 30 shutouts overall and lead the league with a 2.49 ERA. Cardinal pitchers held the opposition to one run 31 times and to two runs in 21 games. Thus, in 82 games—just over half the schedule—opponents scored two or fewer runs. Briles won his first four decisions to push his personal winning streak to 14 games and finished the season with 19 victories. Washburn won 14 games and pitched the first Cardinal no-hitter since Lon Warneke in 1941 when he cuffed the Giants on September 18 (a day after Gaylord Perry no-hit the Cardinals). In the bullpen, Hoerner was 8-2 with 11 saves and a 1.47 ERA.

Although a 2-11 tailspin dropped the Cardinals to

22-21 and into fourth place on May 29, they reversed their slide with a nine-game winning streak and led the league by 10 games at the All-Star break at 53-30. They were 24-6 in July, their best month, and coasted to a September 15 clinching date in Houston.

The Cardinal offense wasn't as explosive as in 1967, falling off in home runs (115 to 73), runs scored (695 to 583) and batting (.263 to .249), but Shannon, Flood and Brock helped pace the attack with timely hitting and speed. Shannon raised his average 21 points to .266, led the club with 79 RBIs and had a torrid stretch of 41 RBIs in just over two months. Flood batted a team-leading .301, and Brock led the league in stolen bases (62), doubles (46) and triples (14).

The 1968 World Series shaped up as a rerun of 1967 as Brock and Gibson led the Cardinals to a three-games-to-one advantage over the Detroit Tigers. In the opener, Gibson mowed down 17 Tigers to set a single-game Series strikeout record and the Redbirds defeated 31-game winner Denny McLain, 4-0. In Game 4, Gibby posted a record seventh consecutive Series triumph and poled his second career homer in Series play (a record for a pitcher) in a 10-1 decision over McLain. Brock doubled, tripled, homered and drove in four runs in the rout. He also swiped his seventh base to tie Eddie Collins' record with 14 career Series steals. And with a single in Game 7, Brock collected his 13th hit to tie Richardson's mark.

Once more, though, the Series stretched to seven games. And once again, Gibson was given the ball in the decisive game, this time against 17-game winner Mickey Lolich, a winner in Games 2 and 5. Through six innings, Lolich and Gibson hurled shutout baseball. Then, with two Tigers aboard and two outs in the seventh, Flood slipped on the soggy Busch Stadium field when he tried to retreat after misjudging Jim Northrup's fly ball. The ball sailed over his head and both runners scored, the only runs Detroit would need in a 4-1 victory.

In an uncharacteristically somber St. Louis clubhouse, the Cardinals reflected on what might have been.

"Look, I don't want to make alibis," Flood said. "I should have made the play. I should have made the play. But I didn't and that's all there is to it."

Gibson merely shrugged off the incident, expressing more disappointment in the lack of offense. "There's no way you can win without scoring some runs. Curt's a real pro. Curt would say it's his fault because that's the kind of guy he is."

Even as losers, the Cardinals maintained a winning attitude. It wasn't the dark hour that everyone would remember. It was something overheard in the clubhouse the year before, something that would echo over time.

"We're the Cardinals!"
"Yeah!"
"We're the best!"
"Yeah!"
"We're the champs!"
"Yeah!"
"EL BIRDOS!"
"YEAH!"

1967
FINAL STANDING

Club	W.	L.	Pct.	GB.
St. Louis	101	60	.627	—
San Francisco	91	71	.562	10½

BATTERS

Pos.	Player	G.	HR.	RBI.	B.A.
1B	Orlando Cepeda	151	25	111	.325
2B	Julian Javier	140	14	64	.281
SS	Dal Maxvill	152	1	41	.227
3B	Mike Shannon	130	12	77	.245
OF	Lou Brock	159	21	76	.299
	Curt Flood	134	5	50	.335
	Roger Maris	125	9	55	.261
C	Tim McCarver	138	14	69	.295
UT	Bob Tolan (of)	110	6	32	.253
	Alex Johnson (of)	81	1	12	.223

OTHER CONTRIBUTORS (20+ Games): Ed Bressoud, Phil Gagliano, Dave Ricketts, Johnny Romano, Ed Spiezio.

PITCHERS

Thr.	Pitcher	G.	W.	L.	ERA
R	Dick Hughes	37	16	6	2.68
R	Nelson Briles	49	14	5	2.44
L	Steve Carlton	30	14	9	2.98
R	Bob Gibson	24	13	7	2.98
R	Ray Washburn	27	10	7	3.53
L	Al Jackson	38	9	4	3.95
L	Larry Jaster	34	9	7	3.02
R	Ron Willis	65	6	5	2.67
L	Joe Hoerner	57	4	4	2.59

OTHER CONTRIBUTORS (20+ Games): Jack Lamabe, Hal Woodeshick.

1968
FINAL STANDING

Club	W.	L.	Pct.	GB.
St. Louis	97	65	.599	—
San Francisco	88	74	.543	9

BATTERS

Pos.	Player	G.	HR.	RBI.	B.A.
1B	Orlando Cepeda	157	16	73	.248
2B	Julian Javier	139	4	52	.260
SS	Dal Maxvill	151	1	24	.253
3B	Mike Shannon	156	15	79	.266
OF	Lou Brock	159	6	51	.279
	Curt Flood	150	5	60	.301
	Roger Maris	100	5	45	.255
C	Tim McCarver	128	5	48	.253
UT	Bobby Tolan (of)	92	5	17	.230
	Johnny Edwards (c)	85	3	29	.239

OTHER CONTRIBUTORS (20+ Games): Ron Davis, Phil Gagliano, Dave Ricketts, Dick Schofield, Dick Simpson, Ed Spiezio.

PITCHERS

Thr.	Pitcher	G.	W.	L.	ERA
R	Bob Gibson	34	22	9	1.12
R	Nelson Briles	33	19	11	2.80
R	Ray Washburn	31	14	8	2.26
L	Steve Carlton	34	13	11	2.99
L	Larry Jaster	31	9	13	3.51
L	Joe Hoerner	47	8	2	1.47
R	Ron Willis	48	2	5	3.38

OTHER CONTRIBUTORS (20+ Games): Wayne Granger, Dick Hughes.

Number 20

Curtain Calls And Free-For-Alls

Mets catcher Gary Carter (left) and Manager Davey Johnson share a post-victory smile, a luxury they enjoyed 108 times in 1986.

The mood at the breakfast table was somber as Ray Knight and his wife discussed his professional future with the New York Mets one morning in the spring of 1986.

"You're going to be the third baseman this year," said Nancy Lopez, a leading money-winner on the Ladies Professional Golf Association Tour who had married Knight in 1982.

"You're wrong, Nancy, no matter what you say," Knight responded.

Knight had good reason to be pessimistic. After coming to New York from Houston in an August 1984 trade, Knight had batted .280 in the final month of that season but struggled through an in-

jury-plagued 1985 campaign with a .218 average. Even worse, the former Astro star had been forced to platoon at third base with Howard Johnson. The man who had replaced Pete Rose at third base for the Cincinnati Reds in 1979 loomed as a strong candidate for the scrap pile when the Mets moved north in April 1986.

Nancy Lopez Knight would have none of that kind of talk.

"I know you can play," she told her 33-year-old husband. "I saw you play at Cincinnati. If there's any justice in this world, you're going to get an opportunity to play."

"There's no way I'll get to play in New York," a

Though he hadn't lived up to his vast potential, young Darryl Strawberry still wielded a dangerous, sometimes awesome, bat.

he was among the Mets' leading hitters with a .292 average.

Even so, many Mets watchers still expected Knight to be released. Almost none of the Mets' brass wanted to keep him. But one man still had faith in Knight—Manager Davey Johnson.

"I had the final word," Johnson said. And when the Mets left Florida for New York, Knight went with them.

It didn't take long for Knight to prove his manager's wisdom. On April 22, the Georgia native hit his fourth home run of the season—only two less than he had hit in all of 1985—to spark a 7-1 victory over Pittsburgh. That triumph improved New York's record to 7-3, tied for first place in the National League East with the St. Louis Cardinals. Three nights later in St. Louis, the rejuvenated third baseman smacked a pair of homers to propel the Mets to their seventh straight win. With Knight leading the way, the Mets went on to sweep four games from the Cardinals. They never looked back in a remarkable season punctuated by intense emotion, tremendous drama and rhubarbs both on and off the field.

Never far from the middle of everything was Knight, who had his manager worried about only one thing after his hot start.

"I'm afraid he's going to break some hands, he hits so hard on his high-fives," Johnson said.

High-fives. Barely a month into a season in which he wasn't even expected to participate, Knight already was becoming known for a practice that would make the Mets one of the most hated world champions of all time.

Though New York had finished second to the N.L.-champion Cardinals in 1985, most forecasters had picked the Mets to tear up the league in 1986. No one had more confidence in the Mets than the Mets themselves, who exploded to a 20-4 start and quickly began displaying the theatrics that generally are reserved for late-season heroism. Full of pride and determination, the Mets greeted each other with high-fives and clenched fists at seemingly every opportunity. The Shea Stadium fans loved it, demanding curtain calls after every home run, no matter how meaningless.

The Mets "took guff for our curtain calls," Knight said. "But you've got to realize that we never wanted to do them. The fans would scream for a guy and he would say, 'I don't want to go out there,' and other guys would say, 'You better get out there.' I know I never felt comfortable doing it."

Not surprisingly, the Mets' showmanship was perceived by other teams' players and fans as hotdogging. With every high-five, slapped back, tipped cap and wave to the crowd, the Mets became increasingly despised by the rest of the National League.

despondent Knight replied. "They've made a commitment to Hojo to play every day. I'll be a platoon player. You can forget that."

In fact, Knight complained, platooning with Johnson looked like a best-case scenario. He was well aware of the rumors that the Mets, who already had shopped him around unsuccessfully that spring, were quite willing to put him on waivers and pay him the final year of his contract just to open another spot on the roster. The thought that he might not even be playing baseball in 1986 left Knight thoroughly discouraged.

"Listen," Nancy said. "I want to talk to you about what you're saying, about (the Mets) eating your contract and (you) not being a part of this ball club. Don't care about what people think. You have to believe in yourself."

That piece of advice stuck with Knight, who approached the rest of spring training with newfound vigor. By the end of the Grapefruit League schedule,

"We know they're good," Cardinals shortstop Ozzie Smith said. "But they act like they have to remind everyone all the time."

The Met who grated on the most nerves was catcher Gary Carter. As a seven-time All-Star with the Montreal Expos, Carter had been nicknamed "Camera" by the Mets, who hated the way the curly-haired Californian's smiling mug always seemed to be facing somebody's lens. But when he was traded to the Mets for four players after the 1984 season, his fierce dedication to winning earned his new teammates' respect. He hit 32 homers and drove in 100 runs in 1985 to lead New York to 98 victories, the most since the 1969 Miracle Mets won 100. They still fell three games short of St. Louis, but the Mets saw that Carter could help guide them to the promised land in 1986, and his cocksure attitude and boyish enthusiasm started rubbing off.

That rubbed a lot of folks the wrong way.

"We'd hate the Mets even if they weren't in first place," one Cardinal seethed. "No one can stand Carter."

Opposing pitchers were infuriated by the 32-year-old catcher's clenched-fist salutes to New York's rabid fans as he rounded the bases, returned to the dugout and then reappeared to the sound of more thunderous applause. And with his teammates following his lead at least to some degree, the Mets collectively came to be labeled arrogant.

"All year we got flak for being arrogant," Knight said. "It was a bum rap. The main reason we weren't liked is that we won so much. . . . When you're a winner, you get noticed more. Every highlight is on ESPN, every high-five, every comeback. Hey, we got excited a lot. Gary Carter, me, Wally Backman, Lenny Dykstra—we're all excitable guys. But we weren't showing anybody up. You win, you're pumped up. It's a genuine reaction. What should we have done, frown?"

Fireballing righthander Dwight Gooden, the best pitching prospect Davey Johnson had ever seen, struck out 68 fewer batters than he had in 1985, but his loyal fans still manned 'The K Korner' at Shea Stadium.

Though Ron Darling got off to a 6-0 start in 1986, Mets Manager Davey Johnson still found reason to criticize the righthander.

Carter, it seemed, was incapable of such a facial expression. But who could blame him for smiling? In leaving Montreal, a city he had called home for 10 years, Carter leaped face-first into the media spotlight on a team that, with him batting fifth and handling a young pitching staff, was ripe for success.

The architect of this team was Frank Cashen, the bow-tied general manager who had been hired by Owners Nelson Doubleday and Fred Wilpon after their purchase of the club in January 1980. New York had finished last in the division three years running, and Cashen, a highly successful sportswriter, publicist, racetrack operator, advertising director and, in particular, executive with the powerhouse Baltimore Oriole teams from 1966-75, was entrusted with the responsibility of resurrecting the Mets.

One of the first acquisitions under Cashen's watchful eye was Darryl Strawberry. Hailed as a "black Ted Williams" while a student at Crenshaw High School in Los Angeles, Strawberry was the first overall pick of the June 1980 amateur draft. The lefthanded batter hit for average and tremendous distance, and when he galloped at full throttle, he was a study in grace and speed. He advanced steadily through the Mets' minor league organization, and after only 16 games at the Triple-A level in 1983, Strawberry was promoted to the parent club to play right field. After a slow start, he finished with 26 homers and 74 runs batted in and was named the league's Rookie of the Year. He matched or bettered those numbers in each of the next two seasons but never quite lived up to the high expectations of both the fans and the organization. Injuries, inconsistency, questionable work habits and moodiness made the tall outfielder the target of more abuse than praise.

"People are always talking about me hitting 50 home runs," Strawberry said. "The pressure has been on me since the day I arrived. Maybe they expected me to hit 50 right away. When they talk about me, they say I should hit .300, 50 homers, drive in 125 to 130 runs and steal 50 bases. That's what they say. It adds pressure."

Two years after adding Strawberry to the fold, the Mets used the fifth overall pick of the June amateur draft to select a player who would have even more effect on the pitching staff than Strawberry had on the lineup. Dwight Gooden.

Davey Johnson first encountered Gooden in St. Petersburg, Fla., shortly after the Mets had drafted the Tampa native in June 1982. Johnson, then an instructor in the Mets' farm system, crouched behind the plate to warm up the righthander. Johnson recoiled from one blazing fastball after another until prudence, plus a tender hand, suggested that he call off the drill. He could hardly believe that the hard-throwing hurler with the fluid mechanics and wicked curve was only 17 years old.

"This guy," Johnson said, "is the best pitching prospect I've ever seen."

Gooden didn't disappoint in his brief stay in the minors. After registering 300 strikeouts and being named the Class-A Carolina League's Pitcher of the Year in 1983, Gooden jumped directly into the Mets' 1984 starting rotation. With a 17-9 record, a 2.60 earned-run average and a league-high 276 strikeouts, Gooden was an easy pick as the N.L. Rookie of the Year, giving New York back-to-back winners. He did even better a year later, winning the league's Cy Young Award with an incredible 24-4 record, 1.53 ERA and 268 strikeouts, all N.L. highs.

"He doesn't have to be compared to anyone," Strawberry said. "Pretty soon, people are going to be compared to him."

Unlike Strawberry, Gooden immediately became the darling of New York. His adoring fans kept track of his whiffs in "The K Korner" at Shea Stadium and showered him with praise. The easygoing youngster may have been a bit uncomfortable with all the commotion, but just like on the mound, he handled the attention with surprising poise.

Almost hidden by Gooden's shadow was another outstanding pitcher whom Cashen had acquired a few weeks before signing Gooden. Ron Darling, the Hawaiian-born son of an Irish father and a Chinese-Hawaiian mother, seemed to have it all. With his olive skin and Asian features, he had the looks of a model. He later married one. An All-America pitcher at Yale, where he studied for three years, he also was blessed with brains and brawn. The Texas Rangers made him the ninth overall pick of the June 1981 amateur draft, but the Mets acquired his services (along with pitcher Walt Terrell) by sending outfielder Lee Mazzilli, a huge favorite at Shea Stadium, to the Rangers in April 1982.

In 1984, his first full season in New York, Darling joined the rotation and won 12 games. He went 16-6 with a 2.90 ERA the next year. It was generally agreed that Darling could be the No. 1 starter on almost any team that didn't feature Dwight Gooden.

The only person who appeared upset with Darling's performance was his manager. Darling got off to a 6-0 start in 1986, but Johnson still was frustrated by the righthander's control problems and tendency to fall behind in the count even while pitching with a comfortable lead.

"He should be better," Johnson said. "He wins because he's a competitor. But it shouldn't be that tough for him. That's what bothers me."

The self-confident Darling let Johnson's harping go in one ear and out the other.

"I seem to take the brunt of the criticism as far as the pitching staff is concerned," he said. "I'm man enough not to get upset by it."

Keith Hernandez was quite upset when he became a Met in June 1983. Cashen's swap of pitchers Neil Allen and Rick Ownbey for St. Louis' standout first baseman was his biggest since his days with the Orioles. And though Hernandez was less than thrilled to be going from the defending world champions to a team that would finish last for the second consecutive year, Mets fans were elated to receive a former batting champ and Most Valuable Player with five Gold Gloves on his mantel.

Cashen had made a steal. Hernandez recovered from the initial shock of the trade and quickly assumed leadership of a club that was loaded with youngsters and had more on the way. Even while enduring insults from St. Louis fans who had been informed that he had been traded for, among other things, allegedly working crossword puzzles in the dugout during practice, and then being called to testify at a 1985 trial in which he admitted using cocaine during his years with the Cardinals, Hernandez was a model of consistency on the field. He hit .311 and knocked in 94 runs in 1984 and followed that up with a .309, 91-RBI season. And as a fielder, he was without peer.

Gold Glove first baseman Keith Hernandez recovered from the shock of being traded by St. Louis and assumed a leadership role for the Mets.

"Keith is the best I've ever seen at digging balls out of the dirt," Johnson said. "But there's more to Keith than that. He's a pro in all aspects of the game. He wins games with his bat, he wins games with his glove. And everything he does is done with enthusiasm and animation. It's very critical for an infield to have spark. Keith shows signs of life and enjoyment in everything he does. That's important."

Cashen's next big trade came in December 1983, and this time he got a Fernandez to go with Hernandez. Two players were dispatched to Los Angeles for Sid Fernandez, a 21-year-old lefthander who wore jersey number 50 in honor of his native Hawaii, the 50th state. "El Sid" had pitched a pair of no-hitters in one season while in the lower reaches of the Dodgers' farm system and had won Texas League Pitcher of the Year honors in 1983. A power pitcher whose fastball moved up through the strike zone rather than down, Fernandez was more of a long-range prospect than Gooden and Darling. He spent parts of the '84 and '85 seasons at the Mets' International League affiliate in Tidewater and opened the 1986 season with 15 major league victories on his resume.

By the time Fernandez joined the organization,

Lefthander Bob Ojeda (left), third baseman Ray Knight and catcher Gary Carter congratulate each other after another Mets triumph.

the Mets were starting to jell. With Davey Johnson at the helm in his first major league managing job, the Mets won 90 games and came in second in 1984, their best finish in eight years. But Cashen, who had picked up Knight late that season, knew he still had work to do if the Mets were to emerge on top.

In December 1984, Cashen plugged a big hole behind the plate by acquiring Carter and added depth at third base by getting Howard Johnson from the Detroit Tigers in exchange for Terrell. Hojo platooned with Knight and batted .242 as the Mets posted their second consecutive second-place finish.

But Cashen, like all successful general managers, still wasn't satisfied. Though Gooden, Darling, Fernandez and righthander Rick Aguilera, who had won 10 games and fashioned a 3.24 ERA as a 1985 rookie, formed a rotation that was second to none, he wanted another lefty to balance his starting staff. He also craved a righthanded-hitting second baseman to alternate with Wally Backman, a slick fielder who hit from both sides of the plate, but with success only from the left side and with power from neither.

Cashen realized his first objective at Boston. In a November 1985 trade that involved eight players but required him to give up no major leaguers, Cashen landed Bob Ojeda. The 28-year-old Californian's five-year record with the Red Sox was only

44-39, but the deal met with general approval from Mets fans. Even Cardinals Manager Whitey Herzog had to tip his cap to the Mets for a deal that made a strong team even better.

"If you're going to get a lefthander," Herzog said, "get one who pitched in Boston. He's got to learn how to pitch just to survive in Fenway Park."

Cashen achieved his second goal in a trade with Minnesota. Again giving up only minor leaguers, he obtained Tim Teufel, a scrappy .265 lifetime hitter who had totaled 24 homers and 111 RBIs as the Twins' starting second baseman the previous two seasons. Teufel solidified an infield that left shortstop, manned by light-hitting, 28-year-old Rafael Santana, as the only weak spot.

With that transaction, Cashen rested. The rebuilding job that he had commenced six years before was finished. His 1986 roster was set.

Batting leadoff was either Len Dykstra or Mookie Wilson, who shared center-field duties. Dykstra, called "Nails" for his tough-nosed approach to the game, was a 23-year-old speedster with a decent glove, an adequate bat and a crooked grin. Wilson, a 30-year-old switch-hitter from South Carolina, was a consistent .275 hitter with a weak arm.

Batting second in Johnson's typical lineup was either Backman or Teufel, depending on the opposing pitcher that day, followed by Hernandez, Strawberry, Carter and 37-year-old left fielder George Foster, a high-paid former superstar with the Cincinnati Reds whose effectiveness was eroding. The bottom third of the order featured either Knight or Howard Johnson, Santana and the pitcher.

Actually, Hojo and 24-year-old Kevin Mitchell played a lot of shortstop in the first half of the season as Johnson tried to field the most potent offense he could devise. Johnson, who had earned a math degree at Trinity University in San Antonio, varied the lineup according to the data spit out by his trusty computer and his own whims.

"It (the lineup) comes from the computer and from my hunches and from who hasn't played and from who needs to play," he said.

In the bullpen, Johnson had a good righty-lefty combination in veteran Jesse Orosco, who had earned 65 saves over the previous three seasons, and 25-year-old Roger McDowell, who had tallied 17 saves as a rookie in 1985. Orosco's fastball and slider and McDowell's sinker baffled batters in the late innings, while righthander Doug Sisk helped out in middle relief.

"This is the best . . . pitching staff I've seen in my 12 years," Hernandez said. "They just take so much pressure off us because they keep us in every game. You know that the starter is going to give you six or seven good innings every time out, and then we've got Roger and Jesse to come in and finish it off. It's just a fantastic staff."

Johnson knew he had something special as he watched his team work out in St. Petersburg before the season. The only scary moment of the spring occurred when Wilson, performing a rundown drill between two fielders, was struck in the eye by a throw from Santana. It took 21 stitches to close the wound, and Wilson was out until mid-May.

But Dykstra was more than willing to play every day and the Mets still ranked as the team to beat in the N.L. East. Johnson was so sure of his club's potential that he set an especially lofty goal. "We don't want to just win," he proclaimed. "We want to dominate."

The Mets did just that from the start. They had a five-game lead by the end of April and a six-game advantage at the end of May. The race was all but over by the All-Star break as the Mets coasted in with a 59-25 record and a 13-game margin over their closest pursuers. "Metsmania" was sweeping the country—like wildfire if you cheered the Mets, like a fungus if you didn't—and the team's perceived arrogance and on-field celebrations were beginning to take their toll. Whenever word came of a fight in a major league baseball game, it was a good bet that the Mets were involved.

"We were pretty intense all year," Backman said. "We had to be after a while. People were gunning for us. They didn't like the way we acted. They

Len Dykstra was a fiery competitor who would do whatever it took to ensure victory.

came at us pretty good. Some of them wanted to fight us because they knew they couldn't beat us playing baseball."

For whatever reason, the Mets fought. On May 27, Dodgers pitcher Tom Niedenfuer, who had just served up a grand slam to Foster, drilled Knight in the elbow with his next pitch. Knight charged the mound and both benches emptied. A similar scene erupted less than two weeks later when Mets first-base coach Bill Robinson incited the wrath of Pirates pitcher Rick Rhoden by questioning him about his alleged habit of scuffing baseballs. It was bench-clearing brawl time again July 11 when Strawberry stormed after Atlanta's David Palmer, who had plunked him with a pitch.

These incidents were little more than shoving matches, but a genuine fight erupted July 22 in Cincinnati. When the Reds' Eric Davis slid hard into Knight at third—according to Ray, Eric also cursed him—Knight responded with a hard right jab to the chin. By the end of the ensuing melee, a number of players on both sides sported bruises as souvenirs of the evening's affair.

Technically, the Mets had provoked only one of the altercations (the brawl with the Pirates), but turning the other cheek was not in their nature. As a result, the Mets were prime candidates for Friday night's main event.

"People on other clubs are looking for us to fight," Backman said.

After the brouhaha in Cincinnati, Reds outfielder Dave Parker certainly was. "I wish we had another series with them," he fumed. "Maybe we could get into another fight. There are too many tough guys over there. I think they ought to be shown there are tough guys everywhere."

The Mets met their match, so to speak, in a highly publicized off-the-field fracas in Houston just after the All-Star break. The night started harmlessly enough with Teufel, Darling, Ojeda and Aguilera visiting a local nightspot to celebrate the birth of Teufel's son. All proceeded peaceably until Teufel was reportedly asked to leave the bar because he was arguing with another customer. Teufel tried to take his drink with him as he left but was informed by an off-duty police officer working as a security guard that Texas law prohibited such a practice. One insult provoked another and before long, all four players and a pair of off-duty officers were going at it. The four Mets wound up behind bars, with Teufel a bit worse for wear, on charges ranging from aggravated assault to hindering arrest. Club officials sprung the four on bond the next day, but Astro fans later delighted in wearing T-shirts that read "Houston Police 4, New York Mets 0."

Another controversy involving the Mets surfaced in early August when Foster was released. The slumping outfielder had been relegated to pinch-hitting duty after the All-Star break and the left-field job was turned over to Mitchell and Danny Heep, who platooned. Foster didn't like it, and it was reported that he blamed his benching and other Mets personnel decisions on racial factors. Foster, who is black, denied making the statements, but Davey Johnson still seethed at the allegations.

"That was maybe the straw that broke the camel's back," said Johnson, who recommended that Foster be released and saw the vacant roster spot filled by Lee Mazzilli.

The Mets, it seemed, could not avoid the glare of the media spotlight—not that they really tried. As the season dragged on toward its inevitable conclusion, the printed page and airwaves became saturated with Mets hawking everything from cars to soap and even performing their own music video. And they were just warming up. When the Mets finished the regular season with a club-record 108 victories and a 21½-game cushion over second-place Philadelphia, that just meant the Mets' publicity locomotive could keep on chugging into the postseason.

Surprisingly, no single Met had a season that could be described as outstanding. New York led the league in batting (.263), runs scored (783), hits (1,462), total bases (2,229) and ERA (3.11), among other categories, but it was a collective effort that produced those numbers.

The only New York batters who led the league in anything were Hernandez (94 walks) and Carter (16 game-winning RBIs, tied with Houston's Glenn Davis). Hernandez (.310) was the only Met regular who broke .300, while Carter (105) was the only Met in triple-digit RBIs. Only Strawberry (27) and Carter (24) surpassed 20 homers. The numbers also were spread fairly evenly around the Mets' superb pitching staff, which was topped by Ojeda's 18-5 record and McDowell's 22 saves, one more than Orosco. Gooden won 17 games and was content to fan 200 batters (68 fewer than the year before) as he altered his approach to pitching.

"I don't worry about strikeouts," he explained. "I'd just as soon throw one pitch and get a ground ball as three for a strikeout."

With all these solid but unspectacular performances, the most dominant team in baseball failed to produce any of the major postseason award winners. None, that is, unless you count Knight's distinction as The Sporting News' Comeback Player of the Year in the senior circuit. And among the non-playing personnel, Cashen was honored as The Sporting News' Major League Executive of the Year for his work in constructing the Mets, who attracted 2,762,417 fans to Shea Stadium, the highest attendance for any New York team in history.

Despite the lack of awards, there was no question that the Mets had dominated their opposition in 1986. But it was their postseason miracle comebacks that made them truly great.

After splitting the first two games of the N.L. Championship Series in Houston, the Mets and the West Division champion Astros went to New York for Game 3. The Mets entered the bottom of the ninth inning trailing, 5-4. Pitching for Houston was ace reliever Dave Smith, who had registered saves in 33 of 39 save situations that season. When Dykstra came to the plate with one on and one out, Houston fans already were beginning to savor a 2-1 lead in the series. But the diminutive Dykstra, who had poked just eight home runs during the regular season, slammed a Smith forkball into the Mets' bullpen in right field to give New York a 6-5 victory.

"The last time I hit a home run in the bottom of the ninth inning to win a game," Nails reflected gleefully, "was in Strat-O-Matic."

Dykstra's improbable homer set the tone for the rest of the postseason. The Astros evened the series with a triumph in Game 4, but the Mets moved one win away from the World Series when Carter, who had been mired in a 1-for-21 slump, won Game 5 with an RBI single in the 12th inning. The playoff series then moved back to the Astrodome, where Houston's Bob Knepper checked the Mets on two hits through eight innings and entered the top of the ninth with a 3-0 lead in Game 6. But key hits by

World Series MVP Ray Knight hugs teammate Gary Carter after the Mets had
dispatched Boston in the final game of the 1986 classic.

Dykstra, Wilson and Hernandez and a run-scoring
fly ball by Knight tied it up and sent the game into
overtime. The Mets went on top, 4-3, in the 14th,
but Houston kept the game going when Billy
Hatcher smacked a solo home run in the bottom
half of that frame. It appeared as if the game would
go on forever until finally, in the top of the 16th
inning, the Mets tallied three times to take a 7-4
lead.

The game wasn't over yet. Orosco, who had allowed Hatcher's game-tying homer two innings earlier, was beginning to tire. The Astros rallied for
two runs and had the potential tying and winning
runs on base when hot-hitting Kevin Bass came to
the plate with two out. But Orosco had something
left in reserve. Heeding Hernandez's advice not to
throw any fastballs, Orosco delivered six straight
breaking pitches to strike out Bass and end the
game. After 16 innings and four hours, 42 minutes
—the longest contest in postseason history—the
Mets had completed an incredible comeback to win
the N.L. pennant.

"The ball's in there—the last ball from the last
strikeout—and it's not leaving my pocket," the

ever-grinning Carter said as the Mets celebrated in
their clubhouse. "I'm going to have all the guys sign
it on the flight home, and I'm never going to let go
of it. That had to be the best game that ever lived."

Carter's desire for a memento autographed by his
teammates typified the Mets' all-for-one-and-one-
for-all camaraderie. They may have been despised
by others, but they liked and pulled for each other.
That unity again was evident when the Mets took
on the Boston Red Sox in the World Series.

The Mets dug themselves a huge hole by losing
the first two games of the Series at Shea Stadium.
Only one team in World Series history—the 1985
Kansas City Royals—had ever come back to win the
Series after losing the first two games at home. But
the Mets stormed back to win the next two contests
at Boston before dropping Game 5. The Series returned to Shea Stadium with the Red Sox needing
just one more victory to wrap up the title.

They seemed intent on icing the Series immediately. Single tallies in each of the first two frames
gave Boston a 2-0 lead. New York knotted the count
in the fifth, but an unearned run put Boston back
on top in the seventh. With Roger Clemens, the

American League's most dominant pitcher, on the mound for the Red Sox, the Mets appeared to be in dire straits.

To the Mets' delight, however, Clemens left the game with a blister on his pitching hand after seven innings. New York promptly tied the game, 3-3, on Carter's sacrifice fly in the bottom of the eighth. After a scoreless ninth, the game went to extra innings.

If either of the contestants loomed as destiny's darling, it was Boston. Dave Henderson, the outfielder whose stunning home run in Game 5 of the A.L. playoffs had forever etched him in New England baseball lore, led off the top of the 10th inning with a circuit blast off Aguilera, New York's fourth pitcher of the night. When Boston added another run to take a 5-3 lead into the bottom of the 10th, the setting was perfect for a fairy-tale finish for Henderson and the Red Sox.

Entrusted with protecting Boston's lead was rookie Calvin Schiraldi, who had become the team's ace reliever after being obtained from New York in the Ojeda deal a year earlier. Schiraldi retired the first two New York batters, Backman and Hernandez, and the latter was so sure that the Mets' well of miracles had run dry that he left the dugout, went to Davey Johnson's office and turned on the TV to watch the Mets' rip-roaring season come to a quiet end.

"I went into Davey's office for a beer," Hernandez recalled. "I was very ticked."

The first baseman's anger turned to renewed hope as he watched Carter and Mitchell rap consecutive singles. Schiraldi then fired two quick strikes past Knight to put the Red Sox one strike away from their first world championship since 1918. But the Shea Stadium fans went crazy when Knight rapped the next pitch into center field for a single, scoring Carter and sending Mitchell to third. That was it for Schiraldi, who was replaced by Bob Stanley.

Facing Wilson, Stanley again put the Red Sox one strike away from the championship—twice. After fouling off Stanley's 2-1 delivery, Wilson fouled off two more pitches to keep the Mets breathing. Wilson's persistence then paid off when Stanley uncorked a wild pitch. Mitchell raced home with the tying run and Knight scampered to second, stirring the crowd into a frenzy.

The most incredible play of all was yet to come. Wilson fouled off the next two pitches, then spanked an easy grounder straight toward first baseman Bill Buckner, normally a solid fielder. Buckner put down his glove but the ball skipped beneath it, giving Knight all the time in the world to jump on home plate with the winning run.

"I thought it was going to be a routine play," Knight said. "When I hit third base, I heard (coach)

Buddy Harrelson yelling, 'Go! Go!' and I looked over my shoulder and couldn't believe it. When I crossed the plate, I had a tremendous feeling of electricity."

The whole club was charged after that spectacular comeback. With the momentum clearly on New York's side, it came as little surprise when the Mets overcame a 3-0 deficit to win the decisive seventh contest, 8-5. Knight led the way with two singles and a home run to raise his Series average to .391. And when it was over, Knight, the guy deemed least likely to retain his job during spring training, was named World Series MVP.

"I've been obsessed this year with coming back," he said. "Tonight just capped it off."

The next spring, Knight was in camp with the Baltimore Orioles after signing a free-agent contract. But he still had warm feelings for the '86 Mets.

"All of those guys had something special," Knight reflected. "I don't know if it came from pulling for one another or not, but there was always the feeling that somebody was going to pull us through. There were all winners on that club—a great professional attitude."

And cocky? Sure. Arrogant? Perhaps. But whatever it was, it worked. The Mets proved they were what they said they were—the best team in baseball.

1986
FINAL STANDING

Club	W.	L.	Pct.	GB.
New York	108	54	.667	——
Philadelphia	86	75	.534	21½

BATTERS

Pos.	Player	G.	HR.	RBI.	B.A.
1B	Keith Hernandez	149	13	83	.310
2B	Wally Backman	124	1	27	.320
	Tim Teufel	93	4	31	.247
SS	Rafael Santana	139	1	28	.218
3B	Ray Knight	137	11	76	.298
OF	Mookie Wilson	123	9	45	.289
	Lenny Dykstra	147	8	45	.295
	Darryl Strawberry	136	27	93	.259
C	Gary Carter	132	24	105	.255
UT	Danny Heep (of)	86	5	33	.282
	Howard Johnson (inf)	88	10	39	.245
	Kevin Mitchell (of)	108	12	43	.277

OTHER CONTRIBUTORS (20+ Games): George Foster, Ed Hearn, Lee Mazzilli.

PITCHERS

Thr.	Pitcher	G.	W.	L.	ERA
L	Bob Ojeda	32	18	5	2.57
R	Dwight Gooden	33	17	6	2.84
L	Sid Fernandez	32	16	6	3.52
R	Ron Darling	34	15	6	2.81
R	Roger McDowell	75	14	9	3.02
R	Rick Aguilera	28	10	7	3.88
L	Jesse Orosco	58	8	6	2.33
R	Doug Sisk	41	4	2	3.06

OTHER CONTRIBUTORS (20+ Games): Randy Niemann.

Number 21

Gas House Gang Rides High

Members of the 1934 Gas House Gang: (Left to right) Dizzy Dean, Leo Durocher, Ernie Orsatti, Bill DeLancey, Rip Collins, Joe Medwick, Frankie Frisch, Jack Rothrock and Pepper Martin.

They were the last bunch you would want to encounter over 167 days of a baseball season—if you were playing baseball. To an economically strapped Depression society of 1934, they were the most effective sports therapy around, a roisterous, grimy, lovable aggregation known as the Gas House Gang.

These St. Louis Cardinals brawled among themselves but went to the baseball wars united behind a bare-knuckles battlefront. They drew fines and suspensions. They went on personal strikes. They dripped with color and perspiration. They were uninhibited, talented baseball professionals who reigned in an era when life moved at a leisurely pace and love of the game was a stronger magnet for gifted athletes than the monetary rewards it offered.

No player symbolized the spirit of the Gas House Gang more splendidly than a gangly 23-year-old whose eccentric conduct and zest for life would illuminate the National League for most of the 1930s. He was a former cotton picker from the Southwest, a child of poverty who answered to the name of Dizzy Dean.

Dean was far removed from the behavioral norm; his antics were ample proof. But once Dizzy took the pitching mound, it was the batter who lost his equilibrium while trying to cope with the big righthander's blazing fastball, his darting curve and the taunts he hurled from just over 60 feet away.

Dizzy was the first and only player who, by his own declaration, had three birthplaces, three birthdates and a pair of names. He eventually clarified that he was born in Lucas, Ark., on January 16, 1911. He merely disseminated other data as "scoops" for newspaper pals. And although christened "Jay Hanna" he assumed the handle "Jerome Herman" to relieve a grieving father. He explained the circumstances to J. Roy Stockton in the St. Louis scribe's book, "The Gashouse Gang":

I was very popular with the neighbors and especially with a man who had a little boy about my age—six or seven, I guess. . . . My name in the first place was Jay Hanna Dean

The pitching aces of the Gas House Gang were 'Me
'n' Paul': 30-game winner Dizzy (right) and
19-game winner Paul Dean.

*and this boy's was Jerome Herman something
or other. I was named after some big shot on
Wall Street—or he was named after me, I
don't know which.*

*Anyhow, this boy Jerome Herman took sick
and died and we sure did feel sorry for his
dad. He just moped around and didn't care
for nothin' no more. So I went to him and
told him I thought so much of him that I was
goin' to take the name of Jerome Herman and
I've been Jerome ever since. He perked up
right away, and I guess wherever he is he's
mighty proud.*

Fact or fiction, the account was typical of this
unrivaled showman. He thrived in an age when em-
broidered tales were enthusiastically accepted. The
more farfetched, the better the laugh—and the better to keep repeating. From the moment he hit the
Cardinal farm system in 1930, Dean had them doubled over with his yarns and unrestrained bragging.
But, as Ol' Diz pointed out, "It ain't braggin' if you
can back it up."

In his first major league appearance, Dean cuffed

the Pittsburgh Pirates, 3-1, with a three-hitter on
the final day of the 1930 season. While the Cardinals entrained for Philadelphia to meet the Athletics in the World Series, Dizzy went home to steal
the pre-Series headlines, perhaps to send a message
to club President Sam Breadon and General Manager Branch Rickey.

"Show me another pitcher in the majors who has
never been defeated," he exulted.

"Sure (the Cardinals) begged and begged me to go
along with them. But, you know, I'm fed up on this
baseball stuff. Us big-league pitchers get rather
bored in time.

"I told Mr. Rickey I would wait until next year
and win him three games in the World Series. I
would have done that this year if they'd allowed me
to work. . . .

"Down there they think I'm good. Well, after seeing several of the big-league teams play . . . I don't
recall seeing any better than myself. I told Gabby
(Street, the manager) I could win him 20 or 30
games next year. And to tell the truth, I don't think
I will be beaten.

"Don't think though that I'm bragging about all
this; I'm just lettin' you in on some inside facts. . . .
Next year, I'm going to be known as "The Great
Dean.""

Unfortunately for Diz, he paraded under that
moniker for Houston in the Texas League. After a
spring camp marked by free spending ("I kept wir-
ing Rickey for the old dough-re-mi"), fast talking
("Those news chaps had to have some stories") and
insubordination ("Gabby can think up more laws
in a minute than an Oklahoma lawyer"), Dean was
dispatched to Houston.

"That's probably a world record," commented
Cardinals pitcher Jim Lindsey. "It's the first time a
club ever lost 30 games in one day."

Dean won 26 games for Houston, locking a spot
on the Cards' 1932 roster no matter what his behavior. In his first major league season, "The Great
Dean" led N.L. pitchers in strikeouts (191) and innings pitched (286) while posting an 18-15 record.
In 1933, he won 20 games and struck out a league-
high 199 batters, including a major league record 17
in the first game of a July 30 doubleheader against
the Chicago Cubs.

"I should have done better," Dean apologized.
"My fastball wasn't breaking just right."

By 1934, Diz had the numbers to back up the
bragging. And when he held court at the Cardinals'
Bradenton, Fla., spring camp, Dean was doing the
bragging for two. "Why, we're going to win 45
games between us this year," said Dizzy, his arm
slung around a 20-year-old rawbone rookie. "If we
don't . . . we'll give the money back to Mr. Breadon,
won't we Paul?"

Hesitating, Paul Lee Dean nodded. The young

The brain trust of the 1934 St. Louis Cardinals: player-Manager Frankie Frisch (left) and coach Mike Gonzalez.

righthander had signed a $3,000 contract after a 22-7 1933 season with Columbus in the American Association. He was judged as hard a thrower—if not harder—than his celebrated sibling. And at 6-foot-2, 195 pounds, he was physically similar. Otherwise, the two brothers were easily distinguishable: Jay Hanna was garrulous, aggressive, the spokesman; Paul Lee was reticent, retiring, the listener.

But Dizzy talked a good enough game for two. "Next to me, I think he will be the greatest pitcher in the world," he said. Then, this multitalented athlete-orator-prophet offered another prediction: The defending World Series champion New York Giants would not retain the N.L. pennant. "It will take 95 games to win the pennant," he asserted knowingly, "and the Giants can't win that many. That's why we'll win."

The manager of the Redbirds read Dean's prophecies with consuming interest. He had traveled the pennant road many times and knew the obstacles and perplexities that were ahead. He had played in seven World Series, four times as a Giant, three as a Cardinal. He was Frank Francis Frisch, the "Fordham Flash," and he was entering his first full

season as pilot of the Gas House Gang after succeeding Street the previous July.

Now 35, Frisch may have lost a step, but he played second base and rapped out base hits in the same aggressive manner that marked his game since he was plucked off the Fordham campus by John McGraw in 1919. He had batted at least .300 in 12 of his last 13 seasons, won the N.L. Most Valuable Player award in 1931 and had become one of the most popular Cardinals ever after arriving from New York in an unpopular deal for Rogers Hornsby following the 1926 season.

Upon taking over as skipper, Frisch outlined his managerial philosophy, an expression of his own fighting attitude that became the essence of the Gas House Gang:

"A winning ball club is made up of good players with good pitchers—that goes without saying. But there's something else, a fighting spirit, a confidence, a determination to pull through. . . .

"The same goes for individuals. There are winning ball players. They may not hit as well or be such capable fielders, but they fight for every game and fight for their club. They have the winning spirit.

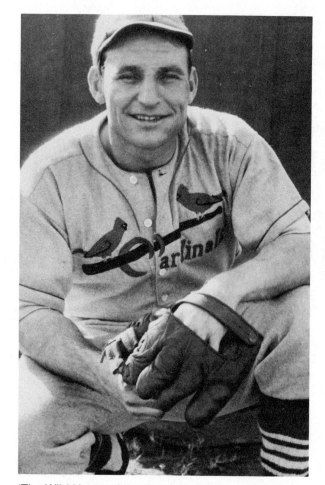

'The Wild Horse of the Osage,' third baseman Pepper Martin, led the Gas House Gang in hustle and horseplay.

"You can search in the records for this spirit and you will never find it. It isn't there. Batting averages don't express it, nor pitching averages, nor fielding averages...."

Frisch also was something of a character himself. A native of New York City, he had a high-pitched nasal twang that soared to dramatic heights when he was emotionally moved. The Dutchman, as Dizzy called him, had a highly developed sense of humor and a temper that could carry him to the brink of apoplexy.

Dizzy Dean's role as ringleader of the Gas House circus was strongly challenged by the team's muscular third baseman, a grinning Oklahoman who frequently proclaimed and set out to prove himself the strongest man in the world. Originally an outfielder, he was like a tornado in clubhouse wrestling matches, much as he had been in the 1931 World Series, when his .500 hitting and five stolen bases helped the Cardinals topple the mighty Philadelphia Athletics.

John Leonard (Pepper) Martin was unrivaled as a scrapping, hustling, sparkplug. He tore into bases

with head-first slides, knocked down line drives with his broad chest and left the field each day with the dirtiest uniform. Off the diamond, he had no equal as a prankster. Dropping waterbags out of upstairs hotel windows was one of his many favorites. Teammates were continually amused and constantly on guard.

"Pepper organized the famous Mudcat Band of humpty-dumpty musicians who serenaded fans before exhibition games," Frisch once wrote. "He strolled along St. Louis streets wearing a sign, 'KICK ME HARD.' He carried sneeze powder in his pocket. He excelled in the art of giving the hotfoot. He forged the name of the latest Public Enemy No. 1 on hotel registers. When lobby sitting bored him, he would stage a fake brawl with a teammate who would pretend to smack him in the face. Popcorn would fall from Pepper's mouth like dislodged teeth, ketchup would drip from his lips like blood. Ladies fainted, Pepper was happy."

Martin loved to race midget cars and ride broncos at rodeos. Whatever was available to while away the idle hours, Pepper was for it, regardless of the risks involved. And in two of his first three full seasons in the majors, Pepper batted at least .300. A better leadoff man could not be found.

Undoubtedly, the Gas Houser with the fastest fists was Joe Medwick, the 22-year-old left fielder. The son of a Hungarian millhand in Carteret, N.J., "Muscles" was well-proportioned at 5-10 and 178 pounds. He attacked a pitched ball—usually a bad one—with uncommon ferocity, rattling the fences with powerful drives as the Cards' cleanup man. In 1933, his first full major league season, the right-handed-hitting Medwick batted .306, pounded 18 home runs and drove in 98.

Woe betide any pitcher—or teammate—who took liberties with Medwick. Early in 1934, he traded punches with Tex Carleton when the Cardinal pitcher tried to order him out of the batting cage; when the Dean brothers stomped toward him in the dugout after he had committed a miscue behind Dizzy, Medwick grabbed a bat and threatened to "separate them forever."

Dizzy found Medwick's pugilistic practices exasperating. "Before you even get to do enough talking to get really mad enough to fight and make a good job of it, Joe whops you and the fight's over," Dean moaned. "That ain't no way to fight."

But above all, Medwick was deeply admired and respected by his teammates for his slashing hitting. "He just stood up there and whaled everything within reach," Leo Durocher remembered. "Doubles, triples, home runs. He sprayed 'em all over every park, and if he had a weakness, it was a ball over the plate."

Medwick's outfield mates were less combative but no less spirited. Ernie Orsatti, the primary center fielder, had joined the Cardinals in 1927 and hit better than .300 five times as a part-time outfielder/first baseman. He was only 5-7½, 150 pounds, but he thundered across the field with breakneck abandon, a throwback to his days as a Hollywood stunt man. Orsatti, in fact, had decided to pursue a career in baseball at the urging of actor Buster Keaton, who had organized a studio team on which Orsatti starred.

Right field was patrolled by Jack Rothrock, who joined the Cardinals in 1934 after a year and a half in the minor leagues. From 1927 through 1931, he had been a versatile switch-hitting infielder/outfielder with the Boston Red Sox. With the Gas House Gang, he was a reliable No. 2 batter.

James Anthony Collins proved a worthy successor to slugging first baseman Jim Bottomley. A switch-hitter, "Rip" batted over .300 in 1931 and 1933. He also packed a wallop that belied his small frame (5-9, 160 pounds), slamming 21 home runs with 91 RBIs in 1932.

Whenever Martin or Dizzy proposed a prank, Collins was a willing accomplice. During one series in Philadelphia in 1936, Martin, Dean and infielder Heine Schuble dressed in workers' overalls and sauntered into a banquet room at the team hotel. Ignoring a convention that was in progress, the "redecorators" began pointing, measuring, moving furniture and eventually arguing over the job at hand. Collins, acting as the foreman, shouted directions and epithets at his crew. Soon, one of the befuddled onlookers recognized Dean and the ball players were called upon to make speeches.

"Rickey always accused me of being the ringleader," Collins said innocently. "I never could understand why he picked on me—unless it could have been because there was considerable truth in his allegations."

Joining Collins, Martin and Frisch in the Cardinals' infield was Leo Durocher, a fashion plate off the field and a viper-tongued battler on it. An adroit fielder, Durocher was the weakest hitter among the regular Redbirds (his best season had been his first in the majors, .270 with the New York Yankees in 1928), but he also was free with advice. For good reason, he owned the nickname "Lippy."

In one game, Dizzy was attempting to escape a tight spot when the Lip grunted orders from shortstop, "Pitch him low, pitch him low."

Stepping off the rubber, Dean turned toward his tormentor, glared for a second then roared for all the park to hear, "Why in the hell should a great pitcher like me listen to a lousy .210 hitter like you?"

When Frisch raced in from second base and echoed Durocher's instructions, Dean turned on the manager with a ready response: "You stick to playing second base and I'll stick to pitching. . . . Tell me

'Muscles' Joe Medwick, the Cardinals' left fielder, needed only a bad ball to hit and one punch to settle a score.

the last time you won 20 games, you old Dutchman."

The Cardinals' catching staff was composed of Virgil (Spud) Davis, a strapping 210-pound veteran, and 22-year-old Bill DeLancey. Davis, who broke into the majors with the Cardinals in 1928, had developed into one of the National League's best hitters with the Philadelphia Phillies, batting no lower than .313 in five full seasons there. He returned to St. Louis after the 1933 season in a deal for Jimmy Wilson—the catcher he had been traded for in May 1928. DeLancey provided Frisch with another long-distance threat after walloping 21 homers and collecting 97 RBIs at Columbus in 1933.

Once past the Deans—or, in Dizzy's words, "Me 'n' Paul"—Davis and DeLancey guided a starting rotation rounded out by righthander Tex Carleton and lefthanders Wild Bill Hallahan and Bill Walker.

Carleton was slender, cool and courageous, a quiet man who let his pitching speak for itself. He notched 10 wins as a rookie in 1932, then 17 in 1933 as the No. 2 starter on the St. Louis staff.

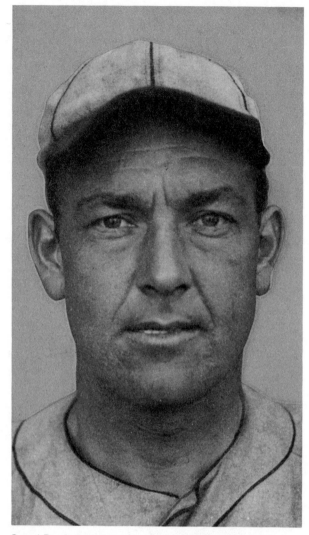

Spud Davis had been traded in 1928 but returned to hit .300 as half of the Cards' catching corps.

Hallahan was deserving of his nickname, but he wasn't so erratic that he was uneffective. He led the National League with 126 walks in 1930 and 112 passes in 1931, but he also topped the circuit in strikeouts both seasons. More important, he chipped in 15 and then 19 victories to help the Cardinals to two N.L. flags.

Walker, a winner of 14, 17 and 16 games for the New York Giants from 1929 through 1931 and twice the league's earned-run champion, was acquired following the 1932 season. Like the rest of the Cardinals, he was set for a big year after a 9-10 season in 1933.

St. Louis, a fifth-place finisher in '33, was picked to finish fourth behind New York, Chicago and Pittsburgh in The Sporting News' annual poll of the Baseball Writers' Association of America. "That's all right with me," Frisch said. "I wouldn't care if they picked us to finish last. If everybody got to thinking that, we might give them a surprise."

What everyone overlooked was the fire that burned deep in the Gas House: "The Gas House may have been a nuthouse, but they played ball for keeps, the way it should be played," Frisch maintained. "It was a club compounded of rawhide, rusty spikes, grit, gall, baseline dust and splinters off outfield fences."

Nine games into the season, however, the Cardinals had lost seven times. Paul Dean worked only two innings in each of his first three assignments and surrendered eight runs. When he gave up five runs in five innings on May 3 against Philadelphia (despite gaining his first major league victory), grave doubts surfaced about his ability. Frisch gave him the acid test May 11 against the Giants and Paul held up with a 3-2, 10-inning decision over Carl Hubbell.

Paul's second big-league victory gave the Cardinals 12 wins in their last 13 games. Bolstered by the league's best hitting attack, they were in first place by the end of May despite the loss of Walker, who suffered a broken forearm May 6 when struck by a Medwick line drive in batting practice. When the Cards entrained for Pittsburgh to begin their June slate, however, Dizzy Dean informed Frisch he'd be without two other pitchers as well—Ol' Diz and Paul were going on strike.

Paul, Dizzy maintained, was due an extra $2,000 in wages that Rickey had promised in March. Until he received it, the Deans wouldn't pitch an inning. On June 1, Dizzy sat in the stands at Forbes Field instead of taking his turn on the mound. The Cardinals lost, 4-3—with Paul Dean in uniform. By the next afternoon, Dizzy was back in the fold, his sympathy strike over.

"Gee, those Cardinals are swell fellows and there never was a fellow like Frisch," Dizzy said. "Isn't he a pip? You know there must be something wrong with anybody who wouldn't pitch his arm off for Old Frank. Show me a guy who says a bad word about Old Frank and I'll bash his face in."

With the Deans leading the way, the Cardinals engaged New York and Chicago in a tussle for the lead. Of the Redbirds' first 33 victories, the Deans accounted for 17. Paul, past the experimental stage, won his first eight decisions.

"It is my judgment that Paul throws a sailer," remarked one Chicago batter. "He comes down half sidearm and the ball seems to dart out from the lower clutch of his fingers. In fact, he hurls the ball out of his sleeve, so to speak."

Even the hurling of the Deans, however, could not hold off the Giants, who took over first place on June 6. A 13-14 pace through June dropped the Cardinals into third place behind Chicago, where they remained for virtually all of July and August.

A string of injuries to Paul Dean, Frisch, Medwick, Martin and Davis could have spelled doom if not for the Redbirds' robust hitting and steady pitching from Dizzy's supporting cast. As August unfolded, Collins (.340), Medwick (.333), Frisch (.309), Orsatti (.306) and DeLancey (.303) soared among the league's hitting leaders. The Ripper had cracked 23 home runs through July as he dueled the Giants' Mel Ott and the Boston Braves' Wally Berger for N.L. power honors. As of August 1, Paul Dean was 12-4, Carleton had won 11 games and Walker was healthy and pitching effectively.

Dizzy was flying high in the popularity polls and the victory column. He shut out the Reds on August 7 for his 20th victory. The next day, he notched his 21st with three innings of relief. And four days later, he and Paul were solidly berthed in the Cardinals' doghouse.

The improbable "Dean Debacle" began August 12 after the Cubs defeated Dizzy and Paul in a doubleheader to drop the Cardinals 7½ games back. With an August 13 exhibition game scheduled against the Detroit Tigers, the Gas Housers immediately entrained for the motor city—everyone except the Deans, that is. Before the Cards returned to St. Louis, Dizzy explained that he had "pulled something" in his elbow; Paul said he had aggravated his previously sprained ankle. Nevertheless, Frisch slapped a $100 fine on Dizzy, $50 on Paul.

The bizarre incident did not end there. On August 14, while the Cardinals warmed up for a game against the Phillies, the Dean brothers failed to appear on the field. Frisch found them half-dressed in the clubhouse.

"You fellows hike out there on the field like the rest of the boys," Frisch ordered.

"Nothing doing," Diz replied. "We've decided the fines against us are unjust. We're not a-goin' to do it. We're quitting."

"Then you're suspended," Frisch shot back. "Take off your uniforms."

Dizzy followed orders and ripped his uniform to shreds. He reached into his locker and subjected his road uniform to the same treatment. "There was a wild scene for a few minutes," The Sporting News reported, "both of the boys upsetting benches and carrying on in a tantrum."

The next day was payday. Dizzy discovered $186 deducted from his check—$100 for the fine, $50 for a day's pay and $36 for the two uniforms. Paul's check was short $70.

Instead of destroying team morale, the mutiny pulled the other Gas Housers closer together. "The fellows are going to work just that much harder for the team," said Durocher, the captain. "It isn't the proper thing for two players to think they are bigger than a ball club . . . you watch our smoke from now on. We'll show those two guys a thing or two."

The Cards showed Dizzy by winning six of seven games during his absence (Paul was pitching by Au-

Switch-hitting first baseman Rip Collins was proof that big surprises (35 homers, 128 RBIs in 1934) sometimes come in small packages.

gust 17). The Great One returned to the mound on August 24, thoroughly repentant with sagging shoulders and downcast eyes. As the game progressed, the prodigal son became the showman once more. He shut out the Giants on five hits, rapped two singles, stole a base and gained his 22nd victory.

After the season, Orsatti pointed to the Dean suspensions as the key to the Cardinal pennant drive.

Determined to prove to their teammates that they were not "quitters," the Deans pitched in and out of turn the rest of the season. After losing both ends of a Labor Day doubleheader against Pittsburgh, the brothers won 12 games as the Cardinals played 20-5 baseball.

"Dizzy pitched 'em daffy and Daffy pitched 'em dizzy," Orsatti said.

The day after that Labor Day setback, however, the Giants swept a doubleheader from the Phillies to go seven games up. "I guess we couldn't ask for much more," Giants Manager Bill Terry said.

The press certainly thought so. In the September 20 issue of The Sporting News, correspondent Dick Farrington wrote:

> Even as this was typed, the Cards had a chance to pull through, but it required a 200 percent Optimist, Rotarian or whatnot to concede that Frankie Frisch's lads would be able to climb over the wall. . . .
>
> Whatever disappointments have been encountered will have to be charged off to the failure of the other hurlers to keep pace with the Demon Deans.
>
> Tex Carleton was under normal weight practically all season due to stomach trouble in the spring and lacked stamina most of the way; Bill Hallahan . . . experienced his poorest season since joining the club, and Bill Walker, just beginning to reach his 1931 form, went out with a broken wrist and was a long time in getting back on the job. On top of this, the two shop-worn veterans, Jesse Haines and Dazzy Vance, did little for the cause.

Setbacks, for sure, but the Cardinals trailed the Giants by only 3½ lengths at that point! They had just won three of four games in New York (September 13-16), the significance of which escaped a clueless Dan Daniel. "Frankie Frisch bade a sad adieu, not only to Harlem, but to the 1934 World Series as well," the venerable scribe wrote.

The Giants peeked warily over their shoulders as the Redbirds charged into Ebbets Field on September 21. Dizzy held the Brooks hitless for 7⅓ innings in the opener and won, 13-0, on a three-hitter. Paul fired a no-hitter, allowing only a first-inning walk, and triumphed, 3-0.

Jay Hanna hailed his brother's achievement with a sparkling Deanism: "Paul didn't tell me he was gonna throw a no-hitter. If I'da known that, I'da thrown one, too."

The Gas Housers kept clawing away, splitting a two-game series with Cincinnati, winning one in Chicago, dividing a pair at home with Pittsburgh and winning the first two games of a season-ending series with the last-place Reds. With two games to play, the Cardinals had caught New York. And the Giants were staring at two games with the pesky but positively dangerous Dodgers, whom Terry had smeared in January by remarking, "Is Brooklyn still in the league?"

The Dodgers pounded home the truth and redeemed Brooklyn's honor by sweeping the Giants, who wound up with 13 losses in their final 21 games. In St. Louis, Paul Dean notched his 19th victory in a 6-1 decision over the Reds on September 29. The next day, Dizzy shut out the Reds, 9-0, for his 30th victory of the season, and the Cardinals claimed their fifth N.L. pennant. The victory was the Cardinals' 95th, the number Dizzy had deemed necessary to win the flag. Furthermore, the Deans had made good on Dizzy's boast of some 45 victories between them.

The rest of the pitching staff had taken its knocks, mostly in the press, but they helped make the Gas House "the gamest team" Frisch ever saw, "the gamest, best bunch of fighters that ever won a league title."

Paced by the extra-base power of Medwick and Collins, the take-the-extra-base philosophy of Martin and the base hits of Frisch and Rothrock, the Cardinals led the league in hits, runs, runs batted in, doubles, stolen bases, slugging average and batting average (.288). They placed second in home runs and triples. Collins led the league in total bases (369) and slugging average (.615) while tying Ott for the home run title (35). Medwick topped the circuit in triples (18). Martin claimed his second straight stolen-base crown (23). Dizzy Dean was named the N.L. MVP and topped the league in victories, strikeouts (195), shutouts (seven) and winning percentage (.811).

Only one more challenge lay ahead: the Detroit Tigers. In their first season under fiery catcher/manager Mickey Cochrane, the A.L. MVP, the Bengals captured their first pennant since 1909. Some observers labeled the Cardinals fatigued and frazzled; what they were was on a roll.

The Gas Housers arrived in Detroit at their intimidating best. With the Tigers taking batting practice at Navin Field, Dizzy appeared in his street clothes, grabbed a bat and barged into the batting cage. "Let a man hit that can hit," he ordered.

After rifling several drives into the bleachers, he taunted Tigers slugger Hank Greenberg. "Throw the bat away," he laughed after looking over Greenberg's hefty stick. "I'm a-pitchin'."

Indeed he did, and with only two days' rest. Before the Cardinals took the field, Frisch ordered: "Don't start figuring the losers' share. We get the big check or they'll laugh us out of baseball." Helped by five Detroit errors and a 13-hit attack highlighted by Medwick's three singles and home run, Dean turned back the Tigers, 8-3, on an eight-hitter although he apologized for not being in

Former Hollywood stunt man Ernie Orsatti played the outfield with reckless abandon while 22-year-old Bill DeLancey (right) shared catching chores with Spud Davis.

"usual shutout form." The opening-game victory was the Cardinals' first ever in Series play.

Lynwood (Schoolboy) Rowe was superb in Game 2, limiting St. Louis to one hit over the final nine innings of a 12-inning contest won by Detroit, 3-2. With Henry, Edsel and other Ford dignitaries crowding the best boxes, one writer noted that the Tigers were like Fords—hard to start but getting there in the end.

Martin and the Cardinals charged ahead in Game 3, however, as the Series shifted to St. Louis. Leading off the Redbirds' first, Martin ripped a line drive into the right-field screen, normally a double at Sportsman's Park. This was the Wild Horse of the Osage, however, and this horse was running wild. Martin slid safely into third base with his patented belly-flop slide, then scored on Rothrock's sacrifice fly. In the fifth, he scored again on

Rothrock's triple after lacing a leadoff double. Paul Dean, meanwhile, was busy shutting out the Tigers for 8⅔ innings before settling for a 4-1 victory.

Detroit submariner Eldon Auker dealt the Redbirds a 10-4 setback in Game 4 as tragedy nearly stalked into the Cardinals' camp. In the fourth inning, the high-spirited Dizzy was sent in to pinch-run for Davis. When Martin grounded to second baseman Charlie Gehringer, Diz raced to second and *jumped* to block Billy Rogell's relay to first. Dean caught the ball square in the forehead and dropped to the ground unconscious. He was carried off the field and rushed to a hospital, where tests revealed no serious damage.

"I saw thousands of stars, moons and all kinds of animals, but no Tigers," Diz said. "I still can't see the Tigers."

Back on the mound the next day, Dizzy dropped a 3-1 decision to Tommy Bridges. Brother Paul, however, squared the Series for the third time in Game 6. He held the Tigers to seven hits and stroked a game-winning single off Rowe in a 4-3 victory.

Sleep was difficult for the Gas House that night. Thousands of Detroit fans congregated outside the Cardinals' hotel, tooting horns, blowing whistles and beating drums. The next afternoon, it was the Tigers who appeared in a daze. Detroit collected only six hits off Dizzy Dean, who rapped a double and single in a seven-run third inning that sent the Redbirds on to an 11-0 victory and their third World Series title.

With the outcome painfully clear by the sixth inning, the mood of the Detroit crowd turned ugly after Medwick slashed a run-scoring triple to right field. Sliding hard into third, Medwick's feet became entangled with third baseman Marv Owen's and kicks were exchanged. "Muscles" scrambled to his feet and both players struck a fighting pose, but peacemakers intervened before blows were struck. When Joe returned to left field in the middle of the inning, he was greeted by a shower of produce, pop bottles and even a monkey wrench.

Twice park attendants cleaned up the debris before Commissioner Kenesaw Mountain Landis summoned Medwick, Frisch and Cochrane to his box.

"Mr. Medwick," the commissioner began, "did you kick Mr. Owen?"

"You're damned right I did," confessed Ducky.

"Then you're out of the game," the Judge replied.

"Why, why, why?" shrieked Frisch.

"Do you want this fine young man to be killed, Frisch?" Landis asked. For one of the few times in his life, the Flash was silenced.

Medwick's bat had thundered all through the Series. Joe led the Cardinal regulars with a .379 average on 11 hits. His five RBIs were second only to Rothrock's six. Collins (.367) and Martin (.355) also rapped 11 hits apiece and combined for seven RBIs.

Frisch and DeLancey, both sub-.200 batters, knocked in four runs each, and Orsatti was steady with a .318 mark. The irrepressible Deans had accounted for all four St. Louis victories. Paul's 1.00 earned-run average was slightly better than Dizzy's 1.73 mark.

As the kindling was split and stacked for another tour through the hot-stove league, Wilbur Wood of the New York Sun paused to reflect on what was sure to be a hotly debated topic:

Granting that the Redbirds are not a great ball club . . . they certainly have the something which makes them a more interesting outfit to watch than perhaps any great club of the past. They are a hell-roaring, hard-riding bunch of baseball cowboys. They can't help it. It's just in them to do things in a way that dazzles the eye.

For color, if not for class, the Cardinals of 1934 achieve top rating. Their dashing play and drastic expedients stood out in sharp contrast against the workaday play of the Tigers, even though some of the Bengals were roused to show their teeth in county fair style, too, as the Redbirds laid into them hand and foot in the desperate struggle for baseball supremacy.

The Cardinals may play county fair baseball. But if that is county fair baseball, it takes real he-men to play it. More power to them. And more power to county fair baseball.

1934
FINAL STANDING

Club	W.	L.	Pct.	GB.
St. Louis	95	58	.621	——
New York	93	60	.608	2

BATTERS

Pos.	Player	G.	HR.	RBI.	B.A.
1B	Rip Collins	154	35	128	.333
2B	Frankie Frisch	140	3	75	.305
SS	Leo Durocher	146	3	70	.260
3B	Pepper Martin	110	5	49	.289
OF	Joe Medwick	149	18	106	.319
	Ernie Orsatti	105	0	31	.300
	Jack Rothrock	154	11	72	.284
C	Spud Davis	107	9	65	.300
	Bill DeLancey	93	13	40	.316
UT	Burgess Whitehead (inf)	100	1	24	.277

OTHER CONTRIBUTORS (20+ Games): Pat Crawford, Chick Fullis, Buster Mills.

PITCHERS

Thr.	Pitcher	G.	W.	L.	ERA
R	Dizzy Dean	50	30	7	2.65
R	Paul Dean	39	19	11	3.44
R	Tex Carleton	40	16	11	4.26
L	Bill Walker	24	12	4	3.12
L	Bill Hallahan	32	8	12	4.25

OTHER CONTRIBUTORS (20+ Games): Jesse Haines, Jim Mooney.

Number 22

Mack Leads His A's To Promised Land

In the early years of the 20th Century, John Wesley Coombs was a star pitcher for the Colby College team in Waterville, Me.

In the same time frame, Thomas McGillicuddy was an innkeeper at Worcester, Mass.

While not attending to his hostel business, McGillicuddy was a regular at baseball games in and about Worcester. He had played the game as a youngster in East Brookfield, Mass., and could discern a prospect from a counterfeit.

Tom had a brother, Cornelius. Some years before, Cornelius had taken compassion on typographers and newspapermen by chopping several syllables from his name and emerging as Connie Mack. Connie was manager of the Philadelphia A's in the young American League and ever-alert for promising talent.

Connie had infinite confidence in brother Tom's recommendations. So, when the hotel keeper told the manager about a young hurler who was baffling New England batters with his fastball and tricky curves, Connie instructed Tom to have the pitcher report to him.

Coombs quickly discovered that he was out of his element in the big city. Geographically, that is. Not professionally.

Trying to solve Philadelphia's public transportation system, Coombs spent an entire morning on street cars that carried him to all points of the municipality instead of to Columbia Park, the A's home grounds. Finally, Coombs found his way to the ball park and into the Athletics' fold.

Without benefit of minor league experience, the 23-year-old righthander made his debut in the majors on July 5, 1906, at Columbia Park against Washington. Philadelphians, known to be tough audiences, were both impressed and pleased. Fazed not one whit by the big-time atmosphere, the former collegian scattered six hits, struck out six batters and walked five as the A's downed the Senators, 3-0.

Coombs won 10 games as a rookie, the most memorable victory occurring in Boston on September 1. In an unfathomable performance, Coombs went all the way in a 24-inning marathon, beating the Red Sox, 4-1. He allowed 15 hits and struck out 18 batters.

Philadelphia's Connie Mack was still in the early years of his long managerial run when his A's emerged as an American League power.

Great expectations followed "Colby Jack" into the 1907 season, but they weren't realized. In fact, the touted pitcher—haunted by control problems—won a total of only 13 games in 1907 and 1908 and was even given a trial as an outfielder before rebounding for a respectable 12-11 pitching record in 1909.

Coombs seemed primed to break loose in 1910. And so did the rest of Mack's Athletics, who had risen from their sixth-place standing of 1908 to second in 1909 and in the process threatened the American League reign of the Detroit Tigers (who outdistanced the A's by 3½ games in '09 for their third consecutive pennant).

With Mack as the guiding force, the A's clearly

Outfielder Danny Murphy (second from left) with the A's $100,000 infield of (left to right) Stuffy McInnis, Frank Baker, Jack Barry and Eddie Collins.

were emerging as a force to be reckoned with. Connie had been a big-league pilot as long ago as 1894, with the National League's Pittsburgh club, and he had won pennants in 1902 and 1905 with the Athletics. There wasn't much Mack hadn't seen or absorbed on a baseball diamond—he first played in the majors in 1886—and his judgment in game situations and on player-personnel matters was widely respected. As the Reach Baseball Guide once reported, ". . . It is not every manager who can direct as well as construct."

As Mack gathered his troops for spring training in 1910, he was able to reflect on a construction project that had begun in 1901, the first year of the American League. Mack, in what would be the first season of an incredible 50-year run as manager of the Athletics, signed former Gettysburg College standout Eddie Plank and introduced the lefthanded pitcher to professional baseball at the big-league level. Plank had few problems with the adjustment, winning 17 games for the '01 A's.

Plank was a fidgeter on the mound, tugging at his cap, hitching his belt, jerking at his uniform and doing whatever else he could to frustrate and perhaps even antagonize the opposition. When he finally unleashed the ball, over-eager batters invariably were off-stride.

The somber-faced Plank evolved into one of the majors' best pitchers. Following his fine rookie year, Eddie posted 20 or more victories in five of the next six seasons. One teammate described him as "not the fastest, not the trickiest and not the possessor of the best stuff, but just the greatest."

Philadelphia's other pitching aces were Charles Albert Bender, a member of the club since 1903; Cy Morgan, who had been obtained from the Red Sox during the 1909 campaign; and Harry Krause, who had spent his first full season with Philadelphia in 1909. Bender and Morgan were righthanders, while Krause was a lefthander.

Bender, a Minnesota-born member of the Chippewa tribe, attended the Carlisle (Pa.) Indian School before entering professional baseball. Mack always referred to him as Albert; to everyone else, he was "Chief."

Bender was only 19 when he won 17 games for Mack as a first-year major leaguer in 1903. Two years later, he posted 18 victories for the pennant-winning Athletics and notched Philadelphia's only World Series triumph against the New York Giants by tossing a shutout. About to start his eighth big-league season, Bender, 18-8 in 1909, was shooting for his first 20-victory campaign.

Morgan, who had reached the major leagues with the St. Louis Browns in 1903, racked up 14 victories for the Red Sox in 1908 and won 18 contests overall in 1909 while dividing his time between the Boston club and the Athletics. Besides his pitching talents, Morgan was a vaudevillian in the winter months and entertained his teammates with minstrel songs and anecdotes during tiring train rides.

Krause, after a four-game stint with Mack's team in 1908, shot into prominence in 1909 with an 18-8 record that featured seven shutouts.

Mack's catching corps consisted of Ira Thomas, Jack Lapp and Paddy Livingston.

The A's infield was made up of veteran Harry Davis at first base and youngsters Eddie Collins, Jack Barry and Frank Baker at second base, shortstop and third base, respectively.

Davis, the A's captain, had topped the American League in home runs in four consecutive years (1904 through 1907), compiling totals of 10, 8, 12 and 8. Having slumped to a total of nine homers in the 1908 and 1909 seasons, Davis remained an outstanding fielder. His cries of "shoot it" gave young infielders the confidence to make hurried throws in tight situations, with the assurance that Davis would somehow come up with the ball.

Davis was 36 years old at the start of the 1910 season. Collins and Barry would turn 23 a few weeks into the season, and Baker was 24.

Nicknamed "Cocky," Collins had joined the A's in 1906 while still a student at Columbia University and played under the name of Sullivan that year in an attempt to protect his collegiate eligibility. In 1909, his second full season in the majors, Collins batted .346.

Eddie's double-play partner, Barry, was another player with a college background. The Holy Cross product was a quality shortstop, though not a robust hitter.

An agile fielder and good baserunner, Baker had shown some punch in 1909 by driving in 89 runs and cracking 19 triples for the A's.

Speedster Rube Oldring, nearing his 26th birthday, was Philadelphia's center fielder. He was flanked by veterans Topsy Hartsel and Danny Murphy, both of whom had been with the A's since 1902. Murphy held down second base in his first six seasons with Mack's team before relinquishing the position to Collins.

The team that Connie Mack herded into Washington for the season-opening game of 1910 was one lucky enough to be part of history. For the first time ever, the President of the United States would be on hand to throw out the ceremonial first pitch on opening day. And while all eyes were transfixed on 300-pound William Howard Taft at the outset of the game, they soon focused on Walter Perry Johnson. Through six innings, Washington's "Big Train" had allowed nary a hit.

"That day Walter Johnson was as fast as I ever saw him," Baker said. Then, recalling his seventh-inning at-bat, Baker said he "hit a fly ball toward right field, where the overflow crowd was several deep in front of the fence.

"It was a common practice in those days for the overflow crowd to open up and let the fielder have a chance to catch the ball when the visiting team was batting and stay closed up when the home team was at bat. That gave the home batters chances to get ground-rule doubles on balls that fell into the crowd.

"Washington right fielder Doc Gessler tried to catch the ball and the crowd opened up for him. But a little boy either got scared or couldn't move fast enough, and Gessler stumbled over him. That ended any chance he had of catching the ball and gave me a double . . . ."

Baker's hit was the only one of the afternoon against Johnson, who emerged a 3-0 winner.

It wasn't exactly a glorious start to the season for the Philadelphia Athletics. But it didn't take long for the A's to get into gear. Three weeks into May, they had reeled off a 13-game winning streak. Included in the skein was a no-hitter by Bender against Cleveland.

"Elmer Flick was the last man to face me," Bender said. "He worked the count to 2 and 2, and then I turned loose with all I had on a fastball on the outside. He took a good cut, but lifted a little foul behind the plate. Ira circled around like a drunken sailor, but finally caught it—and I breathed a big sigh of thankfulness."

By mid-June, Coombs was pitching effectively but not sensationally. Starting, however, on June 22, the day after the Athletics took over first place for keeps, he was all but invincible. He commenced his streak of exceptional pitching by blanking the New York Highlanders and then tossed five shutouts in the month of July. Coombs was rolling, and so were the Athletics (who on the morning of August 1 were 60-30 and atop the American League standings by six games).

Chemistry, his major at Colby, no longer was on Coombs' mind. Finding the right formula for setting down American League hitters clearly was his No. 1 priority now.

"At first," Coombs admitted, "I merely considered baseball as a quick way to make money during the summer months, and still thought of chemistry as my life's work."

The A's were playing well overall now. They proceeded to fashion a 22-7 record in August, extending their league lead to 11 games.

Getting tremendous mileage out of a sharp-breaking curveball, Coombs fired four more shutouts in September. By season's end, Coombs had tossed 13 shutouts—an American League record that still stands—and won 31 games.

After clinching the pennant with 2½ weeks left in the season, the A's set their sights on becoming the first team in American League history to win 100 games. Clarence (Lefty) Russell, a 20-year-old pitcher purchased from the minor leagues, elevated the A's to that lofty figure by shutting out the Red Sox on October 1 in his first big-league appearance. The triumph proved the first and last in the majors for Russell.

The A's wound up 14½ games ahead of second-place New York and boasted a 102-48 final record, a mark built predominantly on extraordinary pitching but also achieved because of a steady, productive offense. Collins finished as the league's fourth-best hitter with a .322 average, Oldring batted .308 and Murphy contributed a .300 mark.

Collins' versatility won him praise from even the toughest critics.

After acknowledging Collins' prowess with the bat (Eddie compiled a .333 career batting average), Detroit Tigers immortal Ty Cobb called the A's infielder "the greatest second baseman who ever played the game." Cobb, not known for doling out compliments, added: "Eddie could do anything and everything. They talk about (Rogers) Hornsby and (Nap) Lajoie as being in a class with him. That's a lot of foolishness. Hornsby and Lajoie had their points, true enough, but for all-round ability, Collins would lose the both of them.

". . . You should have seen the plays he made as a fielder. He could run the bases, too.

"I guess he was the smartest player of them all. That was his strength—headwork. Actually, he wasn't endowed with great natural ability. I mean, he lacked the thing they call style. He had a peculiar loping gait as a runner and he threw the ball with a

The big three of the Philadelphia Athletics' 1910 and '11 pitching staffs were righthanders Chief Bender (above left) and Jack Coombs (left) and lefty Eddie Plank (above). Coombs won 59 games in the two seasons.

sort of pushing motion. In contrast to Lajoie, who was the picture of grace, Eddie was awkward and unorthodox.

"But, in his own way, he always managed to get the job done, and the tougher the situation the better he'd be."

Oldring's big year ended in disappointment.

"After we won the pennant, Mr. Mack arranged exhibitions with a picked team of American Leaguers, including Ty Cobb and Tris Speaker, to keep us in condition (for the World Series against the Chicago Cubs)," said Oldring, reflecting on the fact that the 1910 National League schedule ran a week longer than the American League's slate. "My spikes failed to hold while I was going for a line drive by Speaker, and I fell and fractured a knee. So, I saw the Series from a box, with my knee in a cast."

Murphy, a team player in the truest sense, was in his second full season of outfield play.

"Murphy had been a fixture at second base since 1902, and a mighty good one," Oldring recalled. "Mack was trying to fit Collins into the lineup somewhere (in 1908) and played him every place. At one of our daily meetings, Danny, a really great hitter, suggested that he be moved to right field and Collins take over at second base." The move was implemented.

For Murphy, being a key figure in the Athletics' second-base picture was nothing new. Six years before turning over the keystone position to Collins, he had emerged as the principal successor to Lajoie when the latter went from the Athletics to the Cleveland club.

Murphy's offensive skills weren't immediately apparent when he first reached the majors with the National League's New York Giants, but they shone brightly and quickly when the native Philadelphian broke into the American League. In a total of 176 at-bats with the 1900 and 1901 Giants, Murphy batted .222. Then, after hitting a monstrous .462 in 49 games for Norwich of the Connecticut League in 1902, Danny was obtained that summer by the Athletics and made his A.L. debut on July 8. Playing against the Red Sox and entering the game in the second inning, Murphy went on a 6-for-6 spree that included a bases-loaded home run.

Coombs, Bender and Morgan all fashioned earned-run averages below 1.60 for the 1910 Athletics, and Plank finished just above the 2.00 mark. Coombs' 31-9 ledger was enhanced by a scintillating 1.30 ERA, while Bender put together a 23-5 season that featured a 1.58 ERA. Morgan won 18 of 30 decisions with a 1.55 ERA, and Plank went 16-10 with a 2.02 ERA.

"No pitcher ever gave a manager more than Coombs gave me in 1910," Mack said. And the numbers surely supported Cornelius McGilli-cuddy's claim.

"No better pitcher ever walked out to a mound," third baseman Baker suggested.

Bender had his supporters, too, and Cobb was among them.

"Mr. Mack always matched Bender against the toughest pitchers in the league," Cobb remembered. "There were no soft spots for him. If the White Sox pitched their big wheel, Ed Walsh, Bender went in to oppose him. If Walter Johnson was Washington's starting pitcher, Bender would be in there for the Athletics. Or if Boston started Smokey Joe Wood, Bender was his opponent. That went on for years."

Noting that Plank finished his major league career with 305 victories (while Bender, Eddie's longtime teammate, totaled 208), Cobb lauded the lefthander's record. "Can't take that away from him," the Georgia Peach said. "He had a nice cross-fire style, but Bender had more stuff—a wicked curve and a fastball second only to (Walter) Johnson's."

While the pennant runaway achieved by these Athletics stirred the passions of Philadelphians, A's fans who recalled the Giants' humiliation of their team in the 1905 World Series—Mack's men were shut out four times in five games—weren't content with the A.L. flag. Neither were the A's themselves.

The A's, though, were hurting for the World Series against the Tinker-to-Evers-to-Chance Cubs. With Oldring sidelined, Amos Strunk would be thrust into starting center-field duty in the Series. The 20-year-old Strunk had appeared in just 16 games for the A's during the 1910 regular season. Furthermore, old-pro Plank would be unavailable for postseason action because of an arm ailment.

All was not well with the Cubs, either. Star second baseman Johnny Evers was sidelined because of a broken ankle.

Strunk played creditably enough, collecting three singles, a double and a triple and batting .278 in four games against the Cubs. As for the void created by Plank's absence, well, the A's had no reinforcements on whom to call. Instead, they simply went with their best. And Philadelphia's best was more than good enough.

Incredibly, Mack used only Coombs and Bender on the mound in the 1910 Series. Bender tossed a three-hitter in Game 1, Coombs turned in complete-game victories in Games 2 and 3 (there was one off-day between those contests), the Chief dropped a 10-inning decision in Game 4 and Colby Jack wrapped up matters with a 7-2 conquest in Game 5.

Offensively, the A's got a .429 performance from Collins, a .409 mark from Baker and eight RBIs and the lone home run of the Series from Murphy.

Considering the youth on this team, Mack's charges seemed poised to challenge for American League and major league supremacy for years to

Frank (Home Run) Baker was a hard-hitting third baseman who drove in 115 runs for the 1911 Athletics, while Eddie Collins, a smooth second baseman, was a high-average hitter for the A's.

come. Such an assessment was not without foundation.

The makeup of the 1911 A's differed little from the cast with which Mack started out a year earlier. One principal change in the club occurred approximately one-third of the way into the season when team captain Davis gave way to 20-year-old Stuffy McInnis, who had played a total of 57 games for Philadelphia over the previous two years. First base was a new position for McInnis, who had seen most of his earlier service as a middle infielder and pinch-hitter. Elsewhere, Bris Lord, who had won the left-field job from Hartsel after his midseason acquisition from Cleveland in 1910, again was a front-line player.

The 1911 pennant race was a bit more strenuous for the A's, whose main competition this time around came from Detroit. The Tigers even were atop the American League standings in early August. Cobb and company proceeded to unravel, however; indeed, they came completely undone. By season's end, Philadelphia, showing markedly increased firepower, had run off with the A.L. flag by a 13½-game margin over Hugh Jennings' Tigers. And, for the second straight year, the Athletics had topped the 100-victory mark, compiling a 101-50 record.

Collins and Baker were the big men with the bats

for the 1911 Athletics. Collins hit at a sizzling .365 clip, while Baker emerged as the American League's home run champion with 11 long-distance shots, drove in 115 runs and batted .334. Murphy ended the season with a .329 average, and McInnis proved his mettle with a .321 mark.

The homer crown was a first for Baker, who played most of his big-league career in the dead-ball era.

"Up until I got too old to get around on good fastball pitching, I used a 52-ounce bat," Baker once reminisced. "Honest! You had to hit that ball fair and square and with some weight and power back of it to make it go over a fence.

"Why, you know I swung with all my might at a good fastball, hit it fair and square and was lucky if it bounced against the fence. I hit the fence in Shibe Park (the successor to Columbia Park) 38 times in one year. Eddie Collins told me if I had been hitting the (lively) ball that Babe Ruth hit, every one of them would have gone over the fence."

McInnis' development at first base gave the A's what became known as their "$100,000 infield." The estimated worth of Baker, Barry, Collins and McInnis was an eye-popping figure for that era, but the truly eye-popping thing about this quartet was its all-around skill.

"Gosh, those fellows were great ball players,"

Stuffy later observed. "Collins at second and Barry at short teamed up marvelously. Practice, practice, that's all they did, and when they were off the field they talked about situations that might arise and what they'd do."

McInnis could swing the bat from the outset of his big-league career, and he evolved into one of the top-fielding righthanded first basemen in baseball history. In 14 seasons as a major league regular, he batted above .300 on 10 occasions and was in the .290s three other times. While having some difficulty afield in his early years in the majors, McInnis became a gifted glove man—accomplished to the point that in 1921, while a member of the Red Sox, he committed exactly one error in 152 games (the lone miscue in 150 or more games remains the American League record).

Coombs had another sensational season in 1911, winning 28 games. After three sub-20-victory years, Plank returned to the select figure with a 22-8 mark. Bender won 17 of 22 decisions, and Morgan and Krause combined for 26 triumphs.

The defending World Series champion Athletics would get an opportunity for revenge in the 1911 fall classic. Their opponents would be John McGraw's Giants, who had inflicted such a painful defeat upon the A's six autumns earlier.

Baker stole the show. After the Giants had prevailed in Game 1, New York and Philadelphia were in a 1-1 struggle in the sixth inning of Game 2 when Baker blasted a two-run home run off Rube Marquard. The Athletics held on for a 3-1 victory at Shibe Park, the gleaming baseball palace that they had opened in 1909. The next day, McGraw's team was guarding a 1-0 lead with one out in the ninth when John Franklin Baker forever became Home Run Baker by depositing a Christy Mathewson pitch into the right-field seats. Properly inspired, the A's proceeded to win the contest, 3-2, in 11 innings, and they went on to capture the Series in six games.

Besides his two key homers, Baker hit a Series-leading .375 and drove in five runs overall. Also collecting five RBIs was the 38-year-old Davis, back in the lineup as a fill-in for the injured McInnis. And Barry, coming off one of the best offensive seasons of his big-league career (he batted .265 with 63 RBIs), hit .368 against the Giants.

This time, the A's were forced to employ *three* pitchers to cop the Series crown. Bender won two games, posting route-going victories in Games 4 and 6, while Plank tossed a five-hitter in Game 2 and Coombs went the distance in Philadelphia's 11-inning conquest in Game 3.

Having won two straight World Series crowns, the Athletics were the subject of considerable discussion among baseball people. Just how good was this A's team?

Danny Murphy, a converted second baseman, moved to Philadelphia's outfield and continued his sound work with the bat.

"There were no weak spots that one could indicate with certainty," none other than McGraw himself said in later years. "In the first place, it had wonderful pitching. Very few ball clubs were ever equipped with such pitchers as Bender, Plank and Coombs. All of these were thinking pitchers. In addition, they had the goods physically. A club with a trio of such pitchers would be pretty hard to beat in a season or in a series any time.

"I don't remember ever having seen a much better combination around second base than Eddie Collins and Jack Barry. Then, at third, there was Frank Baker. Stuffy McInnis came along . . . and there was an infield pretty nearly perfect. All of these men . . . knew the tricks of the game in the field.

"The Athletics had a punch at all times. Our pitchers realized that to their sorrow. . . . On the other hand, our batters knew what they were up against when they had to face such pitchers as Plank, Coombs and Bender.

"I have no hesitation in expressing the opinion that the Athletics of that period were one of the greatest ball clubs of all time."

Righthander Cy Morgan wasn't the ace of Philadelphia's staff, but he did total 33 victories in 1910 and '11.

As long on talent as Mack's men were, however, they came up short in 1912. Woefully short. The A's wound up 15 games behind the Boston Red Sox, who got a 34-victory performance from righthander Smokey Joe Wood and stormed to the American League pennant. Philadelphia, in fact, finished third in 1912, one game behind Washington. Not even the .348 bat work of Collins, a .347 average and 133-RBI production from Baker, 101 RBIs by McInnis and a total of 47 victories from Plank and Coombs could avert a drop of two places in the standings.

The Athletics were back atop the American League in 1913 and 1914, despite the fact Coombs made only a handful of appearances in those years because of the debilitating effects of typhoid fever. Baker won the league homer title each season, Collins batted .345 and .344 and Joe Bush, Boardwalk Brown, Byron (Duke) Houck and Bob Shawkey took up the pitching slack created by Coombs' absence. In '13, the A's won the pennant by 6½ games and dismissed the Giants in five games in the World Series. And in '14, they ruled the American League by 8½ games, only to be swept by Boston's "Miracle Braves" in one of the greatest Series upsets of all time.

Mack, distraught over the Athletics' showing against the Braves, soon began to dismantle his club. Collins was traded over the winter of 1914-1915, Bender and Plank took their wares to the Federal League and Baker, mired in a dispute with Mack, sat out the entire 1915 season before being sold to the New York Yankees. Barry and Shawkey also were dispatched by the middle of 1915.

Neither deep disappointment in his club's 1914 finish nor an accompanying make-over of his personnel could overshadow what Mack, the manager who worked in street clothes, had achieved. He had directed his charges to four A.L. championships and three World Series titles in a five-year span, with the 1910 and 1911 seasons standing out because of back-to-back Series crowns and regular-season victory totals exceeding 100. Mack had led with a quiet elegance, his most demonstrative moments often occurring when he positioned his players defensively with a wave of his scorecard or delivered other instructions via the same means.

Mack's guidance wasn't confined to on-the-field endeavors.

"In 1911, after we had clinched the pennant, he (Mack) called me into the office," Bender recalled. " 'I'm counting on you to win the World Series,' he said. 'I'll do the best I can,' I replied.

"Then, he casually asked, 'Albert, how much do you still owe on your house?'

" 'None of your business,' I replied, smiling. He insisted that I tell him. 'It's $2,500.'

"I lost the first game to Mathewson and then won

my next two . . . I pitched the final game and went home to celebrate . . . ."

Bender then received a telephone call from his manager.

"Do you remember that conversation we had before the Series started?" Mack asked the Chief.

No, Bender said, he did not.

The next day, Bender said, Mack "pulled a check out of his desk for $2,500 . . . ."

An appreciative Connie Mack clearly had gotten his money's worth—and then some—from Chief Bender. Just like he had reaped uncommon dividends from the "$100,000 infield," Eddie Plank and that product of Colby College, the ol' chemist-turned-pitcher, Jack Coombs.

1910
FINAL STANDING

Club	W.	L.	Pct.	GB.
Philadelphia	102	48	.680	—
New York	88	63	.583	14½

BATTERS

Pos.	Player	G.	HR.	RBI.	B.A.
1B	Harry Davis	139	1	41	.248
2B	Eddie Collins	153	3	81	.322
SS	Jack Barry	145	3	60	.259
3B	Frank Baker	146	2	74	.283
OF	Bris Lord	72	1	20	.278
	Rube Oldring	134	4	57	.308
	Danny Murphy	151	4	64	.300
C	Jack Lapp	71	0	17	.234
	Ira Thomas	60	1	19	.277

OTHER CONTRIBUTORS (20+ Games): Topsy Hartsel, Heinie Heitmuller, Ben Houser, Paddy Livingston, Stuffy McInnis.

PITCHERS

Thr.	Pitcher	G.	W.	L.	ERA
R	Jack Coombs	45	31	9	1.30
R	Chief Bender	30	23	5	1.58
R	Cy Morgan	36	18	12	1.55
L	Eddie Plank	38	16	10	2.02

1911
FINAL STANDING

Club	W.	L.	Pct.	GB.
Philadelphia	101	50	.669	—
Detroit	89	65	.578	13½

BATTERS

Pos.	Player	G.	HR.	RBI.	B.A.
1B	Stuffy McInnis	126	3	77	.321
2B	Eddie Collins	132	3	73	.365
SS	Jack Barry	127	1	63	.265
3B	Frank Baker	148	11	115	.334
OF	Bris Lord	134	3	55	.310
	Rube Oldring	121	3	59	.297
	Danny Murphy	141	6	66	.329
C	Ira Thomas	103	0	39	.273

OTHER CONTRIBUTORS (20+ Games): Harry Davis, Claude Derrick, Topsy Hartsel, Jack Lapp, Paddy Livingston, Amos Strunk.

PITCHERS

Thr.	Pitcher	G.	W.	L.	ERA
R	Jack Coombs	47	28	12	3.53
L	Eddie Plank	40	22	8	2.10
R	Chief Bender	31	17	5	2.17
R	Cy Morgan	38	15	7	2.70
L	Harry Krause	27	11	8	3.04

Speedy Rube Oldring handled center-field duties for Connie Mack's Philadelphia A's while swinging a productive bat.

Number 23

Giants Rediscover Winning Formula

Frankie Frisch, alias the Fordham Flash, was a composite, do-everything player who quickly won the heart of Giants Manager John McGraw.

John Joseph McGraw, manager of the New York Giants, was tending to routine business matters on a spring afternoon in 1919 when he received a visitor at his office in the Polo Grounds. The caller was Art Devlin, third baseman on pennant-winning Giants clubs of years gone by and now baseball coach at Fordham University.

Devlin got right to the point. "We've got a player who is ready for the big leagues," Devlin said. "You know I wouldn't say that if I wasn't sure of it."

"He must be good," allowed McGraw, interrupting Devlin's oratory.

"He is good and knows he's good," Devlin went on. "I don't mean he's conceited. But he's a ball player and he knows it. There isn't a ball player in the National League who's going to talk him out of it, either."

McGraw was not about to ignore the opinion of a man he esteemed so highly. Since time did not permit him to check the prodigy personally, McGraw assigned the task to a coach. When the aide returned with a report equally as glowing as Devlin's, McGraw concluded that a gem of rare quality was indeed available for the taking.

McGraw caught his first glimpse of the phenom at the completion of the spring term at Fordham. He was a well-constructed chap—5-foot-10, 185 pounds—who spoke with a raspy twang that reflected his New York City roots. A football player of considerable note, the young man drew long, admiring glances when he ran at full-throttle on the gridiron. With good reason, the kid was known as the Fordham Flash.

Frank Francis Frisch was the son of a wealthy lace and linen manufacturer who regarded professional baseball as an unworthy vocation for his heir. He preferred that Frankie join him in business. He withdrew his objections only after he was assured that Frank would sign nothing short of a major league contract with the Giants.

Despite the gaudy reports, Frankie Frisch was not fully prepared to leap into a starting job with the National League club. For one thing, he had limited range afield and therefore was unsuited to play shortstop, his position as a collegian. He was better qualified to play either third base or second, decided McGraw, an accomplished third baseman himself in his prime.

Secondly, Frankie had enjoyed considerable success batting crosshanded. No matter how well he hit using that unorthodox style, he would have to adopt the conventional method. When that was achieved, McGraw suggested that Frisch master switch-hitting. This, too, he accomplished with uncommon quickness.

Frisch made his first appearance in a major league game on June 17, 1919, against the Cubs in Chicago. He pinch-hit for Hal Chase, the picture-perfect first baseman whose tainted reputation would soon lead to his expulsion from the game. Frisch batted against Grover Cleveland Alexander and reached base on an error.

McGraw let Frisch ride the bench for most of the next eight weeks, allowing him to pick up pointers on the major league system and observe the stratagems of the genius known as Little Napoleon.

Frisch, who began to play regularly for the Giants in mid-August, was an instant hit with McGraw. On one of the first balls hit his way, Frankie was the victim of a bad hop. After the smash caromed off his chest, Frisch pounced on the ball and nipped the runner at first base.

McGraw applauded the effort. "If he'd made the play cleanly, I'd have paid no attention to it," the manager said. "But for a kid just breaking in and doing it before a crowd, to get a ball that has gotten away from him, well, he's got guts."

McGraw's admiration for Frisch increased daily. Before long, the Fordham Flash had another nickname. He was known as "McGraw's boy," a tribute to his fiery, win-at-all-costs attitude that reminded Mac of his days with the legendary Baltimore Orioles.

Years later, after Frankie's credentials had been well established, Joe McCarthy paid him the ultimate compliment. Leading up to the point he wished to make, the famed manager observed that every great player had at least one weakness. Then he asked his listeners, "What was there that Frank Frisch couldn't do?"

The question was rhetorical. Frisch could run, field, throw and hit. He was the composite player. He had color, superb competitive fire and a wit that, according to the situation, could slash, humble or amuse.

Frisch came quickly to full blossom as a major leaguer under the astute handling of McGraw. By 1921, playing a majority of his games at third base (but also seeing extensive duty at second base), Frisch had evolved into one of the league's top hitters and run producers. His emergence as a big-leaguer of the first order seemed to coincide with the arrival of shortstop Dave Bancroft in June 1920.

The first two months of the 1920 season had been excruciatingly painful for McGraw. His inner defense was ragged, particularly at shortstop. Veteran Art Fletcher was showing the effects of advancing years. Ground balls that the team captain once gobbled up with ease were now squirming through for base-hits.

McGraw's discontent did not spring from fielding deficiencies alone. He was irritated by the Giants' spot in the second division and positively humiliated by his team's secondary role in the city's baseball rankings.

Since coming to New York shortly after the turn of the century, McGraw had been accustomed to having the larger portion of the publicity pie. He could tolerate the Yankees as long as they played a minor role. Now, however, in 1920, the American Leaguers—Polo Grounds tenants of the Giants, no less—were usurping the acclaim that McGraw considered his birthright. About a dozen newspapermen were chronicling the daily heroics of the Yankees and their new home run sensation, Babe Ruth, while only a handful of reporters were covering the Giants. The disparity cut deeply.

McGraw's distress reached breaking-point proportions in early June. Mac stomped into the office of Charles A. Stoneham and informed the club owner that personnel changes were mandatory if the team hoped to regain its lost prestige. As the first step, McGraw suggested that Stoneham engineer a trade for Bancroft, the highly capable shortstop for the last-place Philadelphia Phillies. "Make 'em an offer they can't refuse" was the thrust of his directive.

Though office hours were over, Stoneham placed a telephone call to William F. Baker and located the Phillies' owner in a Philadelphia restaurant. "We want to make a deal for Bancroft," said Stoneham, adding that the Giants were prepared to send along Fletcher (who at 35 was seven years Bancroft's senior), pitcher Wilbert Hubbell and approximately $100,000.

The financial consideration left Baker speechless. While the subject of money was constantly on his mind, it was because of paucity rather than abundance. The sum of $100,000 could cure a lot of the Phils' fiscal woes, assuming that Baker had heard correctly over the long-distance wires. He asked time to consider the offer and promised to be at the Giants' office by the next morning.

Baker slept fitfully that night. He did not regain his composure until he sat across the desk from Stoneham the next morning and heard the Giants' executive repeat his offer. When the Phils' magnate boarded the afternoon train for Philadelphia, he fairly luxuriated in wealth.

With Bancroft tightening the defense and contributing a .299 batting mark as a Giant, New York

The arrival of shortstop Dave Bancroft in 1920 helped bring the Giants back into the New York baseball spotlight.

leaped from the second division and finished in second place for the third consecutive year.

When the 1921 campaign got under way, Bancroft and Frisch formed a leak-proof combination around second base. George Kelly, the slugging Californian, was at first base and rookie Goldie Rapp at third. The race was not far along, though, before McGraw realized that Rapp was inadequate. Another trade was the only solution. Again, the wily manager and Stoneham turned to their favorite swapper, Baker. When the discussions ended in late June, the Giants had obtained second baseman Johnny Rawlings and veteran outfielder Casey Stengel from the Phillies in a five-player deal that included the packaging of Rapp to Baker's club.

In still another transaction, this one again with the Phillies and hammered out on July 25, McGraw gave up young outfielder Curt Walker and catching prospect Butch Henline in exchange for hard-hitting outfielder Emil (Irish) Meusel. In 1919 and 1920, his second and third full seasons in the majors, Meusel had batted .305 and .309 for the Phillies.

The trade of Meusel kindled screams of disap-

proval in Philadelphia, all aimed at Baker.

"The swapping of Emil Meusel, one of the greatest hitters in baseball . . . for two untried rookies caused waves of indignation among a set of fans already having a nationwide reputation for being gluttons for punishment," reported the correspondent for The Sporting News. "If the Phillies really traded Walker and Henline even up, then the club owner needs a guardian, for the next move might be to trade the franchise for a pen-knife.

"However, nobody here (Philadelphia) believes it was a straight trade, and fans guess that it required from $25,000 to $50,000 of Stoneham's bank notes to swing the smelly deal." It later was disclosed that the Phils received approximately $30,000, plus a third player, pitcher Jesse Winters.

As the result of the dealing, McGraw moved Frisch from second base to third, inserted Rawlings into the lineup at second and installed Meusel in left field, where Irish teamed with George Burns in center and Ross Youngs in right. Stengel, a major leaguer since 1912 and known for his fun-loving ways, was assigned a utility role. "The big asset with Casey . . . is his pep," the New York Tribune reported, "and the Giants certainly need this ingredient . . . ."

McGraw's infield and outfield alignments had gone from very good to downright formidable.

Behind the plate, McGraw divided the catching chores between longtime St. Louis Cardinal Frank (Pancho) Snyder and Earl (Oil) Smith, a garrulous Arkansan who was a continual source of annoyance to his manager. "He's an anarchist," McGraw said of Smith. "He has no respect for law and order."

Smith had no respect for opposing pitchers, either, and that McGraw liked. He had batted .294 for the Giants in 1920 and was hitting well over .300 as the 1921 season moved into August.

New York's pitching rotation consisted primarily of Art Nehf, Jesse Barnes and Fred Toney, all 20-game winners in 1920, and Phil Douglas, a big Southerner who could pitch effectively when he was not on, or recovering from, a "vacation," which was his euphemism for a prolonged bout with demon alcohol.

With his team now well-fortified, McGraw turned his concern to the Giants' position in the standings. After losing three of four games to the Cardinals three weeks into August, New York lagged 7½ lengths behind Pittsburgh. And the Giants and the Pirates were about to start a five-game series.

As the New York players showered and dressed following their final game against the Cardinals, McGraw decided that the hour had come for him to fire all his psychological jets. Another second-place finish just wouldn't get it. Exiting his office, he hailed his troops into silence and addressed them with one of his good old-fashioned speeches. He had the players drooling after painting a glowing portrait of the riches to be won by playing the Yankees in the forthcoming World Series. Then, McGraw changed direction and turned on the vitriol. Years later, Stengel relived the event for New York newspaperman Tom Meany.

"... And now it's all gone," McGraw told Stengel and his teammates, "gone because you're all a bunch of knuckleheaded fools. You've tossed it all away. Pittsburgh is going to come in here tomorrow laughing at us—Pittsburgh is going to take it all. Pittsburgh, a bunch of banjo-playing, wisecracking humpty-dumpties! You've thrown it away. And remember, you've only yourselves to blame."

Just as McGraw had predicted, the Pirates were jubilant and carefree when they sauntered onto the field the next day. Because this was their last scheduled visit of the season to New York, the Bucs posed willingly for photographers who wanted pictures to illustrate projected World Series articles. As they glanced merrily toward the cameras, the Pirates also sneaked glimpses of the Giants seated glumly across the way.

"Look at them," McGraw snarled. "Look at the clowns! Nobody ever had a softer touch than you fellows have today."

McGraw's psychological ploys paid off. In a doubleheader that got the Giants-Pirates series going, New York rolled to 10-2 and 7-0 victories behind the pitching of Nehf and Douglas. Meusel provided the offense, rapping a single, two doubles, a triple and a home run in the twin bill.

As the Giants were congratulating one another over slashing Pittsburgh's lead to 5½ games, McGraw strode into their midst. "I told you fellows last night you didn't have a chance," he snorted. "Well, I was wrong. You have a bare chance . . . ."

Toney, who four years earlier as a member of the Cincinnati Reds had pitched a 10-inning no-hitter against Chicago in a game in which the Cubs' Jim Vaughn hurled no-hit ball through nine innings, was pretty much the whole story the next day. Besides keeping the Pirates' offense in check, he drilled a three-run homer and emerged a 5-2 winner.

McGraw's pitching selection for the fourth game of the series was uncertain. After his sparkling effort in the series-opening doubleheader, Douglas was assumed to be on another of his "vacations." But Phil was available, after all, and he arrived at the Polo Grounds able and eager for the game of August 26. McGraw took Douglas at his word that he was fit to take the mound, and the righthander came through once more. He beat the Pirates, 2-1, as Frisch tripled home one run and scored a second for the Giants.

New York needed one more victory for the series

sweep, one more triumph to vault within 2½ games of the lead. The Giants sent Nehf to the mound for this crucial contest, and the 5-9 lefthander responded with a four-hit, 3-1 success.

Using the five-game sweep as a springboard, the Giants kept on winning. They moved past the Pirates before mid-September and, gaining 11½ games on Pittsburgh in the last five weeks of the season, roared to a four-game margin of victory over the Bucs in the National League pennant race. New York's flag-winning record was 94-59.

With his seventh pennant as the Giants' manager secured, John McGraw turned his attention toward his next objective. The goal—beating the fast-rising Yankees in the World Series—transcended all others in his fabled career as a National League manager, even that of disposing of Connie Mack's 1905 Philadelphia A's in the first sanctioned Series (which the Giants did accomplish, in five games). Conquest of their Polo Grounds houseguests might stem some of the powerful Yankees' ever-growing gate appeal and thereby loosen the American Leaguers' grip on the city of New York. Most of all, though, a decisive victory would catapult the Giants and McGraw to what they considered their rightful place—the peak of baseball esteem—and the manager would be King John once more.

McGraw obviously had the personnel to realize his ambition.

First baseman Kelly, nephew of renowned outfielder Bill Lange of the National League's Chicago club in the 1890s, had batted only .266 with 11 home runs for the 1920 Giants but blossomed in 1921. The 25-year-old San Francisco native belted a National League-leading 23 home runs and drove in 122 runs (the second-best RBI figure in the league). He also compiled a .308 batting average.

Kelly's emergence took some doing. He had batted .158 in a 17-game trial with the Giants in 1915, struggled to the identical figure in 49 games with McGraw's club in 1916, hit .067 in limited duty in 1917 (a year in which he also played briefly for Pittsburgh) and topped the National League in strikeouts with 92 in 1920.

During the tough going, Kelly was the butt of numerous press-box jokes.

"I am ready to step down and let a younger man trail the Giants," wrote one veteran reporter after seeing Kelly collect a rare base hit. "There is nothing more to see."

Kelly, nicknamed "High Pockets" because he stood 6-3, did some talking of his own, particularly on the subject of his strikeout total.

"Look at the number of hits, the number of runs I've driven in," Kelly said. "Then you can see how valuable I was in the lineup. Don't judge me by the number of times I've struck out."

In subsequent years, Kelly further answered his

Hard-hitting Giants outfielder Emil (Irish) Meusel
poses with brother Bob, an outfielder with the
cross-city-rival New York Yankees.

hitting? You're about the worst righthanded hitter I've ever seen.' I made the switch (to hitting from both sides), and averages show the maneuver made a difference of between 60 and 70 points."

Frisch, after batting a creditable .280 in 1920, his first full season in the majors, gave evidence in 1921 of being everything he had been touted to be at Fordham. The 23-year-old Flash batted .341 and, despite clubbing only eight home runs, drove in 100 runs.

Meusel, who had shown signs of his vast potential in three full seasons with the Phillies, turned that potential into reality in 1921 with a magnificent split tour of duty with the Phils and Giants. As a member of the hapless Philadelphia club, the right-handed-hitting Meusel batted .353 in 84 games; with the hard-charging Giants, he was a .329 hitter in 62 games.

Center fielder Burns, twice a National League stolen-base leader, contributed a .299 mark to the Giants' cause in his ninth season as a regular for McGraw. A New Yorker through and through—he was born in the Empire State, received all of his minor league seasoning in Utica and had played solely for the Giants since his arrival in the majors in 1911—Burns was a leadoff man who had the knack of drawing walks and at the same time compiling notable official at-bat totals. Before finishing his big-league career in 1925, Burns would lead the National League in bases on balls five times and top the circuit in official at-bats twice (while surpassing 600 at-bats in a season on seven occasions overall).

McGraw's man in right field, Youngs, was something special. Not only to the Giants, but to Little Napoleon himself.

Not quite 20 years old when he reported to the Giants' spring camp in 1917 after being purchased from the minor leagues the year before, Ross Middlebrook (Pep) Youngs was a sweet-swinging raw talent from Texas. A not-so-surehanded infielder in the minors, Youngs was targeted for outfield duty by McGraw and was sent to Rochester to hone his skills.

"I'm giving you one of the greatest players I've ever seen," McGraw told Rochester Manager Mickey Doolan. "If anything happens to him, I'm holding you responsible." Youngs hit .356 for the International League team and proceeded to win a starting job with the Giants in 1918.

Youngs played with a zeal that won him many fans. Besides proving a terror at the plate, as evidenced by his .351 batting average in 1920 and his .327 mark and 102 RBIs in 1921, Pep was a strong-throwing outfielder who learned to play the caroms off the Polo Grounds' right-field wall with consummate skill. Additionally, he was a good base-stealer.

"He was the greatest outfielder I ever saw on a baseball field," McGraw would say after Youngs

critics with continued high hit and RBI totals combined with markedly decreased strikeout figures.

Rawlings wound up appearing in 86 games for the Giants, batting .267. Including the 60 games he had played for Philadelphia, the veteran of five full major league seasons hit a career-high .278.

Bancroft, like Rawlings an Iowa native, also put together the best year of his career. Playing his seventh season in the big time—he was a rookie regular for the Philadelphia Phillies' 1915 National League champions—Bancroft compiled a .319 batting mark and drove in 67 runs. His emergence as a hitter clearly was the result of hard work.

"It took me nearly six years to learn . . . switch-hitting," said Bancroft, who in his second big-league season had hit a paltry .212. "I was a natural right-hander (at the plate), but around the latter part of the campaign in my last year with Portland of the Pacific Coast League in 1914, one of the older players cracked: 'Why don't you switch to lefthanded

died of kidney disease in 1927 at age 30. "The game was never over with Youngs until the last man was out. He could do everything a baseball player should do, and do it better than most players. As an outfielder, he had no superiors. And he was the easiest man I ever knew to handle ... he never caused one minute's trouble for myself or the club. On top of all this, a gamer ball player than Youngs never played ball."

Teammate Frisch, a no-holds-barred player if there ever was one, said this of the Texan: "Ross Youngs was the hardest-running guy I ever saw, the best at throwing those savage cross-blocks to break up attempts at double plays."

Waite Hoyt, star pitcher for the New York Yankees, called Youngs "a smaller Ty Cobb."

McGraw received tremendous production in 1921 from his catching tandem of Snyder and Smith, who combined for 18 home runs and 96 RBIs. Snyder hit .320, while Smith finished at .336.

While developing into a sound hitter in '21, Snyder had earned raves during his career for his defensive work.

"As a mechanical catcher, Snyder has no superiors and in our opinion no present equals," a national baseball magazine reported while the 6-2, 195-pounder was still a member of the Cardinals. "He is everything that a catcher should be—a sure and efficient backstop, a deadly thrower to bases, a man of tremendous strength and energy, and of a size sufficient to deter any audacious baserunner who might try to sweep the catcher out of the path by a sudden dash of bristling spikes. Snyder has the ideal build and the perfect equipment of mechanical gifts . . . ." Despite his considerable skills, Snyder, who first played for the Cardinals in 1912, was traded to the Giants during the 1919 season.

The "anarchist" label that McGraw bestowed upon Smith grew out of Earl's combative nature, which often surfaced when the Giants' manager sought to call pitches during a game. Smith thought he was perfectly capable of handling that assignment himself, and he and McGraw went jaw-to-jaw on that subject and many other topics as well.

Lew Fonseca, who had made his major league debut with Cincinnati in 1921 and later would win an American League batting championship, remembered Smith as downright ornery.

"He'd flip dirt onto your ankles and down into your shoes when you were hitting," Fonseca recalled, "or he'd squirt tobacco juice up and down your calf, or, to distract you further, he'd go so far as to tip your bat.

"I remember that one time Oil shoved his glove against my bat before I swung. So I took a step back and swung the bat backward instead of forward and jarred the hell out of his mask . . . ."

Perhaps more than being a battler or a good hit-

George (High Pockets) Kelly survived early-career criticism to emerge as the Giants' smooth-swinging first baseman.

ter (his lifetime big-league batting mark was .303), Smith was a winner. In a 12-season career in the majors, Earl played in a total of five World Series with three franchises (the Giants, Pirates and Cardinals).

Snyder and Smith handled a pitching staff that, after producing three 20-game winners in the Giants' second-place season of 1920, managed only one 20-victory hurler in New York's pennant year of 1921. Entering the select circle for the second consecutive season was control artist Nehf, a 29-year-old Indianan who won exactly 20 games.

In 15 major league seasons, Nehf walked only 640 batters in 2,708 innings. In his first full season (1920) with the Giants after being obtained in a trade with the Boston Braves, the little lefthander issued only 45 bases on balls in 281 innings.

"I take no great credit for it," Nehf said of his ability to nick the corner of the plate. "It was a

Fun-loving veteran Casey Stengel provided John McGraw with outfield depth and kept the Giants' locker room in high spirits.

natural pitch for me. I tried one time just to see if I could, and I threw with my eyes closed. I hit the outside corner low in the strike zone, anyway."

Toney, sold from Cincinnati to the Giants approximately 15 months after his historic 1917 duel with Chicago's Vaughn, won 18 games for McGraw's club in 1921. As fate would have it, a Giants legend was instrumental in Toney's development as a pitcher.

"I was a sidearmed pitcher when I went to the majors," said righthander Toney, reflecting on his arrival in the big leagues in 1911 with the Chicago Cubs. "In fact, I almost was an underhanded pitcher.

"But the first year up there I saw Christy Mathewson work a game and he came straight overhand.

Right then I knew I'd have to learn how to pitch overhanded, too.

"It took a couple of years, but I finally mastered it."

The Giants' other two principal starters, right-handers Barnes and Douglas, each won 15 games.

McGraw and the Giants viewed the 1921 World Series not only as an opportunity to rule the baseball world and at the same time reclaim the affections of New Yorkers, but also as a chance to massage their own egos. After all, McGraw's teams had wound up losers in their last four World Series appearances. The Yankees, on the other hand, would be competing in their first-ever Series.

The Yankees did little, initially, to make the Giants feel better about themselves. McGraw's troops lost the first two games of the best-of-nine fall classic—they scored nary a run against Carl Mays or Waite Hoyt—and fell behind, 4-0, after 2½ innings of Game 3. But a four-run third inning and an eight-run seventh that featured Youngs' bases-full triple sent the National Leaguers winging to a 13-5 triumph.

From that point on, the Giants dominated. They captured the Series, five games to three, with Nehf tossing a four-hitter in the 1-0 finale, a game that ended on a stirring note. With one out and Aaron Ward on first base in the Yankees' ninth, Frank Baker strode to the plate. Baker, who as a member of the Philadelphia Athletics had earned his sobriquet of "Home Run" with his long-ball hitting against McGraw's Giants in the 1911 Series, rifled a ground ball on which second baseman Rawlings made a marvelous stop. Rawlings, who fell while lunging for the ball, threw out Baker from a sitting position. On the play, Ward attempted to reach third base but was nailed on first baseman Kelly's on-target throw to Frisch.

Snyder hit a Series-leading .364 for the Giants. Irish Meusel, playing against brother Bob, the Yankees' right fielder, topped all batsmen with seven RBIs while batting a hefty .345. Barnes and Douglas each won two games for the new World Series champions.

As McGraw savored his return to the baseball heights, he also mapped plans for 1922. While Rawlings had delivered as anticipated in the just-concluded season, McGraw thought his infield could be even stronger. If he moved Frankie Frisch to second base, as was his desire, McGraw then would need a qualified third baseman. Mac knew exactly the man he wanted: Heinie Groh, a little fellow who had been a Giant at the beginning of his big-league career before being traded to Cincinnati. As a member of the Reds, Groh had developed into a steady .300 hitter. In fact, he had batted .331 in 97 games for Cincinnati in 1921. To obtain Heinie, McGraw gave up George Burns, one of his favorite

Ross Youngs (left), a talented Texan who played with every ounce of his heart, was a sweet-swinging outfielder, while lefthander Art Nehf was the ace of John McGraw's 1921 and '22 pitching staffs.

persons, catcher Mike Gonzalez and a truckload of cash.

Confident that he now had the finest infield in the league, and perhaps all of baseball, McGraw sailed to Havana and spent considerable time in the casinos and at the race tracks. When he joined his players at training camp in the spring of 1922, he was fully prepared for another pennant run.

In a typical windup to spring training in this era, McGraw and the Giants embarked on a lengthy barnstorming tour. While in Memphis, a city that the Giants' manager always found hospitable, McGraw had an enjoyable stay that exceeded all others in lasting benefits. Old cronies told him about a shortstop with the Little Rock club of the Southern Association and a pitcher/first baseman with a local oil-company team. Mac acted on both tips and, in due course, welcomed to the Giants two future Hall-of-Famers, Travis Jackson and Bill Terry. (Jackson would see his first extended duty with the Giants in 1923, while Terry would work his way into half of the New Yorkers' games by 1924.)

The Giants of 1922 were heavy favorites to repeat as National League titlists, and they pretty much had things their own way for the entire season. The pitching staff gave McGraw the few problems he encountered, but it also was the source of considerable satisfaction.

McGraw suffered a crushing blow in August when Douglas, irate over what he considered unfair treatment from his manager, was permanently barred from baseball after he tried to vent his anger. The pitcher drew the ban from Commissioner Kenesaw Mountain Landis after he wrote a letter to a St. Louis player, a missive in which he offered to desert his team and thereby help the Cardinals in their pennant bid. The letter read in part: "I want to leave here. I don't want to see this guy (McGraw) win the pennant. You know I can pitch and I am afraid that if I stay I will win the pennant for them . . . ." At the time of his ouster from the game, Douglas had an 11-4 record.

Fortunately for the Giants, McGraw had strengthened his mound corps in late July with the acquisition of righthander Hugh McQuillan from the Braves. Toney went to Boston in that swap.

"I hear he's no early-to-bed, early-to-rise fellow, but I'll be able to handle him," McGraw said of McQuillan.

"He hasn't much of a record (5-10 for Boston in 1922)," Stoneham responded.

"I know," McGraw said. "But he's not gaited to pitch for a second-division club. Put him on this club and he'll be a winner."

McGraw's third encounter with a pitcher involved Jack Scott, a hulking, slow-moving right-hander. A 15-game winner for the Braves in 1921, Scott had been traded to Cincinnati before the start of the 1922 season but was released after suffering a mysterious arm ailment and making only one appearance with the Reds. Signed by the Giants at the tail-end of July after convincing McGraw that life had returned to his arm, Scott proved a valuable addition in the heat of the pennant race.

The Giants, who finished seven games ahead of runner-up Cincinnati at season's end, parlayed an explosive offense into their second straight National League flag. Six of the seven players who appeared in 100 or more games for McGraw batted above .320. The biggest all-around thumpers were Meusel, with a .330 average, 16 home runs and 132 RBIs; Kelly, with a .327 mark, 17 homers and 107 RBIs; and Youngs, a .330 hitter who knocked in 86 runs (and stood out on defense, with 28 assists from his outfield station). The lone 100-game performer who wasn't in the above-.320 batting class turned out to be Groh, who finished at .265.

Nehf won 19 games, 24-year-old righthander Rosy Ryan developed into a 17-game winner, Barnes notched 13 victories (including a no-hitter against the Phillies), Scott went 8-2 as a Giant and McQuillan was 6-5 in a New York uniform.

While the World Series was a Yankees-Giants rematch, there was one totally new aspect to the fall classic. For the first time, the Series was presented on radio "to an invisible audience, estimated at five million." Grantland Rice, the noted sportswriter, described the action and, marveled the New York Times, "Not only could the voice of the official radio observer be heard, but the voice of the umpire on the field announcing the batteries for the day mingled with the voice of a boy selling ice cream cones."

What transpired on the field, however, reminded everyone of 1921. The Giants, winners of the final three games of the '21 Series, rolled to a four games-to-none romp—the New York rivals played one tie game—as the fall classic reverted to a best-of-seven format. Irish Meusel again set the run-production pace, driving in seven runs, while Groh batted .474 and Frisch hit .471. Scott and Nehf were pitching standouts, Scott tossing a shutout in Game 3 and Nehf again hurling a complete-game victory in the Series finale.

McGraw would not win another Series. However, he would guide the Giants to N.L. titles again in 1923 and 1924, giving him four consecutive pennants, which remains the National League record to this day.

Finding the kind of skilled players capable of mounting such a pennant streak was a singular attribute of Little Napoleon, who would recruit them, trade for them, make note of them for future delivery, scour the country for them and, as in the case of Frank Francis Frisch, even find them in his own back yard.

In 1921 and 1922, McGraw's knack of finding and developing talent and then riding herd over it had been demonstrated once more.

1921
FINAL STANDING

Club	W.	L.	Pct.	GB.
New York	94	59	.614	——
Pittsburgh	90	63	.588	4

BATTERS

Pos.	Player	G.	HR.	RBI.	B.A.
1B	George Kelly	149	23	122	.308
2B	Johnny Rawlings	86	1	30	.267
SS	Dave Bancroft	153	6	67	.319
3B	Frankie Frisch (2b)	153	8	100	.341
OF	Irish Meusel	62	2	36	.329
	George Burns	149	4	61	.299
	Ross Youngs	141	3	102	.327
C	Frank Snyder	108	8	45	.320
	Earl Smith	89	10	51	.336

OTHER CONTRIBUTORS (20+ Games): Eddie Brown, Bill Cunningham, Alex Gaston, Lee King, Bill Patterson, Goldie Rapp, Curt Walker.

PITCHERS

Thr.	Pitcher	G.	W.	L.	ERA
L	Art Nehf	41	20	10	3.62
R	Fred Toney	42	18	11	3.61
R	Jesse Barnes	42	15	9	3.10
R	Phil Douglas	40	15	10	4.21

OTHER CONTRIBUTORS (20+ Games): Rosy Ryan, Slim Sallee.

1922
FINAL STANDING

Club	W.	L.	Pct.	GB.
New York	93	61	.604	——
Cincinnati	86	68	.558	7
Pittsburgh	85	69	.552	8
St. Louis	85	69	.552	8

BATTERS

Pos.	Player	G.	HR.	RBI.	B.A.
1B	George Kelly	151	17	107	.327
2B	Frankie Frisch	132	5	51	.326
SS	Dave Bancroft	156	4	60	.321
3B	Heinie Groh	115	3	51	.265
OF	Irish Meusel	154	16	132	.330
	Casey Stengel	84	7	48	.368
	Ross Youngs	149	7	86	.330
C	Frank Snyder	104	5	51	.343
	Earl Smith	90	9	39	.278
UT	Johnny Rawlings (2b)	88	1	30	.282
	Bill Cunningham (of)	85	2	33	.327

OTHER CONTRIBUTORS (20+ Games): Lee King, Dave Robertson, Ralph Shinners.

PITCHERS

Thr.	Pitcher	G.	W.	L.	ERA
L	Art Nehf	37	19	13	3.29
R	Rosy Ryan	46	17	12	3.00
R	Jesse Barnes	37	13	8	3.51
R	Phil Douglas	24	11	4	2.62
R	Jack Scott	17	8	2	4.39

OTHER CONTRIBUTORS (20+ Games): Virgil Barnes, Red Causey, Claude Jonnard.

Number 24

Yankees Climb Back To the Top

The 1930 season, dismal and far short of expectations, was drawing to a close. The vaunted New York Yankee machine, not far removed from its once-lofty position atop the baseball world, was sputtering and spinning its wheels in third place, far behind the American League-leading Philadelphia Athletics. Yankee Owner Colonel Jacob Ruppert, displeased with his team's fall from grace, was convinced that a managerial change was in order.

The man on the hotseat was Bob Shawkey, the winning pitcher in the first game played at Yankee Stadium in 1923. Shawkey had taken the Yankee reins before the '30 campaign after the untimely death of Miller Huggins in 1929. He was a nice guy and well-liked by the players, but Shawkey did not command the respect and discipline that Ruppert deemed necessary for his ball club.

So who was available to lead the Yankees back to their rightful position of prominence? Who would command the respect and authority expected by Ruppert and General Manager Edward G. Barrow?

The answer came in late September when the Chicago Cubs announced that Manager Joe McCarthy had resigned and would be replaced by Rogers Hornsby. Though Ruppert had never met McCarthy, he knew enough about the Irishman's background to pique his interest and justify a job interview.

That background included a mediocre minor league playing career that was fueled more by the youngster's intense desire than talent. "I wasn't much of a hitter and I didn't have good speed, either," he said years later. And after 14 years of futility, he finally accepted the fact that his love for the game was not enough to fulfill his dream of making it to the big leagues. So, what about managing?

That thought appealed to McCarthy, who pursued his new dream with the same vigor that he once had pursued ground balls as a hungry young minor leaguer. He continued playing until 1921, but it was his long, consistent managing success, especially at Louisville, that caught the eye of Cubs Owner William Wrigley. The Cubs were in disarray after the 1925 season and McCarthy, despite having no major league experience, was asked to turn around their sagging fortunes.

It was mission accomplished when, in 1929, the

Yankee Manager Joe McCarthy (left) never enjoyed a close relationship with Babe Ruth and pretty much let the slugger go his own way.

Cubs lapped the National League field, winning by 10½ games before losing to the Philadelphia A's in the World Series. But when the Cubs finished second in 1930 and McCarthy had problems with veteran superstar Hornsby, it was time to move on.

But move on where? That question was answered by Ruppert and Barrow, who met with the Philadelphia native in a hotel room of his home city during the A's-Cardinals 1930 World Series. The parties quickly reached accord and a few days later a nervous McCarthy stood before a microphone at the New York offices during ceremonies to introduce him to sportswriters and fans as the new Yankee manager.

Asked to say something to his new employer, Mc-

Joe McCarthy finally settled on shortstop Frank Crosetti (left) and smooth-swinging third baseman Joe Sewell to man the left side of his 1932 infield.

Carthy blurted, "Colonel Huston, I . . ." A roar of laughter cut him short and McCarthy turned flaming red. Colonel Tillinghast Huston, Ruppert's original partner, hadn't been connected with the club for years.

Ruppert found the remark humorous. "Maybe," he said, "McCarthy will be around here long enough so he will get to know me better."

Little did the Yankee owner or anybody else realize that McCarthy would be around for 16 years, long enough to get to know Ruppert very well and to guide the Yankees to eight pennants and seven World Series championships. And all McCarthy knew for sure was that the job he was expected to perform in 1931 would be tough.

"McCarthy," Ruppert warned him when he was hired, "I finished third last year. I realize that you are confronted with problems that it will take you a little while to solve, so I'll be satisfied if you finish second this year. But, I warn you McCarthy, I don't like to finish second."

There was nothing easy about Marse Joe's first year with the Yankees. He faced a monstrous task.

For the last several years, discipline had deteriorated, due in large part to the unbridled lifestyle of Babe Ruth. And the Bambino had fancied himself excellent managerial timber while openly seeking the Yankee job. He was advised, somewhat abruptly, that a man who could not handle himself was incapable of handling others.

Many other Yankees were reluctant to accept the 5-foot-8, 190-pound McCarthy because he had never played in the major leagues. He carried the "bush league" stigma until it was eradicated by the team's success and McCarthy's unswerving devotion to fairness and firmness.

McCarthy was a perfectionist, a hard-driving taskmaster and a fighter. He was proud to be in the major leagues and proud to wear the uniform of the New York Yankees. He expected his players to feel the same way.

His years in the minors taught him to be patient with the mechanical mistakes of young players, but he would not tolerate what he considered "flaws of spirit." When he ran across a disruptive personality, he would send that player packing.

The one exception was the great one—Ruth. Mc-Carthy knew the unique position that Babe held in the hearts of the fans and had no intention of challenging it. He allowed baseball's home run king to call his own shots and never really felt in total control of the Yankees until 1935, when Ruth was released and signed by the Boston Braves.

Changes were inevitable when the 43-year-old McCarthy reported for 1931 spring training and he didn't disappoint. He took one look at players shaving in the clubhouse and issued a ban on the practice. "They're reporting to do a day's work," he informed Barrow. "Why show up at the office needing a shave?"

Card playing in the clubhouse before a game also was forbidden. "Let 'em think baseball," was Mc-Carthy's explanation.

Marse Joe never majored in psychology, but he practiced it constantly. In an early conversation with Barrow, McCarthy suggested that each player wear a uniform a size larger than necessary and that caps be changed from the old square style to the round. These changes, he explained, would make the athletes appear more menacing.

Champions also should be neat on the field, he told Barrow, and he therefore wanted three sets of uniforms available at all times so the Yankees would present a fresh-from-the-showcase appearance.

In accordance with Ruppert's timetable, McCarthy led the Yankees to a second-place finish in 1931. Though Ruth and Lou Gehrig each hit 46 home runs and young Ben Chapman stole 61 bases, the A's still were too strong. The Yankees finished 13½ games behind.

When the Yankees arrived at St. Petersburg, Fla., for 1932 spring training, only four regulars and two starting pitchers remained from the 1927 club that had steamrolled to 110 victories and a four-game sweep of the Pittsburgh Pirates in the World Series. The regulars were Ruth, Gehrig, Tony Lazzeri and Earle Combs. The pitchers were Herb Pennock and George Pipgras.

In the intervening years, the club had added Chapman, Bill Dickey, Joe Sewell, Lyn Lary and two pitchers who would develop into the team's aces—Red Ruffing and Vernon (Lefty) Gomez. Newcomers at McCarthy's second spring camp included Frank Crosetti, a $75,000 shortstop who had batted .343 in the Pacific Coast League; Jack Saltz-gaver, another costly infielder who had batted .340 in the American Association, and Johnny Allen, a 26-year-old righthander who had won 21 games in the International League.

The top reserves were Sammy Byrd, a 25-year-old outfielder who was known as "Babe Ruth's legs" because of his frequent service as a late-inning replacement for the aging slugger; Myril Hoag, a 24-year-old Californian with one year of outfield experience with the Yankees; Arndt Jorgens, of Norwegian birth and great value as a backup catcher for Dickey, and Eddie (Doc) Farrell, a 30-year-old utility infielder who had been in and out of the majors since 1925.

Until the start of the Grapefruit League season, the biggest news from Florida concerned the progress of contract negotiations between Ruth and Ruppert. The Babe had just completed a multi-year pact that paid him $80,000 annually and there was widespread speculation on his pay demand for the new season.

Ruppert anticipated little trouble in signing the 37-year-old Sultan of Swat. The owner hailed the player as "a sensible fellow (with) a fine spirit," hopeful that the Bambino would accept a substantially smaller paycheck in the depths of the Great Depression.

Babe had different ideas. He was still the biggest personality in baseball, the idol of millions of American youths, and he had batted .373 in 1931, with 46 homers and 163 runs batted in. These were not statistics that merited a sizable pay slash.

When two mid-winter meetings in New York failed to produce agreement, negotiations were transferred to St. Petersburg. Days passed without hints of progress. When not at the bargaining table, the Babe worked out at a local gymnasium, "punching the bag, skipping the rope, boxing, wrestling and doing miles of synthetic roadwork on a treadmill."

The exhibition games were underway when Ruth finally agreed to terms. He signed a one-year contract, his first of less than two years since he was acquired from the Boston Red Sox in 1920. It called for $75,000 in pay and a percentage of the gate receipts from exhibition games.

Babe immediately went to the ball park where the Yankees were playing the Boston Braves. He suited up and played the entire 11 innings in a colorless fashion. In six at-bats he walked once and failed to get a hit while fanning twice. In the field, he committed two errors.

But with the Bambino's services secure for another year, New York fans directed their attention to the competition for three infield positions. There was no question about first base. The bag belonged to Gehrig, the indestructible Iron Horse who was midway through his record streak of playing in 2,130 consecutive games.

The three other infield jobs were in dispute. Lazzeri was the incumbent second baseman but he was coming off a substandard 1931 season in which he batted .267 with just eight home runs. It seemed likely that the veteran would lose his job to Saltz-gaver. That would leave Lary, Sewell and Crosetti to battle for the two remaining positions.

Two outfield berths were locked up. They belonged to Ruth and Chapman, who switched off in left and right. Either the veteran Combs or the younger Byrd would patrol center. Dickey, of course, owned exclusive rights to the catching job.

The heart and soul of the Yankees remained Ruth and Gehrig. The sluggers supreme were not always the best of friends, but they were inseparable in the Yankee lineup.

From 1927 through the '31 campaign, Ruth and Gehrig had combined for 451 home runs and 1,577 RBIs. That's an average of 45 homers and 158 RBIs per season per man. No other combination in baseball history has ever come close to matching that offensive consistency. When it came to hitting the pitched ball, both were cool, calculating masters.

But off the field, they were as different as night and day.

Gehrig was a gentle giant, a quiet man who was unassuming and honest to a fault. While Ruth was gathering up headlines and coloring the course of baseball history with his open lifestyle, Gehrig was lurking in the Babe's shadow, content with his station in life.

"I'm not a headline guy and we may as well face it," Gehrig once said. "I'm just the guy who's in there every day, the fellow who follows Babe in the batting order. When Babe's turn at bat is over, whether he strikes out or belts a home run, the fans are still talking about him when I come up.

"If I stood on my head at the plate, nobody'd pay any attention."

The Iron Horse might have been overshadowed by his colorful teammate, but he didn't go unnoticed.

"I didn't manage Ruth at his peak," said McCarthy years after Gehrig had died, "but how could anyone be greater than Gehrig? Look at his World Series batting, .361. He was right at the crest of his career in 1932, and he put on the greatest one-man show I've ever seen. In the four games against Chicago, Lou batted .529 and was personally responsible for 14 runs.

"I often thought that Gehrig felt sorry for opposing pitchers. If he had been hungry for headlines, he would have hit a lot more home runs and for a higher average. When we had a ball game wrapped up and Gehrig had a few key hits, he wasn't nearly so dangerous a batter. I guess he was the kind of fellow who never liked to rub in a defeat or embarrass a pitcher."

Such concerns never bothered Ruth, who attracted headlines like a magnet and always put on a show for his adoring fans. The coolness he sometimes showed to Gehrig usually was attributable to a feeling that he was being upstaged.

Both sluggers were in top form opening day as Yankee ace Lefty Gomez squared off against A's

Veteran Earle Combs, a holdover from the 1927 Yankee team, finally won the 1932 center-field job and continued his .300-hitting ways.

righthander George Earnshaw in a battle of 20-game winners at Philadelphia. What was expected to be a low-scoring pitcher's duel was anything but, with Earnshaw taking the brunt of the Yankees' offensive explosion.

Ruth drove in five runs with two homers and a single and Gehrig pounded out a homer, triple and single in the Yanks' 12-6 victory. Byrd, the starter in center field, hit two home runs and a single.

The Yankees took great pleasure in their clouting carnival and "laughed heartily at the discomfiture of (Philadelphia outfielder) Al Simmons in particular because Al had predicted in a newspaper interview that the Yankees were overrated and would not finish better than fourth."

Of more importance, however, was the opening-day lineup that had Byrd in center, Saltzgaver at second base, Lary at shortstop and Crosetti at third along with regulars Gehrig, Ruth, Chapman and Dickey. It was a lineup that was to change drastically over the course of the season as McCarthy looked for the right combination.

Byrd, the first-game slugger, would soon relinquish his starting job to the veteran Combs. But the 5-10 Georgia product had other means of carving his special niche. As Ruth's late-game caddy, he received a lot of publicity. But his "second career" generated even more.

Byrd retired from baseball in 1936 to become a

Sammy Byrd, who later would forge a career as a professional golfer, was used primarily as Babe Ruth's late-inning defensive replacement.

professional golfer. And he justified that decision by scoring a tour victory in the Victory National Open at Chicago in 1943.

Combs did not have Byrd's golf prowess, but he was a survivor. After seven years as a Yankee starter with a .300-plus career average, the Kentuckian wasn't about to let his job slip away at the tender age of 33. The eight-year veteran bided his time when Byrd jumped off to his blazing start, and when his teammate cooled off, Combs slipped into the lineup and proceeded on his .300-hitting way.

The infield situation was not so easily settled.

McCarthy liked what he saw of the strapping Crosetti, but he couldn't decide whether the 21-year-old rookie was better suited for shortstop or third-base duty. And the jury was still out on whether the San Francisco native could hit major league pitching, even though he had pounded out .334 and .343 averages in his last two seasons for the San Francisco Seals of the Pacific Coast League.

There were other things McCarthy didn't know about the young Italian. Such as Crosetti's determination, consistency and durability, traits that would endear him to his manager and Yankee fans as the starting shortstop for most of the next decade.

McCarthy did know about the veteran Lazzeri, one of the strong men in the Yankees' Murderers' Row lineup of the late 1920s. He knew that it would

be difficult to keep a man of Lazzeri's determination and intense pride out of the lineup after a one-season dip. And, as McCarthy suspected, it didn't take long for Lazzeri to win back his manager and long-time Yankee fans.

That gave the Yankees an all-Italian double-play combination and the fellow San Franciscans formed a fast friendship. They also formed a rock-solid middle infield that would rank among the best in the major leagues over the next six seasons.

When Lazzeri moved the weak-hitting Saltzgaver out of the lineup and Crosetti took over Lary's shortstop position, McCarthy was left with a hole to fill at third base. But the ever-perceptive manager always seemed to be prepared for such emergencies.

In this case, it was Sewell to the rescue. The former Cleveland shortstop was the ace up McCarthy's well-worn sleeve.

Joe Sewell was something of a prodigy when he was introduced to major league baseball in 1920. And what an introduction that was!

The Indians were in the stretch run of a hard-fought American League pennant race when their shortstop, Ray Chapman, became the tragic victim of the only on-field fatality in big-league history. Chapman, batting against Yankee pitcher Carl Mays, couldn't duck away from an inside pitch and was hit on the skull. He died the next day. The Reach's Official American League Baseball Guide described the aftermath of the incident in its 1921 edition:

It cast a gloom over the American League race and so deeply depressed the Cleveland team that it momentarily lost the lead and would have lost the pennant had it not recovered its nerve in time, aided by the acquisition of a competent shortstop in young Sewell from New Orleans.

"Young Sewell" was just a green kid, fresh from the University of Alabama and playing in his first season of professional baseball when news reached New Orleans of Chapman's death. To say that he was surprised when told that Cleveland Manager Tris Speaker had tabbed him to fill Chapman's position was something of an understatement.

"Sure, I was scared when I went up," Sewell said later. "Right in the middle of a pennant race like that, replacing a man who had been killed. The newspapers made a big deal out of this unknown shortstop, me. I had played only 92 games as a pro.

"Cleveland had to get a shortstop somewhere. They had only one extra infielder then and he couldn't play the position. I'd never seen a major league ball thrown until that game against the Athletics.

"My first time at bat, I lined out to center field. Then I singled through the box. My third time up, I

Speedy leftfielder Ben Chapman could swing a big bat and terrorize opposing pitchers and catchers with his baserunning.

tripled over the third baseman's head into left field. After that triple, I wasn't scared any more. 'Shoot,' I said, 'I can play up here.' "

And play he did. Sewell hit .329 in his 22 games with the 1920 Indians and helped them win the A.L. pennant. He didn't hit well in the World Series, but he rebounded in 1921 to bat .318. For the next nine seasons, Sewell batted under .300 only twice, enjoying his best year in '23 when he batted .353.

Throughout his exceptional career with the Indians, Sewell also was noted as one of the game's premier glovemen, one of the toughest players in baseball history to strike out and one of baseball's top ironmen.

At one point, the 5-6, 155-pounder played in 1,102 consecutive games, the third longest streak in baseball history, and during his entire 10-year Cleveland career, the lefthanded swinger struck out only 98 times. Twice he made it through 154-game schedules with only four strikeouts.

But by 1930, the elastic in Sewell's legs was gone and the Indians moved him to third base. By the end of the campaign, he was sitting on the bench. A few months later, the Indians gave him his release.

That's when McCarthy and the Yankees stepped in. They signed the veteran and he rewarded them by hitting .302 and playing a strong third base in 1931. But when 1932 spring training rolled around, Sewell was informed that he would have to make way for the kids.

Still, McCarthy, entertaining doubts about his 1932 infield, took special note of the 33-year-old veteran. "Joe's still quite a ball player, quite a ball player," he said after watching him one day in an exhibition game.

That observation was borne out as the 1932 season progressed.

McCarthy had no doubts about left field or catcher, where Chapman and the steady Dickey performed.

The speedy Chapman had arrived on the New York scene in 1930 as a steel-handed third baseman. He hit .316 in his 138 games that season, but McCarthy took one look at the youngster in '31 and told him to try the outfield. Chapman had no objection; he just wanted to play. And by the end of the campaign, there was little doubt that the outfield is where he belonged.

Chapman was a high-strung youngster with a quick temper. But he also had the quickness and speed to cover a lot of ground and to terrify pitchers and catchers with his baserunning. And his .315 average and 122 RBIs in 1931 had proven to Yankee officials that his batting skills were genuine.

Dickey was entering his fourth season as the Yankees' regular catcher and the 6-1, 185-pounder with the smooth lefthanded swing seemed to be getting better every year.

As a catcher, he ranked among the best. As a handler of pitchers, he had no peer. Dickey, a strong, silent, no-nonsense type, had an uncanny ability for remembering opposing hitters, their strengths and weaknesses, and getting his pitcher to exploit them.

He also had batted over .300 in each of his first three seasons, including a .339 mark in 1930, and was beginning to show signs of increasing his power production. He was, in short, the prototype major league catcher.

But Dickey did have one flaw. He was slow, catcher-slow. That quality wasn't lost on Ruth, who decided to say something one day after watching Dickey get thrown out at third trying for a triple.

"When I came back to the dugout after getting tagged out," Dickey said, "Ruth said, 'Pittridge, I can outrun you.' He called me Pittridge for partridge, which is what some of them called quail, and I was always talking about bird-hunting.

"Of course, that burned me up. Ruth was getting a little old. I couldn't run very fast, but I did think I could outrun Ruth. I said, 'You can't outrun me, either.' He said, 'I'll bet you a hundred I can.' Well, I was just a young fellow, not making a big salary, and a hundred was a lot to me. But you couldn't back off from Babe.

"I said, 'When will we run?' He says, 'Come out early tomorrow and we'll have the race. So all the players heard about it and they came out too.

"I wanted to run 100 yards but he said 75. When we started out, he got a little in front of me. About the 50-yard mark, I went by him. The course went right by the dugout. When we got even with it, he

The Yankees' outstanding starting rotation featured righthanders Red Ruffing (left) and Johnny Allen (center) and lefthander Vernon (Lefty) Gomez.

just turned and ran on into the clubhouse. I didn't mind that. I was glad I beat him. . . ."

Ruth may not have been fast afoot, but his fast 1932 getaway (four homers in his first five games) spawned talk of the Bambino breaking the 60-homer record he had set five years earlier.

Babe quickly quashed that speculation.

"I'm more interested in the Yankees winning the pennant," he said. "There are times when I'll be a lot smarter to swing for singles than to knock the ball into the bleachers. I've an ambition to play in 10 World Series and if we can win this year I will reach that mark. I think my mark of 60 homers in one year is pretty safe without trying to better it."

Gomez, too, jumped off to an impressive start. No longer thin as a rail, the fun-loving lefthander now weighed 175 pounds and evoked unstinting praise from his manager.

"I am willing to predict," said the usually conservative McCarthy, "that he leads the American League lefthanders, including (Lefty) Grove, when the final results are compiled. . . . He was everything that makes for success—speed, curves and almost perfect control. Furthermore, the boy has a world of confidence in himself and as he goes along, that quality will increase."

Gomez, a third-year man who had recorded a 21-9 record in 1931, was the class clown of the Yankee locker room. A master story-teller with a penchant for doing crazy things, Gomez, known as "El Goofy," always managed to keep spirits high and the clubhouse loose.

Gomez was on the hill May 16, a noteworthy day for the 1932 Yanks. For one thing, Lefty's 8-0 conquest of Cleveland lifted the Yankees into first

place, where they would remain for the rest of the season. For another, the shutout enabled the club to tie league records of four consecutive whitewashings and 40 straight scoreless innings. Allen, Pipgras and Ruffing had accounted for the other shutouts.

The Yankees' streak ended the next day when Allen, a rookie righthander with a temper as big as his talent, served up a first-inning home run to Earl Averill. That home run obviously didn't sit well with the youngster, who already had developed a reputation as a bad actor among opposing managers and players as well as umpires.

"The guy thinks he should win every time he pitches," Gehrig once said of the North Carolina native. "And if he loses, it's a personal conspiracy against him."

But Allen didn't lose on this occasion—or many others in 1936. Chapman's mammoth home run gave the Yanks their eighth straight victory and Ruth's 10th-inning homer the next day made it nine while giving the Yankees a sweep of the four western teams at Yankee Stadium. The string finally was snapped May 19 by the Washington Senators.

As the Yankee machine, becoming more efficient and devastating day by day, rolled into June, McCarthy finally was settling on his most productive lineup. That included Lazzeri, who exploded for a homer, a triple, a double, two singles and six RBIs in a 20-13 June 3 Yankee victory at Philadelphia. Lazzeri's performance would have been more noteworthy if Gehrig hadn't chosen that particular game to put on the greatest performance of his career.

Facing Earnshaw in the first inning, the Iron Horse homered over the right-field wall. He repeated that feat in the fourth and the fifth, both times on Earnshaw pitches. After five innings, A's Manager Connie Mack removed the righthander in favor of Lee Roy Mahaffey, a righthander whom Mack regarded as a shade smarter than most pitchers.

As Earnshaw prepared to go to the clubhouse, Mack called him over. "Sit beside me, George," he said. "You've been pitching wrong to Gehrig. I want you to see how Mahaffey does it."

Earnshaw, a graduate of Swarthmore College, did as ordered. In the seventh inning, he saw how Mahaffey did it. Gehrig smacked a fourth home run, this one over the left-field fence. Picking up his glove, Earnshaw stomped out of the dugout, exclaiming to Mack, "I see. He made him change directions."

Ordinarily, Gehrig's four consecutive home run feat would have been recorded in blaring headlines. But June 3, 1932, was not an ordinary day. For on the same day that Lou duplicated an accomplishment that had been unmatched for 38 years, John McGraw retired as manager of the New York Giants after a 30-year rule. Consequently, the big first sacker, who had labored for most of his career under the enormous shadow of Ruth, saw his most notable one-game achievement dwarfed by the resignation of the Little Napoleon, who had dominated New York baseball since 1902.

The Yankee juggernaut rolled on. After games of July 3, the Bombers led second-place Detroit by 9½ lengths. But Jake Ruppert, a world-class pessimist, would have preferred a much larger lead. And after what happened in Washington on the Fourth of July, the owner was convinced that the lead was inadequate, that sinister forces were about to destroy his club.

The Bombers not only lost two games at Washington on Independence Day, but:

• Gomez's winning streak ended at 11 games in the opener and his record tumbled to 14-2;

• Allen, who had won six games, three in a row, lost for the second time;

• Dickey slugged Carl Reynolds, breaking the Washington outfielder's jaw in two places.

Moreover, Ruth and Gehrig were involved in base-line scuffles with Buddy Myer, the Nats' second baseman. In retaliation, Myer slid into first base with spikes gleaming and slashed Lou's pants. It was a nasty situation at Griffith Stadium. Hostility was everywhere. Firecrackers exploded perilously close to Yankee players and Ruppert was certain that the twilight of the New York gods was at hand.

Dickey's one-punch knockout unsettled the baseball community as few events had in recent memory. It was inconceivable to many that the Arkansas native, usually in full control of his emotions, should have been aroused to violence over a collision at home plate.

There *were* provocations, however. The day before at Boston, Roy Johnson slammed into Dickey with what the Yanks regarded as unnecessary ferocity, chipping one of Bill's teeth. That, and other similar incidents, had wearied Dickey of baserunners intent on doing him bodily harm.

The incident occurred when the Senators were comfortably ahead in the second game. Reynolds was on third when the batter missed the pitch on an attempted squeeze play. Dickey's throw toward third base, trying to nail the runner, struck Reynolds on the back. As the runner started for the plate again, Sewell retrieved the ball and fired to Dickey, who was holding the ball as Reynolds crashed into him. Moments later, Reynolds was down and out with a double fracture of his jaw.

When Will Harridge read the umpire's report, the league president came down heavily on Dickey —a 30-day suspension and a $1,000 fine.

Clark Griffith said the penalty was too light.

Reynolds' action, said McCarthy, was "a deliberate attempt to injure Dickey and Reynolds got just what he deserved. I do not favor fist fights on the field, but in the case of Dickey, he had plenty of provocation. He had a narrow escape from serious injury when Johnson bowled him over in Boston and I told him to be on the alert in Washington.

"So when Reynolds, who had no chance to score because Dickey had the ball in his hand, ran into him at top speed, it was not surprising to me that Bill took the law into his own hands. He simply lost his temper as any red-blooded man would do."

With Dickey out of action until August 4, the Yankees called up Eddie Phillips from their Newark farm club to help out Jorgens. The veteran Phillips appeared in nine games during his brief stay and batted .290.

More misfortune struck July 18. In a game against Chicago, Ruth tore the extensor muscles in his right thigh while chasing a pop fly. The Bambino was idle until July 25, when he hit a two-run pinch single at Philadelphia.

By July 28, Ruth was ready for regular duty again. He celebrated with two home runs, a double and seven RBIs in a 10-1 rout of Wes Ferrell at Cleveland.

The Babe's return to the regular lineup was as welcome and as spectacular as that of Dickey on August 4. The catcher marked that occasion with three singles and a grand-slam homer in pacing the Bombers to a 15-3 victory at Chicago.

With Dickey and Ruth again going strong, the Yankee guns continued their rapid fire. By the end of August, all the players were aware that a major league mark was within easy grasp. If they could avoid a shutout in their next three games, the Yanks would break a mark, set in 1894, of scoring in 132 consecutive contests.

Babe Ruth crosses the plate after hitting his 'called-shot' homer in Game 3 of the 1932 World Series as Lou Gehrig shakes his hand and Cubs catcher Gabby Hartnett watches.

The streak was nearly broken September 1, in game No. 131. Blanked through eight innings, the team broke through in the ninth when Ruffing singled home a run. There was more of the same the next afternoon. This time Ruth walked in the ninth and rode home on Lou Gehrig's triple. Last-pitch theatrics were discarded September 3 when Combs hit a first-inning homer against Washington to give the Yanks the record. The Bronx Bombers went on to score in every 1932 game.

Two days later, the Yankees dispelled any illusions Philadelphia might have entertained about winning the A.L. pennant. Before a Labor Day crowd of 70,772, the largest of the season, the Yanks twice crushed the defending-champion A's. Gomez recorded his 23rd victory in the opener while the nightcap went to Allen, the twice-beaten rookie who won his 16th game and 10th in a row.

In high spirits, the Yankees entrained for their final tour of the four western cities. They were 12½ games in front of the second-place A's and even Ruppert displayed an occasional flash of optimism. McCarthy, too, was as upbeat as his cautious nature would permit. If any serious problems existed, nobody was aware of them.

Detroit was the first stop. Arriving there on September 7, the players proceeded to their hotel, where Ruth suddenly was stricken with severe pains in his side. Fearing appendicitis and reluctant to risk surgery in the Motor City, Babe returned to New York to consult the club physician.

Examination revealed that, while Ruth had a touch of appendicitis, surgery would not be required; merely rest and relaxation far from his teammates, who were certain to wrap up the pennant in the next several days.

The Yankees reached that milestone September 13 in Cleveland, with the veteran Pipgras recording a 9-3 victory.

The win was the Bombers' 100th of the year—they had lost 43 times—and gave McCarthy the unique distinction of being the first manager to win a flag in each major league.

Soberly, the Yankees observed their achievement. "If Ruth had been here," wrote the reporter for the New York Herald Tribune, "he would have thought of something to enliven the occasion."

But the Babe was not there. He was still in New York trying to regain his strength. He rejoined the team in Philadelphia on September 21, looking drawn and haggard. In two games at Shibe Park, he collected only two singles.

The Yankees completed the campaign with 107 wins and were 13 games better than the A's. Only the Senators battled the Yankees on even terms in their 22-game season series. The Tigers, White Sox and Red Sox were the easiest marks, losing 17 of 22 games. The Yanks were 16-6 against the Browns, 15-7 against the Indians and 14-8 against the dethroned A's.

Allen led American League pitchers in winning percentage with his 17-4 record and .810 percentage.

Ruffing, the two-time 20-game loser from Boston, was second in the league with a 3.10 ERA while recording 18 victories. Gomez recorded a 24-7 record while Pipgras chipped in with 16 wins.

Hitting honors, as usual, went to Ruth and Gehrig. Ruth batted .341 with 41 homers and 137 RBIs, while Gehrig hit .349 with 34 homers and 151 RBIs. Lazzeri drove in 113 runs and Chapman added 107, while Dickey, Combs and Lazzeri all topped the .300 level.

Now that McCarthy had satisfied two of Ruppert's three requests—a second-place finish in 1931 and a pennant in 1932—he took aim at the third—a world championship. To this order, Ruppert added a time limit. He wanted his title in four games, matching the Yankees' feat against the Pirates in 1927 and the Cardinals in 1928. "I want to have something over which to boast a little to the other club owners," he said.

McCarthy gave his boss exactly what he wanted. And it seemed only fitting that McCarthy's victim was his former club, the Chicago Cubs.

The Cubs outhit the Yankees in the Series opener, but lost to Ruffing, 12-6. Game 2 resulted in a 5-2 Yankee win as Gomez outdueled Lon Warneke.

Almost 50,000 fans packed Wrigley Field for Game 3, which ended in a 7-5 Yankee victory. But this game was special. History remembers it as the one in which Ruth supposedly called his fifth-inning home run.

Universal agreement exists on some points, sharp disagreement on others. It is certain that the score was tied, 4-4, with one out when Ruth stepped into the batter's box. There also is unanimity that the Bambino was being deluged by a shower of profanities from the Chicago dugout. It was that kind of Series. Joe Vila, one of the most highly respected baseball writers of the day, reported in The Sporting News what happened next:

> When Charley Root whipped over a strike on him, the Babe put up one finger on his right hand. Strike two brought up two fingers. A ball and he put up a finger on his left hand. Two balls and up went two fingers on his left hand. And now he wiped his hands on his trousers and pointed toward the distant bleachers. Root wound up and pegged a fast ball—and the Babe hit it out of the park.

Gabby Hartnett, squatting behind the plate when Ruth pointed, reported that Babe accompanied the gesture with the remark that "it only takes one to hit it."

Root denied to his dying breath that Ruth called the home run. "If he had," asserted the pitcher, "I'd have thrown the next pitch at his head."

New York players—Gehrig, Sewell and Ruffing among them—took the affirmative view. Late in life, Ruffing told an interviewer, "After he (Ruth) trotted around the bases he came to the dugout and sat next to me. I said, 'Babe, what if you had struck out?' He said, 'Then I'd have been a jackass.' "

According to some opinions, Babe appreciated the merits of the called-homer story as a vital adjunct to the romance of baseball and permitted it to endure, even encouraged it.

Gehrig, who had witnessed the Ruth drama from the on-deck circle, followed him to the plate and smashed a Root pitch into the right-field seats for his second homer of the game, just as Ruth's round-tripper had been his second of the afternoon.

Though he failed to last the distance, Pipgras received credit for the victory. When he was relieved by Pennock, it marked the first time a Yankee hurler had been lifted in a Series game since the opening contest of the 1927 classic, a stretch of nine route-going performances.

The Bronx Bombers clinched their fourth world championship the next day with their 12th straight Series triumph. Lazzeri cracked two homers and a single in helping the Yanks bury their adversaries, 13-6.

Despite Ruth's Game 3 exploit, the real hero of the Series was Gehrig, who collected nine hits, three homers and eight RBIs in the four games.

For baseball observers, the 1932 Yankees provided a glimpse of the devastating machine that was but a few years away from total domination.

1932
FINAL STANDING

Club	W.	L.	Pct.	GB.
New York	107	47	.695	—
Philadelphia	94	60	.610	13
Washington	93	61	.604	14

BATTERS

Pos.	Player	G.	HR.	RBI.	B.A.
1B	Lou Gehrig	155	34	151	.349
2B	Tony Lazzeri	141	15	113	.300
SS	Frank Crosetti	115	5	57	.241
3B	Joe Sewell	124	11	68	.272
OF	Ben Chapman	150	10	107	.299
	Earle Combs	143	9	65	.321
	Babe Ruth	132	41	137	.341
C	Bill Dickey	108	15	84	.310
UT	Sammy Byrd (of)	104	8	30	.297
	Lyn Lary (ss)	91	3	39	.232

OTHER CONTRIBUTORS (20+ Games): Doc Farrell, Myril Hoag, Arndt Jorgens, Jack Saltzgaver.

PITCHERS

Thr.	Pitcher	G.	W.	L.	ERA
L	Lefty Gomez	37	24	7	4.21
R	Red Ruffing	35	18	7	3.10
R	Johnny Allen	33	17	4	3.70
R	George Pipgras	32	16	9	4.19
L	Herb Pennock	22	9	5	4.59

OTHER CONTRIBUTORS (20+ Games): Ed Wells.

Number 25

Swifties Hustle Into Prominence

Reserves or regulars, the 1942 Cardinals, such as backup first baseman Ray Sanders (above), were a running, never-say-die outfit.

The year was 1942. Winds of war were blowing ill and most eyes were riveted on the European conflict that suddenly had expanded into a global demonstration of power and wits that would consume the United States and its allies for most of the next four years. The nation was naturally tense as young men from all walks of life prepared to do battle in a series of confrontations the U.S. had hoped to avoid.

So far, major league baseball had remained relatively unscathed by world events and Billy Southworth sat back in the St. Louis dugout, consumed by a different kind of war. His young Cardinals were doing battle in an exhibition game and the Redbird manager was taking note of something that had caught his attention during earlier spring workouts. It was instinct, more than anything, that told the veteran baseball man that something was *wrong;* something was *different.*

"Early in the season, I noticed that the ball had changed," Southworth explained some years later. "I saw men hit the ball with everything they had but fail to drive it the distance it used to travel. I decided the ball was not quite as lively. As the sum-

One of the great outfields in baseball history was composed of Cardinals (left to right) Enos Slaughter, Terry Moore and Stan Musial.

mer advanced, I became convinced of this.

"This led to the conclusion that it would be wise to change playing technique to meet the difference in the ball. I don't know how many others met the situation in that way. I saw that the ball was just enough slower to help the runner make third from first on a hit that went on the ground all the way."

Southworth did not realize what impact his astute observation and subsequent style change would have on baseball. But he did know that what he proposed would kindle excitement in St. Louis. His game plan was simple: create a clone of the Gas House Gang, the rag-tag, stick-it-in-your-ear bunch that ruled St. Louis a decade earlier.

So after the lively-ball era of the late 1920s and '30s, more than a few eyebrows were raised in '42 when Southworth's St. Louis Swifties came hustling into the nation's consciousness. They were young, they were brash and enthusiastic and they were dedicated to the Gas House Gang-promoted principle that you do what you have to do to win.

They did and they did.

Toward that end, Cardinal Vice President Branch Rickey had assembled an interesting cast of characters. Though they came from divergent back-

grounds, there were common threads that linked the '42 Cardinals to their pennant-winning destinies.

Most members of the team could run. And they *liked* to run. Their enthusiasm was contagious and they operated at only one speed—fast. Whether hustling down to first base after a walk or turning an outfield mistake into a run, these guys knew how to pressure a defense, and they never let up.

Neither did they give opponents much quarter. They played like a bunch of kids and whether up 14-0 or 2-1, they played with the same conviction and intensity. And likewise if they were on the short end of the score. No deficit was insurmountable.

They were, in short, in love with the game and well-schooled in the spirit with which they believed it should be played.

The inspirational leader of this jackrabbit brigade was one Enos Slaughter, known by teammates and fans as Country. The son of a North Carolina farmer, Slaughter was a man in a hurry. When he took his spot in the outfield, he ran. When he came in at the end of a half-inning, he ran. When he hit a tap to the pitcher, he ran down the first-base line like it was the first leg of a triple. And when he made an out, he didn't drop his head and walk slowly off the field. He ran.

Slaughter was a slashing lefthanded hitter with speed, power, a rifle arm and surprising defensive skills that belied his stocky, 5-foot-9, 190-pound frame. He had arrived in St. Louis in 1938 and quickly won the hearts of Cardinal fans who viewed this brash, 22-year-old youngster as a throwback to their beloved 1934 Gas House Gang. And the comparison was not lost on a couple of old-timers who appreciated the youngster's hell bent style, if not his penchant for doing the little things that would beat their teams.

"He (Slaughter) is the finest example of what it means to do your level best I've ever seen," said Washington Manager Bucky Harris. "He is the best exponent of the desire to win the game has known . . . and I don't except Ruth, Cobb, Lou Gehrig or any other star.

"Slaughter should be held up to every American boy as an ideal. His name should be in school textbooks along with this country's most revered heroes. He never quits. He never will. He won't even let down. . . ."

"He likes to play ball, he gives it every ounce he has every second and he is equipped with all the baseball tools a fellow will ever need," said Boston Manager Casey Stengel. "I give you the greatest competitioner, the greatest team player, Slaughter, I have ever seen. Period."

Slaughter backed up that lofty praise with a .276 rookie batting average in 1938 and then followed up with .320, .306 and .311 marks in the next three seasons. The latter mark came in 1941, a season marred by a broken collarbone, the result of Slaughter diving into the outfield wall trying to make a catch.

As the Cardinals prepared to open the '42 campaign, however, the soon-to-turn 26-year-old was feeling good and ready to contribute to what he hoped would be a championship season.

Anybody who believed Southworth was expecting something less than a championship from his young troops did not know the 49-year-old manager. The 5-10, 170-pound Southworth was baseball's eternal optimist.

Billy the Kid was in his second hitch as Cardinal manager. In 1929, after a glittering career as a major league outfielder, Southworth had piloted the Cards for part of one humbling season. His performance was flawed by inexperience and he was returned to the minor leagues to learn how to handle men.

Southworth was managing smartly in the Cardinal farm system at Rochester in 1940 when he was summoned to St. Louis to replace Ray Blades, and he quickly demonstrated that he had matured sub-

Wiry Marty Marion, alias Mr. Shortstop, was a capable hitter with a glove as smooth as silk.

stantially during his minor league sojourn. He guided the Redbirds to a 69-40 record and third-place finish down the stretch of the '40 campaign, and then followed that with a 97-56 record and second-place finish in 1941. Southworth had become a strict disciplinarian who treated everyone fairly.

If Southworth had one special talent, it was his skill at preparng a team for the season. He worked his athletes longer and harder than other managers, and always on a timetable. His training camps looked more like a school room than a sweat shop.

Billy loved to talk baseball and always encouraged his players to express their opinions. Once, in 1942, when the Cardinals were at a critical point in the season, Southworth was about to insert Ken O'Dea as a pinch-hitter in a game the Cards trailed at Boston.

Suddenly, Billy's attention was directed to second base, where Johnny Hopp was waving his arms frantically. Southworth trotted on the field to consult with his baserunner and was told, "You were busy hitting infield during batting practice and didn't have a chance to watch Ray Sanders."

"What about Sanders?" Southworth inquired.

"He's hittin' like a fool, knockin' the cover off, every time up," Hopp said. "I thought I ought to tell you."

The 1942 Cardinals took off when veteran Jimmy Brown (above) moved to second base, Johnny Hopp took over at first and Whitey Kurowski at third.

Southworth acted on the advice and sent Sanders to the plate instead of O'Dea. Sanders promptly singled home the run and the Cardinals went on to beat the Braves.

Southworth's optimism was being sorely tested as the Cardinals stumbled through the early part of the 1942 season. Though the Redbirds were one game ahead of their 1941 pace by mid-June, the torrid Brooklyn Dodgers were pulling steadily away. The Cardinals' mediocre start could be traced directly to what Southworth perceived as a defensive lapse that had resulted in 20 one-run losses.

So Billy the Kid huddled with Terry Moore, the team's splendid center fielder and captain, and infielder Jimmy Brown, a six-year Cardinal veteran currently playing third base.

"We're a game better than last year," Southworth told his players, "but while we were second or third in double plays, we're last this year."

"Well," said Moore, "let's do something about it."

"Will you feel all right playing second base?" Southworth asked Brown.

"I'll pitch or be batboy if it'll help," Brown replied.

That was what Southworth wanted to hear. He shook up his infield the next day at Philadelphia, replacing Sanders at first with Hopp, benching second baseman Frank (Creepy) Crespi in favor of Brown and putting rookie George (Whitey) Kurowski at third. Only the budding Mr. Shortstop, Marty Marion, retained his starting position.

Marion clearly was the centerpiece of this makeshift infield. But what a centerpiece he was. The wiry 6-2, 165-pound youngster was poetry in motion, baseball's version of the Brahms Lullaby.

"Maybe I'm prejudiced because I see him every day," Southworth said, "but he's the best ever. Yes, he's Mr. Shortstop in person. He anticipates plays perfectly, can go to his right or left equally well and has a truly great arm. Some of the things he does have to be seen to be believed."

That opinion was seconded by venerable Philadelphia A's Manager Connie Mack, who said, "I've looked at a lot of shortstops in my day, but that fellow is the best I've ever seen."

Though his bat couldn't match his fielding magic, Marion, who had reached the major leagues in 1940, was proving to be a .270-range hitter who was capable in the clutch. And, of course, he could run.

So, too, could Brown, who was one of the old men of the club at age 30. Brown originally was pegged as a shortstop when he joined the Cardinals in 1937, but his arm proved inadequate. There was nothing inadequate about how the youngster played the game, however, and he quickly convinced observers that he was a gamer in the tradition of his 1934 predecessors.

Brown, a fiery-tempered North Carolinian who would never back down from a fight, also could hit, as evidenced by his .306 mark in 1941.

Hopp and Kurowski were youngsters intent on taking advantage of their chance to crack the starting lineup. Hopp had alternated between the outfield and first base in the previous two seasons and had checked in with a .303 average while doing fill-in work for 134 games in 1941. He had earned a reputation as a smart, hard-nosed baserunner who could belly-flop his way into the heart of any baseball fan.

Kurowski was something of a medical curiosity. As an 8-year-old in Reading, Pa., he had fallen from a fence and slashed his right wrist on broken glass. He received routine medical care until a severe pain developed weeks later.

Osteomyelitis was the diagnosis. Surgeons removed three inches of diseased bone from his forearm and sent the youngster home with glum predictions for use of the arm.

In time, however, Kurowski's muscles strengthened to the point where he could throw a baseball accurately and hit it with uncommon force. He was a hungry and determined 24-year-old rookie when he took over as the regular third baseman.

The new infield alignment produced the cure that Southworth sought. Though smaller than most first basemen (5-10), Hopp played the position well. Brown, with his knowledge of opposing batters, tightened the defense around second base. Marion was Marion and Kurowski handled everything hit his way with the touch of a veteran.

There was no such need to tighten the outfield defense. Southworth had at his disposal what eventually would rank among the greatest outfields of all time. Slaughter, of course, was in right, Moore in center and a young rookie, Stan Musial, in left.

Musial, the member of that trio destined for the greatest glories, was a 21-year-old Pennsylvanian who only a few years before had dreamed of becoming the next Carl Hubbell.

Musial had won 18 games in a Class D league as a 19-year-old lefthander in 1940. Promotion up the

A pair of good-looking rookies, Stan Musial (left) and Whitey Kurowski, stepped into the Cardinal lineup and helped produce a 1942 World Series championship.

Cardinal ladder was assured until the youngster fell while playing outfield and injured his arm. When he reported to Springfield in the Western Association in 1941, the arm was too sore to pitch. The club was in desperate need of outfielders, however, and Musial filled in—to the tune of a .379 batting average with 26 home runs. A short stint at Rochester of the International League produced more eyebrow-raising hitting and the youngster was called to the parent club late in the '41 campaign.

It didn't take long to impress Southworth. Employing what later would be termed a classic, uncoiling stance and fluid swing, Musial rapped out two hits in his major league debut and went on to

The Coopers, Walker (left) and Mort, a 22-game winner, formed one of the best brother batteries in baseball history.

hit .426 in his late-season stint. When the 1942 season approached, he was being tabbed as the starting left fielder, a decision Southworth would never regret.

The youngster's defensive skills were enormous, but raw. He used speed and instincts to make up for judgment mistakes and Moore took the budding superstar under his wing.

Nobody ever had a better teacher. The Captain, as he was known to his teammates, carried a .284 career average into the '42 campaign, but his capable bat was only icing for Moore's cake.

To say the 30-year-old veteran was a defensive whiz was something of an understatement.

"I don't see how they can rank anybody better than Moore," said former Gas Houser and current Dodger Manager Leo Durocher. "What the heck,

I've got no ax to grind for the guy. He's a swell fellow. But he's on the other team and he's beaten us out of two dozen ball games. But you can't rank anybody any better.

"If a ball is hit in the air, he'll get it. Nobody can do any better than that. Maybe some others will tie him, but I don't see how anyone can beat him."

A man of few words, Moore let his glove do the talking. And his message came through loud and clear as opponents watched him perform magic for the Cardinals' pennant express.

With their infield defense dramatically improved and their jackrabbits defying opposing fielders with their every extra base, the Cardinals' winning pace accelerated. Unfortunately, however, the front-running Dodgers showed no inclination to lose. In fact, even with the Redbirds applying steady pressure, the Dodgers still managed to build their lead to 10 games by August 5.

But Southworth kept assuring his youngsters that there was no way the Dodgers could keep up the breakneck pace that had produced a 71-29 record through their first 100 games. And, he assured them when the Dodgers faltered, they would be in for a pennant fight.

The first indication that Southworth knew what he was talking about came in late August, when the Dodgers arrived in St. Louis for a four-game series. The deficit already had been trimmed, but still stood at 7½ games. The Redbirds would need to win at least three of the four.

Southworth had his aces primed for the Flatbushers. First, the Dodgers would have to face nemesis Max Lanier, a lefthander who had defeated them in three of four starts already in '42 and owned a 20⅓-inning scoreless streak against the Bums. Lanier, never a big winner in his two-plus major league seasons, did have a penchant for coming through in the big game.

And that's exactly what the stocky North Carolina farmer did, stopping the Dodgers on four hits en route to a 7-1 victory. Lanier got more than enough help from Moore, who collected three hits and scored four times.

The Dodger lead was 6½ and now they faced the prospect of trying to beat Mort Cooper, the ace of the Cardinal staff who was en route to a 22-7 record, a 1.77 earned-run average and the National League Most Valuable Player Award.

Big Mort was half of the Cardinals' brother battery that also included Walker Cooper, a 6-3, 210-pound catcher. The Cooper brothers were sons of a rural mail carrier in western Missouri. Mort, the older by two years, was a 6-1 righthander who threw a fastball and forkball with humbling effect.

Though he was in only his second full season in the major leagues, the 27-year-old Walker already was an accomplished prankster and bench jockey.

His favorite stunt was to slip a lighted cigarette into the pocket of an unsuspecting victim. He also was an expert marksman—at spraying tobacco juice on the shoes of opposing batters.

Walker's sharpest barbs usually were saved for Durocher. He was fond of waving a watch in the direction of the Brooklyn manager and yelling, "Hey, Leo, what time is it?" That was guaranteed to raise the hackles of Durocher, who as a Yankee rookie many years earlier, had been accused of swiping Babe Ruth's timepiece, a charge that he denied vigorously.

To some teammates, Walker was known as "Muley," a fitting nickname for one whose obstinacy equalled that of a barnyard beast. He revealed that stubborn streak one summer when the editor of The Sporting News assigned a photographer to snap head shots of all the Cardinal players for an upcoming feature article. All the Cardinals posed willingly except Big Walk. He flatly refused until the editor leaked word to the Redbirds that he planned to run a photo of the south end of a horse heading north over Walker's cutline.

The threat turned Walker into the soul of congeniality.

There was nothing congenial about Walker Cooper when it came to playing baseball, however. He was fast for his size and wielded a dangerous bat with home run potential. Baserunners ran at high risk.

Neither was there anything congenial about Mort once he toed the rubber. Twice he had won 13 games in the high minors and, as a Cardinal starter in 1941, he also posted 13 victories, despite being sidelined six weeks after surgery to remove a growth in his arm.

The pitcher had an affinity for No. 13 dating back to his childhood. He was first attracted to the number when he won a gun in a raffle with ticket No. 13. He used the gun to win two state trapshooting titles. Mort wore uniform No. 13. He was born in 1913, his wife on June 13 and his son on September 13. Not surprisingly, his automobile license plate was 1300.

But the "13 connection" took a backseat to the Cardinals' 1942 pennant chase. Several weeks before his late-August confrontation with the Dodgers, Mort had discarded uniform No. 13 after repeated failures to win his 14th victory. Instead, he donned No. 14, which had been discarded when Gus Mancuso was traded to New York. The trick worked. He won. In his next outing, the hurler wore brother Walker's No. 15. Again success. When Mort hooked up with Whitlow Wyatt August 25 in the second game of the crucial Dodger series, he was wearing O'Dea's No. 16.

It was a match made in heaven. Wyatt, a cunning righthander who had outdueled Cooper, 1-0, at a

Harry Walker (left), Max Lanier (center) and Marty Marion enjoyed bragging
rights after the Cardinals had closed out the Yankees in the '42 Series.

critical juncture of the 1941 pennant race, was at his
best again as a crowd of 33,527 looked on at Sportsman's Park. For 12 innings, the pair waged a classic
duel with neither team able to score.

The Dodgers broke through in the 13th when
Lew Riggs singled home Mickey Owen. The Cardinals, however, were undaunted. They tied the score
in the bottom of the inning on Walker Cooper's
single and won it an inning later when Moore singled with the bases loaded.

The lead was 5½.

Next on tap for the Dodgers was Johnny Beazley,
the Cardinals' spectacular young righthander who
was looking for victory No. 16.

Beazley represents one of the great success stories
in baseball history. He's also a great example of how
fleeting fame can be.

Beazley had pitched without much success in the
minors, first as Cincinnati property and later as a
Cardinal farmhand with New Orleans. It was while
he was pitching with the Southern Association's
Pelicans that Beazley came under the influence of
Ray Blades, the Cardinal manager before South-

worth. Blades taught the youngster that there was
more to pitching than simply firing fastballs past
hitters and literally transformed him into a winner.
After a 16-victory 1941 season at New Orleans,
Beazley was ready to step into the spotlight.

That he did. When the '42 campaign had ended,
the 24-year-old rookie had compiled a 21-6 record
for the best winning percentage in the National
League. His 2.13 ERA was second in the league to
Mort Cooper's 1.77 mark.

He capped off his big season by beating the Yankees twice in the World Series and then packed his
gear for the off-season, secure with the knowledge
that his 1942 success was merely the tip of the ice-
berg.

Beazley, however, was to win only nine more
major league games. A month after the '42 World
Series, the youngster was in the service, preparing
to serve his country during the war. At some point
during his three-year hitch, Beazley threw out his
arm, possibly in a service game in which, out of
condition, he consented to pitch.

When he returned to the Cardinals in 1946, he

Cardinal World Series celebrants (back row left to right) Enos Slaughter, Stan Musial, Johnny Beazley, Whitey Kurowski, (front row) Manager Billy Southworth and Harry Walker.

was only a shell of his former self. He would never return to his 1942 form.

For that one season, however, Beazley was on top of the world and he matched pitches with the Dodgers and Max Macon the night of August 26. Both were outstanding and the game was deadlocked, 1-1, after nine innings. The Cardinals pulled out their 2-1 victory in the 10th when Macon slipped while trying to field a dribble near the mound and allowed the deciding run to score. The lead was 4½.

Though the Dodgers were able to salvage the final game of the series, 4-1, by beating Lanier, who was pitching on short rest, they left St. Louis shaken and sober with the understanding that their once-insurmountable lead was no longer inurmountable. And their pursuers were relentless.

Relentless translated into a blistering stretch run that netted the Cardinals 41 victories in their last 48 games and 43 in the final 51. Their .854 season-ending winning percentage exceeded the run put together by the Miracle Braves, who compiled a .787 mark in coming from behind to win the 1914 Na-

tional League pennant.

When all was said and done, the Cardinals owned a 106-48 record, two games better than the Dodgers' 104-50 ledger, marking only the third time in baseball history that two teams in the same league had won 100 or more victories.

The Cardinals finally caught the Dodgers on September 12 when Kurowski's two-run homer and Lanier's five-hit pitching beat Brooklyn, 2-1, at Ebbets Field. Cooper, wearing Coaker Triplett's No. 20, had recorded his 20th win the day before when he outpitched Wyatt and held the Dodgers to three singles in a 3-0 victory.

When the Redbirds split a doubleheader the next day with Philadelphia and the Dodgers lost twice to Cincinnati, St. Louis grabbed a lead it never lost.

The Cardinals clinched their sixth pennant on the final day of the season when lefthander Ernie White, who had been handicapped throughout the campaign by arm trouble, scattered five hits in pitching St. Louis to a 9-2 victory.

Cooper and Beazley ranked as the top two pitchers in the league and Big Mort led the league in wins, ERA and shutouts (10). Lanier added 13 victories to the St. Louis cause, as did righthander Howie Krist, most of them in relief.

Amazingly, the Cardinals had only two .300 hitters, Slaughter (.318) and Musial (.315). Slaughter was the team's top home run and RBI man with 13 and 98, respectively. The Cardinals' eight regulars hit only 49 home runs and averaged only 61 RBIs.

The Cardinals were understandably proud of their accomplishment, nobody moreso than the never-say-die Southworth.

"We won this one the hard way," he said. "No one won it for us. We went out and won it ourselves . . . and we'll beat the Yankees the same way. One thing this young club isn't afraid of is reputation."

That didn't appear to be the case when the New Yorkers, appearing in their sixth World Series in the last seven years, carried a 7-0 lead into the ninth inning of the opener. The Cardinals had committed four errors and had managed but one hit, a two-out eighth-inning single by Moore, off Yankee veteran Red Ruffing.

But the Yankees quickly discovered that another World Series championship was going to be anything but easy.

A one-out Walker Cooper single and a two-out walk to pinch-hitter Sanders set the stage for five straight Cardinal hits that nested four ninth-inning runs and brought Musial to the plate representing the tying run. The rookie grounded out to end the Yankees' 7-4 victory, but notice had been served.

Beazley pitched the Cardinals to a 4-3 victory in Game 2, White shut out the Bombers in Game 3, the Redbirds outlasted the Yankees, 9-6, in a Game 4 slugfest and the Swifties completed their near-miraculous stretch run in Game 5 when Beazley outdueled Ruffing, 4-2.

The incredible journey to the top of the baseball world had come to a dramatic conclusion. The 1942 Cardinals, who stressed teamwork, speed and more teamwork above all else, had won 47 of their last 56 games and were world champions.

". . . on the Cardinals we play to win games," was the assessment of Musial. "That's always the first consideration; individual averages are secondary. I go out every day to give Billy and the club all I have. And, if the box score shows I've made three hits, well, it doesn't make bad reading."

"I never saw a team play ball like our outfit did in that last month and a half," said Lanier. "It just looked like we couldn't be licked."

How great the running Redbirds might have become except for world affairs in succeeding years made pleasant conjecture in the following decades. But manpower demands of World War II started to riddle their ranks almost before the last cheer had died away.

Beazley enlisted in the Army Air Corps in November. When the Redbirds assembled for spring training in 1943, Moore and Slaughter also were missing. In July, Jimmy Brown was inducted into the service. Even in that depleted state, the Cards won the pennant, but lost the World Series to the Yankees.

White was in military garb by the time the 1944 campaign opened. Still the Cards continued to win. They followed their third straight flag with a Series victory over the St. Louis Browns.

As the war effort escalated in 1945, so did the requisitions on Cardinal personnel. Musial, Walker Cooper and Lanier joined the colors, thereby imposing an even heavier burden on Southworth as he tried for a fourth straight pennant.

Studded with players unfit for military duty or otherwise exempt, the Birds waged a stirring battle for the 1945 pennant before losing out to the Cubs by three games.

When the global guns fell silent and major leaguers returned to the baseball wars, some picked up the thread without a noticeable hitch in their careers. Others, like Beazley, discovered that inactivity had robbed them of their multiple skills.

Those who rejoined the Cardinals celebrated with another flag in 1946. They tied the Dodgers in the 154-game schedule, beat Durocher's gang in a playoff and then vanquished the Boston Red Sox in a seven-game World Series.

How great might they have been except for global conflict? Conjecture lives on.

1942
FINAL STANDING

Club	W.	L.	Pct.	GB.
St. Louis	106	48	.688	—
Brooklyn	104	50	.675	2

BATTERS

Pos.	Player	G.	HR.	RBI.	B.A.
1B	Johnny Hopp	95	3	37	.258
2B	Jimmy Brown	145	1	71	.256
SS	Marty Marion	147	0	54	.276
3B	Whitey Kurowski	115	9	42	.254
OF	Stan Musial	140	10	72	.315
	Terry Moore	130	6	49	.288
	Enos Slaughter	152	13	98	.318
C	Walker Cooper	125	7	65	.281
UT	Frank Crespi (2b)	93	0	35	.243
	Ray Sanders (1b)	95	5	39	.252

OTHER CONTRIBUTORS (20+ Games): Ken O'Dea, Coaker Triplett, Harry Walker.

PITCHERS

Thr.	Pitcher	G.	W.	L.	ERA
R	Mort Cooper	37	22	7	1.77
R	Johnny Beazley	43	21	6	2.13
R	Howie Krist	34	13	3	2.52
L	Max Lanier	34	13	8	2.96

OTHER CONTRIBUTORS (20+ Games): Murry Dickson, Harry Gumbert, Howie Pollet, Ernie White.